DATE DUE			
Aug 5 '65			
Aug 11 '65			
Dec 2 '66			
Jan 4 '67			
Nov 27 '67			
Mar 31 69			
Nov 17 '70			
May 18 '72			
pr 26 7 9			
GAYLORD			PRINTED IN U..S.A.

THE KINGDOM OF GOD
IN THE TEACHING OF JESUS

GÖSTA LUNDSTRÖM

THE KINGDOM OF GOD
IN THE
TEACHING OF JESUS

A History of Interpretation from the Last Decades
of the Nineteenth Century to the Present Day

Translated by
JOAN BULMAN

JOHN KNOX PRESS
RICHMOND, VIRGINIA
1963

Published in Great Britain by Oliver & Boyd Ltd.,
Edinburgh and London, and in the United States
of America by John Knox Press, Richmond, Virginia.

Library of Congress Catalog Card No. 63-16411

A translation of *Guds Rike i Jesu Förkunnelse* ; *tolkningens
historia från 1800-talets sista decennier till våra dagar*, by Gösta
Lundström, published by Svenska Kyrkans Diakonistyrelses
Bokförlag, Lund, in 1947.

The Scripture quotations are from the Revised Standard
Version of the Bible, copyrighted 1946 and 1952 by the
Division of Christian Education of the National Council of
the Churches of Christ in the United States of America, and
used by permission.

ENGLISH EDITION
First published 1963

To
MY WIFE

AUTHOR'S PREFACE

This book, which is here presented in English, was first published in 1947 as a thesis for the degree of Doctor of Theology at Uppsala University. When Messrs Oliver & Boyd offered to undertake its translation into English, I naturally accepted with great pleasure. They also asked me to carry the story of the exegetic interpretation of the Kingdom of God down to the present day. The best method, I felt, was to add to the book as it originally stood, some portions of which had been cut, a postscript dealing with developments in the past fifteen years.

I should like to thank Messrs Oliver & Boyd for undertaking the publication of this book. I should also like to thank the translator, Miss Joan Bulman, and Bo Runmark, Director of Svenska Kyrkans Diakonistyrelses Bokförlag, for their parts in bringing the English version into being.

The object of this study has been to follow the history of the interpretation of the Kingdom of God in the teaching of Jesus down to the present day. The predominant question is what Jesus Himself meant by the Kingdom of God. Other questions which have to be considered are the relations between present and future in Jesus' idea of the Kingdom of God, and Jesus' personal attitude towards the Kingdom He preached. What the conditions for entry into and life in the Kingdom of God, and so the whole ethic of Jesus, mean to us, obviously largely determines the image we form of the Kingdom of God, as also the question of the relation between the Kingdom of God and the Church.

I have done my best to trace the philosophical and theological principles which underlie the work of the various scholars. Often they have obviously not been aware of them themselves, still less acknowledged them. The account has largely had to take the form of a literary survey. Down to the year 1906 chronological order has mainly been followed. The dominating figure during this period is Johannes Weiss. With Albert Schweitzer's monumental work on the history of research into the life of Jesus, which was published in 1906, a new phase set in, in which the most important contributions either were based on or were antagonistic to the eschatological interpretation of Jesus. During this period it has not proved possible to follow the discussion chronologically, and the various authors have consequently been classified together in groups.

GÖSTA LUNDSTRÖM

Strängnäs
August 1962

Contents

List of Abbreviations

BOHLIN, T.   *Kristna Gudsrikestanken = Den kristna Gudsrikestanken under 1800-talet och i nutiden.*

CULLMANN, O.   *Christ and Time.*   Eng. trans. of *Christus und die Zeit.   Die urchristliche Zeit- und Geschichtsauffassung.*

D.L.Z. = Deutsche Literaturzeitung.

E.H.P.R. = Études d'histoire et de philosophie religieuses.

Exp. = The Expositor.

Exp.T. = The Expository Times.

HOLMSTRÖM, F.   *Eskatologiska motivet = Det eskatologiska motivet i nutida teologi: tre etapper i 1900-talets teologiska tankeutveckling.*

J.Rel. = The Journal of Religion.

KÜMMEL, W. G.   *Promise and Fulfilment = Promise and Fulfilment.   The Eschatological Message of Jesus.*   Eng. trans. of *Verheissung und Erfüllung.   Untersuchungen zur eschatologischen Verkündigung Jesu.*

LOHMEYER, E.   *Begriff der Gemeinschaft = Vom Begriff der religiösen Gemeinschaft.   Eine problemgeschichtliche Untersuchung über die Grundlagen des Urchristentums.*

OTTO, R.   *Idea of the Holy = The Idea of the Holy.   An Inquiry into the non-rational Factor in the Idea of the Divine and its relation to the Rational.*   Eng. trans. of *Das Heilige: Über das Irrationale in der Idee des Göttlichen und sein Verhältnis zum Rationalen.*

——*Kingdom of God = The Kingdom of God and the Son of Man.   A Study in the History of Religion,* Eng. trans. of *Reich Gottes und Menschensohn.   Ein religionsgeschichtlicher Versuch.*

——*Life and Ministry = The Life and Ministry of Jesus, according to the Historical and Critical Method.*   Eng. trans. of *Leben und Wirken Jesu nach historisch-kritischer Auffassung.*

R.G.G. = Religion und Geschichte im Gegenwart.

RITSCHL, A.   *Rechtfertigung und Versöhnung = Die christliche Lehre von der Rechtfertigung und Versöhnung.*

SCHWEITZER, A.   *Geschichte = Geschichte der Leben-Jesu-Forschung.*

——*My Life and Thought = Out of my Life and Thought; an Autobiography,* Eng. trans. of *Aus meinem Leben und Denken.*

——*Mystery of the Kingdom = The Mystery of the Kingdom of God: the secret of Jesus' Messiahship and Passion,* Eng. trans. of *Das Messianitäts- und Leidensgeheimnis.   Eine Skizze des Lebens Jesu.*

SCHWEITZER, A. *Quest* = *The Quest of the Historical Jesus: a critical study of its progress from Reimarus to Wrede*, Eng. trans of *Von Reimarus zu Wrede: eine Geschichte der Leben-Jesu-Forschung*.

S.T.K. = *Svensk Teologisk Kvartalskrift*.

Th.Bl. = *Theologische Blätter*.

Th.Lz. = *Theologische Literaturzeitung*.

Th.R. = *Theologische Rundschau*.

Th.W.B.N.T. = *Theologisches Wörterbuch zum Neuen Testament*, ed. G. Kittel.

WEISS, J. *Predigt Jesu* = *Die Predigt Jesu vom Reiche Gottes*.

Z.N.W. = *Zeitschrift für die neutestamentliche Wissenschaft und die Kunde der älteren Kirche*.

Z.Th.K. = *Zeitschrift für Theologie und Kirche*.

Introduction

During the nineteenth century *"Leben-Jesu-Forschung"*—study of the life of Jesus—reached its highest peak. Towards the end of that century increasing doubt began to be felt as to the possibility of writing a scientific life of Jesus. Interest turned instead to the teaching of Jesus, in which the Kingdom of God occupies a dominating position. The question what Jesus meant by the Kingdom of God had been prominent ever since Albrecht Ritschl. As the eschatological interpretation of the Kingdom of God gained ground, this question became really vital.

The aim of the present investigation is to follow the interpretation of the Kingdom of God in the teaching of Jesus down to the present day. The fundamental question has been, What did Jesus mean by the Kingdom of God? Other questions which have attracted particular attention have been the relation between present and future in Jesus' conception of the Kingdom of God, and Jesus' personal attitude towards the Kingdom He preached. It will be necessary, therefore, to linger particularly over the views of research on these questions. Discussion on the Kingdom of God and the Church has been particularly lively during the past twenty-five years. How one interprets conditions for entry into and life in the Kingdom of God, and so the ethics of Jesus, is obviously of great significance to the whole concept one forms of the Kingdom of God. The questions of the Kingdom of God and the Church and of the ethic of Jesus cannot, however, be allowed the same space as those first mentioned. It has been the author's endeavour to try to establish the philosophical and theological principles by which the various scholars have been guided, often without realising it themselves. I am well aware how difficult it is for one who is not a systematic theologian to enter into the realm of systematic theology. Yet the attempt must be made, if we are ever to have any means of establishing whether an interpretation is really an interpretation or whether it is an adaptation and modernisation.

A   I

To achieve the purposes here set out, the book has largely had to take the form of a survey of published works. Up to 1906 chronological order has mainly been followed. The dominating figure here is Johannes Weiss, so that the major space is consequently devoted to him. With the appearance in 1906 of Albert Schweitzer's monumental work on the history of the study of the life of Jesus, a fresh phase begins. The most important contributions made by later research to the interpretation of Jesus' conception of the Kingdom of God are based on and argued around Schweitzer's eschatological interpretation. Here it has proved impossible to follow chronological order. The various interpretations have consequently been grouped together under classified headings.

To set forth at length the author's personal views on the Kingdom of God in the teaching of Jesus would carry him outside the limits he has set himself. Some indication of these views may be gathered from the concluding chapter of this work. They can, of course, also be deduced from the tone of the critical comments.

I

Albrecht Ritschl's Interpretation of the Kingdom of God

D uring the first half of the nineteenth century, both exegetic and systematic theology paid extremely little attention to the idea of the Kingdom of God. Albrecht Ritschl (1822-89) brought about an appreciable change in this state of affairs, in that he made the concept of the Kingdom of God the centre of theological interest and debate by taking the Kingdom of God as one of the focal points in his "elliptical" theology. He became the great "theologian of the Kingdom of God" of the nineteenth century, and his ideas were adopted and further developed by a large school of pupils. Even in Sweden his theology played an important part.

According to Ritschl, Jesus of Nazareth appeared as an Israelite prophet preaching the coming of the fulfilled Dominion of God.[1] The purpose of the divine covenant was now achieved, for when Jesus preached the nearness of the Kingdom of God, this did not mean to Him that the Kingdom belonged to the future, but that the pre-appointed time was now come when the Dominion of God should become effective over His covenanted people, who were called to this, and who had been appointed through God's ordinance. "The expression 'Kingdom of God' means the Dominion of God which is made effective through their will, in accordance with our conviction

---

[1] Ritschl translates βασιλεία τοῦ Θεοῦ as "*Herrschaft Gottes*" (the "Dominion of God") in the Biblical-theological section of *Die christliche Lehre von Rechtfertigung und Versöhnung*, henceforth cited as *Rechtfertigung und Versöhnung*, VOL. II, 4th edn., Bonn·1900, whereas elsewhere he uses the expression "*Reich Gottes*" (the "Kingdom of God").

that the Dominion of God through Christ has established a community which allows itself to be ruled by God."[2]

The historical mission of Jesus was to found the Kingdom of God upon earth. The very works of Jesus brought into being the Dominion of God, for when He healed demoniacs and crushed the power of the devil, the Dominion of God entered into human life (Mt. XII. 28). So by His preaching and His works Jesus proved Himself the bearer of the Kingdom of God. His inmost intention was "through sustained influence to educate a select group of people for entry into the Kingdom of God, which can only rank as the highest Good while at the same time it represents the highest task for its participants."[3] For that reason Jesus called the Twelve together and initiated them into the secret of the Kingdom of God and of His own person. Referring to the group of disciples, Jesus answered the Pharisees that the Kingdom of God was in the midst of those who asked (Lk. XVII. 20 f.). The Beatitudes, also, show that there are men who possess the state of mind that corresponds to the Kingdom of God, and who therefore need no change of heart. Jesus knew Himself to be the Messiah and as such exercised the Dominion of God, which was brought into being in a kingdom of obedient subjects who acclaimed Him as the Son of God and the bearer of God's Dominion. This community had accepted the ethical task of the Kingdom of God.

Thus Ritschl could say that, through the exercise of righteousness, the Kingdom of God would come into being within a short space in the community of the followers of Christ, in a manner that is exemplified by the growth of the seed and the working of leaven on dough.[4] The parables of the mysteries of the Kingdom of God and the Labourers in the Vineyard

[2] *Op. cit.*, p. 30. The Kingdom of God is realised where Jesus is active "in His office of Revealer" (A. Ritschl, *Unterricht in der christlichen Religion*, 3rd edn., Bonn 1886, p. 3).

[3] *Rechtfertigung und Versöhnung*, VOL. II, p. 31. See also *Unterricht in der christlichen Religion*, 7 and 8, where the Kingdom of God is defined as "the *union* of *subjects* bound together by righteous conduct," and is represented as "the spiritual and *moral task* of those gathered together in the Christian community." "Jesus Himself saw in the Kingdom of God (*i.e.* in the realisation of the Dominion of God) the *moral* end of the religious fellowship He had to found, since He understood by it not the common exercise of worship, but the organisation of humanity through action inspired by love" (*Rechtfertigung und Versöhnung*, VOL. III, 3rd edn., Bonn 1888, p. 12. See also pp. 240, 270, 275, 481, etc.).

[4] *Rechtfertigung und Versöhnung*, VOL. II, p. 40.

always signify by "fruit" a human product, springing out of an individual activity, which in turn is called forth by the divine "seed," *i.e.* by the "*Antrieb*" or impulse of the divine word of revelation.[5]

The parables of the Grain of Mustard Seed and the Leaven also indicate that the Kingdom of God will attain its full development only in the future (Mk. ix. 1). At the moment of facing the apparently unhappy outcome of His mission Jesus expressed His certainty that He would one day be revealed as the Lord and King of the Kingdom of God.

When, in Part III of *Rechtfertigung und Versöhnung*, Ritschl gives a definition of the Kingdom of God, this is purely ethically conceived. "The Kingdom of God consists of those who believe in Christ, inasmuch as they treat one another with love without regard to differences of sex, rank or race, thereby bringing about a fellowship of moral attitude and moral properties extending through the whole range of human life in every possible variation."[6]

There are signs, indeed, of a certain tendency in Ritschl to break away from the one-sidedly ethical interpretation of the Kingdom of God, yet this always holds the field.[7] He asserted that the Kingdom of God is a directly religious conception, as is shown by the original expression: Dominion of God. This clearly indicates a force coming from God and directed towards man. The Kingdom of God is partly the highest Good, partly also the common task of humanity, since the Dominion of God is only to be found where men obey God. These meanings are mutually interdependent. Therefore also the Kingdom of God is revealed as a religious conception of secondary importance as compared with justification and atonement, in which there is no room whatever for independent human activity.[8] The ethical task envisaged for the Dominion of God rests on the independence and responsibility of God's subjects. When Ritschl tried to

---

[5] *Unterricht in der christlichen Religion*, p. 3.

[6] *Rechtfertigung und Versöhnung*, VOL. III, p. 271.

[7] The ethical interpretation of the Kingdom of God comes out most strongly in the first edition of *Rechtfertigung und Versöhnung*, in which the realisation of the Kingdom of God is clearly shown as a result and a product of a common human ethical activity (*op. cit.*, 1st edn., pp. 20, 250), whereas the religious aspect is more strongly emphasised in later editions.

[8] *Op. cit.*, VOL. II, p. 30.

emphasise the religious character of the Kingdom of God in this way, it was clearly in order to stress that relations between men in the Kingdom of God are dependent on God. But "religious" here hardly means more than passive as opposed to active.

It is important to bear in mind that Ritschl always held firmly to the Kingdom of God as a sociological entity, even though he inclined now and then towards an individualistic interpretation of Christianity. It is in the work of his pupils that a purely individualistic interpretation of Christianity and the Kingdom of God first begins to appear.

Ritschl's conception of the Kingdom of God is to the last degree *this-worldly, monistic,* and *ethical* in character.[9] The Kingdom of God, which is our immediate possession, is absolutely uneschatological. Ritschl's interpretation of the Kingdom of God springs not so much from the concept of the Kingdom of God to be found in the Gospels, as above all from his philosophical attitude. It has, indeed, been demonstrated how closely Ritschl's interpretation is linked with the concept of the Kingdom of God developed by Kant.[10] To Kant the Kingdom of God is "a general combination instituted for the express purpose of avoiding what is evil and cultivating what is good in mankind, taking the form of an existing and constantly expanding society and concerned solely with the general support of morality":[11] it is "a people of God standing under ethic laws, a republic under ethic laws."[12] The concept of the Kingdom of God is, for Ritschl as for Kant, essentially an ideal belonging to an ethically-determined society, or a vision of a human culture pervaded by ethical purpose. It bears the stamp of Kant's this-worldly interpretation of the Kingdom

[9] F. Holmström, *Det eskatologiska motivet i nutida teologi, tre etapper i 1900-talets teologiska tankeutveckling,* Stockholm 1933, henceforth cited as *Eskatologiska motivet,* p. 66.

[10] I. Kant, *Die Religion innerhalb der Grenzen der blossen Vernunft,* Reklam, the third part of which carries the sub-title: *Die Gründung eines Reiches Gottes auf Erden* (The Foundation of a Kingdom of God on Earth). With regard to Ritschl's interpretation of the Kingdom of God and the sources of it see J. Weiss, *Die Idee des Reiches Gottes in der Theologie,* Vorträge der theol. Konferenz zu Giessen, No. 16, Giessen 1901, pp. 110-55; G. Aulén, *Den kristna gudsbilden genom seklerna och i nutiden. En konturteckning,* Stockholm 1927, pp. 322-4; A. Nygren, *Filosofisk och kristen etik,* 2nd edn., Stockholm 1932, pp. 204 f.

[11] Kant, *Die Religion innerhalb der Grenzen der blossen Vernunft,* p. 97.

[12] *Op. cit.,* p. 104.

of God, and not of the Kingdom of God as taught by Jesus. The effect of this dependence on German idealistic philosophy, primarily on Kant, is that Ritschl's interpretation of the Kingdom of God becomes a modernised adaptation. Ritschl himself seems to have been quite unaware of having fallen into conflict with the New Testament statements about the Kingdom of God, but believed on the contrary that his ideal of an ethical and cultural humanity derived from the teachings of Jesus. Because of this philosophical preoccupation his concept of the Kingdom of God has nothing whatever of that quality of glowing expectation of the establishment of the Kingdom in the future; rather he regards the Kingdom as something the Christian already possesses, identifying it with the group of disciples. The distinction between present and future has for him no deep-seated significance. The distinction he is concerned with is that between time and eternity. Nor is there either, therefore, any place in Ritschl's interpretation of Jesus for a "salvationary" mode of approach.

Notwithstanding all the criticisms that can be levelled at Ritschl's interpretation of the Kingdom of God, it remains to his credit that he brought the subject to the forefront of theological discussion. It would in any case have been highly remarkable if he had achieved full insight into what the Kingdom of God really meant for Jesus, at a time when the problem had not yet received any attention from theologians.

It would lie outside the scope of the present study to follow in detail the further development of Ritschl's idea of the Kingdom of Heaven by his pupils. We can only mention here J. Kaftan's attempt to reformulate the concept of the Kingdom of God in religious terms.[13] He defined the Kingdom of God as "the highest good" which God bestows, but it is therefore at the same time an ethical ideal which Christians are collectively to bring about. The Kingdom of God becomes both gift and task.

Ritschl's dominating influence on the interpretation of the Kingdom of God comes out clearly in the Bible theologies

---

[13] J. Kaftan, *Das Wesen der christlichen Religion*, Basle 1881, 2nd edn., 1888. See also T. Bohlin, *Den kristna Gudsrikestanken under 1800-talet och i nutiden*, henceforth cited as *Kristna Gudsrikestanken*, Lund 1928, pp. 56 ff.

of the second half of the nineteenth century, by H. H. Wendt,[14] W. Beyschlag,[15] and B. Weiss,[16] even though these show definite tendencies to part company with Ritschl. A typically Ritschlean interpretation of the Kingdom of God is to be found in K. Lühr,[17] F. Traub,[18] the Englishman J. Orr,[19] and the American H. C. King.[20]

The Ritschlean theology gained entry into Sweden chiefly through Pehr Eklund of Lund and Fredrik Fehr of Stockholm,

[14] H. H. Wendt, *Die Lehre Jesu*, 2 vols., Göttingen 1886-90, 2nd edn. 1901; Eng. version: *The Teaching of Jesus*, trans. J. Wilson, Edinburgh 1892-3, defines the idea of the Kingdom of God as "a state of ideal and blessed fellowship of God, with a people attached to Him in true obedience" (Eng. trans., VOL. I, p. 212). The Kingdom of God is a kingdom of ethical nature in so far as it is realised already here in time, but it also necessarily includes the element of the full salvation which God bestows on "the members of the Kingdom" (p. 382). The Kingdom is therefore also a coming heavenly kingdom, (p. 377). For this combination of future and present, Wendt offers a purely psychological explanation: "Jesus possessed . . . in His personal piety, from the first, too keen a consciousness of an already existing state of gracious fellowship with His Father in Heaven, too rich an experience of the possession of Divine power and of guidance by the fatherly love of God, and too firm confidence in the accessibility of this blessed state to all other men, to lead Him to believe or to proclaim the Kingdom of God to be a merely future and heavenly one, and not rather as being in essence already in course of realisation here upon earth" (p. 400). With regard to Wendt's attitude to Ritschl, see Bohlin, *Kristna Gudsrikestanken*, pp. 191-9.

[15] W. Beyschlag, *Neutestamentliche Theologie oder Darstellung des Lebens Jesu und des Urchristentums nach den neutestamentlichen Quellen*, 2 vols., Halle 1891-2; Eng. version: *New Testament Theology, Or Historical Account of the Teaching of Jesus and of Primitive Christianity according to the New Testament Sources*, trans. N. Buchanan, 2 vols., Edinburgh 1895.

[16] B. Weiss, *Lehrbuch der Biblischen Theologie*, 6th edn., Stuttgart and Berlin 1895, 7th edn. 1903; Eng. version: *Biblical Theology of the New Testament*, trans. D. Eaton and J. E. Duguid, Edinburgh 1882-3. There are those who are already in the Kingdom of God (Mt. XXI. 31, XI. 11). "Already they have part in this kingdom; in their fellowship it begins to be realised," Eng. trans., VOL. I, p. 68.

[17] K. Lühr, "Das Bild Jesu bei den Eschatologen," in *Protestantische Monatshefte*, 1903, pp. 64-78. The Kingdom of God is "the communion of a People of God bound together in righteousness and love and so blessed by God" (p. 68).

[18] F. Traub, "Die Gegenwart des Gottesreiches in den Parabeln vom Senfkorn und Sauerteig, von der selbstwachsenden Saat, dem Unkraut und dem Fischnetz," in *Zeitschrift für Theologie und Kirche*, henceforth cited as *Z.Th.K.*, 1905, pp. 58-75. Jesus saw the emergence of the Kingdom of God in the communion of those who believed in the Messiah, even though He did not always see it so.

[19] J. Orr, "Kingdom of God, of Heaven," in *A Dictionary of the Bible*, ed. W. Hastings, VOL. II, Edinburgh 1899, 6th imp. 1905, pp. 844-56. The Kingdom of God is identified more or less with the Church, even though "the Kingdom of God is a wider conception than that of the Church" (p. 854). "The Church is, as a society, the visible expression of this kingdom in the world; is indeed the only society which does formally profess . . . to represent it" (p. 855).

[20] H. C. King, *Ethics of Jesus*, New York 1910. The Kingdom of God is the highest good, the rule of love in the life of the individual and the community.

even though these were not in every respect thoroughgoing followers of Ritschl. Both S. A. Fries and Nathan Söderblom were also obviously influenced by the great Göttingen theologian. S. A. Fries gave the following definition of the Kingdom of God: "The Kingdom of God, which consists of righteousness, peace and joy in the Holy Spirit . . . consists of all those who trust in God in His highest revelation in Jesus Christ, and who love one another as brothers."[21]

As to Söderblom, about the end of the eighteen-eighties and the beginning of the eighteen-nineties he found Ritschl's concept of the Kingdom of God a help towards understanding the person of Jesus, for at that time he regarded the question of who Jesus was as identical with the question of what Jesus aimed at with His mission.[22] The aim of Jesus was to preach and found the Kingdom of God on earth, and His disciples have for all time the task of realising the Kingdom of God in faith and obedience. Söderblom later called this "harsh but sound theology of the Kingdom of God" both "indispensable" and "incomparable."[23]

[21] S. A. Fries, *Guds Rike*, Stockholm 1910, p. 626.

[22] With regard to Söderblom's attitude towards Ritschl and his interpretation of Jesus in general see A. Fridrichsen, "Söderbloms Jesustolkning. En forsknings-uppgift," in *Religion och Bibel*, 1, 1942, pp. 58-63. How Söderblom was later obliged, under the influence of J. Weiss, to abandon the Ritschlean positions is discussed in connexion with the account of the debate on the Kingdom of God during the eighteen-nineties.

[23] N. Söderblom, *Gå vi mot religionens förnyelse?* Uppsala 1919, pp. 10 f.

II

The Individualistic and Spiritual
Interpretation of the Kingdom of God

Whereas the Kingdom of God, which to Ritschl was a sociological entity, occupied a dominating position in his system, it meant little to his most outstanding pupil, Wilhelm Herrmann, who was indeed regarded by orthodox followers of Ritschl as the great destroyer of the master's theology. Where we do encounter the idea of the Kingdom of God in Herrmann, it is adapted along individualistic and spiritual lines. Jesus meant by the Kingdom of God "the rule of God which man may see and experience—above all, therefore, the rule of God in man's own heart."[1]

What Ritschl wanted to emphasise, in calling his theology "elliptical," was that Christianity always has two focal points, the one religious justification, and the other ethical—the Kingdom of God; and just as an ellipse cannot exist without its two focal points, so Christianity cannot be clearly defined without its two. That Ritschl did not always succeed in holding these two ideas in juxtaposition is another matter, but the intention would seem to be clear. Adolf Harnack, on the other hand, sought to present the teaching of Jesus as three spheres, each of which is so constituted that it embodies and fully expresses the whole teaching of Jesus.[2] These spheres are:

[1] W. Herrmann, *Dogmatik, mit einer Gedächtnisrede auf Wilhelm Herrmann von M. Rade*, Gotha 1925, p. 25; Eng. version: *Systematic Theology*, trans. N. Micklam and K. A. Saunders, London 1927, p. 46. In his *Ethik*, Tübingen 1901, 6th edn. 1921, we encounter the idea of the Kingdom of God "only indirectly and at the same time modified, in fact like the idea of a moral community in general" (Bohlin, *Kristna Gudsrikestanken*, p. 164).

[2] A. Harnack, *Das Wesen des Christentums*, 1900; 71st thou. Leipzig 1927; Eng. version: *What is Christianity?* trans. T. B. Saunders, London and New York 1901.

(1) The Kingdom of God and its coming; (2) God the Father and the infinite value of the human soul; and finally (3) The higher righteousness and the commandment of love.

The teaching of Jesus on the Kingdom of God has, according to Harnack, two poles. On the one hand the coming of the Kingdom is revealed as a purely future event, and the Kingdom itself as an outward Dominion of God; on the other it is something inward and already in being, it holds its entry already in the present. This pole, that the Kingdom does not come with outward manifestations but that it is already there, was the real view of Jesus. The Kingdom of God is in reality a still, powerful divine force in the hearts of men. It comes when it makes its entry into the individual soul. The Kingdom of God is, therefore, the dominion of the Holy God in the individual heart. It is God Himself in His power. Everything here turns on the soul and God, on God and the soul. Jesus Himself was upborne by the consciousness that God is always near. The Kingdom of God as interpreted by Harnack becomes transformed into the spiritual communion of the soul with God. All the dramatic and eschatological features are relegated to a lower plane.

An interesting point is Harnack's constant uneasiness in face of the eschatological doctrine. He could not avoid issue with it, for the discussion on the eschatological character of the Kingdom of God was in full swing. But he tried to defend himself. In 1900 we find him stating that the exhortation to repentance clothes itself in every age in such phrases as: The last hour is at hand, or, This is the eleventh hour. The whole dramatic eschatological apparatus with its expressions such as "The Kingdom of God is at hand," "The end is nigh," has this purpose of pressing home the necessity for repentance.[3] A few years later he declared[4] that in the teaching of Jesus

---

[3] *Op. cit.*, (Eng. trans.), pp. 40 f.

[4] A. Harnack, *Dogmengeschichte* (Grundriss der theol. Wissenschaften, VOL. IV, PT. 3), 4th edn., Tübingen 1905, pp. 14 f. In the 2nd edn. of *Lehrbuch der Dogmengeschichte* (Samml. theol. Lehrbücher, VOL. I, Frieburg i. B. 1888, 2nd edn. 1888, 4th edn. 1909), Harnack wrote (p. 56): "Jesus preached the Kingdom of God as something future and yet present, as something visible and yet invisible," he said in the 4th edn. of the same work in 1909 (p. 71): "Jesus preached the Kingdom of God, which is opposed to the kingdom of the devil and so also to the kingdom of the world, as something future and invisible, yet it was present and visible; for men heard His preaching, in which the kingdom came like a hurricane, and they saw Him and His works." And (p. 67): "The gospel came into the world

there are static elements, such as the Lord's Prayer and the Sermon on the Mount, which find their most succinct expression in the statement that God is the Father of man, but that these are embedded in an impulsive, flaming, world-abandoning element the source of which lies in the doctrine of the Kingdom of God. The Gospel thus came to the world as an apocalyptic message and an eschatological movement, but there was to Harnack no shadow of doubt that the static elements were the essential ones to Jesus.

Harnack stands out as the foremost and most influential representative of this purely individualistic, spiritual, uneschatological interpretation of Jesus, to which Jesus stands as the pre-eminent religious personality, as a religious hero above all others in the history of mankind. Harnack was not without forerunners and has found a long succession of followers in practically every country right down to the present day.

J. Wellhausen published in 1894[5] a picture of Jesus which corresponds in intention with Harnack's later ideas. It is the picture of a religious personality. Jesus takes His place in the ranks of Old Testament prophets such as Amos, Hosea, Isaiah, and Jeremiah, whose assurance of God never falters. So too Jesus stands there, strong and clear-eyed, as the true man and hero who fought a hard battle against His opponents, in particular the Pharisees. The most important thing to His disciples was not what He taught but the impress of His personality, in which He gathered the eternally true, the human and divine under the burning-glass of His individuality. He fulfilled the ideal of humanity.[6] No one before Him had so rejoiced in goodness in peace of conscience.[7] When Jesus proclaimed the imminent coming of the Kingdom of God, He could not have meant by the Kingdom anything other than what His contemporaries understood by it. But the Kingdom

---

as an apocalyptic-eschatological message; apocalyptic and eschatological not merely in form, but also in content." See W. Bousset's criticism in *Theologische Rundschau*, henceforth cited as *Th. R.*, 1901, pp. 95 f.

[5] J. Wellhausen, *Israelitische und jüdische Geschichte*, Berlin 1894. Wellhausen altered his viewpoint considerably in the various editions in the chapter "Das Evangelium."

[6] " 'Ecce homo'—a divine wonder in this age and in these surroundings," *op. cit.*, p. 317.

[7] "But he *enjoyed* piety as no one ever before him in peace of soul and a good conscience towards God," *op. cit.*, p. 312.

does not come through a happy chance, Jesus makes it the object of endeavour. Jesus not merely prophesies its coming but "draws it onto the earth through His transcendence, He plants at least the seed."[8] The new age begins with Him, and the Kingdom, which is already at hand but which is to be fulfilled in the future, is nothing else but the communion of love between free people, who are the children of God. The religion of the Gospel is individualism. The celebrated Old Testament scholar seems, when he wrote this, not to have doubted for a moment that the liberal image of Jesus is an adequate expression for the very inmost intentions of Jesus. But to us today Wellhausen's presentation seems more like German idealism read into the Gospel than the actual Gospel picture of Jesus and the Kingdom of God He preached. What we have here is the ideal man of Goethe and Carlyle.

Later Wellhausen was driven to assert that the Kingdom of God only occupies a secondary position in the teaching of Jesus.[9] Only in Mk. VIII. 27-X. 45 do we find any direct instruction on the coming Kingdom of God, but he regarded both this and the Christological sayings here as community theology.

The underlying aim of the individualistic interpretation of the Kingdom of God was to find the religious content behind the historically-conditioned ideas, and to free the former from the latter. Thus B. Duhm declared that Jesus did indeed adopt the old conception of the Kingdom of God, but without the apocalyptic form, for His was "a purely religious hope."[10] What this means in purely idealistic terms is that Jesus transferred the centre-point of religion from the historical people of Israel to within the soul of man. But one cannot for that reason ignore the fact that the Kingdom of God is also an objective entity, which is to be established on the renewed earth by outward cataclysms. This view depends, however, on Jesus' idea of the world. Not to compromise Jesus too much, Duhm adds: "Possibly, of course, we might venture to think that Jesus would not have held to this form of expectation, if He could have seen the earth as we see it."[11]

[8] *Op. cit.*, p. 314.

[9] J. Wellhausen, *Einleitung in die drei ersten Evangelien*, Berlin 1905.

[10] B. Duhm, *Das kommende Reich Gottes*, Tübingen 1910, p. 33; Eng. version: *The Ever-Coming Kingdom of God*, trans. A. Duff, London 1911, p. 73

[11] Duhm, *op. cit.*, (Eng. trans.), p. 79.

The Kingdom of God becomes in the end, as for Wellhausen, "the fellowship of those free spirits who have communion with God."[12] But it does not come of itself. "We must work hard, to build up our own life; we must fight and so grow strong and then ripen like true men. All the time we must pray like children: 'Father, Thy Kingdom come'."[13]

Johannes Müller exercised a strong influence not merely on the educated laymen he gathered together at Schloss Elmau, but on a wide circle of theologians too. Here I will only mention Martin Dibelius, who is palpably under the influence of Müller's thought. The aim of Müller's instruction was not to impart theoretical knowledge but to kindle personal life in those who wish to find themselves. What Jesus was interested in was life. He tried to enlighten mankind "through new, through truly personal being,"[14] in which men become like children, direct, simple, impulsive. Jesus came into the world as an inexhaustible source of divine life-energy. Whenever He approached, a strange stir ran through the people. All who entered the radius of His personality were affected by the divine vibrations. What this means to us, Müller expresses thus: "We must place ourselves under the impact of His personality, as it reaches us from the Gospels, the source of His history, and must surrender ourselves unresistingly for Him to work upon."[15] Real life is only to be attained through an "attitude of life" (*"Lebenshaltung"*), not through repentance and such things. The ethical teaching of Jesus is not ethics, not a message, but impulses sent out by Jesus to bring the hidden forces in the human soul to living and creative development. Only so is a state of soul achieved that gives stature to our life. This is "new being."

The Kingdom of God becomes to Müller "the hidden life-force of the All,"[16] that shapes life. It reflects Jesus' presentation of the unutterable He experienced within Him, and which He saw breaking forth. The world renewal which Jesus offers is that personal life develops in all circumstances and sets its stamp upon them. Jesus preached the dawning of the day of God, but to Müller this means that He "irradiated

[12] *Op. cit.*, p. 86.   [13] *Ibid.*

[14] J. Müller, *Von den Quellen des Lebens. Sieben Aufsätze*, 4th edn., Munich 1914, p. 60.   [15] *Op. cit.*, p. 258.

[16] J. Müller, *Die Bergpredigt, verdeutscht und vergegenwärtigt*, 1906, 5th edn., Munich 1919, p. 31.

man with His sanctity and led him forth into the new life."[17]

Jesus here has nothing left of that which is characteristic of Him in the Gospels. He is the Son of Man, which means simply that He is the true man. He is man according to God's plan, who can infuse the new, the truly human nature into seekers who wish to become true men.

The Kingdom of God is not by any means the dominating centre-point of the teaching of Jesus, but the gospel is Jesus Himself; His personality is the new creative force which has entered into history (W. Heitmüller[18]). This view, in which the personality of Jesus is transcendent, is to be found not only in such writers as A. Hausrath, A. Hauck, and Arnold Meyer; its influence may be seen even in the conservative Theodor Zahn,[19] not to mention the dominating position this picture of Jesus occupied in popular presentations of the first few decades of the present century. We find it all over the world. As examples may be mentioned in France A. Réville and A. Causse; in England J. E. Carpenter, C. W. Emmet, Lily Dougall, J. Mackinnon; in Scotland A. B. D. Alexander;[20] and in Italy P. Chiminelli and A. Chiapelli. In America a liberal spiritualised representation of Jesus became very prevalent in the twentieth century in conjunction with the

[17] *Op. cit.*, p. 34.

[18] W. Heitmüller, *Jesus*, Tübingen 1913. The psychological view of the Kingdom of God comes out clearly in Heitmüller: "Thus Jesus set himself to reshape and increase the heritage received. The idea began to emerge that the glorious future already entered into the present. It was not a recognition won by thought, but, like most of Jesus' flashes of prophetic insight, the involuntary, inevitable illumination from His own experience. He experienced in Himself the subjugation of the hostile powers, the devils; He experienced in Himself and through Himself what the Kingdom would bring; He lived as though the Kingdom of God were already realised; He saw beginnings full of promise even in the circle of His own followers; He began to regard Himself as the Messiah: then the inherited idea of the Kingdom of the future inevitably, perhaps to His own astonishment, became transformed into a belief in its fulfilment in the present, even though at first naturally only in embryo" (pp. 144 f.).

[19] T. Zahn, *Grundriss der neutestamentlichen Theologie*, Leipzig 1928, emphasises how the mission of Jesus is itself the appearance of the Kingdom of God, since the word preached by Jesus establishes the dominion of God in the hearts of those who receive the word in faith. According to Zahn, Jesus called Himself "Son of Man" because He knew that the true nature of man had come to perfection in and through Him (p. 21).

[20] A. B. D. Alexander, "The Kingdom of God and the Ethics of Jesus," in *The Expository Times*, henceforth cited as *Exp. T.*, 1928-29, pp. 73-7. "The eschatological interpretation of the Gospels confuses colour with form, by-product with main intention. . . . He (Jesus) was essentially a Reformer and a Revealer of eternal values" (p. 75).

"Social Gospel":[21] the outstanding names are W. P. Du Bose,[22] B. W. Bacon, E. I. Bosworth, W. H. Robinson,[23] H. J. Cadbury,[24] and F. C. Grant.[25]

In depicting the character and personality of Jesus eschatology is thrust aside (J. Ninck, F. Rittelmeyer), though Jesus is represented as a man of will with a passionate, proud, kinglike will (K. Weidel). That the whole problem of the character of Jesus has been falsely posed is shown by the degree of modernisation that is necessary in order to force Jesus into this mould. When finally Ninck, for example, declares that one cannot understand the self-awareness of Jesus without believing in the divine in man, it is obvious that this interpretation of Jesus has its roots in idealistic philosophy.[26]

[21] A. C. Purdy, "Das Neue Testament in der amerikanischen Theologie," in *Th. R.*, N.F. III (1931), pp. 367-86.

[22] W. P. Du Bose, *The Gospel in the Gospels*, London and New York 1906. "Jesus Christ has not come so much to create the kingdom of God without us, as to create within us the power to see it. I am come, He says, that they which see not may see. What He saw and what He would have us to see is: all the eternal love that God the Father is, *ours*; all the infinite grace that God the Son is, ours; all the perfect fellowship or oneness with ourselves that God the Holy Ghost is, ours. If all this is ours, then all things are ours, and all blessedness ours" (p. 96). Du Bose may be regarded as a forerunner of Vilhelm Grønbech.

[23] W. H. Robinson, *The Parables of Jesus in their Relation to His Ministry*, Chicago 1928. "For Jesus the Kingdom of God was a spiritual thing. It was a communion of souls founded on sacrifice and love" (p. 44). "For Jesus the Kingdom of God was a present spiritual force" (p. 51).

[24] H. J. Cadbury, *The Peril of Modernizing Jesus*, New York 1937.

[25] F. C. Grant, *The Gospel of the Kingdom*, New York 1940. The Kingdom of God immanent, not apocalyptically but religiously. Jesus did not give Himself out to be the Messiah.

[26] M. Maurenbrecher asserts in *Von Nazareth nach Golgatha, Untersuchungen über die weltgeschichtlichen Zusammenhänge*, Berlin-Schöneberg 1909, that Jesus regarded religion and morals from the point of view of those without possessions. The atmosphere of guilt is gone. God the Father cares for all and forgives all who repent. See also A. Schweitzer, *Geschichte der Leben-Jesu Forschung*, Tübingen 1913, henceforth cited as *Geschichte*, pp. 570 ff.; R. Eisler, *Ἰησοῦς βασιλεὺς οὐ βασιλεύσας, Die messianische Unabhängigkeitsbewegung vom Auftreten Johannes des Täufers bis zum Untergang Jacobs des Gerechten nach der neuerschlossenen Erobung von Jerusalem des Flavius Josephus und den christlichen Quellen.*, Rel. wiss. Bibliotek, Heidelberg 1929-30; Eng. version: *The Messiah Jesus and John the Baptist*, trans. A. H. Krappe, London 1931. Eisler regards Jesus from a one-sidedly political Messianic viewpoint. Jesus was a small man. His sense of inferiority explains, among other things, the eschatological hope of the time of salvation which is to come through the miraculous power of God, and His Messianic self-awareness, which compensated for His physical insignificance. The Kingdom of God is not transcendent but is "a political, moral and religious state of people here on earth" (Eng. trans., p. 346). Once men have attained the knowledge that they are the children of God and live as brothers, they have entered into the Kingdom of God. Everyone has the law in his own conscience; by following it here and now, the Kingdom of God can be realised. It lies in every man's power to build the Kingdom.

III

The Social Interpretation of
the Kingdom of God

The social interpretation of the Kingdom of God which emerged in various forms both in Europe and America, is obviously intimately connected with the theology of Albrecht Ritschl. Just as by him, the Kingdom of God is conceived as the common moral task of humanity.[1] Any full account of the social interpretation of the Kingdom of God would fall largely outside the framework we have set ourselves, which is to trace the different interpretations of Jesus' teaching on the Kingdom of God. There is throughout this movement little if any attempt to reach an exegetic understanding of what Jesus meant by the Kingdom of God, or to set this against its historical background. The only Kingdom of God this movement could see in the teachings of Jesus was an immediate, practical force operating in the present.[2] The influence this interpretation had, however, particularly in America—the "Social Gospel"—was so great that we would not feel justified in altogether passing it over.

[1] Bohlin, *Kristna Gudsrikestanken*, pp. 347 f.: "Ritschl actually to a large extent prepared the way for this movement" (the religious-social movement in Germany and German Switzerland), "both indirectly, by his critical attitude towards the ascetic, world-denying, pietistic ideal of life, and also more directly by the strong emphasis he placed on the eternal life as a spiritual possession 'in this world,' and on the idea of the nature of the Kingdom of God—as is most clearly apparent in its original expression—as the common moral *task* of Christianity." W. Rauschenbusch, *A Theology for the Social Gospel*, New York 1922, p. 139, n. 1, comments favourably on Ritschl's idea of the Kingdom of God, although the social perspective does not receive full justice.

[2] Even works by members of this movement which take the form of a commentary on the Scriptures, have all of them a practical religious purpose, as for example L. Ragaz, *Die Gliechnisse Jesu*, Berne 1944, where this is shown already by the question and answer form.

The Interpretation of the Kingdom of God by the Social Movement in Germany and Switzerland

In Europe the social interpretation of the Kingdom of God found its main adherents in Germany and Switzerland, though it also reached Sweden.[3] The two dominating figures in this German and Swiss religious-social movement were Johann Christoph Blumhardt and his son, Christoph Blumhardt.[4] Brought up in the eschatological atmosphere of Württemberg Pietism, the elder Blumhardt entertained a deep belief in the imminent actual appearance of the Kingdom of God. About the turn of the century the younger Blumhardt became converted to a belief in an organic development of the Kingdom of God in terms of this world. This change was also marked by his becoming an active member of the Social Democratic political party. The younger Blumhardt's conception of the Kingdom of God was strictly practical. The Kingdom of God, which occupies the central position in his theology, is conceived as a spiritual reality, active and creative in the present moment. It is not in Heaven that the Kingdom of God is to be established, for there the will of God already prevails, but here upon earth. Blumhardt declared accordingly: "It is of tremendous importance to labour for the earth, it is not heaven that is to be conquered, but earth."[5] The victory of the Kingdom of God does not presuppose or lead to any cessation of the world of time or history, but involves a re-creation of this world in and by the conquest of sin and death and the realisation of a perfected active life of mankind in God, whereby the whole of existence is placed in the service of God and reveals the glory of God. The universality of the Kingdom of God is asserted against all individualistic thirst for salvation. Jesus will not exclude anyone at all from the Kingdom, not even His enemies. In support of this interpretation Blumhardt

[3] As exponents of religious socialism, who strongly emphasise the Kingdom of God on earth, may be mentioned: in England, J. R. Campbell; in France, Wilfred Monod and Elie Gounelle; in Holland, R. Backer; in Denmark, F. Linderberg and to a certain extent V. Ammundsen. In Sweden the ideas of this movement are chiefly represented by "Förbundet för kristet samhällsliv" (The Association for Christian Social Life), founded in 1918, and numbering Natanael Beskow, Sam. Thysell, and Sigurd Westman among its members.

[4] This account of the Blumhardts is based on Bohlin, *Kristna Gudsrikestanken*.

[5] Chr. Blumhardt, *Predigten und Andachten aus dem Jahre 1888 bis 1896*, Erlenbach-Zürich and Leipzig 1925, p. 513.

quoted Lk. xvii. 21, where "in the midst of you" refers to the
Pharisees, or the enemies of Jesus. Though His enemies are
bound with the bonds of Satan, Jesus still sees within them the
germ of the Kingdom of God.

The significance of Jesus for the Kingdom is that in Him
God sowed a seed of the Kingdom of God that is to grow still
greater. "With Jesus God has sowed a seed in the human
race, this seed is to come to growth within individual men,
that the Kingdom of God may grow from all individuals;
from you and me, from Jews and heathens, from the pious and
from the godless it shall grow. That will be the wonder, when
the Kingdom of God appears, that it has been created not
from any one great man, but that it is something living, that
grows and lives from millions of men."[6] The Kingdom of
God will reveal itself with increasing power on earth, until all
will realise that Jesus Christ has triumphed in mankind and
that God has become the King of all the world, and His will
prevails everywhere. No one will ever be able to escape His
influence. The goal is the realisation of heaven on earth, a
new inconceivable reality that embraces all and everything
and, where the good has won complete victory, a new history
that will be purely and exclusively the history of *God* in
mankind.

It is important to note that the younger Blumhardt, like
his father, emphasised strongly that the Kingdom of God is not
a product of human progress but is a gift from God, something
from on high. But even though ultimately it is God who Himself creates the Kingdom, it is also certain that He expects
the co-operation of mankind for the Kingdom to become reality.
It is to His co-operators that He entrusts the cause of the
Kingdom. The community of Christ is God's temple on earth,
and without such a temple the Kingdom of God cannot
appear on earth. By abandoning itself to God's will and
awaiting the Kingdom of God the community draws this down
to earth and into humanity. The Kingdom of God does not
come suddenly and unexpectedly through some catastrophe
or some great ultimate miracle, but it comes little by little, as
through a slow development in every sphere of life the way
is prepared for the coming of the Kingdom in perfected form.

[6] Chr. Blumhardt, *Vom Reiche Gottes*, Berlin 1925, p. 29 (quoted after Bohlin,
Kristna Gudsrikestanken, p. 352).

Chr. Blumhardt therefore vigorously asserted that Jesus sought not merely the salvation of individuals but a re-creation in the spirit of the Kingdom of God of all existing political and social institutions with Jesus as Lord on earth: in social life, in politics, in home and family, in manners and customs. It is a "Kingdom of God on earth." The peculiar quality of this interpretation of the Kingdom of God is above all the connexion between future hopes and present social need. Thus the younger Blumhardt wrote: "You know well that I await the future of Jesus Christ—it is the fire of my heart— but where do I await it? I do not look up to heaven; there, where the multitudes of people perish in their misery, there do I look, there must He appear, or it is not Jesus."[7]

However strongly it is emphasised that God and only God can establish the Kingdom, the idea of human co-operation and of the gradual emergence of the Kingdom of God preclude any idea of anything miraculous. The Kingdom of God becomes an ethical goal as it was for Ritschl, even though Blumhardt displayed an altogether different eschatological fire, for this Kingdom of God that is to come on earth was still for him a thing of the future, and he longed for its coming as ardently as ever any Christian during the early days of the Church.[8]

The foremost pupil of the younger Blumhardt was the Swiss, Leonard Ragaz, who revered his teacher as though he were a man in line with the prophets, the Apostles and the reformers. Ragaz now set out to carry the work of his great master farther.

He said it is stated in the Gospels beyond all question that Jesus, in common with the whole of early Christianity, lived in expectation of the immediate appearance of the Kingdom of God at the Parousia.[9] One cannot read very far in Ragaz's writings without becoming aware that here is the genuine eschatological atmosphere. He will say, for example, that only those who reach out towards the future, can understand

---

[7] Chr. Blumhardt, *Ihr Menschen seid Gottes*, Erlenbach-Zürich and Leipzig 1936, p. 328.

[8] Bohlin, *Kristna Gudsrikestanken*, p. 362. Apart from L. Ragaz, the best-known representative of the religious-social movement in Switzerland is H. Kutter.

[9] L. Ragaz, *Du sollst. Grundzüge einer sittlichen Weltanschauung*, 2nd edn., Ossmanstedt bei Weimar 1911, p. 85.

Jesus.[10] As the One who is to come, God shall be justified. His creation is not yet complete, and God has not yet said His last word; but God is a living God and His work of creation continues.[11]

God who is holy, sovereign, and exalted above the earth, establishes His Kingdom here on earth. Neither the New Testament nor the Old knows of anything else but "a coming of the Kingdom on earth for the establishment of the dominion of God."[12] The phrase that is constantly recurring is: "The Kingdom of God on earth." What Jesus taught is precisely the Dominion of God on earth, which comes about through God's will being done on earth as it is in heaven. "What did Jesus seek?" asks Ragaz. The answer is: "Nothing for Himself, we repeat it, not a position of power, nor honour for Himself, nor confession of His person, no, it was something quite other He sought: the Kingdom of God on earth. The cause of God, that it should grow, should triumph, that God should become manifest and fill the earth, that to Him was all. The Kingdom of God, that is the dominion of God on earth. There should reign on earth the all-powerful God, so that no other power should be of any account as against Him; there should reign the just and holy God, so that all that is just and good should flourish victorious and His will be done on earth as it is in heaven; there should reign the Father, and therewith all should become good and light, pain and death be broken and life and joy become manifest to the ends of the earth. Under the eye of the Father a human Kingdom, in which the children of God have their being in purity and strength, in goodness and trust, counting themselves and others noble and feeling themselves one family, the members of the House of God— that was His will and His promise. And therewith the fulfil- ment of all the hopes of the Fathers and the redemption of all peoples! That was what Jesus sought."[13]

How, then, is the coming of the Kingdom of God on earth visualised? The Kingdom of God has become an historical reality in Jesus, and its forces will stream from Him into and

[10] In a sermon he exhorted the congregation: "Keep forward-looking, forward- striving, grow ever more hopeful ! We can never hope enough, for we have a great God" (Dein Reich komme, 2nd edn., Basle 1911, p. 544).

[11] Ragaz, op. cit., p. 542.

[12] Ragaz, Die Gleichnisse Jesu, p. 29.

[13] Ragaz, Dein Reich komme, pp. 7 f.

interpenetrate the whole world of mankind, though all the time retaining their own peculiar quality. This supernal force which streams into humanity is clearly thought of more or less in terms of a new form of life, a new kind of existence, in which men are freed from all that binds them, freed from sin, hatred, the oppression of the world and of death, freed from the service of Mammon and of the individual self, but united in a kingdom of freedom, purity, righteousness, and love. It is above all the weak and insignificant who will receive the Kingdom, for the strong do not think they need it.

Ragaz stoutly denied that the Kingdom of God could be created here on earth by human activity. No, it is God Himself who creates His Kingdom. "The Kingdom of God will be brought to pass through God Himself, we can do nothing, save offer ourselves as fellow-workers."[14] God creates His Kingdom even through His enemies.[15] Yet it was hard for Ragaz to maintain this view, that God creates His Kingdom Himself through sovereign acts, when he stressed man's co-operation as strongly as he did. The coming of the Kingdom of God becomes dependent on the creative and directive activity of the individual.

But what is even more serious is that the Kingdom of God sometimes becomes in his presentation an absolutely unqualified force. Thus in his passionate polemics against the concept of the Kingdom of God being constrained to fit the ideas of a given Church or community, Ragaz can declare that everything that is created works, willy-nilly, for the Kingdom of God. The winds, the waves, and the forces of nature work for the Kingdom of God! "The scholar pursuing some new scientific truth works for the Kingdom of God, for that too will somewhere take its place in the service of the creating God; the inventor of a new machine that makes possible processes that could not be achieved before, works for

[14] L. Ragaz, *Weltreich, Religion und Gottesherrschaft*, VOLS. I-II, 1922, p. 80 (quoted according to Bohlin, *Kristna Gudsrikestanken*, p. 393).

[15] "God creates His Kingdom of three kinds of men. He creates it through those who are summoned, called, appointed, *those who obey Him*, above all through the great Prophets and Apostles, but also through the unknown witnesses and doers of his Will. He creates it, in so far as those who are summoned, called, appointed, refuse the call, through their *opponents*, yes, *enemies*—who are often, however, their best friends and most beloved sons. And He creates it through those who are summoned, called and appointed, who are *awakened* by their apparent opponents" (*Die Gleichnisse Jesu*, p. 126).

the Kingdom of God—for industry, too, is the handmaiden of God; every workman who helps to build a tunnel, a bridge, a ship, works for God, for even through railways, ships and roads will the dominion of God come; every worker, man or woman, who works with head, hand or heart, works for God, if they work rightly. Every good thought that passes unseen through the heart of man, works for God. They work most for His Kingdom who overcome themselves, hold themselves pure and bring their sacrifice in love. They hasten its coming most. They are the nobility of the Kingdom. At their head stands Jesus Christ, who loved the most."[16]

It is, of course, true to say that Jesus, too, is a prophet, indeed the prophet of prophets, but at the same time He transcends everything that prophets and "prophethood" stand for.[17] But when Ragaz refuses to consider seriously the idea that Jesus regarded Himself as the Son of Man, he is approaching suspiciously close to the thought-processes of Johannes Müller. The Kingdom of God is on its way to losing its supra-worldly quality and becoming a general creative force of no particularly specified quality. Jesus becomes the first representative on earth of a new kind of life, which in the end is to rule the earth. This new kind of life is "the Kingdom of God on earth."

"The Social Gospel"

Nowhere has the social interpretation of Christianity gained so much influence as in America. The American theologian, H. J. Cadbury, declares: "The Social Gospel, which meets such coolness from continental theologians generally, has for a generation been the staple diet of American liberals. From every college pulpit, in every Church conference it has been proclaimed as *the* gospel of Jesus."[18] When the "Social Gospel" appeared, towards the end of the nineteenth century, this interpretation of Christianity by no means lacked forerunners.[19]

[16] Ragaz, *Dein Reich komme*, p. 55.   [17] Ragaz, *op. cit.*, p. 8.
[18] Cadbury, *The Peril of Modernizing Jesus*, pp. 94 f.
[19] H. R. Niebuhr, *The Kingdom of God in America*, Chicago and New York 1937, pp. 161 ff.; G. Hammar, *Christian Realism in contemporary American Theology. A study of Reinhold Niebuhr, W. M. Horton and H. P. van Dusen, preceded by a general and historical survey*, Uppsala 1940, pp. 151 f. For the history and teachings of the movement see above all C. H. Hopkins, *The Rise of the Social Gospel in American Protestantism 1865-1915*, New Haven 1940.

The reasons why the "Social Gospel," with its expectation of the early establishment of the Kingdom of God on earth, acquired such a dominating position are by no means to be sought primarily in its theology as such, but in a number of contributory factors of an economic and social nature. Here we will only mention American optimism in general, which waxed fat on the boom that preceded the economic depression of 1929, a widespread popular philosophy embracing a biological theory of evolution, and, in certain circles, revivalist movements which had the effect of encouraging hopes that the Kingdom of God was approaching on earth.[20]

Among its exponents may be mentioned F. G. Peabody, Shailer Mathews, and the great name of the movement, Walter Rauschenbusch.[21] Shailer Mathews provided the following definition of the Kingdom of God: "By the Kingdom of God Jesus meant *an ideal* (though progressively approximated) *social order in which the relation of men to God is that of sons and* (therefore) *to each other, that of brothers.*"[22] Mathews considered that the social approach is most apparent in Jesus' conception of the Kingdom of God. That Jesus meant a society by the Kingdom of God, is to Mathews proved by the position which the Kingdom as ideal occupies in relation to the present social order. The old social order was governed by selfishness and hatred, whereas the new is under the universal dominion of love, in which God is Father and all men are brothers. The inmost essence of Christianity can therefore be expressed by the words "The fatherhood of God and the brotherhood of men."

W. Rauschenbusch saw that Jesus did not appear in the capacity of a social reformer, but, like the rest of the movement, he wanted to find general principles for his social programme in the teaching and life of Jesus, which he could then apply to

[20] Niebuhr, *op. cit.*, p. 154; Hammar, *op. cit.*, pp. 155 f.

[21] S. Mathews, *The Social Teaching of Jesus*, New York 1897. Mathews later modified his views in *Jesus on Social Institutions*, New York 1928. F. G. Peabody, *Jesus Christ and the Social Question*, New York 1900. W. Rauschenbusch's most important work is *A Theology for the Social Gospel*. With regard to literature see above all S. Mathews, "The Development of Social Christianity in America during the past twenty-five years," in *The Journal of Religion*, henceforth cited as *J. Rel.*, VII (1927), pp. 376 ff.

[22] *The Social Teaching of Jesus*, p. 58. Among the theologians Mathews quotes in support of his definition are such decided followers of Ritschl as B. Weiss and Beyschlag.

the economic system and social policy of the present-day world. With naïve optimism Rauschenbusch actually declared in 1912 that the hardest part of the work of Christianising the social order was already accomplished.[23] The Kingdom of God, which is the heart of the teaching of Jesus, is presented as the lost social ideal of Christianity. Rauschenbusch even declared that the teaching of the Kingdom of God "is itself the social gospel."[24] This ideal now awaits its imminent realisation. The Kingdom of God is to be created on earth. That it is possible for existing society to put into effect the ethic of love that confronts us in the Sermon on the Mount, is a conviction held by all representatives of this movement in common.

The Kingdom of God means that humanity organises itself according to the principles of love and solidarity. The task of believers is to work out the coming of this Kingdom, and the ennoblement of culture and of society is regarded as an element in this coming. The source of inspiration in this work for the Kingdom of God is primarily faith in the divine love, but also a conviction of the natural goodness of the world and of individuals. Soon the Kingdom of God will be organised here on earth. This Kingdom of God as proclaimed by "the Social Gospel" has been defined by one Dutch theologian as "a God-filled humanity living in a righteous social order."[25]

That this interpretation loses sight of the eschatological nature of the Kingdom of God, in the sense that the Kingdom of God is something different in quality from all human institutions and cultural values, would appear obvious. Nor is the "love" that is spoken of as being the fundamental principle of the Kingdom, anything more than a general feeling of "good will." The traditional apocalyptic and eschatological element in the Kingdom of God has no serious influence on the social theories of Rauschenbusch and his followers, but is regarded by them more as a part of the inevitable shell of Judaism that must always exist. Jesus' social teaching is absolutely independent of this element, since it is based on timeless principles which are applicable to all ages. Jesus solved the conflict between ideal and reality by a practical, *i.e.* psychological, method. He lived Himself,

[23] Hammar, *Christian Realism*, p. 155.
[24] Rauschenbusch, *Theology for the Social Gospel*, p. 131.
[25] Viisser't Hooft according to Hammar, *op. cit.*, p. 156.

and taught others to live, as though the Kingdom of God had already come.

Jesus is even characterised as "the most thorough-going democrat that has appeared in human history."[26] One is tempted to ask whether Jesus really had any social gospel to proclaim. The answer depends upon what one means by "social." The word can, of course, be used in a sense in which it is applicable to Jesus, but in the sense in which we normally use it, it is an anachronism to speak of a "social" Gospel. The "Social Gospel" modernises Jesus and reads into the Gospel ideas which properly belong to optimistic American philosophy and anthropology. With evolutionary ideas abroad in the world, Rauschenbusch was even capable of declaring that the idea of the Kingdom of God was the result of expressing the theory of evolution in religious terms.[27] At the root of the "Social Gospel" we find a moral, humanistic, and immanent conception of God, as is always the case with liberal theology not only in America but everywhere else.[28]

It cannot be denied that the "Social Gospel" has a certain eschatological fire, but the Kingdom of God it proclaims is a kingdom on earth, with too little if any of the quality of eternity.

[26] Cadbury, *The Peril of Modernizing Jesus*, p. 204. Cadbury mentions as typical a reference in the index of a book on religious education: "Kingdom of God, see *Democracy.*"

[27] W. Rauschenbusch, *Christianizing the Social Order*, New York 1912, p. 90.

[28] Hammar, *Christian Realism*, p. 157.

IV

The Eschatological Interpretation
of the Kingdom of God
before Johannes Weiss

Interpretation of Jesus during the nineteenth century had been almost completely de-eschatologised. We cannot here go into the causes for this at any length. We will merely point out that, whereas a definite eschatological vein is observable among certain followers of Pietism, chiefly in the form of a longing for the millennium on earth (Chiliasm)— notably in the Alsatian, Philip Jakob Spener, and his friend, Johann Wilhelm Petersen, as well as in Württembergian Pietism—both Frankish Pietism and Zinzendorff with the Moravian Brethren remained unaffected by this in any way. The de-eschatologising of Christianity by the Moravians, which also had a perceptible influence on Schliermacher, obviously left its mark on the interpretation of Jesus during the past century in a decisive way.[1]

It is, therefore, extremely interesting to see how opposition gradually grew up from circles in which eschatological hope had obviously remained alive, even though the main stream of theology had gone a different way.

Even J. A. Bengel (1687-1752), who was a member of the Württembergian Pietistic movement, and later the so-called first Tübingen school, whose foremost name was J. T. Beck (1804-78), opposed the current spiritualisation of New Testament eschatology, stressing the realistic significance of the eschatological sayings. J. G. Herder (1744-1803) recognised

[1] W. Nigg, *Das ewige Reich, Geschichte einer Sehnsucht und einer Enttäuschung*, Erlenbach-Zürich 1944, pp. 268-95.

the eschatological character of Jesus' teachings,[2] while in 1863 E. Renan called attention to the eschatological aspect of the Jesus tradition.[3]   In 1864 T. Colani, realising the essentially Jewish character of the Jesus of the Gospels, felt called upon to eliminate the eschatological sayings from the text by critical procedure as not genuine,[4] while G. Volkmar provided a spiritualised explanation of them.[5] Even where it was asserted that the eschatological sayings must be taken in a literal sense (W. Weiffenbach),[6] this by no means meant the emergence of an eschatological interpretation of the Kingdom of God, though it was a step in the right direction.

Even though leading theologians during the latter half of the nineteenth century lacked understanding of the realistic eschatology of the New Testament, with its strong tension between a now and a perfected then, and consequently either eliminated the eschatological sayings by textual criticism or modified them, there are nevertheless indications that Biblical realism still remained alive in certain quarters.   In 1878 A. Wabnitz presented his thesis on "L'Idéal messianique de Jésus" in Montauban,[7] setting forth essentially the same view as J. Weiss defended later in 1892.[8]   Württembergian Pietism had always been characterised by a strongly eschatological atmosphere and a realistic expectation of the impending appearance of the Kingdom of God.   The realistic eschatological conception of the Kingdom of God that survived in certain Biblicistic and Pietistic circles broke forth here and there like a spring

[2] C. C. McCown, *The Search for the real Jesus: a century of historical study*, New York 1940, p. 242.

[3] E. Renan, *La Vie de Jésus*, Paris 1863; Eng. version, *The Life of Jesus*, London 1864. See also Fridrichsen, "Söderbloms Jesustolkning," pp. 58-63.

[4] T. Colani, *Jésus-Christ et les croyances messianiques de son temps*, Strasbourg 1864. See also A. Schweitzer, *Geschichte*, pp. 222-4. It is perhaps worth noting that Colani was brought up a strict Pietist, although he later adopted a definitely liberal attitude (*Religion und Geschichte im Gegenwart*, henceforth cited as *R.G.G.*, 2nd edn., VOL. I, p. 1705).

[5] G. Volkmar, *Jesus Nazarenus und die erste christliche Zeit, mit den beiden ersten Erzählern*, Zurich 1882.

[6] W. Weiffenbach, *Die Wiederkunftsgedanken Jesus, nach den Synoptikern kritisch untersucht und dargestellt*, Leipzig 1873.

[7] A. Wabnitz, *L'Idéal messianique de Jésus*. Thèse, Montauban 1873 or 1878. (J. Weiss, in *Theologische Literaturzeitung*, henceforth cited as *Th.Lz.*, gives the date of publication as 1878, whereas *R.G.G.*, 2nd edn., VOL. v, p. 1722, gives 1873. The work is not available in Sweden.)

[8] In *Die Predigt Jesu vom Reiche Gottes*, henceforth cited as *Predigt Jesu*, Göttingen 1892, 2nd edn. 1900.

sent up as a reminder of its existence by some forgotten under-
ground river. It has been shown that O. Schmoller, forerunner
of J. Weiss, was influenced by Württembergian Pietism.[9]

It must also, however, be pointed out that New Testament
research was obliged in the course of its own internal development to take up the eschatological sayings of Jesus for re-
assessment. About the middle of last century the favourite
subject of study had been the life of Jesus. Th. Keim and
H. J. Holtzmann had drawn the portrait of Jesus that was to
be accepted for more than a generation by so-called liberal
theology as representing "the historical Jesus."[10] This portrait
meets us everywhere, and was regarded by the widest circles
as representing the historical Jesus as opposed to the dogmatic
Christ. When opposition set in and declared: "*Vita Jesu
Christi scribi nequit*" (Ritschl, Harnack, and others), theological
writers set themselves, instead of writing the life of Jesus, to
present His teachings, or else they concentrated on the figure
of Jesus as religious personality and hero. In so doing they
no longer based themselves on both St John and the Synoptic
Gospels, but exclusively on the latter. But if the sources
became more limited, they were obliged nevertheless to give
renewed thought to the contents of the teaching of Jesus.
When in addition they began to investigate the position of
Jesus with regard to the eschatological and Messianic ideas
of His time, the stage was set for the rediscovery of the
basically eschatological character of His teaching; for once
the connexion was realised between the Gospels and Jewish
apocalyptic and eschatological thought, it was not so easy
simply to modify and modernise the eschatology of the
Gospels.

Basing himself on the investigations of E. Schürer,[11] W.
Baldensperger showed in 1888[12] that the title "Son of Man,"

---

[9] H. E. Weber, "Die Kirche im Lichte der Eschatologie," in *Neue kirchliche
Zeitschrift*, 1926, pp. 302 f.

[10] Schweitzer, *Geschichte*, pp. 210 ff.; E. von Dobschütz, "Der heutigen Stand
der Leben-Jesu-Forschung," in *Z.Th.K.*, N.F. v (1924), p. 67; F. Loofs, *Wer ist
Jesus Christus ?*, Halle 1916, pp. 39-43.

[11] E. Schürer, *Geschichte des jüdischen Volkes im Zeitalter Jesu Christi*, VOL. II, 2nd
edn., Leipzig 1888, pp. 417 ff.

[12] W. Baldensperger, *Das Selbstbewusstsein Jesu im Lichte der messianischen Hoffnungen seiner Zeit*, Strassburg 1888. Baldensperger had previously been strongly
under the influence of Ritschl, on whom he wrote a monograph, *Die Theologie A.
Ritschls*, 1883. Before Baldensperger the Jewish-Christian theologian, A. Edersheim

with which Jesus associated Himself, was a pre-Christian, Jewish, apocalyptic title for the Messiah, which derives, not from the political ideals of the Messiah-king, but from Daniel's thought-world, which was also the origin of the pattern currently accepted at the time of Jesus: this age and the age to come.

But when it came to applying his insight into the eschatological character of the Son of Man and defining Jesus' conception of the Kingdom of God, Baldensperger proved unable to turn his knowledge of late Jewish eschatology and apocalyptic to account, and the current theological views retained the upper hand. In conformity with Ritschl, he defined the mission of Jesus as "laying the foundation of the Kingdom of God."[13] According to Baldensperger, however, Jesus' conception of the Kingdom of God was not homogeneous, for the Kingdom of God is partly something spiritual, a dominion of God in the human heart, and partly something which has outwardly observable signs. Baldensperger's explanation of this was that the transcendent idea of God prevented Jesus from regarding the Kingdom of God as purely spiritual and inward.

Jesus' teaching of the Kingdom of God undoubtedly had Messianic and eschatological background and colour, and He believed in a coming outward manifestation of the Kingdom of God as deeply as in His Messianic position as the Son of Man. This hope of the outward fulfilment of the Kingdom at the Parousia, which was close, Jesus always clung to firmly. The Kingdom of God would come through a final intervention by God, which would end the existing order of things and allow a new and definitive world, freed from sin and suffering, to take its place. Before His death Jesus saw the Kingdom of God still more transcendentally as the Kingdom of Heaven. Notwithstanding the delay in the coming of the Kingdom, it would yet come, for with Jesus, the promised Messiah, the Messianic epoch had once and for all begun, and it inevitably brought with it the end of the present age and the beginning of a new.

(1825-89) had made use of the apocalyptic material in his *Life and Times of Jesus, the Messiah*, London 1883. See W. Sanday, *The Life of Christ in recent Research*, Oxford 1907, p. 48.

[13] Baldensperger, *Das Selbstbewusstsein Jesu*, p. 107.

Baldensperger did not do justice to these Messianic and eschatological elements, but regarded the spiritualistic conception of the Kingdom as being dominant in Jesus. His evidence for this is chiefly Lk. xvii. 21. The Kingdom of God is therefore mainly, even if not exclusively, as Jesus experienced it within Him, peace and faith. The Kingdom, originally concretely conceived, has become an invisible, spiritual good. The idea has been transposed "out of the category of *place* into that of *quality*."[14]

The meeting-point in which these two sides of Jesus' conception of the Kingdom of God unite is to be found in His deep "sense of God."[15] It was this that enabled him, while associating himself with the Messianic faith of the Synagogue, yet to spiritualise this faith by His own inward experience. To Baldensperger it is the non-eschatological system of thought with its "spiritualised idea of the Kingdom" that in the end, in spite of hints of a more realistic view of eschatology, remains the distinctive thought of Jesus.

The fundamental error in Baldensperger's interpretation of Jesus is that he distinguished the eschatological Son of Man from the eschatological Kingdom of God. The Kingdom of God is placed, so to speak, outside Jesus, whereas in the Gospel it is concentrated precisely in Him. It is therefore also completely meaningless to speak of any change-over from spatial to qualitative terms, since both the Son of Man and the Kingdom of God, which enters into this world, are the "altogether other" that confronts us in Jesus.

In 1889 the "Society in The Hague for the Defence of the Christian Religion" held a prize competition for treatises on the teaching about the Kingdom of God in the New Testament. Both E. Issel[16] and O. Schmoller[17] were awarded prizes. Issel defined the Kingdom of God as a religious conception. It comes into being entirely through God, but the task of the disciples was to propagate that state of mind that expresses itself in submission in faith under God and humble service to one's nearest, in order that the Kingdom of God might grow in the world. One of the merits of Issel's work is that it set

[14] *Op. cit.*, p. 110.
[15] *Op. cit.*, p. 114.
[16] E. Issel, *Die Lehre vom Reiche Gottes im Neuen Testament*, Leiden 1891.
[17] O. Schmoller, *Die Lehre vom Reiche Gottes in den Schriften des Neuen Testaments*, Leiden 1891.

forth clearly the dualism between the Kingdom of God and
the Kingdom of Satan. His chief shortcoming is that he
never realised that to Jesus the Kingdom of God was
eschatological.

O. Schmoller is generally regarded as a very insignificant
forerunner of J. Weiss and is dismissed in a few lines. Yet
he championed with great energy, and in strong opposition to
the prevailing Ritschlean and liberal theology, the view that
the Kingdom of God in the Gospels is a religious, eschatological
conception. That so little attention has been paid to his
treatise is probably due to the fact that it is so crammed with
definitions that it makes rather dry reading. It is also lacking
in clarity and breadth. Although Schmoller had so little
influence on future developments, we will include him in spite
of everything among the forerunners of Weiss.

Schmoller stands in clear-cut opposition to the Ritschlean
conception of the Kingdom of God. The Kingdom of God is
not an active condition of mankind but "a condition into
which one is placed,"[18] and is therefore not a task but a gift.
The coming of the Kingdom is not something inward but an
objective, *historical* act of *salvation*, an historical manifestation
of salvation by God which is altogether independent of man's
repentance. Not even the righteous man is in the Kingdom
of God because he is righteous: he will enter it only when the
Kingdom of God comes and this belongs entirely to the future,
for Jesus prayed: "Thy kingdom come."

The Messiah has come already, but it does not follow from
this that the Kingdom is also here. The proclamation that the
Kingdom of God has come near, must be understood exclusively
eschatologically; "a nearness and a coming of the βασιλεία τοῦ
Θεοῦ in the full, definitive sense" is what is intended here.[19]
When the Messiah returns, the Kingdom of God will follow
as a supernatural cataclysm, which will transform existing
conditions. Schmoller interpreted the sayings on the presence
of the Kingdom of God entirely in terms of the future. As
victories over powers hostile to God, the exorcisms were
nothing more than a preparation and an example, a prolepsis
of what is to come at the Parousia, namely the Kingdom of
God, and are therefore also "a surety of the coming of the

[18] Schmoller, *op. cit.*, pp. 21 f.
[19] p. 72

βασιλεία τοῦ Θεοῦ."[20]   One cannot say that a sort of Kingdom of God has come, that is to hold force for the present, but only that a prelude has been shown of the whole, full Kingdom of God.[21]   The casting out of the demons is a part of the final salvation.   The end of time belongs to the present—or, better expressed, the present belongs already to the end, just as the dawn is part of the morning, which brings with it the sunrise.

The Kingdom of God in the teaching of Jesus is not a moral organisation of men, it is no community.   The fellowship of the disciples of Jesus is not the same as the Kingdom of God, but constitutes "the fellowship of the Kingdom of God in process of becoming."[22]   The disciples are the real aspirants to the Kingdom of God, and in them therefore the coming "members of the Kingdom of God" are already present, but only in them.

With the eschatological view that Jesus held, it is quite inconceivable that the Kingdom of God should grow or develop in any way, since Jesus always thought of the Kingdom as absolute and complete.   What will develop is not the Kingdom of God but the circle of disciples who are qualified for the Kingdom, when it comes through an act of God's sovereign will.

The task of Jesus in this aeon was to prepare mankind for the coming of the Kingdom of God.   But as the actual sending of the Messiah was an objective, salvationary act of God, the coming of the Messiah heralded and prepared the way for the coming of the Kingdom.   His coming was the surest security that the Kingdom will come, and it quite simply cannot fail to come.   The death of Jesus was also necessarily bound together with the coming of the Kingdom of God.   Owing to the redemptive and covenantal character which the death of Jesus had, it too served to prepare, inaugurate and guarantee the coming of the Kingdom of God.   The effect of the death of Jesus is the most powerful prolepsis of the coming of the

---

[20] p. 103.

[21] p. 141.   Schmoller translates ἔφθασεν (Mt. xii. 28) as "is anticipated," "has found its prelude" (p. 140).   H. Gunkel, Reviews of E. Issel, O. Schmoller, J. Weiss; "Die Lehre vom Reiche Gottes, in Th.Lz., 1893, p. 42, commented that the Kingdom of God is already in the redeeming miracles of Jesus, as a foretaste of what is to come, but at the same time as a sure sign of what is to come.

[22] Schmoller, Die Lehre vom Reiche Gottes, p. 127.   "The communion of the Kingdom of God" is "the disciples of Jesus led to their goal, perfected" (ibid.).   In the group of disciples the Kingdom of God is reflected in present time (p. 128).

C

Kingdom. Through it men receive the full salvation of the Kingdom of God, even though they themselves are not in the Kingdom.

Because of Schmoller's association with Württembergian Pietism it was natural for him to think in terms of historical redemption in considering the Kingdom of God in the teaching of Jesus. The time of waiting lies ahead, and through the coming of the Messiah the time of fulfilment is now here. The end, the fulfilment will soon come, for the Messiah has come. The end-time has thus begun and brings with it all that belongs to it. So Schmoller linked together the Messiah and the Kingdom of God. They both belong to the end-time, but Schmoller would have nothing to do with any concentration of the Kingdom in the Messiah. Therefore neither could he come to any understanding of the Church as an eschatological entity, even though the attempt to associate the band of disciples with the purely future Kingdom of God foreshadows later lines of research. The futurist line of interpretation of the Kingdom of God has not, indeed, in general made any attempt to explore the relation between the Church and the Kingdom of God. The fear of falling into Ritschlean modes of thought probably acted as a deterrent. What one misses above all in Schmoller is that he made no attempt to set Jesus' conception of the Kingdom of God against its religious historical background, and that he gave so little idea of the meaning of the Kingdom of God. In order to make the Kingdom of God entirely of the future, he forced the material altogether too much, as do all his followers, and simply disregarded any sayings that did not fit into his scheme.

V

The Interpretation of the Kingdom of God
by Johannes Weiss

Johannes Weiss's contribution to the discussion in 1892[1] attracted attention in quite a different way from Schmoller's treatise. His style is far richer and has a fire and intensity such as one does not often find in works of this kind. Weiss confessed himself that the book was born of a personal conflict. Convinced as he was that his master and father-in-law, Albrecht Ritschl, had been right in placing the concept of the Kingdom of God in the forefront, he was disturbed to find that Ritschl's idea of the Kingdom of God, and the Kingdom of God in the teachings of Jesus, were two quite different things. The roots of Ritschl's idea of the Kingdom were to be found, not in the Gospels but in Kant and the theology of enlightenment. Weiss now set out to establish the original historical meaning that Jesus attached to the Kingdom of God, without dragging in modern and (to Jesus) alien ideas. He cut Jesus, indeed, completely free from modern thought by pointing out unequivocally the gulf that divided the New Testament teaching from the current interpretation of it. His main concern was to show that, according to Jesus, the Kingdom of God is *not* the result of immanent development, but of the miraculous intervention of God.[2] Schmoller's work gave him the courage to publish his sketch, which he had written independently.

The question how far Jesus was influenced by contemporary Jewish ideas about the Kingdom of God is not discussed, as

---

[1] *Predigt Jesu.*
[2] See Weiss's own statement in *Th.Lz.*, 1895, p. 645.

Weiss's primary aim was to understand Jesus' teaching of the Kingdom of God in its own essence. He based his views on the Synoptics, though adopting a somewhat critical attitude towards Matthew, as also towards the customary form of introduction of the parables of the Kingdom of God.[3]

The keynote of the teaching of Jesus is, according to both Mark and Q, that *the Kingdom of God is at hand,* ἤγγικεν ἡ βασιλεία τοῦ Θεοῦ *(τῶν οὐρανῶν)* (Mt. x. 7; Lk. x. 9,11; cf. Mk. vi. 10-11). The meaning is perfectly clear, that the Kingdom of God or the Dominion of God has come so close that it stands at the door but is not yet *here.*[4] The similarity between Mt. xii. 28 and Lk. xi. 20 is striking: "But if it is by the spirit of God [Lk. the finger of God] that I cast out demons, then the kingdom of God has come upon you."[5] The masses among whom Jesus and the disciples performed their missionary work would grasp what it meant, and understand from the healings that the Kingdom of God was quite close, or perhaps already there. This Kingdom of God is not a moral ideal which mankind must bring about, but the highest religious good, which God bestows under certain conditions.

Whereas Jesus generally characterised the Kingdom of God as coming, there are sayings which represent the Kingdom as already realised. The question is, in what sense Jesus spoke of a

[3] Weiss considered Matthew to be very late and to have a "strongly ecclesiastical, catholic attitude" (*Predigt Jesu,* 2nd edn., p. 38). Certain passages in Mt. which are frequently quoted to illustrate Jesus' idea of the Kingdom of God (Mt. xiii. 24-30, 36-43, 47-50, red. xxv. 31-46), must be used with great caution. In Mt. xiii. 41 we find the Pauline conception of a Kingdom of Christ, to be replaced by a Kingdom of God. The introductory words: ὁμοία ἐστὶν ἡ βασιλεία or such-like are very indefinite and are sometimes used by the Evangelists where there is no question at all of the Kingdom of God, whereas they may omit to use them where the parable is quite clearly a parable of the Kingdom of God.

[4] "The Kingdom (or the Dominion) of God has come so close that it stands at the threshold. So the βασιλεία is not yet *here,* but very near" (*Predigt Jesu,* 1st edn., p. 12). The expression "Kingdom of God" is earlier than "Kingdom of Heaven" (p. 9).

[5] Weiss also finds linguistic reasons for the similarity between ἤγγικεν and ἔφθασεν. Both words may be derived from the Aramaic מְטָא, which in Dan. iv. 8 is translated by Theodotion as ἔφθασε, whereas LXX has ἤγγιζε. The same verb is translated by LXX as ἦξει (Dan. iv. 21) and παρῆν (Dan. vii. 13), which indicates not merely closeness but actual contact. Theodotion has in both cases ἔφθασε(ν). If the Aramaic מְטָא were at the root of both ἤγγικεν ἐφ' ὑμᾶς ἡ βασιλεία τοῦ Θεοῦ (Lk. x. 9) and ἔφθασεν ἐφ' ὑμᾶς ἡ βασιλεία τοῦ Θεοῦ (Lk. xi. 20), both sentences would mean the same: the Kingdom has come immediately close to you; it is touching you already.

presence of a Kingdom of God, and whether it can be the same
as the sense in which the term is now used.   The weightiest
argument for rejecting the long series of attempts at a solution
which aim at identifying the Kingdom of God with the group
of disciples or seeing the Kingdom realised in them (Ritschl,
B. Weiss and others), is provided by the prayer: "Thy kingdom
come."[6] To the disciples the Kingdom was not yet there, not
even in its beginnings, so that it could also be said: "Seek his
kingdom" (Lk. XII. 31). Neither are there different degrees
of its coming, as would be the case with a development in this
world, for either the Kingdom is there or it is not yet there;
to the disciples and the early congregations it was not yet
there.

In finding an answer to the question, in what sense Jesus
spoke of a presence of the Kingdom of God, it is equally useless
to say that this is a paradox, for that is a modern way of looking
at things and cannot be applied to Jesus.   What seems to us
a paradox was to Jesus plain fact.

In the cosmology of Jesus there was a clear-cut dualism
between mutually opposed world powers: the Kingdom of God
and the Kingdom of Satan fought for supremacy.   By His
works, above all the casting out of the demons and the healing
miracles, Jesus overcame the power of Satan.   This background
struggle provides the key to Jesus' sayings about the Kingdom
of God as already present.   Because through His actions the
power of Satan, who is the origin of all evil, had been broken,
He could in moments of prophetic enthusiasm, exalted by
the knowledge of victory, speak of the Kingdom of God as
already present.   To Weiss there was thus no question of an
actual presence of the Kingdom of God, but only of a subjective
experience on the part of Jesus.   Jesus saw the presence of the
Kingdom of God proleptically.   (Cf. Schmoller.)

But these sayings about a present Kingdom of God are only
in a minority.   Beside them stands the great bulk of sayings
that speak of the Kingdom as something to be established in a
nearer or more distant future.   The relation between present
and future is summarised thus: The kingdom of Satan is
already crushed, the dominion of God already gains ground,

[6] "Jesus did not say: Thy kingdom grow, Thy kingdom be fulfilled, but: Thy
kingdom *come*. *To the disciples* the βασιλεία was not yet there, not even in its
beginnings, so that even for them the words were: ζητεῖτε τὴν βασιλείαν (Lk. XII.
31)." *Predigt Jesu.*, p. 17.

but as an historical fact it is not yet there; the Kingdom of God, as Jesus expected it, is not yet established on earth.

When and how is the Kingdom of God to be established according to Jesus? If the time of its coming could be reckoned out, its establishment would be man's work, but as to Jesus this was entirely a work of God, no one can reckon out the time when the Kingdom will come in its glory and the world be transformed (Mt. xix. 28). Jesus could only imagine, however, that this was to happen in His generation. Before the Kingdom can be established the Last Judgment will have taken place, in which the fate of each individual will be decided, whether the path is to lead to Life or to Gehenna (Mk. ix. 43 ff.).

Jesus did not need to explain at any length what this coming Kingdom meant. People knew that the Dominion of God was the antithesis of everything that exists at present and would give freedom from all sorrow, from enemies, and oppressors. Jesus painted in restrained colours the glories of the Messianic redemption. Even though He associated Himself with current conceptions, His greatness lies in the modesty, restraint, and sobriety that characterise Him in this respect. He kept all the more firmly in view the essentially religious quality of the Kingdom of God and the moral preparation for its coming. His teaching is therefore a call to the rejection of worldly things and to the most intensive preparation for the Kingdom of God. The new righteousness that Jesus demands is not moral perfection, which the "members of the Kingdom" possess in the Kingdom of God, but the righteousness that is a condition for entry thereto (Mt. v. 20) and is the result of repentance. Weiss prefers therefore to speak, not of the righteousness *of* the Kingdom of God, but of righteousness *for* the Kingdom of God. The new righteousness cannot be separated from its religious, *i.e.* eschatological, basis: Repent, *for* the Kingdom of God is at hand. The nearness of the Kingdom of God is the motive for the new morality (Lk. xii. 57-xiii. 9).

The things of this world, which is doomed to destruction, have lost all value. Now they can only hinder. Cast them, therefore, from you and seize with both hands this new thing that is to come from above. "Seek first the kingdom of God and its righteousness!" Jesus' commands are, from this point of view, not the prescription for a moral society that is to persist, but a hint to the few who know: "Now everything rests on the edge of the sword."[7]   At any moment this world may perish and the Kingdom of God come, which is altogether supra-worldly, and which stands in radical opposition to this world.   Thus Jesus, according to the Synoptics, stands revealed as a radical, world-despising preacher of repentance.

Jesus' attitude towards the Kingdom of God is characterised by the fact that it is He who prepares the way for the Kingdom, in that He casts the ruler over the present aeon from his seat (Lk. x. 18 ff.)—He never speaks of Himself as the founder of God's Kingdom—and that He preaches the gospel of the coming Kingdom.   This preaching does not differ in principle from that of the Baptist, who also preached repentance and the nearness of the Kingdom.   The actual establishment of the Kingdom will come about through the miraculous intervention of God.   He can do nothing for the development of the King- dom but has to wait, like everyone else, until God seizes ultimate power.[8]   Jesus is now a rabbi and a prophet, but unlike John the Baptist He knows that the time will come when He will be raised up before all the people as the Son of Man. Jesus *is* a prophet before the eyes of everyone; He will *become* the Son of Man, either now during His lifetime or, as grew ever clearer to Him, after He had passed through death.[9]

When Jesus calls Himself the Son of Man it is, therefore, not merely in the sense of a simple "I" (Mt. xi. 19; Lk. vii. 34) or in the sense of "man" (Mk. ii. 28), but the Passion and Parousia sayings show that Jesus characterised Himself as He who had the right to the Messiah-title Son of Man.   Jn. v. 26 f., whether the words were actually spoken by Jesus or not, shows us the lines along which we must interpret the Synoptic

[7] *Op. cit.*, p. 49.

[8] "As Jesus now is, a rabbi, a prophet, He has nothing in common with the Son of Man except the claim to *become* such.   He cannot even intervene at all in the development of the Kingdom of God; He has to wait until God definitively seizes dominion again, just as the people" (*op. cit.*, p. 24).

[9] "He *is* a prophet before the eyes of all, He will *become* the Son of Man, either in His lifetime or, as seems ever more certain to Him, after He has passed through death" (*op, cit.*, p. 54).   "Jesus is actually the Son of God during His mission, He breathes and lives in the blessed consciousness of enjoying the fullest confidence of His Father.   But He is not yet 'Son of Man,' so long as He has not obtained the authority of the Messianic Judgment.   But He has, on the other hand, a claim to this authority, because He is the 'Son of Man.'   We see, then, that Jesus has already now this dignity, but it is the dignity of the Pretender, the Inheritor. The dominion, the heritage, belongs to him already, but he has not yet entered into it" (*op. cit.*, p. 59).

sayings about the Son of Man. Jesus during His mission is the Son of God; He lives in the certainty of having the full confidence of the Father. He is not yet the Son of Man, so long as He has not received authority to hold the Messianic Judgment. But He has the claim to it, since He is the Son of Man. Thus He has the claim as He who is to inherit the dignity of the Son of Man. The heritage, the dominion, are His, but He has not yet taken them in possession. Now He is a rabbi, one day He will appear as the Messianic Judge and King, who shall gather the people before His throne. Only those whom God has appointed will have part in the dominion over the citizens of the Kingdom (Mk. x. 40). The Twelve, who endured all the trials of Jesus, will have dominion with Him over the twelve tribes of Israel and their foremost task will be to judge (Lk. xxii. 28). This knowledge that He would one day become the Son of Man Jesus had by virtue of His baptismal experience.

Just as Weiss depicted Jesus' relation to the Kingdom of God on the basis that this is something entirely in the future, so also with the relation between the disciples and the Kingdom of God. The Kingdom bestowed by God which, before His death, He entrusted to His disciples, is not the Kingdom itself but an invisible crown, an inner claim to the Dominion.

To the mind of Jesus the Kingdom of God is not something subjective, inward, spiritual, but the objective Messianic Kingdom which is most often represented as a territory one enters into, or a land one has part in, or a treasure that descends from heaven. Even Jesus' Messiah-consciousness, which found expression in the title Son of Man, was still bound by the transcendental, apocalyptic nature of the conception of the Kingdom of God. Realisation of the Kingdom is entirely God's affair.[10]

Although Weiss thus sees the eschatological nature of Jesus' teaching of the Kingdom of God as the historical reality, he cannot accept this teaching as being generally applicable or as the basis for systematic theology; on the other hand the

---

[10] "What can be achieved by men by violence and tumult may be a kingship such as David's, perhaps quite a splendid kingdom. God will establish the Kingdom of God without human arms, without horse or rider, but simply with His angels and with supra-worldly forces. To hope for the Kingdom of God in the transcendental sense of Jesus and to make revolution are two things as different as fire and water" (*op. cit.*, p. 40).

teaching of man's relationship towards God as that of children to Father is generally applicable in a religious and moral sense.

To sum up: The main features of Weiss's interpretation of the Kingdom of God are, that the *Kingdom of God* is represented throughout as a *religious* and *not an ethical entity*; it is of purely future reference; the Kingdom of God is the great final miracle. Weiss does not deny the presence of the Kingdom, but only on this interpretation: that the Kingdom of God is so near that it can be said to be already here and Jesus already experienced its nearness. All human activity with regard to the establishment of the Kingdom is dismissed, both for Jesus Himself and His disciples; Jesus had only to wait. The kingdom of Satan is everywhere in direct opposition to the Kingdom of God. The nearness of the Kingdom of God is the *motive* for the new morality. Jesus is now a prophet and teacher, but He is at the same time the claimant to the throne of the Kingdom of God; He is the Son of Man to be, the *Messias designatus, Messias futurus*.

Weiss was completely bound by this view of his. He shared with other purely futuristic interpreters of the Kingdom of God the difficulty of solving the relationship between the present and the coming Kingdom of God, which is involved by the purely futuristic interpretation of Jesus' position as Son of Man only when the Kingdom has been established. The question of the relationship between the disciples and the Kingdom of God is hardly dealt with at all. The new righteousness of Jesus certainly cannot be regarded exclusively from the angle that the Kingdom will soon come in its glory.

The greatest merit of Weiss's interpretation of the Kingdom of God is undoubtedly that, although his theological and philosophical aims drew him in another direction, he nevertheless allowed the *majestas materiae, i.e.* the words of the text, to take priority over his own pet theories which, however, still have the upper hand in his systematic presentation of the Kingdom of God.

VI

The Debate on the Kingdom of God from Johannes Weiss to 1906

The Debate on the Kingdom of God during the Eighteen-Nineties

Johannes Weiss's sketch on the Kingdom of God was an attack on the whole idea of Jesus held by the liberal theology of the day, whose representatives were also its most eager opponents in the lively discussion which followed. One of the main points at issue was the question of the Jewish and non-Jewish elements in the Kingdom of God as seen by Jesus. If it were admitted that He shared the ideas of His time on the Kingdom of God, then the only alternatives seemed to be either to admit that the Kingdom of God was purely religious, purely supernatural, purely eschatological, or else to say that the eschatological Kingdom of God was of minor importance and was not by any means the centre of Jesus' teaching. In the latter case the distinctive elements in Jesus were held to be His teaching of the already present Kingdom of God, His uneschatological belief in God the Father (Bousset), and His exalted ethic. There were also a number of scholars who completely rejected Weiss.

First we will say a few words about the last-named group, which is by no means homogeneous. H. H. Wendt[1] in his contribution of 1893 only slightly modified his previously expressed opinions. J. Köstlin[2] emphasised the immanent

---

[1] H. H. Wendt, "Das Reich Gottes in der Lehre Jesu," in *Christliche Welt*, 1893, pp. 338-42, 361-5, 386-91, 410-13, 434-9. See also *id.*, *Die Lehre Jesu*, 2nd edn., 1901.

[2] J. Köstlin, "Die Idee des Reiches Gottes," in *Theologische Studien und Kritiken*, 1892, pp. 401-73.

character of the Kingdom of God, while J. Stalker[3] rejected any sort of eschatological interpretation of it. A. Klöpper[4] opposed Weiss, asserting that the Kingdom of God is primarily something present, which undergoes an organic development towards the perfection which is its goal. What is characteristic of Jesus is the fundamental reshaping, deepening and spiritualisation which He gave to the conception of the Kingdom of God in historical time. Klöpper therefore had to reject completely any attempt to explain away the sayings about a present Kingdom of God as being merely proleptic, paradoxical, and designed to confound their hearers.

W. Lütgert's work on the Kingdon of God,[5] published in 1895, took but little account of the problems brought to the fore by Weiss. Hardly any scholar is mentioned except A. Schlatter. Lütgert asserted that Jesus followed firmly in the eschatological tradition. The relation between the Kingdom of God and eschatology cannot, he said, be resolved by claiming that Jesus rendered subjective or spiritualised the Israelite hope of the Kingdom of God.[6] But when Lütgert sets out to elaborate the relation between the present and the future Kingdom of God, the Kingdom fails to preserve its basic eschatological character. The Kingdom of God, which has now become something invisible, can be possessed by man already now, not merely in hope but in reality, so that he can enter into it. The Kingdom of God, indeed, stands open, because God forgives sins.[7] Since the Kingdom of God is already present, eternal life, too, is something that one can possess already.[8] But this view considerably reduces the importance of the coming of the Kingdom at the end of time, the only significance of which is that the invisible Kingdom becomes visible, so that, according to Lütgert, the

---

[3] J. Stalker, *The Christology of Jesus: being His teaching concerning Himself according to the Synoptic Gospels*, London 1899. According to Stalker, Schmoller's and Weiss's conception of the Kingdom of God makes Jesus into a fantastic dreamer, caught up in delusions, such as we could not possibly accept as the Redeemer of the world.

[4] A. Klöpper, "Das gegenwärtige und zukünftige Gottesreich in der Lehre Jesu bei den Synoptikern," in *Zeitschrift für wissenschaftliche Theologie*, 1897, pp. 355-410.

[5] W. Lütgert, *Das Reich Gottes nach den synoptischen Evangelien, Eine Untersuchung zur neutestamentlichen Theologie*, Gütersloh 1895.

[6] Lütgert, *op. cit.*, p. 98.

[7] *Op. cit.*, p. 104.

[8] *Op. cit.*, p. 127.

transformation of the world can notwithstanding the presence
of the Kingdom, be designated the coming of the Kingdom
of God.[9]

A number of leading New Testament scholars adopted an
intermediate standpoint. They recognised Jesus' connexion
with late Jewish eschatology and apocalyptic, but emphasised
that in Jesus there were two systems of thought: one uneschatological, world-accepting, the other eschatological, world-
denying (Bousset), or put another way: a spiritual and a
supernatural conception of blessedness (Titius). Jesus was
seen in the form of a religious personality, the sanctity of whose
life sprang from His certainty of the fatherly goodness of God
and an enduring nearness to God, and from His consciousness
of being the Son of God. There is nothing strange or mysterious about the nature of God, according to Jesus. God is
pure love. Eschatological considerations are thus left out of the
picture altogether and so cannot affect the view that is taken
either of Jesus as a whole or, consequently, of the Kingdom
of God either.

Wilhelm Bousset, Weiss's foremost opponent, published his
answer[10] in the same year, 1892, as Weiss's own book appeared.
The title itself indicates both the basic attitude and the attitude
towards the particular problem. According to Bousset, Jesus
must be considered against the background of the late Judaism
in which He grew up. Late Judaism had evolved the ideas
of a "this side" and an "other side", but it is important to bear
in mind that the apocalyptic hope lies not so much in the
future as in the beyond.[11] To understand Jesus one must
realise that the fundamental characteristic of late Judaism
was a leaning towards the transcendental, the supranaturalistic,
which as applied to the concept of God according to Bousset
involved a spiritualisation. As it can be shown that to Jesus
the eschatological expectations were entirely free of political
or national issues, and that He taught no intermediate kingdom

---

[9] *Op. cit.*, p. 149.

[10] W. Bousset, *Jesu Predigt in ihrem Gegensatz zum Judentum, Ein religionsgeschichtlicher Vergleich*, Göttingen 1892.

[11] Bousset, *op. cit.*, p. 22. "The apocalyptic hope lies, not in the future, but in
the beyond, its fulfilment is expected to be brought about by an out-and-out
miracle of God, involving the destruction, or at all events the violent upheaval,
of heaven and earth. The 'miraculous' which to the prophetic hope is an addition,
an adornment, becomes here the substance."

but lived in the immediate anticipation of the ultimate things, this means that the process of spiritualisation of future hopes had progressed and in Jesus reached perfection. "This perfection of the process of spiritualising future hopes was a creative act."[12] This argument made it possible for Bousset to retain the whole of the liberal image of Jesus.

Jesus possessed the certainty of living in the Messianic age, as His reply to John the Baptist shows (Mt. XI. 2 ff.). One of the surest things, Bousset declared now, before Wrede's influence had made itself felt, is that Jesus confessed to being the Messiah before the disciples and the High Priest. The certainty of the blessedness of the age to come had its roots in this Messianic atmosphere. The tension between present and future was gone. Jesus heard already the murmuring of a new age, indeed He lived in the new age. The gulf between present and future no longer exists but has been bridged over, which to Bousset means that ideal and reality had become united with one another.

From this image of Jesus, which to Bousset represented the original or "modern" representation—the front, so to speak, of the Jesus image—he turned now to the reverse side and set himself to trace the connecting links running back from Jesus to Judaism, stressing in particular the other-worldly features. The life of Jesus was determined by a conflict between an "on this side—on the other side"; he expected an early end to this present age through a sovereign act of God. This Jewish side had often been erroneously thrust into the background, but Bousset did not intend to be guilty of the same error. What he wanted to emphasise was that the distinctive feature of Jesus, the faith in God the Father, becomes a complete mystery if one tries to build it on the hope Jesus embraced.

The Kingdom of God was always seen by Jesus from the angle of the ruler and not of the area ruled over, and should according to Bousset be translated "the Dominion of God." Its essential element is righteousness, so that seeking the Kingdom of God and seeking its righteousness become synonymous terms.

How, then, did Bousset regard the relation between future and present in Jesus' idea of the Kingdom of God? Neither the sayings about the coming nor the present Kingdom of

[12] *Op. cit.*, p. 84.

God can be eliminated by critical procedure, he said. The difficulty is that Jesus did not establish any doctrine about the Kingdom of God. All we find is bold paradoxes, brief mysterious hints, which is completely in accordance with the prophetic nature of Jesus' mission. Both Mt. xii. 28 and Lk. xvii. 20 f. point to the presence of the Kingdom of God, while Mt. xi. 2 cannot possibly speak only prophetically of a coming Kingdom of God. The casting out of demons and other miracles by Jesus and His disciples had broken the power of Satan, so that Jesus could say: "If it is by the Spirit of God that I cast out demons, then the Kingdom of God has come upon you," and could behold Satan fall like lightning from heaven (Lk. x. 18). When Jesus saw the victories in the struggle against Satan, He could say: the Kingdom of God has come; a beginning has been made in the establishment of the miraculous Kingdom of God, and in the light of this vision He could compare the Kingdom of God, which is some day to come in glory through a miracle of God, with the seed that ripens quietly and slowly, with the grain of mustard seed that grows into a great tree, with the leaven that leavens the dough, with the treasure in the field and the pearl of great value that a man finds. Thus through the ministry of Jesus the "miraculous dominion of God"[13] has begun, and will reach its perfection when heaven and earth pass away. The sayings that the Kingdom has come and has been established by Jesus are expressions of the bold premonitions He had, and which made it possible for Him to reveal the secrets of the Kingdom of God. The Kingdom was to Jesus a *mysterium*, a still, invisible work which no one can bring on by force but which grows and extends its activities.[14] The Kingdom is present where only two or three are gathered together in Jesus' name, just as when people gather together under the shade of the mustard tree. Bousset asks whether Jesus might not have designated life in the security and peace and childlike directness of faith in God the Father—the life to which He trained His followers—as a life in the Kingdom of God and a seizing of the Kingdom of God in the present. That Bousset would answer the question

---

[13] *Op. cit.*, p. 98.

[14] "To Jesus the thought that, with His works, and in particular the works connected with the purely human, personal, moral side of His nature the Kingdom of God was come, the miraculous Dominion of God had begun to be fulfilled, was not out of reach" (*op. cit.*, p. 100).

in the affirmative is obvious from his whole outlook.[15] He also detects in the Kingdom of God an austere, this-worldly strain, in which the main emphasis is laid on personal religion and moral conduct.

Bousset showed similar tendencies in his account of Jesus' view of His Messianic task. By using the title Son of Man of Himself, Jesus laid claim to the special dignity of the Son of Man of the Book of Daniel and uttered a protest against a political ideal of kingship. The task of the Son of Man was to serve and to give his life as a ransom for many. But one must remember that Jesus used the title in a sense entirely His own. Implying originally a transcendental, other-worldly figure, He used it to signify and characterise His own unique position and task in the present. The eschatological element in the Son of Man is completely volatilised in Bousset's presentation, and Jesus' Messiah-consciousness becomes nothing more than a general expression for what Jesus at bottom always was, namely a man who stood close as no one else to God, the Heavenly Father.

A question one cannot help but ask is, How did Bousset imagine the presence of the Kingdom of God? He never saw it as something actually present.   On the contrary.   "The sayings of Jesus are tremendous flashes of intuition which move mysteriously through His utterances, He speaks of the mystery of the Kingdom of God."[16] By intuition, one might perhaps say, Jesus conceived the eternal and saw it as something that is present in a hidden way, present as an idea that will some day become reality, which will happen when the Kingdom is established in glory. But in this way one loses altogether the strong eschatological tension between a now and a then, which characterises the whole Gospel picture of the Kingdom of God. The tension, instead of being between a now and a then in time, becomes one between time and eternity, idea and

---

[15] "Even as He preached to the weary and heavy-laden the faith in the heavenly Father, to the poor the gospel according to which those who hunger and thirst learn a new righteousness, as He built up by quiet, unobtrusive labour of the most personal nature the community of His disciples, He saw in these His acts the beginning of that Dominion of God which will attain final perfection with the destruction of heaven and earth. Or would this thought have been completely unacceptable to Jesus ? That one can no longer claim, if one admits the possibility of the thoughts outlined above, that Jesus saw the beginning of the miraculous Dominion of God as having come with the casting out of devils" (*op. cit.*, pp. 98 f.).

[16] *Op. cit.*, pp. 100 f.

reality.   Bousset's solution is seen to be inspired by the philosophy which J. F. Fries developed and which Bousset as well as R. Otto adopted.   In this, intuition is regarded as a basis of higher knowledge.   It is only intuition that can throw a bridge between the eternal and the temporal.   "By intuitions we relate the eternal to the temporal, we see in the temporal broken rays of the eternal."[17]

A. Titius's[18] presentation of the teaching of Jesus was more evangelical, as is shown at once by the fact that he laid the main stress on the word "salvation."   The real heart of the Gospel was to him the fatherly goodness of God and the position of the disciples of Jesus as the children of God,[19] while he was inclined to thrust aside the Parousia thoughts of Jesus and spoke of "the painful prick of the Parousia idea."[20]   The idea that the Kingdom of God is near has no independent significance in explaining the outlook of Jesus as a whole. The eschatological element is, however, important in that it focuses attention on what is essential and intensifies the frame of mind which Jesus, in view of His whole outlook, must demand.   The eschatological element provided a ferment in the preaching and way of life of Jesus, but His belief in the nearness of the end did not furnish him with anything which He could not have derived directly from His idea of God.[21]   Titius considered that the Kingdom of God tended in the mind of Jesus to become purely transcendental, while the idea of the Kingdom of God as something to come in the future no longer had the same significance for Him as it had for Judaism.   The Kingdom of God is in a certain sense, namely a spiritual sense, already present in the now.

Johannes Weiss's main contention was that the Kingdom of

[17] W. Bousset, "Kantisch-Friessche Religionsphilosophie und ihre Anwendung auf die Theologie," in *Th.R.*, XII (1909), p. 482. A. Hering, "Die Idee Jesu vom Reiche Gottes und ihre Bedeutung für die Gegenwart," in *Z.Th.K.*, 1899, pp. 472-513, agreed in the main with Bousset's interpretation.

[18] A. Titius, *Die neutestamentliche Lehre von der Seligkeit und ihre Bedeutung für die Gegenwart*; VOL. I, *Lehre Jesu vom Reiche Gottes*, Freiburg i. B. and Leipzig 1895.

[19] Titius, *op. cit.*, p. 193.

[20] *Op. cit.*, p. 183.

[21] "Never, in seeking an understanding of Jesus' way of life or of His moral-religious demands, were we driven to fall back on His conviction of the nearness of the end. . . . The conviction of the nearness of the end has accordingly no independent value for the explanation of His outlook as a whole, but is a feature of His basic religious thought, to which it is completely subordinate" (*op. cit.*, p. 180).

God is not the result of an immanent development but that it comes about through the direct intervention of God. E. Haupt, in his book published in 1895, entirely agreed with this.[22] But on the other hand he attacked what he regarded as the unbridled exegeticism which celebrates its witch's sabbath in the sphere of eschatology. The main question is how much and in what way Jesus was influenced by the ideas prevalent in the Judaism of His day, and one cannot simply take it for granted that all ideas that were current in Judaism were automatically shared by Jesus. In a number of passages we have to consider the Kingdom of God in relation to the present. When, for example, Jesus says that the Kingdom of God is near, this can be interpreted as a purely future reference, but it need not be. For even if the Kingdom of God comes with Jesus, then it should come as the result of His own activity. Now there are, however, according to Haupt, a number of passages which beyond all question imply the coming of the Kingdom of God purely eschatologically (e.g. Mt. xvi. 28, xxv. 1, xxvi. 29; Lk. xxii. 18, 29). In seeking an explanation of this inconsistency on the subject of the Kingdom of God, Haupt rejected the attempts that had often been made to explain it away by saying that a development had taken place in the mind of Jesus with regard to the Kingdom of God, for one can just as well claim that Jesus preached a present Kingdom of God at the beginning as at the end of His ministry. Haupt began his enquiry contrary to custom, with the sayings about a present Kingdom of God. Jesus saw the essence of the Kingdom of God in what had been given to humanity through His mission, and in comparison with that everything connected with the final fulfilment falls into the background. Fulfilment lies with Jesus. What had been hoped for the future, is already now reality. At this moment He gives to the poor, the heavy-laden and the sinners the greatest of all gifts: communion with God. "Where He is, there is the Kingdom of God; with His mission its realisation has been set in motion, God has begun to bring about his Kingdom. . . . The decisive step has been taken by God: the

---

[22] E. Haupt, *Zum Verständnis der eschatologischen Aussagen Jesu in den synoptischen Evangelien*, Berlin 1895. "The coming of the Kingdom of God is to Jesus at every stage a divine act. Its fulfilment is not the result of immanent development, but of a miraculous intervention by God" (p. 52).

D

heavenly realms are opened. Thus the Kingdom of God is present to faith, and yet it remains in the future, at least as concerns its all-round manifestation."[23] The Kingdom of God, which is a purely supra-worldly gift, is thus present in Jesus, and its coming is entirely associated with His person. The Kingdom of God and Jesus are alternative terms, the one cannot be imagined without the other. This means that everything that Jesus took over from Judaism has acquired an entirely new meaning. The eschatological sayings, even the Parousia sayings, must be interpreted "symbolically." Symbolism is the individualised and plastic expression for religious and moral ideas. The first thing is to recognise this symbolic form as form, and then to seize the transcendent reality behind it and the gift of salvation that is given.

Haupt's interpretation of the Kingdom of God proves, then, in spite of certain acknowledgements to J. Weiss, to be purely spiritual. The present Kingdom of God becomes the communion with God which Jesus transmits. What Jesus says of the perfected Kingdom of God only carries to its ultimate conclusion what is already reality: communion with God. This communion with God is the highest thing there is and nothing can surpass it. If the Kingdom of God exists in this way once and for all in the person of Jesus and if He gives it to His own, then the future element in the Kingdom of God ceases to be of any importance whatever.

The concluding passage of Haupt's treatise reveals his whole attitude on Jesus in a lightning-flash. It runs: "It is not for us of today to tear away the symbolic wrappings: at best we should only exchange one image for another. What we must do is to recognise the symbolic form as such, and regard not it, but the transcendental reality contained within it, not the earthly element, but the heavenly good enclosed in it, as the bringer of salvation. We need not make excuses for the Lord Christ for His eschatology, because He too was bound by the limitations of His time: in this sphere too He towered above His time, and His eschatological sayings take their full share of the authoritative weight of all His words, because of His person in general."[24]

When the chief pioneer of the religious-historical school,

[23] Haupt, op. cit., pp. 51 f.
[24] Op. cit., p. 102.

H. Gunkel,[25] expressed himself on the question of the Kingdom of God, he criticised Weiss on the grounds that he represented Jesus' ethics as too remote from the world, and underestimated the heroic element in Him. It is not eschatology that forms the body of Jesus' teaching, as one might easily be led to believe by Weiss's account, only at the end of which is any mention made of the fatherhood of God or the ideal of loving one's enemy. Gunkel said that Bousset saw more clearly than Weiss. He gave a broad survey of the use, both religious and secular, of the word βασιλεία both in the Old Testament and late Judaism and in the New Testament. The great question is, whether the Kingdom of God in the teaching of Jesus is to be understood eschatologically or not, and here the main points to be considered are firstly what βασιλεία means and secondly what is meant by the Kingdom of God and what place it occupies in the teaching of Jesus. One must, said Gunkel, also bear in mind that, as the various ideas connected with the Kingdom of God are of different origins, they only form a very loose cohesion. But here it must be recorded against him that the fact that the several elements in a system of thought are of different origin by no means means that they cannot constitute a firm inward unity. So that to have traced the early history of the idea of the Kingdom of God is not to say that one has understood what the Kingdom of God means in the teaching of Jesus. But this sort of illogical reasoning is often to be found in the early years of the history of religion. Although the picture that Gunkel draws of the personality of Jesus is outstandingly liberal, he emphasises that the Kingdom of God is far more than the individual hope.

By the time H. J. Holtzmann, the "past master" of liberal theology, entered the discussion in 1897, it had to some extent died down.[26] His writings are strongly influenced by Ritschl and Kaftan. That the Kingdom of God is of heavenly origin and heavenly nature is shown by the third petition of the Lord's Prayer, which further develops the preceding petition about the coming of the Kingdom. The Kingdom of God is defined as the divine order, coming from heaven and entering into the present reality, in which the determining factor is the will

---

[25] H. Gunkel, Reviews of E. Issel, O. Schmoller, J. Weiss: *Die Lehre vom Reiche Gottes*, in *Th. Lz.*, 1893, pp. 39-45.

[26] H. J. Holtzmann, *Lehrbuch der neutestamentlichen Theologie*, Freiburg 1897.

of God.[27] The condition for entering into the Kingdom is to practise righteousness. The Kingdom is represented as the highest good (cf. J. Kaftan), and so becomes the comprehensive expression for the final fulfilment of God's purpose with the world. "The Kingdom of God is as much gift as task," Holtzmann declared.[28]

The Kingdom of God can also be regarded as an ethical community, even though this is not immediately apparent in the term itself, for if the Kingdom of God is wherever God's will is done on earth, then it corresponds to the totality of all those through whom the will of God comes to fulfilment, *i.e.* the Kingdom of God is a community. Jesus gathered together the disciples so that they shall be with him in the Kingdom, when God allows this to come. They have already now a foretaste of the joy that will be in the heavenly bridechamber (Mk. II. 19). They see what prophets and righteous men have sought in vain to see (Mt. XIII. 16), and share in the freedom from sabbath and temple duty which the King of the kingdom has. In the age to come they will be the real rulers (Mt. XIX. 28, XXIV. 45-7, etc.). But when Jesus sent them out, it was not to found a Church, but that they should be His helpers in spreading the good tidings. Holtzmann approached a modern understanding of the idea of the Church, but when later he came to define wherein the task of the disciples consisted, all eschatological considerations vanished. Their task was to bring about the regeneration of the life of the Jewish people (the Salt, Mt. V. 13; the Leaven, Mt. XII. 33), and to make the Jewish people sound.[29]

Other theologians, trying to explain the contradiction between a present and a coming Kingdom of God, have fallen back on such pairs of opposites as idea—reality, or form—content. Holtzmann, however, considered that the answer has to be sought historically, in a distinction between the times of success and triumph in the life of Jesus, and those of struggle and defeat. The teaching of the present Kingdom of God belongs to a time when Jesus still saw an earthly future, a wide field for His life's work, before Him, whereas the teaching of

[27] The Kingdom of God is "the Divine Order entering from heaven into the present reality, into the things of this side" (Holtzmann, *op. cit.*, VOL. I, p. 191).
[28] *Op. cit.*, p. 200.
[29] Jesus' task was "to inspire the great community of the people of God already in existence, to bring them health and strength" (*op. cit.*, p. 210).

the Kingdom to come belongs to a period when He had grown familiar with the thought of a swift and violent end to His career. During the days of His success He could think of the coming of the Kingdom as though it were already there. Later on, the gap between what is and what is to come became so great that the apocalyptic aspect had to emerge. God will bring to fulfilment in the future what He has begun with His Messiah.[30] But one must always remember that the interval of time between the present and the coming Kingdom was to Jesus always short, for it was in His own generation that the Kingdom was to come. But if it is only a short time until the Kingdom shall be established in glory, then, argues Holtzmann, future and present are brought so close together that the present can be regarded as the end, just as today already belongs with tomorrow.[31] In this way the clearcut distinction in the Gospel between what is and what is to come is blurred and lost.

The distinctive element in Jesus is to be sought, says Holtzmann, not in those passages in which the perfected Kingdom is painted in earthly colours drawn from the world of apocalyptic imagery, but only in those where it is represented as already present but hidden, yet even so growing and ripening.[32] For the Kingdom of God grows

[30] "Then" (*i.e.* so long as the call to the Kingdom of God met with response) "He could think of the coming of the Kingdom of God as being near, indeed as being here. Now, on the other hand" (*i.e.* when Jesus met with indifference and lack of understanding) "the gulf between what is and what is to be had become as great to Jesus Himself as it had been to the authors of the whole apocalyptic thought themselves" (*op. cit.*, p. 317). Similar ideas are to be found in O. Schmiedel, *Die Hauptprobleme der Leben-Jesu-Forschung*, Tübingen 1902, 2nd edn. 1908, and R. Otto, *Leben und Wirken Jesu nach historisch-kritischer Auffassung*, Göttingen 1901; Eng. version: *Life and Ministry of Jesus according to Historical and Critical Method*, henceforth cited as *Life and Ministry*, trans. H. J. Whitby, Chicago 1908. Holtzmann's views on eschatology underwent a certain change. In "Die gegenwärtige Stand der Leben-Jesu-Forschung", in *Deutsche Literatur-Zeitung*, henceforth cited as *D.L.Z.*, XXVII (1906), p. 2420, he asserted that strong "futuristic tones" can be heard from the very first page of the Gospels.

[31] "But then both elements draw so close together that today becomes part of tomorrow, present time may be regarded as end time" (Holtzmann, *Lehrbuch der neutestamentlichen Theologie*, VOL. I, p. 222).

[32] "The distinctive element in the thought-world of Jesus is to be sought, not at that extreme where the picture of the fulfilled Kingdom of God is painted with earthly colours from the Apocalyptic image-world, but only at that other where an already present, yet hidden Kingdom ripens towards fulfilment" (*op. cit.*, pp. 336 f.). Cf. W. Baldensperger, *Das Selbstbewusstsein Jesu im Lichte der messianischen Hoffnung seiner Zeit*, p. 199.

without any human aid to an ever richer form, and comes
to full maturity only through the indwelling power of God
(Mk. IV. 26-29).

Holtzmann saw clearly that to Jesus the Messianic title, Son
of Man, stood in the closest possible relationship to the Kingdom of God. Jesus is and is called the Son of Man, in the
first place everywhere where He preached, appeared, and
spread the Kingdom of God by forgiving and healing, teaching
and suffering, and in the second place and above all when He
comes upon the clouds to fulfil the Kingdom of God. But the
essential thing with Jesus is not that He saw Himself as the
Son of Man, but that He saw Himself as the Son of God, which
is due to His direct experience of God the Father in the depths
of His soul.

Holtzmann's interpretation of the Kingdom of God occupies
an intermediate position. Although he regarded the Kingdom
as being to Jesus something still to come, he blunted its eschatological character by setting the present and the coming Kingdom quite close together. One must also ask by what right
he divided up the texts so as to relate the teaching of the
present and the coming Kingdom to different periods in the
life of Jesus. In spite of attempts to throw off the Ritschlean
interpretation, Holtzmann still shows signs of its influence, in
particular in his characterisation of the Kingdom of God as a
"task" and as a moral community.

The scholars who ranged themselves on the side of Weiss
form quite a small group: W. Wrede, G. Dalman, G. Schnedermann, F. Krop, and E. Stapfer. W. Wrede, who is often
regarded as the opposite number to Schweitzer, the consistent
eschatologist, being the foremost representative of a purely
uneschatological interpretation of Jesus, asserted nevertheless
in 1894 that the Kingdom of God must be understood as
something purely religious, purely supernatural, purely
eschatological.[33] When Jesus spoke of the Kingdom of God
He thought, like the Jews, of the coming glorious Kingdom

[33] W. Wrede, " Die Predigt Jesu vom Reiche Gottes," lecture given in 1894, in
Vorträge und Studien, Tübingen 1907, pp. 84-126. "The main problem is solved,
once it is realised that the idea 'Kingdom of God' must be understood as purely
religious, purely supernatural, purely eschatological" (p. 113). Cf. also p. 93.
Wrede speaks of "the Kingdom of God coming soon, suddenly, once and for all"
(p. 99). "It (the Kingdom of God), when it comes, is all at once in the midst
of you, sudden, surprising, unmistakable" (on Lk. XVII. 21, p. 111).

which God Himself shall establish.[34]   The Kingdom of God
stands at the very threshold and will soon be here, but *is* not
therefore here yet. (Mk. I. 14 f.; Lk. XIX. 4, XXI. 31).[35]

What is new and startling in the teaching of Jesus on the
Kingdom of God is not, says Wrede, any particular statements
on the nature of the Kingdom, but the fact that the time of
waiting is past, and that God must soon reveal Himself. Jesus
proclaimed that the Kingdom of God is at hand. Not the
Kingdom, but the nearness of the Kingdom is the burden of
the message. To prepare oneself rightly one must believe this
gospel and repent, for with the Kingdom comes judgment.
There can only be question of a present Kingdom of God in
terms of a Kingdom soon to come. It is the supra-worldly
Kingdom to come that is itself present. This is not in any
way to deny that the Kingdom belongs entirely to the future.
To explain this paradox of the relation of the Kingdom of
God to the present and the future, Wrede quotes again the
image that had been current ever since Schmoller of the dawn
that is followed by the morning. It heralds the morning and
at the same time is part of the morning.[36]   The Kingdom is
already apparent. A proof of its nearness is that the heavenly
forces are in action, casting out demons.[37]   But Wrede warns

[34] With reference to the phrase ἤγγικεν ἡ βασιλεία Wrede asks: "But what
sort of Kingdom is it, that has come near?" and the answer is: "Any idea of a
fulfilment of the Divine Will growing up within men, of an ethical dominion of
God in them, is excluded clearly enough by the context. When the 'It is near' is
followed by a 'Repent,' then it is clear that a state of mind pleasing to God is
regarded as a condition for participation in the Kingdom, and cannot therefore
itself be the Kingdom. But the idea of a communion of hearts with God, to be
brought about by Jesus in this aeon, is also quite remote and arbitrary. The
Kingdom is the Kingdom expected among the people, supernatural, eternal,
linked up with the Last Judgment, appearing suddenly and full of power, the
same Kingdom of whose nearness John the Baptist spoke, according to Matthew,
in no other sense than of the nearness of the Last Judgment" (Wrede, *op. cit.*,
p. 95). "From the beginning, then . . . in view of the whole outlook of Jesus, any
conception of the Kingdom of God is ruled out which envisages a prolonged
development in this world, a gradual expansion taking place in history" (pp.
97 f.).

[35] "It (the Kingdom of God) stands indeed at the threshold, but just for that
very reason is *not yet here*" (*op. cit.*, p. 94).

[36] "Only because we know that the morning itself will directly follow the dawn,
can we say that it is already here" (p. 99).

[37] "The casting out of the demons is nothing but a prelude, a dawn, a precursor,
of the coming Kingdom of God which is close at hand. For that very reason,
however, it may also be regarded as a *sign* and *presage* of its coming. The heavenly
forces of the Kingdom will soon be apparent; so they are evidence of its nearness"
(*op. cit.*, p. 99). Wrede is cautious about extending to the whole activity of Jesus

us strongly against using individual sayings, which contrary to the weight of tradition speak of a presence of the Kingdom of God, as a basis for building far-flung theories about this particular teaching being the distinctive message of Jesus.

If Jesus held this eschatological view consistently, it must also necessarily have coloured the view He took of His own position. Wrede, therefore, considered that, as the Kingdom of God is purely to come, the same must also apply to the Messiah: Jesus will become the Messiah only in the future. But His person is decisive for the coming of the Kingdom, and whoever recognises His dignity, has therein the most vital pledge that the Kingdom really is quite near.

The features distinctive to Jesus in relation to the expectations of His time are, to Wrede, (1) the idea that the Kingdom of God is near, (2) the knowledge Jesus had that He Himself had ultimately to prepare the way for the Kingdom, and that He would one day bring it, (3) that His hopes were entirely unpolitical, and (4) finally that the ethical level He demanded rises to heights previously unknown.

Wrede, who appeared later[38] as the most out-and-out opponent of a Messianic consciousness in Jesus, and who was capable of violently distorting the texts in order to make his interpretation fit, showed already in his interpretation of the Kingdom of God in 1894 the same tendency to eliminate or disregard sayings in the texts which are not in line with the consistency of thought he assumed Jesus must have had.[39]

G. Dalman carried out a thorough investigation into the meaning of the word *malkut* in the Old Testament and in

---

what applies only to the actual miracles. The preaching of Jesus is not, like the miracles, in itself a supernatural phenomenon, but points towards a supernatural Kingdom. "Nevertheless it might, in my opinion, be possible in certain connexions that His teaching, too, occasionally, though certainly only occasionally, might be seen in the light of a present Kingdom of God," namely on the one hand in so far as it is inspired by "a secret spiritual force," and on the other in so far as the glad tidings could be regarded as the coming of the Messianic age (p. 106). It is not, however, this that is important but the knowledge that one stands at the end of time, seeing already the first rays of the rising sun and hearing the distant thunder of the coming Judgment (p. 107).

[38] W. Wrede, *Das Messiasgeheimnis in den Evangelien. Zugleich ein Beitrag zum Verständnis des Markusevangeliums*, Göttingen 1901.

[39] "The purely eschatological interpretation of the Kingdom of God in the sense laid down rules out any other interpretation of the idea by Jesus, save at the price of a violent inconsistency in Jesus Himself (Wrede, *Vorträge und Studien*, p. 108).

Judaism, and came to the conclusion that it always means "kingly rule" ("*Königsregiment*") and never "kingdom,"[40] for an Oriental kingdom, even today as in antiquity, is not a state in our sense of the word, not a constitutionally ordered nation or country, but is rather the area over which the power of the king or prince extends. Dalman found it strange that the expression "Kingdom of God" is used in the Synoptics to signify the area ruled over.

Dalman asserted, following J. Weiss, that the Kingdom of God was to Jesus a purely religious conception. It is a gift of God and is always regarded as an eschatological entity, which may be spoken of as present only in the sense that the end is approaching. Both the meaning of the term and its use linguistically were new and distinctive to Jesus, even if the expression derives from Daniel.[41]

The name of G. Schnedermann very seldom appears in the theological discussion; he is not mentioned at all by Albert Schweitzer. He did, however, clearly recognise the connexion between Jesus and the ideas of His time on the subject of the Kingdom of God, and drew the necessary conclusions. He believed himself to have proved in 1893, as against Schmoller and J. Weiss, that Jesus, like His contemporaries, held the Jewish conception of the Kingdom of God. The Kingdom is eschatological *because* the Jewish belief was that the Kingdom would come at the end of history, in the days of the Messiah.[42] Jesus saw "an order of things near in which God the Lord of Israel would be proclaimed King, first over Israel, then over the world; a world kingdom of the God of Israel."[43] The essential part of this belief, which Jesus shared with His people,

---

[40] G. Dalman, *Die Worte Jesu. Mit Berücksichtigung des nachkanonischen jüdischen Schrifttums und der aramäischen Sprache*, VOL. I, Leipzig 1898, p. 77; Eng. version: *The Words of Jesus*, trans. D. M. Kay, VOL. I, Edinburgh 1902, p. 94.

[41] "The theocracy about to make its entrance into the world was something more than a gratifying realisation of the hope entertained regarding it; it was a creative force bringing new ideas in its train" (*op. cit.*, Eng. trans., p. 139).

[42] G. Schnedermann, *Wie der Israelit Jesus der Weltheiland wurde*, 2nd edn., Leipzig 1912, p. 17. G. Schnedermann, *Jesu Verkündigung und Lehre vom Reiche Gottes in ihrer geschichtlichen Bedeutung*, Leipzig 1893-95, states, VOL. I, p. 132, that Jesus "adopted the idea of the Kingdom of God from the people of His time with all its distinctive qualities, among them a not inconsiderable national-political element." G. Dalman, *Die Worte Jesu*, p. 139, n. 3, quotes a statement of Schnedermann's: "The Kingdom preached by Jesus was none other than that so long desired by His people, the Kingdom of God for Israel."

[43] *Wie der Israelit Jesus der Weltheiland wurde*, p. 17.

was that God, the God of Israel, would become King (*e.g.* Ob. xxiv; Ps. xcvi. 10) and that His kingly dominion would in future be more clearly manifest than before through the mediation of the Messiah, the King of the End-Time.

Jesus, then, gave no new teaching about the Kingdom of God. He did not explain the nature of either the Kingdom of God or God Himself. The heart of His teaching was "the religious proclamation of a supernatural, factual manifestation of God to be fulfilled for the yearning people of God, and the moral demands arising therefrom."[44]

It is generally believed to have been Ritschl who made the concept of the Kingdom of God the central concept of Christianity, but Schnedermann believed it would be found in the future that the credit for this should go to Kant.[45] The chief feature of the Gospel teaching about the Kingdom of God is that the Kingdom is actually *coming* through Jesus, who is the Messiah. The new element is thus not the concept of the Kingdom of God but the qualifying statement that it is coming, or, better expressed, that it has come near. The time of fulfilment is now here. The tremendous effect of the teaching of Jesus is due to this unique statement, that the Kingdom has come near; hopes and longings are about to be satisfied.

As a prophet Jesus taught how one must enter into the Kingdom, and Israel will enter first. But Jesus was not only a teacher. The title, Son of Man, which Jesus used with great caution, indicates "the dignity of the Messiah to be."[46]

That some French theologians should have completely accepted Weiss's interpretation of the Kingdom of God seems only natural since, as we have already seen, French Protestant theology was decidedly sympathetic towards eschatology during the decade that led up to Weiss. F. Krop,[47] who was entirely on Weiss's side, declared that the Kingdom of God and the Kingdom of Heaven are completely synonymous terms and equally original. The Kingdom of God is a territory in

---

[44] G. Schnedermann, *Das Jüdenthum in den Evangelien. Eine Einführung in das geschichtliche Verständnis des Lebens Jesu*, (2nd edn. of *Das Judentum und die christliche Verkündigung in den Evangelien*, 1884), Leipzig 1900, p. 251.

[45] G. Schnedermann, *Über den jüdischen Hintergrund im Neuen Testament*, Leipzig 1890, p. 10.

[46] *Wie der Israelit Jesus der Weltheiland wurde*, p. 29.

[47] F. Krop, *La Pensée de Jésus sur le royaume de Dieu d'après les évangeles synoptiques. Avec un appendice sur la question du "Fils de l'Homme,"* Paris 1897.

which God rules and His will is done. It belongs entirely to the future. Krop states: "Jesus always regarded the Kingdom of His Father as being to come. At no moment during His ministry did He regard it as present."[48] The Kingdom of God is an entirely supernatural, eschatological entity, the appearance of which would mean "a complete upheaval of the existing order of things."[49]

E. Stapfer, professor to the Protestant Faculty in Paris, was also in favour of a purely eschatological interpretation of the Kingdom of God.[50] When Jesus spoke of the Kingdom of God, He had in mind the whole of time from the first moment to the last. Jesus did not found the Kingdom of God through His teaching, nor did he give it its laws. Neither does it develop gradually, though the number of those who shall enter into it grows. For the Kingdom is not a spiritual or moral state which is realised by Jesus in the present and which develops invisibly in the consciences of His disciples. But what Jesus spoke of is the sudden, final catastrophe, which man is to prepare for now. This catastrophe, however, is not immediately imminent, for there is still time to prepare. But when the Kingdom comes, it will do so through a sudden transformation, and the Kingdom is a quite different world from that which exists now, with a new order of things, which will be realised on the transformed earth at the coming of the Messiah at the end of the present age.

After the publication of H. J. Holtzmann's contribution in 1897, the discussion on the Kingdom of God died down considerably. In England during the nineties it attracted remarkably little attention.[51] The only contribution of any importance is that of R. H. Charles, who defined the Kingdom of God as "the community in which the divine will was to be realised on earth as it is already in heaven."[52] The two aspects of the Kingdom—part present, part to come—Charles related

---

[48] Krop, *op. cit.*, p. 80.   [49] *Op. cit.*, p. 58.

[50] E. Stapfer, *Jésus-Christ, sa personne, son autorité, son oeuvre*, Paris 1896-98.

[51] W. Sanday, in *Life of Christ in Recent Research*, p. 59, explains with regard to Weiss, *Predigt Jesu*, that he "unfortunately missed the first edition when it came out; there is no copy in the Bodleian and I have not been able to find one in Oxford." He succeeded in borrowing a copy from F. C. Burkitt of Cambridge.

[52] R. H. Charles, *A Critical History of the Doctrine of a Future Life in Israel, in Judaism and in Christianity. Or Hebrew, Jewish and Christian eschatology from pre-prophetic times till the close of the New Testament canon. Being the Jowett Lectures for 1898-99*, London 1899, p. 314. Charles's interpretations present similarities to H. J. Holtzmann's.

to different periods in the activity of Jesus. At first Jesus saw
the Kingdom of God as already present (Mt. xi. 4-6, xii. 28;
Lk. iv. 18 f., xvii. 21; Mk. i. 15, and the parables of the Kingdom of God in Mk. iv and Mt. xiii), and through His own
indwelling divine power it would come gradually to fulfilment.
In Jesus the Kingdom of God was already present. This
present Kingdom was to Charles something inward and
spiritual. It was just before His death that Jesus began to
speak of the Kingdom of God as something that is to come. He
saw that it could not be realised in its perfected form otherwise
than in the future. This coming Kingdom is something outward and visible, and this Kingdom God will establish Himself
at the end of time (Mt. xxiv. 29; Mk. ix. 1; Lk. xiii. 28 f.,
xiv. 15). But Charles believed there are suggestions here and
there that the Kingdom will not come through a catastrophe.
It will gradually transform and renew the life of mankind and
of the world (the Grain of Mustard Seed). Qualifications for
entry into the Kingdom are purely ethical and spiritual, so
that the difference between Jews and heathens will disappear.

In Sweden, Nathan Söderblom was so deeply influenced by
Weiss that he found himself obliged to abandon the Ritschlean
positions. Ritschl had indeed performed a great service by
showing the importance of the idea of the Kingdom of God,
but he "is also the past master among modern theologians in
the art of forcibly injecting his own ideas into the Scriptures,"
Söderblom wrote in 1898. "Jesus and the Apostles did not
preach the Kingdom of God as a comprehensive term for the
moral progress of Christian humanity." Söderblom emphasised rather "the eschatological, transcendental, incommen-
surable character of the Kingdom of God."[53] The Kingdom
of Heaven which Jesus preached involved "something *coming*,
a tremendous, closely imminent world catastrophe, in face
of which the decision must be taken . . . a coming, eschatological act, which will introduce a new way of life and the
expectation of which dominates the horizon."[54]

In logical contradiction of Jesus' teaching that the Kingdom
of God will come soon, the Gospel also speaks of a *present*
Kingdom of God. If Jesus had only preached the Kingdom
of God as something to come, He would have been merely

---

[53] N. Söderblom, *Jesu bergspredikan och vår tid*, Stockholm 1899, 2nd edn.,
Malmö 1930, p. 62.   [54] *Op. cit.*, p. 63.

a prophet. But "He knew, however, that He Himself was the Messiah and that the Kingdom of God was therefore already present."[55]

When Söderblom later came to decide what was in the deepest sense distinctive of Jesus, he did not do the eschatological element full justice. What was new and distinctive about Jesus was according to Söderblom, not the eschatological teaching and not the fact that Jesus, in consequence of His Messiah-consciousness, made the coming Kingdom of God present, but it is individualism that is the real, inalienable heritage of Christianity. The eternal value of the individual human soul is the leading thought in the whole teaching of Jesus. The value of eschatology is that it lends to ethic a tremendous intensity.

To Söderblom, the value of the eschatological interpretation of Jesus is that it brings out the greatness of Jesus, which is to him the kernel of the problem of Jesus. Söderblom held firmly to the eschatological interpretation of the Kingdom of God and urged its importance for Christianity at the present time.[56] On the occasion of the Ecumenical Conference in Stockholm in 1925 he declared: "The eschatological interpretation of the good tidings about the dominion of God is not merely of historical importance for a correct understanding of the origins and early ideas of Christianity, but it also provides a healthy corrective to the culture-happy religion which waxed fat during the golden age of discoveries, technical progress, material abundance and education."[57]

The Debate on the Kingdom of God from 1900 to 1906

In 1900 J. Weiss published a second edition of his treatise on the Kingdom of God. In this the ideas were more fully developed, and the discussion of other theological works, which in the first edition was very brief, was greatly expanded. The

[55] *Op. cit.*, p. 66. The Kingdom of God is present in and with its founder: Christ. Söderblom cites Mt. xvi. 13, xii. 28; Lk. xi. 20; and Mt. xi. 5.

[56] N. Söderblom, "Jesus eller Kristus? Den snara väntan i evangeliet," in *När stunderna växla och skrida*, VOL. II, 3rd edn., Stockholm 1935, pp. 275-301. The essay is devoted to Johannes Weiss, "the man who, of living theologians, has made the most important contribution to research into the life of Jesus" (p. 291). Söderblom also stresses that "to our generation a realisation of the basic eschatological element comes as a necessary awakening" (p. 301).

[57] N. Söderblom, *Kristenhetens möte i Stockholm augusti nittonhundratjugofem*, Stockholm 1926, pp. 259 f.

Old Testament material above all was dealt with in detail. Weiss's position was in the main unchanged. He deplored the fact that, after the publication of the first edition of his book, discussion on the Kingdom of God unfortunately concentrated disproportionately on the unprofitable question: Is the Kingdom of God something still to come, or is it already here? Weiss did not feel himself responsible for this; too much had been made of the differences. The crucial point was not whether the Judgment is nearer or farther away, but that the Kingdom of God is now quite definitely coming. The time of waiting is past. The turning-point is here. Salvation is no longer dream but reality. In comparison with this certainty, which nothing can disturb, it is quite immaterial whether one says that the Kingdom is near, or that it is already here. It is merely a heightened expression of the general certainty that the Kingdom is near, when Jesus now and then in prophetic exaltation leaped over the brief period of waiting, as though He were already at the goal. It is a question of change of atmosphere but not of different dogmatic views.[58] But the teaching of the Kingdom to come is the normal, whereas the proleptic sayings are the exceptions. Both quantitively and materially the futuristic sayings predominate, for the basic atmosphere is always hope.[59] Certain aspects of Jesus' teaching lie quite outside the eschatological teaching, such as the greater part of His ethics and the dual command of love, on the basis of which alone the Christian ethic could live for all time. Weiss was evidently anxious to remove the impression of

[58] Weiss, *Predigt Jesu*, 2nd edn., pp. 69 ff.: "In comparison with this unshakeable *certainty* it is immaterial that He now says, it is near, now, it is already here. It depends on the circumstances, on the mood of the moment, which expression He chooses. When storm-clouds gather and flashes of lightning already flicker on the horizon, one might say: A storm is coming. But one might also say, proleptically: The storm has come. Or, when the sun shines warm and bright for the first time and the first buds open, one generally says: Spring is coming. But who would carp at the exultant spirit that, in these first signs, welcomed the whole of spring as though it were already there in all its glory? It is a matter of temperament and of the vividness of the experience. So in the same way it is merely an intensification of the general certainty when Jesus now and then, in joyful, prophetic exaltation, leaps over the brief span of waiting as though He were already at the goal. It is a question of nuances of feeling, not of different dogmatic attitudes." Weiss cites also passages in the Old Testament to which exactly the same applies (Joel II. 1; Ezek. VII. 7, LXX).

[59] "On the other hand it is equally beyond question that Jesus says elsewhere that the Kingdom of God is already come: ἔφθασεν ἡ βασιλεία τοῦ Θεοῦ" (*Predigt Jesu*, p. 69).

Jesus, apt to be given by the first edition, as a gloomy prophet of doom and an ascetic. Here Jesus is shown as the harmonious teacher of wisdom, who at certain periods of His life uttered " 'maxims' full of the purest, deepest wisdom, which betray no trace of eschatological tension, but merely state simply and calmly what His pure, clear, divinely-inspired mind perceived as self-evident."[60]

This second edition of Weiss's book introduced to some extent a new phase in the debate on the Kingdom of God. The eschatological interpretation gained ground. O. Holtzmann admitted that eschatology is not an incidental offshoot of the teaching of Jesus, but the cornerstone of it all.[61] At the same time he asserted that the Kingdom of God is already present, because the Messiah is present, for the two belong together. "Since the Messiah Himself belongs to the eternal world of the future, it is impossible for Him to sojourn upon earth without even now communicating and dispensing to His surroundings some of the blessings of that future world."[62] When it comes to explaining this further, however, Holtzmann falls back on a purely individualistic interpretation: the teachings of Jesus, he says, can bring about such a happy change within a man that one can say that he already lives in the Kingdom of God. Weiss's influence is clearly apparent, however, when he admits that the sayings about a present Kingdom of God stand almost directly side by side with those that speak of a sudden appearance of the Kingdom.[63]

O. Pfleiderer held that the teaching of the *coming* dominion of God was the normal with Jesus, whereas the proleptical sayings constitute the exception.[64] In 1901 P. Wernle published a clear and concise account of Jesus' eschatological conception of the Kingdom of God.[65] The sayings which refer to the future predominate, and they occur throughout the

---

[60] *Op. cit.*, pp. 135 f.

[61] O. Holtzmann, *Leben Jesu*, Tübingen and Leipzig 1901, pp. 123 f. Eng. version: *The Life of Jesus*, trans. J. T. Bealby and M. A. Canney, London 1904, p. 166.

[62] Holtzmann, *op. cit.* (Eng. trans.), p. 252.   [63] *Op. cit.*, p. 253, n. 2.

[64] O. Pfleiderer, *Das Urchristentum, seine Schriften und Lehren in geschichtlichem Zusammenhang*, 2nd edn., Berlin 1902, VOL. I, p. 618; Eng. version: *Primitive Christianity. Its Writings and Teachings in their Historical Connections*, trans. W. Montgomery, London and New York 1906-11, VOL. II, p. 402.

[65] P. Wernle, *Die Anfänge unserer Religion*, Tübingen and Leipzig 1901, 2nd edn., 1904. Eng. version of 1st edn.: *The Beginnings of Christianity*, trans. G. A. Bienemann, London and New York 1903-4.

whole of Jesus' activity from beginning to end. "Thus, then, the message of Jesus retains its eschatological character from first to last. It is the announcement of the end, of the near approach of the judgment and of the Kingdom, and such it remains."[66] The Kingdom of God, which comes without human effort, is regarded as altogether supernatural. Ethics are among the conditions for sharing in this coming aeon, but brotherly love and purity of heart will not bring the Kingdom to the world, for "they do not drive out devils, they leave the course of the world unaltered."[67] Jesus, however, regarded His work not merely as a preparation for but also as the beginning of the arrival of the new world. The sayings about a present Kingdom of God burst forth from Jesus at moments of particular exaltation when the sense of the littleness of the present was forgotten in the greatness that the Father was now allowing to come about through Him.[68] The influence of Weiss is evident here.

Unquestionably the most important contribution to the discussion at the beginning of the twentieth century was the sketch of the life of Jesus published in 1901 by the twenty-six-year-old Albert Schweitzer.[69] This first draft of a "consistently

---

[66] *Op. cit.*, 2nd edn., p. 49.   [67] *Op. cit.*, pp. 53 f.

[68] *Op. cit.*, pp. 44 ff. Wernle warns against building up psychological fabrications on inadequate foundations in an attempt to reconcile contradictory sayings by the assumption that Jesus, in the face of death, had altogether abandoned the idea of a present Kingdom of God. In his *Jesus*, Tübingen 1917, he emphasises that the answer to the question why the Kingdom of God had already appeared, is always: Because the Messiah has come. This presence can only be grasped by those who have faith. That the Kingdom of God in the teaching of Jesus can be at once a present and a coming entity, Wernle explains on psychological grounds, in spite of the fact that in other connexions he warns against this. One moment Jesus' gaze is fixed on the hopeful small beginnings of the Kingdom of God in the present, the next, the forces hostile to God force themselves on his attention and then the Kingdom of God is banished into the future and the small beginnings are lost sight of. Beside the eschatological figure of Jesus stands the figure of Jesus as the Redeemer of souls, the Son of God. It is, says Wernle in 1917, precisely the figure of the historical Jesus and His personality that gives us the key to the understanding of Christianity and its triumph. So that, in spite of a definitely eschatological conception of the Kingdom of God, Wernle retains unaltered the attitude of the turn of the century. In connexion with Wernle mention should also be made of his *Die Reichgotteshoffnung in den ältesten christlichen Dokumenten und bei Jesus*, Tübingen and Leipzig 1903. A. Schweitzer's classification of Wernle among the opponents of an eschatological interpretation of Jesus (*Geschichte*, pp. 246 ff.) does not apply to the latter's interpretation of the Kingdom of God. Wernle defended himself against this charge (*Th.Lz.*, 1906, p. 503).

[69] A. Schweitzer, *Das Messianitäts und Leidensgeheimnis, Eine Skizze des Lebens Jesu*, Tübingen and Leipzig 1901, 2nd edn. 1929; Eng. version: *The Mystery of*

eschatological" interpretation of Jesus introduced a new element that was to prove of decisive importance for future developments. The interpretation of the Kingdom of God given in this work is the same as in Schweitzer's great later work,[70] so that we will not discuss it in detail here. The reason why Schweitzer's first publication attracted so little attention is undoubtedly that Wrede's book on the Messiah, published the same year,[71] deflected interest from consistent eschatology to consistent scepticism.

A remarkable change is noticeable in W. Bousset, who in 1902 came out entirely on Weiss's side.[72] Βασιλεία, says Bousset, should be translated "the dominion of God," though he is rather doubtful about the passages which speak of entering into the Kingdom, as there the idea of locality predominates. The basic character of the Kingdom of God is eschatological. "Like the whole of his age, Jesus expected the *miraculous* Kingdom of God, not a new state of affairs that would develop out of the existing state in which it had been immanent, He expected the Kingdom of God, not a Kingdom at which men had built and toiled, He knew nothing of any immanent transfiguration and transformation of the world, to Him as to His age the world was only fit to be destroyed, He taught His disciples to save themselves by escaping from this world into the altogether new state of things that was soon to come. In this sense He taught His disciples to pray: Thy Kingdom come. If He spoke of this βασιλεία here and there as though it were already present, that does not alter the eschatological nature of His teaching. Thus Jesus saw in His casting out of the devils a sign of the immediate nearness of the Kingdom of God, indeed of its presence (Mt. XII. 28, *et par.*).[73] Bousset's

---

the Kingdom of God: the secret of Jesus' Messiahship and Passion, henceforth cited as *Mystery of the Kingdom*, trans. W. Lowrie, London 1956.

[70] A. Schweitzer, *Von Reimarus zu Wrede, Eine Geschichte der Leben-Jesu-Forschung*, Tübingen 1906; Eng. version: *The Quest of the Historical Jesus: a critical study of its progress from Reimarus to Wrede*, henceforth cited as *Quest*, trans. W. Montgomery, 3rd edn. London 1954.

[71] Wrede, *Das Messiasgeheimnis in den Evangelien*.

[72] W. Bousset, "Das Reich Gottes in der Predigt Jesu," in *Th.R.*, v (1902), p. 437, n. 1.

[73] Bousset, *op. cit.*, p. 438. The parables of Jesus never taught an immanent Kingdom of God, evolving here on earth through the aid of human intervention. Even the parables of the Treasure and the Pearl are not concerned with "a present good," but the disciples are "to dedicate their whole earthly lives to the object of future participation in the Kingdom of God" (p. 439). In the parables of the

E

strong insistence that the Kingdom of God is something miraculous and transcendental is in keeping with the religious philosophy of Fries, which he adopted. A comparison with Rudolf Otto springs to mind. Even the ethic of Jesus is completely eschatological in tone. Its command runs: For the sake of the blessedness of the Kingdom of God, abandon this miserable world altogether.

As a general summing up of Bousset's interpretation of Jesus, it can only be said that, in spite of his altered attitude on the Kingdom of God, he remained true as before to the old liberal traditions.[74] The picture of Jesus as a whole remains very much the same in all Bousset's works, even though on the question of Jesus' Messiah-consciousness his ideas grew steadily more radical, until in the end he felt compelled to deny it altogether.

In America even such a typical representative of the Social Gospel as S. Mathews[75] now came out with the view that the eschatological interpretation of the Kingdom corresponded to the original ideas of Jesus. He did not think one could speak of a presence of the Kingdom in any other sense than that, when Jesus preached the Kingdom, there were those present who would enter into it when it was revealed.

That Reformed theology should put forward champions of a definitely eschatological interpretation of the Kingdom of God is hardly surprising, if we remember how even before J. Weiss this movement had clearly grasped the futuristic nature of the Kingdom of God. A typical representative is the Swiss, R. du Pasquier,[76] who considered we must admit the fact that to Jesus the Kingdom of God was something future.[77] Jesus did not found the Kingdom on earth, but proclaimed its

---

Self-growing Seed, the point to be stressed is not the quiet growth, but the way the harvest comes quite suddenly without human intervention, and to the great surprise of the farmer is already there. One cannot force the Kingdom of God; soon, after one night, it shall be there.

[74] With regard to Bousset's interpretation of Jesus see also his *Jesus*, Religions-geschichtliche Volksbücher, I. 2-3, Tübingen 1904, 4th edn. with intro. by Schmidt, 1922; Eng. version: *Jesus*, trans. J. P. Trevelyan, ed. W. D. Morrison, London and New York 1906.

[75] S. Mathews, *The Messianic Hope in the New Testament*, Chicago 1905. Mathews also asserts that the Messiah is eschatological, since the Kingdom is so (p. 114).

[76] R. du Pasquier, *Le Royaume de Dieu dans la prédication de Jésus*, Lausanne 1906.

[77] "We have to admit that, to the mind of Jesus, the Kingdom of God is still to come" (du Pasquier, *op. cit.*, p. 77).

imminent appearance. But not only that. Jesus declared the presence of the Kingdom of God under certain circumstances. This presence was entirely spiritual. Jesus saw the Kingdom as present in the power of God which vanquished demons and which He transmitted, and even in the acts of grace which accompanied these powers. In this spiritual coming of the Kingdom Jesus saw the first appearance of the Kingdom of God, and "the first appearances of the Kingdom are the guarantee of its glorious coming at the end of the world: that is the chief teaching of the parables of the Kingdom."[78] Du Pasquier denied that Jesus ever, in a sort of prophetic rapture, experienced the Kingdom as present. That the Kingdom of God now manifested itself as a force, which to Him was the same as its spiritual presence, constituted the prelude to its miraculous coming in glory.[79]

How the leading exegetic theologians regarded the question of Jesus about the turn of the century and during the early years of the present century is shown with all possible clarity by A. Jülicher's account of the Kingdom of God and of Jesus.

When in 1899 he published the second part of his study of the parables,[80] it might have been expected that the eschatological idea of the Kingdom of God would have exercised a decisive influence on his interpretation, but this is not the case. The Kingdom of God, according to Jülicher, is an exclusively supernatural idea, which realises itself entirely without human aid, but it is nevertheless not merely a future entity but exists already here on earth. As prophet of the Kingdom of God Jesus was upheld by a rock-fast faith in His ideal; against all indifference and all hostility He opposed His triumphant: we still have the Kingdom of God.

---

[78] *Op. cit.*, p. 239.

[79] In opposition to J. Weiss's view that Jesus in moments of prophetic transportation experienced the Kingdom as present. Cf. Schmoller's comments in *Die Lehre vom Reiche Gottes in den Schriften des neuen Testaments*, pp. 148-54.

[80] A. Jülicher, *Die Gleichnisreden Jesu*, Tübingen 1888-99, 2nd edn., 1910. On the question of Mk. IV. 26 ff. Jülicher says: "But it is certain, according to this parable, that to Jesus the Kingdom of God did not mean merely a coming entity, but was already here, on earth—for in heaven there is no growth and expansion—that it continues to increase and its limits to expand, and that no inertia or hostility can prevent its attaining certain fulfilment. . . . So in the parable of Mk. IV. 26 ff. we encounter the rocklike faith of the prophet of the Kingdom of God in His ideal: as against the indifference, the workaday attitude, the avowed hostility of the majority, a triumphant, confident: The Kingdom must remain to us" (VOL. II, p. 546).

In 1906 Jülicher published a more detailed interpretation of Jesus.[81] The central core of the Gospel is the expectation of the Kingdom of God, which has a genuinely Jewish colouring. Jesus' idea of the Kingdom of God differed, however, from that of the Jews in that He brought the Kingdom into the present and into the course of history.[82] The most important innovation, however, was the introduction of the theory of evolution into the idea of the Kingdom of God.[83] The task of Jesus was to bring in and establish the Kingdom, and even if we have to abandon the title "Son of Man" as a Messianic title used of Himself by Jesus, it still remains a fact that He entered into Jerusalem and was crucified as the Messiah, and accepted from Peter the designation Messiah. Jesus thus allocated to himself the most important rôle next to God in the Kingdom of God.

Jülicher quite correctly set the Kingdom of God and the Messiah in very close relation to one another. As the Messiah and the Kingdom of God cannot exist without one another, the Kingdom also is there, because the Messiah is there. Admittedly it is not visible to those who cannot see the high position of Jesus, but the leaven is also invisible, that is hidden in the meal and there carries out its work. The generation to which Jesus was sent, had in Him the Kingdom amongst them. It was for them to see what was in Jesus: "to recognise the spirit of the Kingdom that resided in Him, to approach Him inwardly."[84] Future and present were united in the person of Jesus, for He belonged to them both. When finally Jülicher comes to define what it is that is new in Christianity, he finds it in Jesus Himself and His personality. He has carried the moralisation of religion through to the end. This interpretation reveals the religion of Jesus as the religion of humanity, and every eschatological feature has disappeared.

[81] A. Jülicher, "Die Religion Jesu und die Anfänge des Christentums," in *Die Kultur der Gegenwart*, VOL. I, PT. 4, Berlin and Leipzig 1906, 2nd edn. 1909, pp. 42-131.

[82] Mk. IV. 26 ff., which Jülicher describes as the profound parable of the seed ripening without human intervention, might mean the "damping of exaggerated eschatological expectations" (*op. cit.*, p. 55).

[83] "(He brings) the Kingdom to some extent into the present, and allows the idea of evolution, which was diametrically opposed to all Jewish ideas of the Kingdom, to enter into the Kingdom of God" (*op. cit.*, p. 56).

[84] *Op. cit.*, p. 59.

VII

The Futuristic Interpretation of
the Kingdom of God

Albert Schweitzer was the first to attempt to interpret the whole teaching of Jesus in exclusively futuristic terms. Previously even those who most clearly saw that Jesus' idea of the Kingdom of God was eschatological, had still tried to find room for other, uneschatological thoughts in His teaching. Schweitzer cut out all compromise, root and branch. Almost everyone who has written on the subject since has been obliged to reckon with him. Though it took a little time for the discussion to get into its stride, it has been waged all the more intensively ever since. An important factor here has been that researches into the history of religion have thrown an entirely new light on the eschatology of Jesus.

Whereas hitherto we have followed chronological order, from now on we will consider our authors in groups, arranged according to their interpretation of the Kingdom of God.

Albert Schweitzer

Even those theologians who stressed the eschatological nature of Jesus' idea of the Kingdom of God, had also recognised the essential Jewishness of His view of the ultimate. No one had ever so completely denied that Jesus in any way diverged from the Jewish idea of the Kingdom of God as Albert Schweitzer. According to him, the fault with J. Weiss and his followers was that they related eschatology merely to the teaching of Jesus instead of allowing His basically eschatological outlook to colour the whole of His public activity. They let Jesus speak and think eschatologically on certain main points, while for the rest they presented His life as uneschatologically as modern historical theology itself. To Schweitzer it seemed almost inexplicable that the eschatological school, with its insight into Jesus' teaching on the Kingdom of God, should not have immediately realised the "dogmatic" element in the history of Jesus, for eschatology is nothing but dogmatic history which enters into and elevates natural history.[1] Schweitzer asks whether it is not really the only possible reaction, that one who expected His Parousia at any moment should be governed in His acts no longer by the natural course of events, but by this expectation alone. The explanation of Jesus' activities from this dogmatically eschatological angle he calls "the solution of consistent eschatology."

Even as a young student, in 1894, he had been filled with doubt, on reading Mt. x-xi, regarding the prevailing theory of the priority of the Mark text and the whole conception of the life of Jesus that had been built up on this basis.[2] In commissioning the disciples Jesus predicted that the Kingdom of the Messiah would appear before they had even made their way through the towns of Israel. These predictions, which reveal the strong eschatological tension in which Jesus lived, could not have been put into His mouth later. If we fit Mt. x-xi into the historical framework of Mark, which is reliable, we begin to get some idea of the public activities of Jesus and His attitude towards the purely eschatological Kingdom of God.

The account of the Kingdom of God as seen by Jesus, and of the attitude He Himself adopted towards the Kingdom He preached, which Schweitzer gives in his monumental study of research into the life of Jesus, may be summarised briefly as follows. Like John the Baptist, Jesus expected that the Kingdom of God, and therewith the super-earthly state of the world and of the elect of humanity, would appear at any moment. Then He and the elect would enter into the heavenly existence.

The Kingdom of God is an essentially supernatural event, an end to the present age. Its arrival is imminently close but always coming. The Kingdom of God can, therefore,

---

[1] "Eschatology is simply 'dogmatic history' which breaks in upon the natural course of history and abrogates it" (*Quest*, p. 349).

[2] A. Schweitzer, *Aus meinem Leben und Denken*, Leipzig 1932; Eng. version: *Out of my Life and Thought, An autobiography*, henceforth cited as *My Life and Thought*, trans. C. T. Campion, New York 1949, pp. 5-8.

never be in the strict sense of the word present in the life of
Jesus. The parables in Mk. IV do not speak of natural growth
and natural development, but stress the wonder that, through
the power of God which is active, the one thing follows the
other at its appointed time. But what is the initial fact
(*"Anfangstatsache"*) after the occurrence of which the Kingdom
of God shall come, as surely as harvest follows sowing? Why,
simply that it is sown! According to Schweitzer Jesus cannot
here have meant anything else but the eschatological movement
of repentance evoked by the Baptist and now intensified by
Himself, which by the power of God forces the Kingdom
of God to come, just as the sowing, which is done by man,
brings forth the harvest through the same infinite power.[3]
He who now sees the seed sown in the earth, expects with the
earthly harvest the heavenly one, *i.e.* the revelation of the
Kingdom of God. Here the connexion is not merely symbolic
and analogical, but temporal and real. The exhortation to
His hearers was, therefore: Ye who have eyes to see, read in
the harvest which is ripening upon earth, what is being prepared in heaven! *At the time of the harvest the Kingdom of God
shall come.* When that comes, the Kingdom of God will also
be here. It is as near as that.

The disciples were sent out to preach: "Repent, for the
Kingdom of God is at hand!" It was a flying mission, the
purpose of which was to proclaim swiftly to Israel what was
to come. Even with Jesus' preaching of repentance the Kingdom would dawn; "The host of penitents is wringing it from
God, so that it may now come at any moment."[4] The secret
of the Kingdom of God, that now, at harvest-time, the Kingdom would come, could be hidden no longer (Mt. x. 27) but
had to be revealed. "The 'is near' had turned to an 'is here'."[5]
Jesus would not see His own again in this age, for before they
had hastened through the towns of Israel, the Parousia of the
Son of Man would have come, which is both logically and

---

[3] "The movement of repentance evoked by the Baptist and now intensified by
His own (Jesus') preaching. That necessarily involves the bringing in of the
Kingdom by the power of God; as man's sowing necessitates the giving of the
harvest by the same infinite Power. Anyone who knows this sees with different
eyes the corn growing in the fields and the harvest ripening, for he sees the one
fact in the other, and awaits along with the earthly harvest the heavenly, the
revelation of the Kingdom" (*Quest*, pp. 354 f.).

[4] *Op. cit.*, p. 356.

[5] *Geschichte*, p. 405.

temporally identical with the coming of the Kingdom. Jesus had thus hoped to be transformed, during the absence of the disciples, into the Son of Man. But when the hope was not fulfilled, and they returned without the Parousia having taken place, Jesus broke off His activities in Israel and withdrew into heathen territory. Jesus' hopes of the coming of the Kingdom of God now underwent a change. He explained to Himself the failure of the Kingdom of God to appear. How? *The secret of the Passion* supplies the answer.

Because Jesus' idea of the Kingdom of God was altogether dogmatic, the mystery of suffering was already present in the mystery of the Kingdom of God, inasmuch as the Kingdom could not come unless the "Affliction" had taken place (Mk. VIII. 34-8). But now this had not come, and therefore the Parousia could not come. Jesus was compelled in the end to give up hope that the Affliction, without which the Kingdom could not come, would come of itself. When it did not come, this could only mean that an act (*"Leistung"*) was required. The movement of repentance had not been enough. This did not mean, however, that the Kingdom of God was not near at hand, but that God had heard the Lord's Prayer, in which Jesus had prayed with His followers for the Kingdom and at the same time for deliverance from *peirasmós*, and that with regard to the time of trial God in His mercy had decided otherwise and had marked out a different path.[6] As He who was to rule over the children of the Kingdom, Jesus had to give His life for them, for "the many" (Mk. X. 45, XIV. 24) and by His blood to make the atonement that these would have had to make through afflictions and tribulations, for the Kingdom could not come unless the debt were paid. When Jesus went to His death, He did so in order to force forth the Kingdom, which would be taken in possession by "the many" for whom he died, *i.e.* those predestined for the Kingdom. Jesus does not die in order that this one or that one may come into the Kingdom of God; "He provides the atonement in order that the Kingdom itself may come."[7] When Jesus went up for the last time to Jerusalem, He was forced to do so not from any historic-empirical necessity, but from a dogmatic and eschatological one: He must die in order to compel the

[6] *Quest*, p. 387.
[7] *Op. cit.*, p. 388, n. 1.

coming of the Kingdom. In Is. LIII Jesus had found the answer to His question as to how God intended to bring forth the Kingdom.

In Jerusalem Jesus did no teaching in the real sense of the word, but He prophesied in parables the great "tribulation" that was to come (Mk. XII. 1-12), exhorted His hearers to watch for the Parousia, described the Judgment that the Son of Man was to hold, cleansed the Temple and silenced His opponents before all the people. He was condemned and executed as the Messiah, now that the secret of the Messiahhood had been revealed. His public ministry had then lasted less than a year. Jesus saw Himself, not as the Messiah but as the "Son of David," who was to be exalted and transformed into the Son of Man mentioned in Daniel, who was of divine nature. That was His Messianic secret (Mk. XIV. 60) which Peter betrayed to the other disciples, whereas to the people Jesus remained to the last day of His life the prophet from Nazareth, and it was He, the Son of David, and not the Messiah, whom they acclaimed when Jesus rode into Jerusalem. To Jesus Himself the entry was a Messianic act, in which His self-awareness showed forth, as previously in the commissioning of the disciples, the declaration that the Baptist was Elijah, and in the feeding of the five thousand by the lakeside. The betrayal by Judas lay in the fact that he revealed the Messianic secret to the enemies of Jesus. "Jesus died because two of His disciples had broken His command of silence: Peter when he made known the secret of the Messiahship to the Twelve at Caesarea Philippi; Judas Iscariot by communicating it to the High Priest."[8]

This interpretation of the Kingdom of God and the Son of Man by "thorough-going eschatology" as being purely to come, dominates also the interpretation of the new righteousness preached by Jesus and of Church and sacrament. The preaching of the new righteousness of necessity belongs together with the preaching of the nearness of the Kingdom. As the idea that the Kingdom was to be realised eschatologically was the basis of Jesus' teaching, so the whole of His ethic falls under the heading of repentance in preparation for the coming of the Kingdom. "The repentance in expectation of the Kingdom" contains within itself all ethical demands; "as

[8] *Op. cit.*, p. 394.

repentance unto the Kingdom of God the ethics also of the Sermon on the Mount is Interim ethics."[9] To Jesus there was no morality of the Kingdom of God, for in the Kingdom of God all natural states were abolished (Mk. XII. 25). Repentance and service even to humiliation and death led merely to the boundary of the Kingdom. Jesus' ethic is not the ethic of the Kingdom of God but serves merely until the Kingdom, which is imminently near, shall arrive. Jesus' moral demands relate only to inward preparation for membership of the coming Kingdom and the declaration of righteousness at the Judgment.

In the great Church saying (Mt. XVI. 18 f.), which Schweitzer considers to be a saying of Jesus, the Church is a pre-existent entity, which is to be revealed at the end of time and is completely synonymous with the Kingdom. At the "supper on the shores of Genezareth"[10] Jesus consecrates the participants to participate also in the coming Messianic banquet, and gives them the assurance that those who have been with Him at table here shall also be with Him in glory. Actually the meal is an indirect revelation of the secret of the Messiahship. At the Last Supper Jesus is to say that He will not drink again of the fruit of the vine, until He drink it new in His Father's Kingdom. This again indicates that the Kingdom of God is immediately imminent.

The original feature of Schweitzer's interpretation of the Kingdom of God is not so much the strong emphasis on *the Kingdom of God as the great ultimate miracle* and a supernatural world condition, which Weiss, Wrede, and others had already insisted upon, even though they allowed a certain latitude to the idea that Jesus in moments of grace saw the Kingdom as

[9] *Mystery of the Kingdom*, pp. 97 f. The search for any previous occurrence of the expression "interim ethics" has proved unavailing. Schweitzer states that he coined the expression himself (*Geschichte*, p. 595). F. Kattenbusch says that he does not know who coined the expression (*Zeitschrift für die neutestamentliche Wissenschaft und die Kunde der älteren Kirche*, henceforth cited as *Z.N.W.*, 1911, p. 275). The term means, according to Schweitzer, "that the ethical demands of Jesus all aim at inner preparation for membership of the coming Kingdom and ultimately at justification at the judgment. That is as much as to say that to Jesus an ethic of the Kingdom of God did not exist. This presupposes a supernatural state of the world, in which mankind has lost its earthly mortality, and stands transfigured beyond struggle and sin, good and perfect in every way like the angels" (*Geschichte*, p. 595).

[10] *Mystery of the Kingdom*, pp. 168-74. *Geschichte* has the designation "The Supper by the Seashore," p. 421.

present, but rather Schweitzer's view that Jesus tried by His activities *to force the coming of the Kingdom*, first by the movement of repentance and then by His death. To support this development in Jesus Schweitzer based himself on Mt. x-xi, which, however, is quite clearly a later composition made up of separate sayings of Jesus.[11] Schweitzer's construction of the life of Jesus is consequently in danger of reading into the Gospel a line of development that the text by no means justifies. His interpretation of Jesus is distinctly one-sided. One reason for this is Schweitzer's lack of insight into the late Jewish eschatology on which he makes Jesus entirely dependent. This eschatology is to Him exclusively transcendental, Danielian; but a long struggle had been fought out between this and the prophetic, more or less earthly and political type of eschatology.

The decisive criticism of Schweitzer is, however, that even if the Gospel does express the Jewish hope of the future, the centre of interest is not the Messianic age to come. The centre of interest is Jesus' work among His people, in the light of which the picture of Jesus as a whole must be seen. The centre of interest is thus the overwhelming happenings which the historical Jesus saw taking place before His eyes as He went about His mission: "The blind receive their sight and the lame walk, lepers are cleansed and the deaf hear, and the dead are raised up, and the poor have the good news preached to them" (Mt. xi. 5). To the primitive congregation it was the resurrection of Jesus, and not his Parousia, that was the dominating consideration. Among the sayings of Jesus Himself there are obviously some that refer to the present Kingdom of God, side by side with those that represent it as coming. Jesus' position as the Son can only be properly understood in the light of what happened in and through His activity among the people. The presence sayings cannot therefore in any way be eliminated from the teachings of Jesus without distorting the whole Gospel picture.[12]

When Schweitzer faces us with the alternative: either an eschatological or an uneschatological interpretation of Jesus,

[11] The form critics and above all K. L. Schmidt have shown how little historical value the framework of the story of Jesus has in establishing the chronology of the life of Jesus.

[12] For criticism of Schweitzer see above all O. Cullmann, *Christus und die Zeit, Die urchristliche Zeit- und Geschichtsauffassung*, Zürich 1946; Eng. version *Christ and Time*, trans. Floyd G. Filson, London 1951, pp. 84 f. and a number of other places.

he thrusts a wrong answer upon us by framing the question wrongly. One is driven into an "either—or" where it should be a "both—and."

One feature that plays a great part in Schweitzer's account of the history of the study of the life of Jesus and of the Kingdom of God is a sort of semi-Hegelianism. He maintains that, if a thesis is thought out "to the bitter end," it is freed of its anti-thesis, though without there being then any synthesis between thesis and antithesis. The thesis is nullified. As a modern thinker and theologian, Schweitzer cannot accept the realistic eschatology which, according to him, Jesus embraced. The process of thought described above helps him out of this diffi-cult dilemma. By allowing eschatology free rein exegetically, we are freed from the bonds of eschatology. For the sake of truth we are obliged first to emphasise and then to sacrifice eschatology. So the religion of Jesus, which is the religion of love, is freed of its dogmatic trappings, and the late-Jewish eschatological outlook collapses. The mould in which the casting was made has been broken. We are now at liberty to let the religion of Jesus become a living force in our thought, as its purely spiritual and ethical nature demands.[13] "This is Schweitzer's attitude: eschatology is as exegetically funda-mental as it is theologically impossible. As exegetists and historical investigators we must unconditionally accept escha-tology radically without any half-measures whatever. We must look the fact in the face that the faith of Jesus and the Apostles was entirely conditioned by eschatology. As modern theologians we have no use for it."[14]

The consistent interpretation obviously embodies an in-consistency, if one is to reject theologically what one has shown historically to be the central idea of the Gospel. Schweitzer finally ends up with a quite different element— "reverence for life"—which he separates out from the his-torical kernel; but this he reaches by way of a purely philoso-phical argument, and not by way of the Christian Gospel as such.

Even though this was not to be apparent all at once, Schweitzer's great work on the study of the life of Jesus was

[13] *My Life and Thought*, pp. 58 f.

[14] O. Linton, "Eskatologien som exegetiskt och systematiskt problem," in *Svenskt Teologisk Kvartalskrift*, henceforth cited as *S.T.K.*, 1942, p. 304. Cf. Cullman, *Christ and Time*, p. 30.

epoch-making. He achieved what no one before him had done: he destroyed once and for all the liberal image of Jesus as personality and hero, and showed us that our ordinary yardsticks are of no use at all when it comes to measuring the Jesus of the Gospels. He has to be understood eschatologically, even though the whole image of Jesus which then forces itself upon us only increases the distance between us and the historical Jesus of Nazareth.

The Debate on Schweitzer's Interpretation of Jesus

The German theologians rejected Schweitzer's interpretation of Jesus to a man. We cannot, of course, here enter into their criticism of Schweitzer's account of the history of the study of Jesus, but must keep to the question of the Kingdom of God. Here his basic fault, according to P. Wernle,[15] is his view that Jesus tried to force the coming of the Kingdom of God. The impression given by the sources is rather that the coming of the Kingdom is at the free discretion of God, even though mankind may seek it and pray for it. By the very fact of praying for the Kingdom, indeed, they recognise the free power and grace of God. Almost with one voice the Germans declared that one cannot possibly close one's eyes to the fact that there are other features in the teaching of Jesus besides those which are determined by eschatology. It is the non-Jewish, the human, the eternal, all that which is not bound by time, that one must regard as the cornerstone of the teaching of Jesus. It was only to be expected that Schweitzer would come up against that criticism, so long as the power of liberal theology remained unbroken. H. J. Holtzmann,[16] A. Jülicher,[17] H. Windisch,[18]

---

[15] P. Wernle, Review of Von Reimarus zu Wrede, in Th. Lz., 1906, pp. 501-6. To try to describe the person of Jesus in Schweitzer's catch-phrases is "the perversity of all perversities and a betrayal of sound human understanding as of all depth of vision" (p. 504).

[16] H. J. Holtzmann, "Der gegenwärtige Stand der Leben-Jesu-Forschung," in D.L.Z., xxvii (1906), pp. 2357-64, 2413-22, 2477-83, 2541-46. See also id., Lehrbuch der neutest. Theologie.

[17] A. Jülicher, Neue Linien in der Kritik der evangelischen Überlieferungen, Giessen 1906, pp. 1-13. "Astonishing originality informs what is really a work of fiction that Schweitzer offers us in his 19th chapter as the result of his study of the life of Jesus. It is interesting only as testimony to a blazing imagination and intense will-power" (pp. 3 ff.).

[18] H. Windisch, review of A. Schweitzer, Von Reimarus zu Wrede, in Th.R., 1909, p. 146.

H. Weinel,[19] E. von Dobschütz,[20] as well as the conservative
P. Feine[21] and the Catholic scholar A. Meyenberg,[22] all agreed
in their criticism. As concerns the Kingdom of God they
declared unanimously that it is not a purely eschatological
entity as Schweitzer presented it.

Schweitzer's work received nothing like the attention in
Germany that one might have expected. One reason was
unquestionably the theological situation in Germany during
the years just preceding the First World War. The discussion
on the historical existence of Jesus, initiated by A. Drews and
his followers, reached its climax about the year 1910 and
occupied the majority of leading theologians (A. Jülicher,
J. Weiss, H. Weinel, E. Klostermann, P. W. Schmiedel,
M. Dibelius, H. Windisch, W. Bousset, E. Troeltsch and
others), as is shown by the flood of treatises on the subject
which was now printed. After the War crisis theology, the
question of pneumatic or historical interpretation of the Bible,
and form criticism, attracted all the interest. When, about the
middle of the nineteen-twenties, the question of Jesus, and
with that the question of Jesus' conception of the Kingdom
of God, began to receive attention again, theologians were no
longer bound by Schweitzer's opinions. But the great mark
he has left behind him is shown not least by the fact that
no one can any longer dismiss the eschatology of Jesus with
just a few words. Its significance, both for Jesus and for the
whole New Testament, is a question that has to be grappled
with.

In England, where an English translation of Schweitzer's
book was published in 1910,[23] it had a much more favourable

---

[19] H. Weinel, *Biblische Theologie des Neuen Testaments, Die Religion Jesu und des Urchristentums*, Tübingen 1911, 2nd edn. 1913.

[20] E. von Dobschütz, "The Eschatology of the Gospels" in *The Expositor*, henceforth cited as *Exp.*, Ser. VII, No. 9, 1910, pp. 97-113, 193-209, 333-47, 398-417, and in book form, London 1910; and "Der heutige Stand der Leben-Jesu-Forschung," in *Z.Th.K.*, *N.F.V.*, (1924), pp. 64-84.

[21] P. Feine, "Die konsequente Eschatologie," in *Neutestamentliche Studien Georg Heinrici zu seinem 70. Geburtstag . . . dargebracht*, Untersuchungen zum Neuen Testament, No. 6, Leipzig 1914, pp. 201-7. Mt. x is the Evangelist's composition for the Apostolic and post-Apostolic mission. The Kingdom of God was not to Jesus a purely eschatological entity. If Schweitzer were right, then Jesus would be nothing but an apocalyptic visionary, neither has he succeeded in showing how it was possible for such tremendous effects to follow from the activities of Jesus.

[22] A. Meyenberg, *Leben-Jesu-Werk*, Lucerne 1922-32.

[23] *The Quest of the Historical Jesus*, trans. W. Montgomery.

reception. W. Sanday,[24] the standard English exegetist of the day, and F. C. Burkitt,[25] had prepared the way; the latter had written the preface to the English edition. At the Cambridge Church Congress of 1910, a number of leading English theologians, among them C. Gore, J. H. Bernard, R. H. Charles, and V. H. Stanton, read papers on Schweitzer and his theory.[26] The realistic Englishmen decided that Schweitzer keeps closer to the text than do most critical research scholars; nor does he, as so many others have done, reduce the person of Jesus to merely human proportions, but allows Him to keep the exalted stature He has in the Gospels. Another merit of Schweitzer's is that he is able to link quite naturally the eschatology and Christology of the Synoptists with that of St Paul and St John. Besides, the freshness and force of his style could not help but tell in his favour.[27] Even the Catholic

[24] Sanday, *The Life of Christ in Recent Research*. In a review of W. Sanday, *Christologies Ancient and Modern*, 1910, in *Journal of Theological Studies*, IX (1909-10), pp. 584-6, W. R. Inge deplored the fact that Sanday's *Life of Christ* was responsible for a wave of enthusiasm in England, which would not otherwise have occurred, for Schweitzer's book, *Von Reimarus zu Wrede*, "a production which I am old-fashioned enough to think blasphemous. It has now appeared in English, not, as might have been expected, under the auspices of the Rationalists' Press Association, but with commendations from Divinity Professors of both our great Universities" (p. 586).

[25] F. C. Burkitt, *The Gospel History and its Transmission*, Edinburgh 1906. The 2nd edn. of 1907 speaks of "A. Schweitzer's admirable history of the attempts to write a Life of Jesus" (p. viii). Wherever the New Testament speaks of growth and harvesting, it is always the Last Judgment that is referred to. "The End has not come yet. The Kingdom of God remains a theory of the future" ("The Eschatological Idea in the Gospel," in *Essays on some Biblical questions of the day, by members of the University of Cambridge*, ed. H. B. Swete, London 1909, p. 211. F. C. Burkitt, "The Parables of the Kingdom of Heavem," in *The Interpreter*, 1910-11, pp. 131-48; God himself will bring in the Kingdom of God when the time is ripe. This is "a new state of things which should follow on after the present state of things had vanished in catastrophe, after the day of God's Judgment" (p. 148). In view of the nearness of the Kingdom, everything else must be abandoned in preparation for the catastrophe (the Treasure, the Pearl). Until the great final catastrophe comes, Jesus is not the Messiah. He borrowed from the Book of Enoch the ideas in which He clothed His idea of Himself. "He had arrived at the conviction that He was the Chosen of God, but as yet the end had not come. He was not yet the Messiah. But He was the Son of Man who was destined to become the Messiah" (p. 136). This fact explains the secret of the Messiah. See also F. C. Burkitt, *Jesus Christ. An historical outline*, London 1932.

[26] E. C. Dewick, *Primitive Christian Eschatology*, Cambridge 1912, p. 111, n. 1.

[27] Sanday, *The Life of Christ in Recent Research*, pp. 88 f.: "1. He (Schweitzer) keeps much closer to the text than most critics do; he expressly tells us that his investigations have helped to bring out the historical trustworthiness of the Gospels; 2. He does not, like so many critics, seek to reduce the person of Christ to the common measures of humanity, but leaves it as he finds it; 3. By doing this, he is

modernist, G. Tyrrell,[28] was convinced of the superiority of the eschatological interpretation.

But the first enthusiasm gradually subsided. A few years later W. Sanday was slightly embarrassed at having allowed himself to be carried away so unreservedly by his approval of Schweitzer's interpretation.[29] The chief fault that he now saw in him was "a tendency to push things to extremes at the dictates of logical consistency." Others who were now also critical are E. C. Dewick,[30] B. H. Streeter,[31] P. Gardner,[32] C. Emmet,[33] M. Jones,[34] and the American H. B. Sharman.[35]

In France, Schweitzer's influence on the interpretation of Jesus was not inconsiderable.[36] In Scandinavia, which at this time was strongly under the influence of German theology, he was coldly received. Nathan Söderblom,[37] for example,

---

enabled to link on, in an easy and natural way, the eschatology and Christology of the Gospels to the eschatology and Christology of St Paul and St John." See also A. M. Ramsey, *From Gore to Temple*, London and New York 1960, pp. 17 ff.

[28] G. Tyrrell, *Christianity at the Cross-Roads*, London 1909, 4th imp. 1913. Tyrrell compares the "eschatological Jesus" with the Catholic Jesus and finds that Catholicism is closer to the historical Jesus than modern liberal Protestantism, since it has preserved transcendentalism in its conception of Jesus.

[29] W. Sanday, "The Apocalyptic Element in the Gospels," in *Hibbert Journal*, x, No. 1 (1911), p. 84.

[30] Dewick, *Primitive Christian Eschatology*.

[31] B. H. Streeter, "Professor Burkitt and the Parables of the Kingdom," in *The Interpreter*, 1910-11, pp. 241-7. Also *id*, " Synoptic Criticism and the Eschatological Problem," in *Studies in the Synoptic Problem. By members of the University of London*, ed. W. Sanday, London 1911, pp. 423-36. Also *id*. "The Historic Christ," in *Foundations, A Statement of Christian Belief in terms of Modern Thought, By Seven Oxford men*, London 1912, pp. 73-145. According to Streeter, Jesus adopted a very reserved attitude towards Jewish apocalyptic ideas.

[32] P. Gardner, "The Present and the Future Kingdom in the Gospels," in *Exp.T.*, xxi (1909-10), pp. 535-8.

[33] C. Emmet, *The Eschatological Question in the Gospels*, Edinburgh 1911. Schweitzer's Jesus is a caricature.

[34] M. Jones, *The New Testament in the Twentieth Century. A Survey of recent Christological and Historical Criticism of the New Testament*, London 1914. Jones is prepared to accept an eschatological explanation of Jesus, but not the "consistent" one.

[35] H. B. Sharman, *The Teaching of Jesus about the Future according to the Synoptic Gospels*, Chicago 1909, p. 327. "He (Jesus) opposed clearly and strongly the eschatological and catastrophic conceptions of the Kingdom held by John the Baptist and his contemporaries."

[36] According to S. J. Case, "The Life of Jesus during the last quarter-century," in *J.Rel.* v. (1925), p. 571, interest in eschatology dominated the discussion on Jesus even in America during the years 1906-14.

[37] N. Söderblom, in *När stunderna växla och skrida*, VOL. II, p. 298: "Eschatology is no universal explanation of the sayings of Jesus or His self-estimation. It leads us deeper into many obscure sayings and gives a stark, impressive unity to much in the behaviour of Jesus that had previously appeared merely incidental

campaigned strongly against consistent eschatology, which did not help us to understand the secret of the person of Jesus.

Albert Schweitzer's Pupils

"Consistent eschatology" as formulated by Schweitzer has only attracted a small number of really faithful adherents. J. Warschauer[38] tried to write a complete life of Jesus from the angle of consistent eschatology. The attempt only showed up the unreasonableness of the interpretation. F. Buri[39] and above all Martin Werner[40] vigorously championed Schweitzer's interpretation of Jesus.

Werner entirely accepts Harnack's thesis that Christian dogma is a product of the Hellenic spirit working upon the basis of the Gospel, but believes that Harnack falsely determined this basis as being the teaching of Jesus, whereas it should be a universal, in itself non-dogmatic gospel. Jesus was completely under the influence of late Jewish apocalyptic eschatology, and the question of historical dogma is: "How in early Christianity was the eschatology of late Jewish apocalyptic thought made current in the form of imminent expectation?"[41] The objective criterion for historicity is the form in which the late Jewish apocalyptic eschatology—in particular that of Enoch—appeared in Jesus, namely "as the object of the immediate expectation."[42] Since the mind of Jesus moved

---

or strange. . . . Familiarity with the personal life even of humbler actors in a great historical event should show how impossible it is to do it justice through such a simple explanation as the eschatological atmosphere where Jesus is concerned."

[38] J. Warschauer, *The Historical Life of Christ*, London 1927. The book is an attempt "for the first time to apply Schweitzer's thesis to the whole Gospel story" (pp. vii f.). There is a strong element of liberalism in Warschauer's theological attitude.

[39] F. Buri, *Die Bedeutung der neutestamentlichen Eschatologie für die neuere protestantische Theologie*, Diss. Berne, Zürich 1934. On p. 25 Buri confesses himself a complete follower of Schweitzer's. The essence of New Testament eschatology is "the New Testament expectation of the imminent end of the world, grown out of the intense eschatological tension brought about by historical illusion" (p. 29).

[40] M. Werner, *Die Entstehung des christlichen Dogmas problemgeschichtlich dargestellt*, Berne and Leipzig 1941, p. 77, at the end of the chapter "Die 'konsequent-eschatologische' Auffassung des Urchristentums als dogmengeschichtlicher Ansatzpunkt": "The theory of consistent eschatology is historically in truth so magnificently demonstrated and justified that it must be recognised as the ultimate historical solution of the problem of the historical Jesus and of early Christianity."

[41] Werner, *op. cit.*, p. 28.

[42] Werner, *op. cit.*, p. 67.

F

entirely along the lines of the apocalyptic of Enoch, He embraced a purely futurist conception of the Kingdom of God. The whole eschatology of Jesus was expectation of the immediately impending Parousia, when the Kingdom of God should come. Not one single passage in the Synoptic tradition speaks clearly and definitely of the presence of the Kingdom. The early Christian Christology was Angelic Christology. As an Angel or a Prince of Angels the Son of Man formed part of the world of creation, and as the Elect of God He took His place as supernatural world-ruler over the new, supernatural aeon of the coming world, subjugator of the Satanic powers and judge of the world.[43]

Even if only a small number of scholars actually accepted Schweitzer's dogmatic eschatological interpretation of Jesus, there was a far larger number who maintained that the Kingdom of God in the teaching of Jesus is exclusively futuristic, and that the sayings about the nearness of the Kingdom say no more than that it stands at the threshold and can be expected at any moment. Such sayings as Mt. xii. 28 and Lk. xvii. 20 f. they either remove by critical procedure or give them a purely futuristic interpretation.

The former course is taken by A. von Gall in his major work on the history of religion, published in 1926.[44] Jesus' hope of the Kingdom of God had nothing in common with the hopes of the Jewish people, but was the product of Persian influence and was completely transcendental, other-worldly in the full sense of the word. God's kingship was something supra-worldly, heavenly, which only the future would reveal.

[43] M. Werner's "angel-Christology" has been severely criticised. See W. Michaelis, *Zur Engelchristologie im Urchristentum, Abbau der Konstruktion Martin Werners*, Gegenwartsfragen biblischer Theologie, VOL. I, Basle 1942. It is stated on p. 187 that "early Christianity knew no angel-Christology." See also Hj. Lindroth, "Det kristna dogmat och kristendomens aveskatologisering," in *S.T.K.*, 1943, p. 91. For criticism of "consistent eschatology" according to Werner see W. Michaelis, *Der Herr verzieht nicht die Verheissung, Die Aussagen Jesu über die Nähe des Jüngsten Tages*, Berne 1942.

[44] A. Freiherr von Gall, *BASILEIA TOU THEOU, Eine religionsgeschichtliche Studie zur vorkirchlichen Eschatologie*, Religionswissenchaftliche Bibliotek, VOL. VII, Heidelberg 1926. Von Gall considers that it is only Mt. xii. 28 (Lk. xi. 20) and Lk. xvii. 20 f. that might be taken to mean that the Kingdom of God is something that reaches into the present. But Mt. xii. 28 originates from the early congregations, for as Mk. iii. 25 shows, the passage originally ended with vs. 26 (Lk. xi. 17). Lk. xvii. 20 f., on the other hand, presages nothing more than the sudden and unexpected appearance of the Kingdom (pp. 473 ff.).

The Kingdom of God was never something present, but always to come and, as it was connected with the end of the world, eschatological. Two passages in the Gospel, von Gall considers, give binding evidence that Jesus saw Himself as the Son of Man, namely Mt. XVI. 16, the confession of Peter, for which the Matthew text is the most original, and Jesus' confession before the High Priest (Mt. XXVI. 64). Jesus had seen the Parousia and the judgment by the Son of Man standing at the very threshold.

W. Michaelis insists that Jesus must be consistent and His teaching on the Kingdom of God homogeneous. But Jesus' idea of the Kingdom of God was not consistent, in the sense in which Schweitzer uses the word.[45] To John the Baptist the Kingdom of God was exclusively an eschatological entity, coming at the end of time. The same applies to Jesus, when He prayed: "Thy kingdom come." A number of sayings in the Synoptic Gospels can only be interpreted eschatologically. Jesus speaks of the coming "close of the age" (in Mt. XIII. 39 and elsewhere), which brings with it "the day of judgment" (Mt. X. 15, XI. 22 and elsewhere), and the Parousia of the Son of Man (Lk. XVII. 22, 24, 26, 30 and elsewhere). The Kingdom of God also belongs to the end of time, as is shown by the connexion between Mt. XVI. 27 (et par.) and the following vs. 28, which speaks of the Son of Man coming in His Kingdom. Typically eschatological are Mk. IX. 1 and Lk. XXII. 18. A further proof that Jesus spoke of the synchronism of the Parousia of the Son of Man and the coming of the Kingdom is the wording of the prayer: "Remember me when you come in (with) your kingly power" (Lk. XXIII. 42). In all this there is

---

[45] Among Michaelis's works which deal with Jesus and the Kingdom of God should be noted in particular, *Täufer, Jesus, Urgemeinde. Die Predigt Jesu vom Reiche Gottes vor und nach Pfingsten*, Neutestamentliche Forschungen, ed. O. Schmitz, Ser. 11, No. 3, Gütersloh 1928, and *Reich Gottes und Geist Gottes nach dem Neuen Testament*, Basle 1931. He gives a complete interpretation of the parables of Jesus in *Es ging ein Sämann aus, zu säen, Eine Einführung in die Gleichnisse Jesu über das Reich Gottes und die Kirche*, Berlin 1938, and *Das hochzeitliche Kleid, Eine Einführung in die Gleichnisse Jesu über die rechte Jüngerschaft*, Berlin 1939. In his work, *Der Herr verzieht nicht die Verheissung*, of 1942, he maintains his previous interpretation of the Kingdom of God but dissociates it definitely from Schweitzer's "consistent" eschatology, as he has been driven to do by M. Werner: "It is one of the great weaknesses of so-called consistent eschatology that it interprets the expectation of the end by Jesus and the New Testament exclusively in the light of the late Jewish conception of the end of the world" (*op. cit.*, p. 74, p. 12, n. 25). See also on the Kingdom of God Michaelis "Zur Frage der Äonenwende," in *Theologische Blätter*, henceforth cited as *Th. Bl.*, 1939, pp. 113-8.

complete agreement on the matter of the conception of the Kingdom of God and its futuristic nature between John the Baptist and Jesus. But what distinguishes them is that Jesus spoke of *Himself* as the one whose coming was at hand.

Now it might be supposed, says Michaelis, that the teaching of Jesus would sometimes lose its exclusively eschatological character, and that it must contain also uneschatological elements, to which passages other than the definitely eschatological ones in the Synoptics would testify. Is there, side by side with the purely eschatological sayings about the Kingdom, even one saying of Jesus about a Kingdom of God which will become reality during the period of Jesus' lifetime? There are a number of sayings about entering into the Kingdom of God. Of all these "entry" sayings it may be said that the time of entering into the Kingdom, even where the future tense is not specifically used, is identical with the "end time" towards which men look and in anticipation of whose swift arrival they must now repent.[46] Equally the "Theirs is the kingdom, of heaven" of the Beatitudes does not refer to something already possessed, but provides "a guarantee of future possession."[47]

The parables of the Kingdom of God have often been quoted in support of the non-eschatological interpretation of the Kingdom. Michaelis holds that the Treasure and the Pearl are neutral in regard to the eschatological nature of the Kingdom and merely emphasise its absolute value. In the Net (Mt. XIII. 47-50) and the Weeds among the Wheat (Mt. XIII. 24-30) the wording itself does not leave room for anything but an eschatological interpretation. The Self-growing Seed

---

[46] With regard to the "entry sayings" Michaelis says: Mk. IX. 47 refers clearly and definitely to the Judgment and not to any present Kingdom of God, as is shown by the fact that the alternative to entering into the Kingdom of God is to be cast into hell fire. When Jesus says: "Unless your righteousness exceeds that of the scribes and Pharisees, you will never enter the kingdom of heaven" (Mt. V. 20), He is not speaking of any qualification for membership of a present Kingdom of God but of the Judgment with its testing of righteousness. Mt. VII. 21 must be paraphrased so: Only he that does the will of my heavenly Father shall pass through the Judgment and then enter into the Kingdom. In Mt. XVIII. 3 entry into the Kingdom is dependent on receiving it like a child. "The 'receiving' of the Kingdom does not conflict with its eschatological character" (*Täufer, Jesus, Urgemeinde*, p. 66). "The time of this entering in is . . . obviously identical with the end of the world towards which man's mind must be directed and on account of which he must now, immediately repent" (*op. cit.*, p. 67).

[47] *Op. cit.*, p. 68.

does not speak of a development of the Kingdom by itself in time, in such a way that the growing seed would represent the Kingdom. The seed is rather, as in the Sower, the gospel of the Kingdom, *i.e.* the call to repentance.[48] The parable stresses that the ultimate revelation of the Kingdom depends on the effectiveness of the call to repentance. The Leaven and the Grain of Mustard Seed also refer to the effect of the gospel of the Kingdom. Michaelis is obliged, like so many others, to represent a number of parables which expressly state that they refer to the Kingdom of God, as referring only to the gospel of the Kingdom of God, in order to fit them into his interpretation, which would otherwise come up against difficulties.

The most difficult passages to get away from, in any attempt to manoeuvre out of the sayings about the presence of the Kingdom, are undoubtedly Mt. xii. 28, Mt. xi. 2 ff., and Lk. xvii. 20 f. Michaelis says of the first, that Jesus *must* have regarded the exorcisms of the demons from an eschatological angle (cf. Lk. x. 18). They are indications that the end is approaching, but by no means that the Kingdom is present in time. "The coming of the Kingdom at the end of time" is at hand.[49] The contested ἔφθασεν ἐφ' ὑμᾶς cannot mean anything else but "has come close" (as in Mt. iv. 17 and elsewhere). When it comes to forcing Jesus' reply to the Baptists' question into the "end of the world" interpretation, Michaelis uses the same argument as with regard to Mt. xii. 28. Jesus simply cannot, as He expected the eschatological Kingdom of God, have considered it possible that it could be realised in the present.[50] Lk. xvii. 20 is got around in the usual way:

[48] "Actually the Kingdom of God cannot be meant, as the Kingdom of God is an entity which, closely linked as it is with Doomsday, can only be expected from Doomsday (Lk. xxi. 33), namely the unrestricted dominion of God which becomes manifest when God becomes 'all in all' (1 Cor. xv. 28) and not a Kingdom that emerges in history and expands. So also the parable of the Self-growing Seed cannot imply the Kingdom of God itself, but, as the parable according to its introductory words is meant to refer to the Kingdom of God, it can only be to the preparation for the coming of the Kingdom, in other words the preaching of the Kingdom" (*Es ging ein Sämann aus, zu säen*, p. 56). The comforting knowledge the preacher must have, is that the harvest will come (p. 61).

[49] Michaelis, *Jesus, Täufer, Urgemeinde*, p. 74.

[50] John the Baptist's question is paraphrased by Michaelis as follows: "Are you, as you claim to be, he that is to come, whose coming on earth I have prophesied? Are you he, whose consciousness of mission gives him the certainty that at the end of time he will appear as the Messiah? Or is it another, whom we must expect?" Jesus' answer is paraphrased as follows: "That I am he whose coming to the Judgment you and all others await, that my consciousness of mission confirms

an imaginary "suddenly," "unexpectedly," or some such word, is interpolated, giving the following reading: one cannot calculate the end of the world, that brings with it the Kingdom of God, for behold, the Kingdom of God is, whenever it comes, all of a sudden among mankind.

The conclusion Michaelis comes to is that not one single passage in the Synoptic tradition represents the Kingdom as clearly and irrefutably present. Rather the teaching of Jesus is consistent and in accordance with the preaching of John the Baptist, in that it places the time of the coming of the Kingdom as the closely imminent but still future end of the present age. "The Kingdom of God in the teaching of Jesus cannot be thought of as future in any other sense than as coming at the approaching end of the world. The futurity of the Kingdom is the futurity of the end of time, which will be brought about catastrophically by an act of God. A presence of the Kingdom could therefore only be spoken of in so far as its 'end of the world' character allowed."[51] We cannot speak of a present Kingdom of God, but only of present signs of a Kingdom that will come at the end of time.[52] It is God who brings about the Kingdom without human activity. All that men can do is to spread word of the nearness of the Kingdom, and wait and prepare themselves for its coming. That is the only work that they can do "for" the Kingdom of God.[53]

Jesus placed Himself in relation to the Kingdom in the only sense that is possible, from the angle of the purely and exclusively eschatological interpretation of the Kingdom of God: He was conscious of being the *Messias designatus*.[54] Ever since His baptismal experience it had stood clear to Him that He was destined to be the Messiah.

The whole of Jesus' preaching and His view of Himself were thus inspired by certainty of the "nearness of the end."

---

by divine authority the identity of my person with the ultimate Messiah, that is shown by my acts which, although such acts are prophesied for the end of the world, are intended to serve as signs of the end and as proof of my authority" (*op. cit.*, p. 93).

[51] Michaelis, *op. cit.*, p. 82.

[52] Of the "present character" of the Kingdom we can only speak in this sense, "that we speak of present, temporal 'signs' of the Kingdom that is to come at the end of time, and that these present 'signs' serve to confirm the absolute certainty of the nearness of the end" (*op. cit.*, p. 86).

[53] Michaelis, *Das hochzeitliche Kleid*, p 112.

[54] Michaelis, *Täufer, Jesus, Urgemeinde*, pp. 86 f.

The Kingdom of God had accordingly only one form to Jesus, and could have no other but the "exclusively eschatological."[55]

Criticism of Michaelis can be brief. His main fault is that he first restricts the definition of eschatology, and then forces the texts to fit. He considers, in fact, that eschatology covers only two possibilities: future or present. Having established that Jesus, in common with John the Baptist, expected the end of the world to come soon, he can see no possibility of any modification. Jesus has to be as limited in His ideas as Michaelis. To achieve this logical consistency, all the traditional passages which might be interpreted as representing the Kingdom as present, must be twisted to support Michaelis's view. The parables about the Kingdom become parables about the *gospel* of the Kingdom and the Church.

French exegetic criticism of the eschatological interpretation of Jesus mostly followed the tradition of A. Wabnitz and W. Baldensperger, and was sympathetic to the ideas of J. Weiss (F. Krop, E. Stapfer, R. du Pasquier). Schweitzer's influence is perceptible here. The Kingdom of God is presented throughout as something purely futuristic and transcendent. Even such mutually divergent scholars as A. Loisy, C. Piepenbring,[56] Ch. Guignebert,[57] H. Monnier,[58] M. Goguel

---

[55] *Op. cit.*, p. 85.

[56] Even though C. Piepenbring, *Jésus historique*, Bibliothèque de critique religieuse, 26, 27, Paris 1909 ; Eng. version: *The Historical Jesus*, trans. L. A. Clare, London and New York 1924, draws a different picture of Jesus from Loisy, representing Him as a dreamer caught up in the visionary world of His day, he agrees entirely with Loisy in his conception of the Kingdom of God: "Jesus never believed Himself to be the actual Messiah in His lifetime, but regarded Himself as the Messiah of the future. . . . He expected the full and complete manifestation of the Messiah as of the Kingdom of God, in the future" Eng. trans., pp. 116 f. Piepenbring is a typical rationalist and his work is of little value in New Testament research.

[57] Ch. Guignebert, *Jésus*, L'Évolution de l'humanité, Synthèse collective xxxiv, Paris 1933; Eng. version: *Jesus*, trans. S. H. Hooke, London 1935, is mainly influenced by the literature of the years 1900-13, his principal teachers being Schweitzer and Loisy. Practically nothing remains of the religion of Jesus. Guignebert regards the Kingdom of God as entirely futuristic. "The Kingdom is primarily and essentially the material transformation of this present evil world" Eng. trans., p. 341. "The Kingdom of Jesus' expectation was an *eschatological* Kingdom, the gift of divine grace, to be established by the miraculous interposition of the divine will" (p. 351). Any sort of consciousness of mission in Jesus is denied. "There can be no question, therefore, that in Jesus we are dealing with a prophet, a herald of the expected Kingdom," (p. 295). For criticism of Guignebert see P. Dor, *Le Royaume de Jésus et la passion selon M. Guignebert*, Paris 1939.

[58] H. Monnier, *La Mission historique de Jésus*, Paris 1906, 2nd edn. 1914, p. 215: "Apart from the exceptions which I have analysed, and which are not inconsistent

and J. Hering agree on a purely futuristic interpretation of the Kingdom of God.[59]

Loisy, who describes himself as a follower of the critical tradition of Renan,[60] and who defends Schweitzer's thesis, maintains that it is necessary to present Jesus as Schweitzer does in order to be able to assert His historical existence.[61] He defines the Kingdom of God as a principally spiritual and moral reality, which comes into being exclusively through the power and will of God.[62] The Dominion of God shall be revealed through a sudden transformation of things and the exaltation of the Messiah. The by nature eschatological Kingdom of Heaven is now only an object of hope. The gospel has often been regarded as an anticipation of the Dominion of God, in the sense that the latter has already begun, even though it has not yet actually been established. The gospel must then be one with the Kingdom. It is indeed true that preparation and fulfilment cannot be separated from one another, but even if the transition from the gospel to the Dominion of God takes place in a moment, that moment is still decisive, for until the age of glory comes, the Kingdom of God is not here. Jesus compared the Kingdom to a great

---

with the idea of a future Kingdom, there is no authentic text in the Gospel which refers to a present Kingdom."

[59] There are, of course, exceptions. As examples of a different interpretation may be mentioned: H. Clavier, *La Notion de Dieu dans l'enseignement de Jésus*, Études théologiques et religieuses, Montpellier 1932, pp. 50-77, and *L'Accès au Royaume de Dieu*, Études d'histoire et de philosophie religieuses, henceforth cited as E.H.P.R., No. 40, Paris 1944, in which he comes forward as defender of a non-eschatological interpretation of Jesus. All the eschatological terms which Jesus used could just as well be interpreted non-eschatologically. The Kingdom of God is a spiritual, present entity.

[60] A. Loisy, *Mémoires pour servir à l'histoire religieuse de notre temps*, VOL. III: 1908-1927, Paris 1931, p. 437; also in *Journal de psychologie normale et pathologique*, XX (1923), p. 330: "Renan has been my master in Bible criticism."

[61] In *Autour d'un petit livre*, Paris 1903, Loisy asserts that one must defend Schweitzer's theory if one is to maintain the historical existence of Jesus at all.

[62] A. Loisy, *Les Évangiles synoptiques*, Cheffonds 1907-8, VOL I, pp. 251 f.: "Christianity, then, came into the world as a message from God on the near future, and when one sets out to define its essence in the light of history, one finds nothing more nor less than the idea of the Kingdom, which is in itself a future good, even though this future good should not in any way be anything but the consecration of the righteousness acquired in the present. It is precisely this ultimate consecration of the righteousness acquired in blessedness that the Gospel proclaims." See also VOL. I, pp. 232, 237. It is to misrepresent both the Gospel and the idea of the Kingdom of God, to summarise the teaching of Jesus as faith in God the Father. This faith is not the dominion of God, but only one of its conditions (p. 237). Cf. A. Loisy, *L'Évangile et L'Église*, Cheffonds 1892, p. 48.

feast, but as the invitation to a feast is not the feast itself but is a necessary preliminary to it, so is also the gospel to the Kingdom: it is a necessary preliminary that must go before, but it is not the Kingdom itself. As disproportionate as is the relationship between the tree and the little mustard seed it has grown up from, or between the leavened meal and the leaven, so also is the relation between the Kingdom and the Gospel. The gospel is the seed to which God gives growth, and the harvest-time depends entirely upon God. Jesus does not speak, in the parables of the Kingdom of God, of the gospel and its development in the world, but compares the gospel with the Kingdom which is to come soon and unexpectedly with the Parousia.

Only by repentance can man enter into the Kingdom. Repentance is a sort of inner renewal, which brings with it a change of life. The Kingdom of God belongs to those whom God has forgiven, and God forgives everyone who trusts in His mercy. Hope of the Kingdom requires that the present life be ordered in love towards God and one's neighbour.

Jesus appeared as messenger of the Kingdom of God and as the preacher of hope; He was the interpreter of all that hope of the Kingdom stands for. It is worth noting that Loisy represents Jesus as founder of the community of the faithful, which was soon to become the community of the elect. Jesus possessed Messianic consciousness. He was the Son of God. [63] But as the Kingdom of God is purely eschatological, so also is the Messiah. Jesus had not yet entered into that office for which He was destined by providence. Jesus was the Son of God, in so far as He was predestined to become the Messianic King. [64]

---

[63] "Whatever may have been the mystery of His personal conscience, the Saviour presents Himself as the agent of the Kingdom, the preacher of the great hope, the sower who will be the harvester. He is not the revealer of a single and unique truth which, perceived by the conscience of each individual, will bestow on him the plenitude of the heavenly Kingdom, but He is the interpreter of all that is contained in the hope of the Kingdom, the ordainer of the society of the believers, soon to become the society of the elect. His function is social and universal, as the hope of the Kingdom is collective; His action must not be purely inward, but will make itself felt in the objective reality of the Kingdom; and it is in the future that His quality of Messiah, Son of God, will appear, in conformity with the eschatological nature of the heavenly Kingdom" (Loisy, *Les Évangiles synoptiques*, VOL. I, p. 252).

[64] "Jesus, then, was Son of God in that He was predestined to the Messianic royalty, and He was so, too, through the inner feeling that united Him with God the author of this vocation" (*op. cit.*, p. 243).

Jesus scarcely used the title Son of Man, as Son of God corresponded better with the direct relationship to the heavenly Father in which Jesus felt Himself to stand. Jesus did not regard His death as a necessary part of His Messianic activities. He reckoned with the risk that He might be killed, but He never saw His death as the act of salvation that was the object of His life-work. The idea of the suffering Messiah, which is linked up with the conception of the Son of Man, was born within the community.

Maurice Goguel has, by his comprehensive and varied authorship, won a name for himself as France's leading New Testament exegetic critic. His conception of Jesus' idea of the Kingdom of God is explained in his highly original work published in 1932.[65] Goguel emphasises strongly that to Jesus the Kingdom of God was never a spiritual or inward reality, which revealed itself to those who had been freed from the world and from evil. No more was it the ideal community of the disciples.

In the existing world God does not rule wholly and un-restrictedly. When the Kingdom is established the power of Satan will be destroyed; to Jesus this power was manifest not in the fact that heathens ruled over the Chosen People, but in the dominion of sin. Then God's right to rule shall be transformed into ruling. Jesus conceived the Kingdom of God differently from His contemporaries. He saw in it the realisation of God's will, and not the divine power that was called into service by the Jewish people to satisfy its hatred and ambition. The change in the conception of the Kingdom of God was due to the fact that Jesus' conception of God influenced and transformed it. For God was to Jesus not the stern Judge but above all the Father, who is good and merciful and loving. So that all the passages about the external enemies of the Jewish people being destroyed, are eliminated. To Jesus the establishment of the Kingdom meant nothing less than that a whole new world and a new world order would become reality through the intervention of God Himself.[66]

[65] M. Goguel, *La Vie de Jésus*, Paris 1932, which forms the first part of *Jésus et les origines du christianisme*, 1932. How Goguel could take upon himself to write a life of Jesus from a psychological angle, so to speak from within, cannot be discussed here. He considers himself justified in placing together chronologically sayings which show similarity of subject-matter.

[66] "The Kingdom of God is transcendent through its origin and not through the place where it will be established. To Jesus, too, the Kingdom of God is a

Goguel maintains that Jesus did not see this Kingdom of God as already present, not even in a limited and hidden form.[67] The Kingdom of God was purely eschatological. It had no place in this world. It would come suddenly and unexpectedly through the all-powerful intervention of God Himself. To begin with Jesus expected that the end would come soon (Mt. x. 23), later that only a few of His followers would live to see the Parousia (Mk. ix. 1), until in the end He could not at all determine the time of the end of the world (Mk. xiii. 33) that was to bring with it the revelation of the Messiah, the resurrection and the judgment. Even if Jesus believed that the Kingdom was near, He never attempted to indicate precisely when it would come, or, like the Jewish apocalyptic writers, to describe the signs that would precede the coming of the Kingdom, and by which one could reckon how far the time was spent.

Jesus had a Messianic consciousness. Otherwise it would be impossible to explain the origin of the faith in the Resurrection, and the birth and development of Christianity. Moreover there is the evidence of Mk. x. 35-43, the casting out of the demons and the Messianic entry into Jerusalem. Jesus claimed before the High Priest that He would come again as the Son of Man. Some day, then, he was to become the Son of Man; He spoke of Himself already in an anticipatory way

---

new order of things which will be realised by an act of God. The Kingdom of God is the new order of things that will be established when the present world comes to an end" (Goguel, *op. cit.*, p. 547). See also *id.*, "Eschatologie et apocalyptique dans le christianisme primitif," in *Revue de l'histoire des religions*, 1932, p. 393: "Jesus made of the Kingdom of God neither a spiritual reality which was born and would be called upon to develop in the hearts of the believers, nor an ideal society made up of those who accept His teaching and follow Him, a society which would be called upon to co-operate. The Kingdom of God is to Him a new order of things which, at a given moment, will be established at one blow on earth and in which the will of God will not be obstructed by any obstacle, either of men or things."

[67] With regard to Lk. xvii. 20 f., Goguel states that the text says that the Kingdom of God is "within you," and not "in the midst of you" (*La Vie de Jésus*, p. 552). As the words were said to the Pharisees, "in you" cannot mean "in your hearts." To understand the meaning it is necessary to point out that Jesus' teaching of the Kingdom of God was essentially practical. "On the lips of Jesus, the term 'the Kingdom of God' often carried a sense very close to 'condition of entry into the Kingdom of God.' If one bears in mind, in addition, the fact that in Aramaic the same form expresses present and future, one comes to the conclusion that the meaning of this saying of Jesus is: 'The Kingdom of God, that is to say the possibility of entering into it, will be in you' " (*ibid*).

as this Son of Man, but only to those close to Him, who were also the only ones who could have understood. Jesus, then, according to Goguel, saw Himself as the *Messias designatus*. His task during the time He spent among the people was to preach the necessity for repentance, *i.e.* the necessity for preparing oneself for the Kingdom of God and the Judgment. He prepared people so that, when the Kingdom came, they would be able to enter into it, but that is quite a different thing from preparing the Kingdom or hastening its arrival, as Schweitzer's interpretation of Jesus according to "consistent eschatology" would have us believe.

It is always one of the assumptions of the purely futuristic interpretation of the Kingdom that Jesus' conception of the Kingdom of God was consistent. Jesus had only one conception of the Kingdom, the eschatological, which teaches "a visible and sudden coming of the '*malkut*,' complete and not intra-mundane" (J. Hering).[68] The Kingdom of God means an objective, metaphysical transformation of the world. The Son of Man shall bring the originally purely supra-worldly Kingdom of God into the visible world. Jesus according to Hering sometimes hinted at the coming identity between Himself and the Son of Man.

British theologians, after Sanday's and Burkitt's enthusiastic reception of Schweitzer's theory, mostly opposed a purely futuristic interpretation of the Kingdom of God. An exception, however, is the Scottish scholar, E. F. Scott,[69] later active in Canada, to whom the idea of the supernatural coming of the Kingdom necessarily involves that it is still to come.[70] The Kingdom of God is so close that its power can be felt. "The Kingdom . . . is imminent."[71] Scott admits that there are authentic sayings which appear to confirm that Jesus saw the

[68] J. Hering, *Le Royaume de Dieu et sa venue, object de l'espérance de Jésus et de S. Paul*, Thèse, Strasbourg, E.H.P.R., No. 35, Paris 1937. Hering maintains that even the parables of the Kingdom of God in Mk. IV and Mt. XIII, as well as Lk. XVII. 20 f., correctly interpreted, support a purely futuristic idea of the Kingdom of God. For the latter reference see J. Wellhagen, *Anden och Riket, Lukas religiösa åskådning med särskild hänsyn till eskatologien*, Uppsala 1941, p. 99.

[69] Among the works of E. F. Scott may be mentioned *The Kingdom and the Messiah*, Edinburgh 1911, and *The Kingdom of God in the New Testament*, New York 1931. The latter work deals exhaustively with the historical background to Jesus' idea of the Kingdom of God. The purely futuristic interpretation of the Kingdom of God is not so strictly applied here.

[70] Scott, *The Kingdom of God and the Messiah*, p. 104.

[71] *Op. cit.*, p. 112.

Kingdom as already present. But on closer investigation it is found that none of these confirm an actual beginning of the Kingdom. The disciples can bring the Kingdom closer by praying and longing. Jesus believed that by sacrificing His life He would bring about the great transformation (Lk. xii. 50; Mt. xx. 22; Mk. x. 45, xiv. 17, 25). In Scott's interpretation Jesus is shown as having expressed His message throughout in terms of Jewish eschatology.[72] In these circumstances Scott's interpretation could only be decidedly futuristic.

This applies to a still greater degree to the American scholar, Shirley Jackson Case, leader of the so-called Chicago school, who in 1927 published a new biography of Jesus.[73] The method Case evolved is generally known as the "social-historical."[74] The best evidence of historicity is to be gained not by the aid of form criticism, but by establishing a correspondence between Jesus and the social environment in which He lived. If only that is to be regarded as historical in the teachings of Jesus which does not diverge from the current ideas of His time, it follows inevitably that the Kingdom of God in the teachings of Jesus must be represented by Case as purely futuristic. Case entirely ignores the fact that late Judaism in some cases speaks of a present Kingdom of God. If one had asked Jesus what He placed first in His teaching, He would

---

[72] *Op. cit.*, p. v.

[73] S. J. Case, *Jesus, A New Biography*, Chicago 1927. Among Case's other works may be noted *The Historicity of Jesus*, Chicago 1912, *The Evolution of Early Christianity*, Chicago 1914, and *The Social Origins of Christianity*, Chicago 1923. In these three works the way is prepared for his method, the new "social historical" method which is fully applied in *Jesus, a New Biography*, in *Experience with the Supernatural in Early Christian Times*, New York 1929, and in *Jesus through the Centuries*, Chicago 1932.

[74] Case sums up the new method as follows: "Every statement in the records is to be judged by the degree of its suitableness to the distinctive environment of Jesus, on the one hand, and to that of the framers of Gospel tradition at one or another stage in the history of Christianity, on the other. When consistently applied, this test will prove our safest guide in recovering from the present Gospel records dependable information regarding the life and teaching of the earthly Jesus" (*Jesus, A New Biography*, p. 115). Among Case's followers in the matter of the method may be mentioned firstly D. W. Riddle, author of the standard work of the Chicago school: *Jesus and the Pharisees*, Chicago 1928, and F. C. Grant, H. J. Cadbury and C. G. Cole. The school prides itself on being earlier than form criticism. "Actually what has been called the 'Chicago school' anticipated the German work, and in fact it goes beyond *Formgeschichte* in emphasising certain important factors" (D. H. Riddle, "The bearing of recent Gospel research upon the study of the teaching of Jesus," in *J.Rel.*, 1934, p. 151). The name of the school originates from H. J. Cadbury, *J.Rel.*, 1920, p. 300.

probably have answered that purely formally it was "His announcement of the imminence of the Kingdom of Heaven."[75] But Jesus was not primarily interested in confirming the eschatological hope or elaborating its ideas; eschatology was to Him a further argument to support the demand for a righteous life.

Jesus regarded Himself as the prophet who had to announce the closely impending Kingdom of God and its demands. Even if He connected the coming of the Son of Man with the establishment of the Kingdom, this by no means meant that He applied the title to Himself. Case considers it improbable, not to say impossible, that Jesus designated Himself the Son of Man. The view of the apocalyptic tradition was that the Son of Man would remain hidden with God in Heaven until the Day of Judgment, when he would reveal Himself on earth. Jesus would be quite uninterested in "Messianic self-interpretation."[76] Case believes the new Christian Messianic faith to have been born among the disciples as a result of the shock they received at the death of Jesus and what followed thereafter, but it was not the personal religion of Jesus.

When Case is frequently praised by his followers for having given an original interpretation of Jesus which is neither orthodox nor liberal but which provides an accurate picture of the historical Jesus, one can only say that this is manifestly incorrect. The difference between the liberal Jesus-picture of the turn of the century and that of the Chicago school is extremely slight. Case also endeavours, as was done at the turn of the century in Europe, too, to make the historical Jesus the basis of modern Christianity, as when he says: "The religious messages and attitudes of the Jesus of history, not the overlay presented by devotion, tradition, or ecclesiasticism, are the values to which the modern disciple should return."[77] What gripped the disciples once and for all was the dynamic quality about the person of Jesus. Religion was to Jesus essentially a matter of experience, based on the spiritual impulses of the inner life.[78] As a final comment on this

---

[75] Case, *Jesus, A New Biography*, p. 419.

[76] *Op. cit.*, p. 377. "Jesus . . . was more interested in God and the Kingdom than in creating a new Messianic official. God was the only Messiah they needed in the 'world to come' " (*ibid*).

[77] D. W. Riddle, "Jesus in modern Research," in *J.Rel.*, 1937, p. 179.

[78] Case, *Jesus, A New Biography*, pp. 387 ff.

interpretation of Jesus one can only say that Case's presentation demonstrates with all possible clarity how impossible it is to interpret Jesus and His conception of the Kingdom of God without the conception of the Son of Man and of the Church.

To conclude, a word about another purely futuristic interpretation of the Kingdom of God on American soil, namely that of B. S. Easton, which is strongly influenced by German form criticism. Easton, who maintains that the Kingdom of God was to Jesus purely transcendental, and that its full descent in the present age would mean not the transformation but the destruction of the world, admits that there are sayings of Jesus about a present Kingdom.[79] But these do not in any way clash with the futuristic sayings, for no one expected that the full coming of the Kingdom would take place immediately. On the contrary, there would be a whole succession of divine acts leading up to the final perfection. But these are always closely linked in a fixed temporal succession, so that it is possible to speak of the first stage in this series as the coming of the Kingdom.[80] Here Schweitzer's mechanical conception makes itself felt again. Once the eschatological events have been set in motion, the whole series of them must be released right down to the coming of the Kingdom.[81]

[79] B. S. Easton, *Christ in the Gospels*, New York 1930, p. 160. "The phrase, 'The Kingdom of God is at hand,' meant to everyone who heard it, 'The end of the world is at hand,' and could not possibly have any other significance."

[80] Easton finds support for his interpretation in the parables of growth (the Leaven, the Grain of Mustard Seed, the Self-growing Seed). "God's initial act has been performed and, as soon as its consequences have been felt, the next act will follow: 'When the grain is ripe, at once he puts in the sickle, because the harvest has come.' In so far as the power of God's act is manifested in the work of Jesus, the Kingdom may be said to have 'come in contact' with men (Mt. XII. 28); in so far as Jesus' disciples have shared in their power which He has brought, they may be said to be 'in' the Kingdom" (Lk. VII. 28, x. 11, x. 20). Easton, *op. cit.*, p. 163.

[81] Among exponents of the purely futuristic interpretation of the Kingdom of God may be noted also the Dutchman K. E. Proost, *De Bergrede, hare herkomst en strekking*, Amsterdam 1914—he is a devoted pupil of J. Weiss—and J. C. Wissing, *Het begrip van het Koninkrijk Gods, vooral met betrekking tot de religienssocialen in Zwitzerland*, 1927.

VIII

Interpretations of the Kingdom of God which allow Eschatology only to Part of the Teachings of Jesus

We have seen how a number of scholars tried to escape from the eschatological picture of Jesus drawn by Johannes Weiss by declaring that eschatology only had significance for a part of His teaching, while large sections were quite untouched by it. These latter sections were generally represented as being those which showed Jesus' inmost intentions most clearly. Most typical of this interpretation is Bousset. Among the exegetists of the turn of the century we may also mention E. Haupt and H. J. Holtmann. One might have thought that Schweitzer with his consistently eschatological interpretation of Jesus, applying eschatology not merely to Jesus' conception of the Kingdom of God but also to His view of Himself, would have struck the death-blow to any attempt at reaching a solution of the Jesus problem along those lines. This is, however, by no means the case. E. von Dobschütz[1] attempted such a solution in 1910, J. Weiss[2] in 1913, while

---

[1] E. von Dobschutz, "The Eschatology of the Gospels." A brief summary is given in "Zur Eschatologie der Evangelien," in *Th.St.Kr.*, 1911, pp. 1-20. It seems symptomatic that the work was first published in England. Interest in the question of the Kingdom of God was keener there, thanks to Schweitzer's influence, than in Europe in general.

[2] In J. Weiss's last contribution to the question of Jesus in his article "Das Problem der Entstehung des Christentums" in *Archiv für Religionswissenschaft*, 1913, he points out how the Synoptists poured the whole teaching of Jesus into the framework of the teaching on the Kingdom of God, whereas a large part of it, such as most of the parables, is not dominated by the idea of the Kingdom of God. Many of the sayings of Jesus are thus altogether uneschatological, in spite of the fact that the tradition in its entirety is eschatological. Weiss characterises the question of the relationship between the eschatological and the

Hans Windisch[3] followed the same path in 1929 in his inter-pretation of the Sermon on the Mount, in which he detected two main currents in the teaching of Jesus, one eschatological and one non-eschatological.

Ernst von Dobschütz

When von Dobschütz came to grapple with the problem of eschatology in the Gospels, it was not on the basis of any particular group of the sayings of Jesus. He distinguished three separate currents in the teaching of Jesus: (1) the timeless-ethical, (2) sayings which apply entirely to the future, and (3) "transmuted" eschatology, *i.e.* what one expects to be mani-fested in the future in an outward manner, the individual has already received in the present in an inward manner. The disciples of Jesus in the company of their Master enjoyed the community of God and therewith the blessedness of the coming Kingdom already in the present, but this did not prevent Jesus exhorting them to pray for the outward and visible coming of the Kingdom.

Von Dobschütz considered it to be established beyond any argument that the Kingdom of God is in its origin a thoroughly eschatological conception. The Kingdom does not come through our efforts; we have to wait until God brings it. Jesus spoke of Himself as the Son of Man (Mk. xiv. 61). But this does not mean that Jesus saw Himself as the Messiah only in the time to come, as the *Messias destinatus, Messias futurus*, so

---

uneschatological element in the teaching of Jesus as a still unsolved problem. Its solution must lie in the person of Jesus and in faith in Him. Belief in the person of Jesus meant more to the disciples than hope of the imminent coming of the Kingdom. He regarded Himself as the Son of Man and stood as a surety for the Kingdom of God. That Jesus became the centre of the whole eschatological movement is due, according to Weiss, to the fact that He already lived in God in the present moment. The strong emphasis on the significance of the person of Jesus for any understanding of the Kingdom of God and of His whole mission is, of course, nothing new in the debate on the Kingdom of God, though it also to a certain extent heralds the strongly Christocentric interpretation of the eschatological teaching of Jesus during the nineteen-twenties and thirties. But at the same time Weiss clearly regards Jesus in the light of a religious personality. It is His purely personal fire and joy that gives its supreme driving-force to the movement that emanated from Him.

[3] H. Windisch, *Der Sinn der Bergpredigt, Ein Beitrag zum geschichtlichen Verständnis der Evangelien und zum Problem der richtigen Exegese*, Untersuchungen zum Neuen Testament, Leipzig 1929, 2nd edn. 1937.

G

that He would be His own Forerunner, His own John the Baptist.[4] Such an interpretation precludes not only Jesus' own view of Himself but also the trial and sentence passed on Him. Jesus claimed to be the Messiah and spoke at the same time of His return in power and glory, which would occur in His own generation.[5] This eschatology helped Jesus to understand Himself and His own position and at the same time provided the reason for the exhortation: Be prepared, for the Kingdom of God is at hand.

But side by side with these purely futuristic sayings about the Kingdom of God are others which represent the Kingdom as present and Jesus as the Messiah, who now fulfils the Old Testament hope in its true form and brings salvation in its very deepest meaning. When Jesus casts out the evil spirits the powers of the Kingdom are active. The Kingdom is present in His acts (Mt. xii. 28). Nor have we any right to evade the significance of Lk. xvii. 20 f., that the Kingdom of God is something inward. It is from the heart of man that evil thoughts proceed (Mk. vii. 15, 21), i.e. it is in the heart that the devil wields his power. Therefore it is also, according to von Dobschütz, in the heart of man that the Kingdom must be established. The Kingdom of God belongs to present time (Mt. xi. 12), and as present it is something inward, an experience of joy. Again in Mk. x. 15 and in iv. 30-2 (the Grain of Mustard Seed and the Leaven)[6] it is a question of an inward experience of the Kingdom of God, which can be attained already in the present, before the Kingdom is revealed in its outward, eschatological form.

Jesus is more than one of the citizens of the Kingdom, He is its King (Lk. vii. 19; Mt. xi. 3 f.). The disciples saw in Him the unique and ultimate bringer of salvation (Mk. viii. 27 ff.). Jesus came to perform what was awaited for the end-time. The Messianic Judgment, which is a selection between people (Mk. xxiv. 40 f.; Lk. xvii. 34), takes place now, when Jesus

[4] Von Dobschütz, "The Eschatology of the Gospels," p. 201.

[5] "It is quite certain, I should think, that Jesus claimed to be the Messiah. But it is equally certain that He speaks of His coming in glory and power" (von Dobschütz, op. cit., p. 202).

[6] Jesus speaks in these parables not of His gospel but of the Kingdom of God, "illustrating its extensive and intensive power. The conclusion is inevitable that it is by His preaching that the Kingdom comes, or rather, is present. . . . The effect of His preaching is that inward experience of man which we found identified with the notion of the kingdom in two former sayings" (op. cit., p. 339.).

calls some to follow Him (Mt. viii. 22) but leaves others, when He compels the unwilling but rejects the willing. The meal that belongs to the Messianic time takes place already now, when Jesus sits at table with publicans and sinners and says that they will enter into the Kingdom of God before the elders of the people (Mt. xxi. 31 f.).[7]

All these sayings point in one direction: Jesus is the Messiah, who judges and gives salvation. He is the stumbling-block for certain groups, but gives joy and happiness to others. As He Himself is the Son, so also His disciples as sons are free of all restrictions and from paying tax (Mt. xvii. 26). Surrounded by His disciples Jesus represents the new Messianic age. He is the Bridegroom and His followers are the children of the bridechamber (Mk. ii. 19 f.). Jesus declares that something new has come in with Him, in relation to all that went before Him.

All this material, of which we have just given a brief resumé, shows, according to von Dobschütz, beyond all argument that in the teaching of Jesus there is a distinct current to which He gives the name "transmuted eschatology." When he then proceeds to explain that by this term he means that what was regarded in Jewish eschatology as coming at the end of the world is thought of here as already present and existent during the lifetime of Jesus, one feels completely in agreement with him and wonders whether he may not be about to shed a completely new light on the subject, which will do away altogether with the false alternatives of a purely futuristic eschatology. The Kingdom of God appears to be conceived as something qualitatively new which comes through the Messiah already here and now. It is not merely something which is to come, not merely the final miracle without any real connexion with the present time, even if it is near, and Jesus, who preaches now, will one day become the Son of Man.

But the pleasure is short-lived. One soon discovers that von Dobschütz, bound as he was by the limitations of liberal theology, evidently could conceive of the presence of the Kingdom of God as an actual presence during the time when the Messiah lived among His people. For "transmuted eschatology" also means that what one expected as an outward

7 Cf. A. T. Cadoux and C. H. Dodd.

transformation is conceived as something inward. Not every-one can see what is already there, but the disciples can. They recognise Jesus as the Messiah, the Elect of God, and His company are able to rejoice at all the happiness the Messianic age brings with it. The presence of the Kingdom of God became to von Dobschütz an experience in the hearts of the disciples when they felt that the gifts of the Kingdom of God were given already now. This also comes out clearly in the exegesis of the various sayings quoted in support of the inter-pretation. If we leave out the psychological explanation and the talk about the inward experience of the presence of the Kingdom of God, we undoubtedly find here many points of contact with C. H. Dodd's "realised eschatology" and the interpretation of many sayings given by Joachim Jeremias.[8]

The real meaning of "transmuted eschatology" becomes clearer when this system is set in relation to the futuristic view of the Kingdom of God and the Messiah. Then we are told: "The two groups are quite distinct and are to be kept separate. Neither may be reduced easily to the other without violence being done to the tradition, nor can we put aside one of them as a later addition or transformation, both being attested by our best sources."[9] The aim of a sound interpretation must be to give full value to the various groups in the teaching of Jesus. Here the explanation is left to the non-eschatological group.[10] Jesus preached, or more correctly represented, a new relation-ship with God. He lived in uninterrupted communion with God. If He saw Himself as the highest point in His people's religious development, He could only see Himself as the one who stood at the meeting-point of two different ages. Therefore also His return must come soon. But the hope of what is to come becomes hardly more than an adjunct to the eschato-logical relationship in which Jesus stood to the world, if one understands eschatology in its "transformed" form. Faith in the Father implies that Jesus believed that God cannot leave His work unfinished. God must bring it to completion ac-cording to His promise. The salvation which Jesus gave during

[8] J. Jeremias, *Jesus als Weltvollender*, Beiträge zur Förderung christlicher Theo-logie, VOL. XXXIII, No. 4, Gütersloh 1930.

[9] Von Dobschütz, "The Eschatology of the Gospels," pp. 344 f.

[10] It is stated on p. 399 that "we found (this non-eschatological group) to cover the most space and to be of the highest importance."

the days of His earthly life was exclusively an inner experience of the individual, but it will become a collective and outward fact when the Kingdom of God is established in glory. It is thus in the end the uneschatological image of Jesus as the religious personality who lives in a relationship with God never before attained, that unites in itself the different groups of sayings of Jesus in the tradition.[11]

Hans Windisch

The whole idea of the value and importance of eschatology changed radically at the beginning of the nineteen-twenties. Up till then it had mostly been regarded as an historical feature of the Gospel which could not be accepted in a modern pre-sentation of Christianity. During the nineteen-twenties and thirties eschatology came to be regarded instead as the essential content of the Gospel, that was valid for all ages. Now limiting or denying the eschatological character of the Gospel was considered to be an adaptation and weakening, instead of a merit. Windisch adopted a critical attitude towards this view. It is the duty of scholars to determine what the text says without allowing themselves to be bound by any modernisation, not even an eschatological one. It is false to say that a non-eschatological attitude involves a moralisation and humanisation of the Gospel, since it can be proved on investigation that the Gospel contains both moralistic and humanistic elements. "Even in an eschatological age the theology of the moment must not form a preconceived standard of scholarly Bible research."[12]

From an unprejudiced investigation of the Sermon on the Mount in Matthew, Windisch came to the conclusion that this, in common with all the longer speeches in this particular Gospel, is full of eschatological expectation, but that the Evangelist also made use of a great deal of material which was

---

[11] Among followers of von Dobschütz's interpretation should be mentioned in particular a number of English and American theologians such as C. C. McCown, *The Promise of His Coming, A historical interpretation of the idea of Second Advent*, New York 1921, and H. R. Mackintosh, "The Eschatology of Jesus," in *Exp.* Ser VIII, No. 10, 1915, pp. 97-116. A. C. Headlam, *The Life and Teaching of Jesus*, 3rd edn., London 1936, has a similar classification of the sayings on the Kingdom of God to von Dobschütz's.

[12] Windisch, *Der Sinn der Bergpredigt*, p. 8.

originally not at all eschatological and gave it the eschatological stamp.[13]   All the sayings of Jesus can, of course, be included in the eschatological sphere, but many can also be
removed from it, either because they were not originally
eschatological or because the eschatological element is not
essential and can consequently be detached from them.   The
two main currents in the Sermon on the Mount and in the
teaching of Jesus in general should thus be: firstly the elevated
and radicalised teaching of wisdom, secondly the prophetic-
eschatological teaching of salvation and judgment.   What
unites these two currents is chiefly that they have in common
"the idea of God conceived in its purity."[14] which intensifies
the demand for radical liberation from everything that opposes
God.   But here there is also a difficulty which it is hard to
overcome, for the said two currents have been independent
from the start.   Windisch seems inclined to believe that
Matthew eschatologised a number of wisdom sayings.   Sayings
in which eschatological terms do not occur should not be
interpreted eschatologically either.

   It is quite self-evident to Windisch that Jesus' idea of the
Kingdom of God was eschatological.[15]   In the Sermon on the
Mount we cannot detect any softening of the eschatological
character of the Kingdom of God.   But in the theological
exegesis, Windisch asks us to bear in mind that *malkuth* in the
Talmud signifies throughout the Dominion of God, which is
realised when mankind takes to itself the law of God.   He who
here accepts the Dominion of God as a little child enters into
the transcendental Kingdom.   We experience the Dominion
of God here, but wait for its full realisation which will take
place on the other side of all history.   The Kingdom of God
has another meaning too.   It is fellowship with God.   But to
see God, which is the highest longing of all the children of God,
is granted only to the pure.   Therefore a process of purification
has to precede entry to God; this is achieved "in obedience

[13] Windisch finds in Mt. VI. 25 ff. "an outlook permeated through and through
with strong religious optimism, a sort of piety of enlightenment" (*op. cit.*, p. 17).
   [14] *Op. cit.*, p. 20.
   [15] H. Windisch, "Die Sprüche vom Eingehen in das Reich Gottes," in *Z.N.W.*,
XXVII (1928), p. 164: "The 'Kingdom' is the great state of blessedness at the end
of the Day, to which all prophets and apocalyptists testify.   Whoever has anything
to say on the entry thereto, places himself thereby in the prophetic tradition,
explains it or carries it further."

towards God, in living our lives as the children of God, whereby our likeness to God develops step by step."[16]   This by no means precludes that this process is eschatological, for the truly pure heart is one of the eschatological things that no eye has seen. All that God creates in the temporal world is merely promise. The real fulfilment can only come when the temporal ceases to be.

This theological interpretation reveals Windisch's idealistic preconceptions with all possible clarity.   The eschatological sayings are thrust aside.   What is important is not Jesus' teaching about the Kingdom of God but His witness to God, the absolute Lord, the Creator, the Father, the Redeemer and Judge, and Jesus' self-awareness as the one who is to end the succession of God's witnesses.[17]

---

[16] *Der Sinn der Bergpredigt*, p. 174.

[17] In *Jesus und der Geist nach synoptischen Überlieferung*, Studies in Early Christianity, ed. S. Jackson Case, New York 1938, pp. 207-36, Windisch makes some interesting points in connexion with Mt. xii. 28 (Lk. xi. 16) to which little attention has been paid.   G. Sevenster, *Ethiek en eschatologie in de synoptische Evangelien, Een studie over het typische in Jesus' zedeleer*, Diss., Leiden 1929, stands close to Windisch and carries out his aims.

IX

Interpretations in which the Kingdom of God is conceived primarily as a Present Entity

Research in England

Certain English theologians have interpreted the Kingdom of God as a present entity, allowing its futurist character to sink altogether into the background. According to the principles of modern English exegetics, as set forth in E. Hoskyns's and F. N. Davey's study of the New Testament in 1931,[1] tradition is right when it speaks of the Son of Man having now come in humility but that He will come again some day in honour and glory. These two comings are linked together by the fact that Jesus ascribed to Himself the title Son of Man. At the same time it is strongly emphasised that with Jesus the Dominion of God breaks in from another world into this world, and that the coming of Jesus is the intervention of God Himself in the life of the world.[2] Miracles, parables, and wisdom sayings all have a Messianic background. They are the actions and words of the Messiah who fulfils the Old Testament hope and comes with the Kingdom of God, which is now present.[3] God has intervened in history in a decisive

[1] E. Hoskyns and F. N. Davey, *The Riddle of the New Testament*, London 1931.

[2] "Mark clearly means by his double Christology that in Jesus the rule of God did break into this world from the other. The Son of Man has power *on earth*. The Kingdom of God *is* upon you. The bridegroom *is* present" (*op. cit.*, pp. 156 f.). . . . "His (Jesus') coming is the intervention of God in the world" (p. 157).

[3] The parables of sowing, growth and harvesting (the Sower, the Self-growing Seed, the Grain of Mustard Seed, the Weeds among the Wheat) have Old Testament parallels (Hos. II. 21-3; Jer. XXXI. 27 f.; Is. LV. 10 f., XXXII. 13 ff.; Jer. LI. 33; Joel III. 12 f.; Hos. VI. 11) which "almost demanded a Messianic application" (*op. cit.*, p. 185). "This Christological penetration of the Parables renders them everywhere less illustrations of moral or spiritual truths which are easy of understanding than an integral element in the revelation of God which is taking place in Palestine with the advent of the Messiah in His humiliation. Their understanding therefore depends upon the recognition of Jesus as the Messiah and upon the recognition of the Kingdom of God which is breaking forth in His ministry" (p. 188).

manner, and the time of fulfilment is here, for the Messiah is come. Christology is not some later addition but was there from the beginning of the Synoptic tradition.[4]

As English theology in general is dominated by the doctrine of the Incarnation in a quite different way from Continental theology,[5] this doctrine has also affected the idea of the Kingdom of God among modern English theologians, in particular T. W. Manson, A. T. Cadoux, and C. H. Dodd. Different as are their interpretations of the Kingdom of God, there is no mistaking the significance of the doctrine of the Incarnation in their theology.[6] There is also a general tendency to dissociate Jesus from late Jewish apocalyptic and emphasise how He transformed the idea of the Kingdom of God.[7]

A. T. Cadoux

A. T. Cadoux[8] is in many respects a forerunner of C. H. Dodd, though with the fundamental difference that he completely disregards the eschatological character of even the present

[4] "At no point is the literary or historical critic able to detect in any stratum of the Synoptic material evidence that a Christological interpretation has been imposed upon an un-Christological history" (op. cit., p. 207).

[5] Mysterium Christi, Christological studies by British and German theologians, edd. G. K. A. Bell and Adolf Deissmann, London 1930, p. 127. In Essays on the Trinity and the Incarnation, by members of the Anglican Communion, ed. A. E. J. Rawlinson, London and New York 1928, the purpose of the Incarnation is represented throughout as being to bring eternal life into the temporal world. L. S. Thornton, The Incarnate Lord, An essay concerning the Doctrine of the Incarnation in its relation to Organic Conceptions, London 1928, maintains that "This Kingdom is also incorporated into history. It is not simply proclaimed in expectation and promise. It is present in fulfilment; for it is a present reality to the mind of Jesus. The secrets of the Kingdom are His. He knows its treasure and possesses it. Its reality is beyond time and change, beyond historical succession. Yet it is embodied in Him who knows it thus" (p. 168). "In the Messiah and His life-story the Kingdom is concretely embodied with its double revelation of God and man" (p. 169). "The Kingdom of God was incorporated into history in its ultimate individual form in the life-story of the Incarnate Lord" (p. 425).

[6] The same applies also to more popular accounts. D. Edwards, The Shining Mystery of Jesus, London 1928, writes (p. 95): "Jesus came not only to reveal, but to empower; not only to teach disciples, but to create a divine fellowship; not only to announce a Kingdom yet to come, but to constitute that Kingdom, as being Himself the Beloved Son of the Heavenly King."

[7] This applies not only to the above-mentioned scholars but also to others such as V. Taylor, Jesus and His Sacrifice, A study of the Passion-sayings in the Gospels, London 1937, and the American F. C. Grant, The Gospel of the Kingdom.

[8] A. T. Cadoux, The Parables of Jesus, Their art and use, London 1930, and The Theology of Jesus, London 1940.

Kingdom of God, on which Dodd lays strong emphasis with his theory of "realised eschatology." Jesus aimed with His teaching to reach the whole of His people, with its Temple "a house of prayer for all peoples" and Jerusalem "the great King's town," the capital of the Kingdom of Heaven. The aim of Jesus was to gather together the masses, calling upon them to seize the opportunity and enter immediately and wholeheartedly into His service, so that Israel should find its real greatness by serving the nations with the gifts with which God had blessed it, and so gain the world. Jesus looked upon His own lifetime as a time of harvest (Mt. ix. 37 f.; Lk. x. 2), and the Kingdom of God would come as the harvest—"a slow, mysterious process that suddenly presents itself as a great opportunity calling urgently for man to do his part."[9] The parable of the Self-growing Seed is an assurance that the Kingdom of God is present, for it speaks also of the ripe harvest. It is for man to "put in the sickle" at the right moment. He knows little of how the seed grows, but he knows when and how to act, and that is as important as nature's part in bringing the seed to ripeness.[10]

The coming of the Son of Man is usually regarded as the end of the world and the Day of Judgment, but according to Cadoux this represents rather a further opportunity, as is shown by the constantly repeated exhortation to watchfulness in connexion with the Day of the Son of Man. A saying such as Mt. xxiv. 40 f.: "Then two men will be in the field; one is taken, and one is left. Two women will be grinding at the mill; one is taken, and one is left," did not originally apply to the Judgment but was intended as an exhortation to service in the sense: "And if anyone forces you to go one mile, go with him two miles" (Mt. v. 41).[11]

---

[9] *The Parables of Jesus, Their art and use*, p. 164.

[10] Of Mk. iv. 26-29 Cadoux says: "There can be no reasonable doubt as to the point of the parable. It is the co-operation of man with the mysterious power of nature; both factors are emphasised unmistakably—'the seed springs and grows up, he knoweth not how', 'the earth bringing forth fruit of herself'; yet it is man who 'cast the seed into the ground' and at the right moment 'immediately putteth forth the sickle.' Man knows little, but he knows when and how to act, and this is as necessary as nature's power of bringing to ripeness" (*op. cit.*, p. 162). The parables of the Kingdom of God: the Pearl, the Treasure, the Grain of Mustard-Seed, the Leaven, the Sower, are arranged by Cadoux under the heading: "Parables of Israel and the Peoples."

[11] Not even the saying in Mk. xiii. 15 f. about the man on the housetop refers to Judgment Day but merely to seizing the opportunity. The meaning is the

In Mk. IX. 1 and XIII. 20 Jesus implied a coming generation even after the entry of the Kingdom of God. The coming of the Kingdom is not "the final consummation of the Kingdom, but only an important event in its progress."[12]

Everything in Cadoux's interpretation of Jesus is fitted to this one theme: to seize the opportunity that is given now to follow Jesus in service. That this complete "de-eschatologisation" of Jesus' idea of the Kingdom of God, which to be carried through requires a violent adaptation of the sayings of Jesus as recorded by the Evangelists, is a modernisation, can hardly be open to question. The Kingdom of God as taught by Jesus is left completely in the air when it is cut off like this from its connexions with late Jewish eschatology, and its interpretation is left entirely to the discretion of the individual scholar.

T. W. Manson

T. W. Manson[13] distinguishes three groups in the sayings of Jesus: (1) polemic, (2) sayings addressed to the general public, mostly figurative sayings and parables, and (3) sayings to the disciples. He claims that the subjects Jesus dealt with are treated differently according to the audience they were addressed to. Furthermore, there is a quite clear and definite

---

same as in Lk. IX. 62: "No one who puts his hand to the plough, and looks back, is fit for the kingdom of God." "The man on the housetop saw his opportunity and ran to it; here the opportunity seeks the man and makes its selection. The penalty of the others is that they are left, and are glad to be so; it is the parable of the Net again. So we have the two sides: the man who is ready to seize the opportunity is the man the opportunity seizes" (*op. cit.*, p. 196). Neither do Lk. XVII. 22 f., XII. 35-46; Mt. XXIV. 34-41; Mk. XIII. 34-7, refer to the Last Judgment.

[12] *The Theology of Jesus*, p. 30.

[13] T. W. Manson, *The Teaching of Jesus, Studies of its form and content*, Cambridge 1931, 2nd edn. 1935, reprinted 1943. Manson works here on the basis of the four-source hypothesis developed by B. H. Streeter, *The Four Gospels, A Study of Origins, Treating of the manuscript tradition, sources, authorship and dates*, London 1924, 5th imp. 1936. The four sources of the Synoptic Gospels are Mark (Mk.), sayings common to Mt. and Lk. (Q), material peculiar to Matthew (M), and material peculiar to Luke (L). Other works by Manson which deal with Jesus are: *Christ's View of the Kingdom of God, A Study in Jewish Apocalyptic in the mind of Jesus Christ*, London 1918; the Commentary on Mark in the joint work: H. D. A. Major, T. W. Manson, and C. J. Wright, *The Mission and Message of Jesus, An exposition of the Gospels in the light of modern research*, London 1937, and *The Servant-Messiah, A Study of the Public Ministry of Jesus*, Cambridge 1953.

break in the teaching of Jesus between the time before and after Peter's confession of Him as the Messiah at Caesarea Philippi. Only after this did Jesus speak of God as the Father, and then only to His disciples. Whereas previously he had taught the coming of the Kingdom of God, he spoke now, after Peter's confession, of those who enter into the Kingdom and of Himself as the Son of Man. To the disciples' confession of their teacher is added now a new quality, the faithfulness and devotion of the subject to a king, who is the Anointed of God. "It was in fact the recognition of the Kingdom in the person of Jesus: and with the recognition the Kingdom could be said to have come."[14] The Kingdom is here regarded as something altogether spiritual, as a personal relationship between king and subject, in which it is God's part to rule, and man's to recognise God as ruler. As the Kingdom of God is in essence the rule of God as a personal relationship between God and the individual, the whole question of whether it is present or to come goes by the board. It is independent of temporal or spatial conditions. God's claim on mankind that they should obey Him applies for all time. Everywhere where this call of God's is heard and the rule of God accepted in obedience, the Kingdom of God is a present reality.

What Jesus taught about the eternal rule of God is coloured throughout with the intensity with which He in His own life accepted that rule. All the sayings about the Kingdom must be interpreted in the light of Jesus' unique devotion to the will of God, the heavenly Father and King. "Thy will be done" is a paraphrase of the petition "Thy kingdom come," and is the essence of the teaching about the Kingdom of God.

But against God stands Satan, and between these two contesting powers stands mankind, which must give to one or the other its faith and loyalty. Man must make his choice, and no sacrifice is too great for the object of sharing in the Kingdom of God (Mk. ix. 43 ff., x. 29 f., viii. 34 ff.). Man's ultimate fate rests on this decision for or against God.

Manson develops his ideas of the Kingdom of God on earth in connexion with the idea of the "Remnant." That God is

---

[14] Manson, *The Teaching of Jesus*, p. 130. "Peter's confession may fairly be regarded as just that acknowledgement that was needed to make the Kingdom *de jure* into a Kingdom *de facto*" (p. 131).

King is made manifest on earth in one people, whose King God is. In Israel the whole people as such was originally regarded as Jahweh's people and Jahweh was its King, *i.e.* no other qualifications were valid but membership of this people. But when the demand is raised for obedience and devotion, the number of those who pass the test is reduced. The Kingdom of God then becomes the ideal for an elect section of the people, the righteous "Remnant." The archetype of strict Judaism is to be found in Ezekiel, according to which the "Remnant" is to enjoy salvation, whatever may be the fate of the rest of the world. The remnant is a "saved Remnant." The archetype of what Manson calls Evangelical Christianity is to be found in Deutero-Isaiah, where the Remnant is a "saving remnant" which brings mankind under the rule of Jahweh, but this, however, does not come about through states being forced to submit to Jahweh's rule but through individuals being induced voluntarily to accept the King of Israel as their King. The idea of the "Remnant" is further developed under late Judaism, and the true Israel becomes something quite different from Israel according to the flesh.

Jesus saw the "little flock" as the first manifestation of the Kingdom in the world, and it is the instrument in the hand of God for a still greater manifestation, *i.e.* the coming fulfilment. It is the growth of this community that is described in the parables of the Self-growing Seed, the Grain of Mustard Seed and the Leaven. But this community is not the same as the Kingdom of God, it is a manifestation and product of it. The Kingdom of God is, wherever God's will is done on earth as it is in heaven.[15] But it is the Messiah who realises the Kingdom through utter obedience to the will of God, through voluntarily identifying His will with God's. The Kingdom of God on earth manifests itself in the society of those who follow the Messiah and take upon themselves the yoke He bears.[16] Jesus is the first-born of many brothers. He is the founder and perfecter of the faith.

[15] "In the light of this unique devotion and loyalty to the heavenly King all the words of Jesus concerning the heavenly Kingdom are to be read and interpreted. The essence of his preaching of the Kingdom is in the words 'Thy will be done'; all the rest is commentary" (*op. cit.*, p. 161).

[16] "It cannot be too strongly emphasised that the society is not the Kingdom, but only a manifestation or product of it; and that membership of the society is not entrance into the Kingdom, but only a result of entrance" (*op. cit.*, p. 134).

Jesus accepted the Dominion of God completely and when He invited men to follow Him in trust and obedience to God, this was nothing new but only what any ordinary rabbi might have demanded. What was new was that Jesus demanded devotion to Himself, and made this equivalent to devotion to the Kingdom of God. But he who would follow Him must also be prepared to lose his life in order to find it, and he that would be first in the community must be the servant of all. The principle that he who serves is greatest, is embodied in the Son of Man, who came to serve and to give His life a ransom for many.

But what, then, does the "Son of God" mean according to Manson? The Son of Man is the final term in a long development which runs through the "Remnant" of Isaiah and the "Servant of Jahweh" of Deutero-Isaiah, to the "I" of Daniel, where the Remnant idea is fundamental. The "Son of Man" of the Gospels is another embodiment of the Remnant idea. The Son of Man, like the Servant of Jahweh, is an ideal figure who is responsible for the manifestation of the Kingdom of God on earth in a people wholly devoted to the heavenly King.[17] The Son of Man is thus a collective entity even to Jesus, just as the Son of Man is in Daniel. But how, then, is one to explain the fact that in the Gospel the expression "Son of Man" is so often used by Jesus quite unmistakably as a self-designation? Jesus' mission was to create the Kingdom of the holy ones of the Highest, and so to realise in Israel the ideal embodied in the term. Jesus tried to achieve this in two ways: first by preaching, which covered the whole people; then, when this attempt failed, by consolidating the faithful group of the disciples in order to make of that the "Remnant." In the end, when it became clear that not even the disciples could reach the ideal, He stood there alone and embodied in His own person the perfect human answer to God's kingly claims and demands on man. The road to the Cross was a road on which Jesus grew more and more alone until at the end He stood absolutely alone, "at the cross he alone is the Son of Man, the incarnation of the Kingdom of God on earth."[18] The Passion and death of Jesus were the birthpangs of the Son of Man. The

[17] "The Son of Man is, like the Servant of Jehovah, an ideal figure and stands for the manifestation of the Kingdom of God on earth in a people wholly devoted to their heavenly King" (op cit., p. 227).

[18] Op. cit., p. 235.

Cross was the key that opened the Kingdom of God to mankind. Jesus' death achieved what Jesus' teaching had not been able to do. By dying Jesus brought the Son of Man into existence, and gave to this dream-figure a body, a local habitation, and a name.[19] It is the Church, His own body, the head of which He is Himself. Thus Manson traces the connecting line from Jesus as the incarnation of the Kingdom of God on earth down to St Paul.

Even the fulfilment Manson interprets in accordance with his view of the Son of Man as the "Remnant." At the fulfilment the Remnant is to be made righteous, as Daniel describes. But the fulfilment is not in any sense a compensation for sufferings in the present, but is the result of them. The Remnant must serve and sacrifice in order that better times may come. The Kingdom of God is the Suffering Servant, which grows during the intervening time until the day of harvest. Fulfilment is the conclusion to what is already a reality in the now. How and when this happens is wholly unimportant. What matters is that fulfilment *comes* some day.

According to Manson there are thus three mutually independent conceptions of the Kingdom of God, firstly as an eternal fact, secondly as a manifestation in the present life of mankind, thirdly as the fulfilment that belongs to the future.

Manson's interpretation of the Kingdom of God is highly manipulated. The turning-point is Peter's confession, for the Kingdom of God is presented differently before and after this: before as coming, and after as an entity one enters into. If we take Mark as a basis, as Manson does, then Mk. ix. 1 should be the last saying that speaks of a coming of the Kingdom of God; all the rest, from ix. 47 onwards, should speak of entry into the Kingdom. Even though there is no mention of entry into the Kingdom in the first half of Mark, Mk. i. 15

---

[19] "At this stage in the life of Jesus," *i.e.* when Jesus replies to the High Priest (Mk. xiv. 62), "we have in fact reached the point at which the Son of Man becomes an individual person, not by a process of speculation, but by logic of facts; not in apocalyptic theory, but in life. 'Son of Man' in the teaching of Jesus is a symbol for the Remnant in the purest and noblest form in which it could be conceived. His claim to the Messiahship is a claim to be the head of the Remnant in virtue of fulfilling those ideals. And now standing alone against the world, he *is* the Remnant, he is the Son of Man because he alone is equal to the claims of the Son of Man ideal. Son of Man and Messiah have been united in one person, his person" (*op. cit.*, pp. 267 f.).

can just as well refer to the Kingdom as coming, and Mk. IV does not directly speak of the Kingdom as coming. Even in the second half there are sayings about the coming Kingdom of God. In Mk. XIV. 25 the Kingdom of God is unquestionably to be taken futuristically. "Entrance sayings" such as Mk. IX. 47, X. 15, 23-5 set forth conditions for entry into the Kingdom, but could just as well refer to a coming Kingdom as a present one. But the real weakness of Manson's critical procedure lies not in points of detail such as these, but in the fact that he draws far too sweeping conclusions from the internal arrangement of Mark and the other sources. All that Manson's method brings to light is at most the theology of the Evangelist Mark, for the Gospel is built up on a theological and catechistical framework. Sayings from the other sources are usually to be found in typical settings.

It is chiefly, however, the interpretation of the Son of Man as the "Remnant," as applied by Manson, that arouses objections. It is perfectly true that what O. Cullmann calls a "progressive reduction" had taken place with regard to the conception of the Son of Man.[20] When the people of Israel as a whole did not fulfil its mission, a "Remnant" stepped in to deputise for the people. This "Remnant" was concentrated and reduced to one person who alone assumed the rôle of Israel—in Deutero-Isaiah to the deputising, suffering "Servant of the Lord" and in Daniel to the Son of Man, the people of the most High. This one man steps into history as Jesus of Nazareth, who fulfils at once the mission of the suffering Servant of God and of the Son of Man. That the collective ideas are, therefore, of decisive importance for a correct understanding of the idea of the Son of Man, seems obvious. The people and the "Remnant" are always present in the Son of Man.[21] Whether Jesus during His ministry brought about this reduction we have spoken of, is another question. What basis is there in the Gospels for supposing this to be so? The texts offer no possibility of such an interpretation, least of all as Jesus saw His mission as being concerned with the lost sheep

[20] Cullmann, *Christ and Time*, pp. 116 f.

[21] C. H. Dodd, *The Parables of the Kingdom*, London 1935, p. 96: "Although the Son of Man is now identified with Jesus Himself, so much of the earlier idea persists, that His followers are associated with Him in His reign." See also O. Cullmann, *Königsherrschaft Christi und Kirche im Neuen Testament*, Theologische Studien, ed. Karl Barth, VOL. X, Zollikon-Zürich 1941, p. 37.

of the House of Israel. The judgments He passed at the end of His life show how bound up He was with Israel as a collective entity, as is also shown by the fact that He chose twelve apostles. Jesus said that He was come to give His life a ransom for "the many," for humanity. It has indeed been denied that the idea of the "Remnant" had any significance at all for Jesus.[22] The fact that Jewish notions of the Son of Man originate from Dan. VII. 13, where he is a collective idea, does not prove that Jesus did not interpret the Son of Man individually, as that is clearly the way He wished to express His idea of the Messiahship.[23]

Manson's interpretation is a manipulation. Nothing remains of the expectation of an imminent end to the world. The real explanation of Manson's interpretation of Jesus is undoubtedly to be found in the Incarnation theology he embraces, and which can be detected in a number of places in his presentation. The eternal Dominion of God takes physical form on earth in a people who, however, do not live up to God's demands, so that in the end it is Jesus alone who stands there as the incarnation of God's Dominion. He is the first-born of many brothers, and the Dominion of God is incarnated in His Church, which is His body.

C. H. Dodd

The most consistent attempt to present the Kingdom of God as a wholly present entity is that made by C. H. Dodd in 1935.[24] In the Judaism of the time of Jesus there were two distinct and different ways of speaking of the Kingdom of God. God is the King of Israel and His Dominion is real so long as Israel is obedient to the divine will as revealed in the Torah. To

---

[22] A. Oepke, "Jesus und der Gottesvolksgedanke," in *Luthertum*, 1942, pp. 33-62, states: "Nowhere do I find any support for the theory that Jesus associated Himself with the idea of the Remnant. Paradoxically He addressed Himself not to the 'Remnant,' but rather to those who were excluded from the Remnant theology of the synagogue, the *Amme Haarez*. Those claiming to be the 'Remnant' were indeed the sharpest opponents of the coming Kingdom of God" (p. 45).

[23] J. Schneider, Review of T. W. Manson, *The Teaching of Jesus*, in *Th.Lz.*, 1932, pp. 556-9: "It is perfectly possible that Jesus understood Himself and His followers as the holy 'Remnant.' Then indeed a great line would run from the Old Testament to Jesus and on to St Paul. But it is difficult to imagine that Jesus connected the title 'Son of Man' with this idea. This self-designation of Jesus is an expression of his own Messiah-consciousness" (p. 558).

[24] Dodd, *The Parables of the Kingdom*, 3rd edn. 1936.

H

submit to the law is to take upon oneself the Kingdom of Heaven. In this sense the Kingdom of God is a present fact. But in another sense the Kingdom of God is something that will be revealed in the future. God is King not only over Israel but over the whole world. This dominion will one day be a dominion not merely *de jure* but *de facto*. Man hopes for the Kingdom of God in the future and prays: "May He establish His dominion during thy lifetime and during thy days and during the days of the whole House of Israel." Both of these views are to be found in Jesus. The rabbinical expression "To take upon oneself the Kingdom of Heaven" has its parallel in Mk. x. 15: "Whoever does not *receive the Kingdom of God* like a child shall not enter it." The prayer that the Lord shall establish His Dominion has its parallel in the prayer: "Thy kingdom come."[25] The apocalyptic prophecies of a coming, final manifestation of God's Dominion beyond time and space are reflected in such sayings as Mk. ix. 1; Mt. viii. 11; Mk. ix. 43-7, x. 17, 24, 25. In such sayings as these, the Kingdom of God fits completely into the Jewish pattern. The Kingdom of God is to be received here, and its blessings shall be enjoyed at the end of time by those who fulfil the necessary conditions.

But there are sayings of Jesus which do not fit into the Jewish framework. "If it is by the finger of God that I cast out demons, then the Kingdom of God has come upon you" (Lk. xi. 20). Here it is not a question of having God for King in the sense that man obeys His commands. No, the sovereign power of God is active, and man encounters this power of God in activity in the world. "The Kingdom of God is at hand" (Mk. i. 14 f.; Lk. x. 9-11) does not mean that the coming of the Kingdom is something that is dependent on human behaviour.[26] Whether man repents or not, it is here.

[25] *Op. cit.*, p. 42. In *History and the Gospel*, New York 1938, p. 177, Dodd makes even this prayer relate to the present and not the future, for only the present can, according to Dodd, make contact with God's redemptive activity.

[26] Dodd translates ἤγγικεν ἡ βασιλεία τοῦ Θεοῦ as "The Kingdom of God has come" (*The Parables of the Kingdom*, pp. 44 f.). He supports this translation on the grounds that both כְּנַע and מְטָא are normally translated in LXX as ἤγγίζειν

and φθάνειν, both of which mean "to reach," "to arrive." "It would appear therefore that no difference of meaning is intended between ἔφθασεν ἐφ' ὑμᾶς ἡ βασιλεία τοῦ Θεοῦ and ἤγγικεν ἡ βασιλεία τοῦ Θεοῦ. Both imply the 'arrival' of the Kingdom. With an eye on the presumed Aramaic original, we should translate both: 'The Kingdom of God has come' " (p. 44). It is, however,

Jesus did not preach the Kingdom of God as something that was to come in the near future but "as a matter of present experience."[27] He said: "Blessed are the eyes which see what you see" (Lk. x. 23 f.; cf. Mt. xiii. 16 f.). What the disciples "see and hear" is the coming of the Kingdom of God. What prophets and kings have desired to see and what is greater than the prophet Jonah and the wise king Solomon, is the coming of the Kingdom of God. The same applies to the saying about John the Baptist (Mt. xi. 2-11; Lk. vii. 18-30). John is greater than any prophet, because he immediately precedes the great divine event, the coming of the Kingdom of God. The implication is clear: John has carried out his predestined part, and the Kingdom of God has come; after John, the Kingdom of God.

Dodd believes that, on the basis of the above sayings, he has succeeded in demonstrating reasonably clearly that, in the earliest tradition, Jesus was regarded as the one who proclaimed that the Kingdom of God, the hope of many generations, had finally come. "It is not merely imminent, it is here."[28] However we may attempt to reconcile these sayings with those that speak of the Kingdom of God as an object of hope and expectation, we have no right to adapt them, as consistent eschatology did, or to omit them altogether. "Whatever we make of them, the sayings which declare the Kingdom of God to have come are explicit and unequivocal. They are, moreover, the most characteristic and distinctive of the Gospel

---

by no means certain that ἤγγικεν in Mk. i. 15; Mt. x. 7, and ἔφθασεν in Mt. xii. 28, should be translated in the same way. On the contrary, there is much to suggest that, as Mt. x. 7 and xii. 28 belong to Q, a difference in meaning is actually intended, so that ἐγγίζειν would have its ordinary meaning, "to come close." Dodd's conclusions from LXX have also been contested by J. Y. Campbell, in *Exp.T.*, xlviii, (1936-7), pp. 91 f., and K. Clark, in *Journal of Biblical Literature*, lix (1940), pp. 367 ff. See also W. G. Kümmel, *Verheissung und Erfüllung, Untersuchungen zur eschatologischen Verkündigung Jesu*, Abhandlungen zur Theologie des Alten und Neuen Testaments, edd. W. Eichrodt and O. Cullmann, vol. vi, Basle 1945; Eng. version: *Promise and Fulfilment. The Eschatological Message of Jesus*, trans. D. H. Barton, London 1957, henceforth cited as *Promise and Fulfilment*. For further literature see Wellhagen, *Anden och Riket*, pp. 124 ff. B. T. D. Smith, *The Parables of the Synoptic Gospels, A critical study*, Cambridge 1937, adopts a more antagonistic attitude (p. 78, n. 1). R. N. Flew, *Jesus and His Church, A study of the idea of the Ecclesia in the New Testament*, London 1938, pp. 31 ff.: "The Kingdom has come in the person of Jesus. Its blessings can be enjoyed now, through faith. But it has not fully come. The final consummation is delayed."

[27] Dodd, *Parables of the Kingdom*, p. 46.
[28] *Op. cit.*, p. 49.

sayings on the subject. They have no parallel in Jewish teaching or prayers of the period. If, therefore, we are seeking the *differentia* of the teaching of Jesus upon the Kingdom of God, it is here that it must be found."[29]

When Jesus declares that the Kingdom of God has come, He throws out of gear the whole eschatological system according to which the coming of the Kingdom of God is the coming End. "The *eschaton* has moved from the future to the present, from the sphere of expectation into that of realised experience."[30] In seeking for the meaning of Jesus' idea of the Kingdom of God, it is useless therefore to look for it in the apocalyptic speculation that sees the future only in terms of the imagination, for Jesus speaks of something that from one side at least was an object of experience. For the coming of the Kingdom of God is manifest in the series of historical events comprised in the activity of Jesus. The ministry of Jesus is "realised eschatology," *i.e.* the forces of the world to come intervene and force themselves upon this world in a series of events which have never taken place before and can never be repeated, but which are now in progress in the actual process now taking place. The coming of the Kingdom of God is according to Jesus not something which happens instantaneously but is "a complex of interrelated events including His own ministry, His death, and what follows, all conceived as forming a unity."[31] In the whole life and ministry of Jesus, God confronts man with His Kingdom and His power. Our world has thus become the scene of a divine drama, in which the eternal is revealed.[32] It is essential, therefore, to make up one's mind now, for the moment of decision has come. That is "realised eschatology."

By means of His parables Jesus tried to help mankind to see that in that which is now taking place before their eyes, in the miracles, in the summons which, if it is accepted, brings with it blessedness and, if it is rejected, obduracy, in the crucifixion and the affliction of the disciples, God confronts the people with His Kingdom. If the Kingdom of God is thus in a sense identified with Jesus and His cause, then we must understand and interpret the parables in the light of the situation which existed during the ministry of Jesus. That is

[29] *Op. cit.*, p. 49.
[30] *Op. cit.*, p. 50.
[31] *Op. cit.*, p. 185.
[32] *Op. cit.*, p. 197.

their *Sitz im Leben*. The sayings of Jesus were uttered during a brief period of intense "crisis," but the tradition was shaped during a period of increasing community life, which was looked upon as the interval between two crises, one past and one to come. Jesus did not teach anything about a Second Advent or a Parousia, but He taught: "The Kingdom of God has come."[33]

The many sayings that speak about a second Advent Dodd tries to get round by explaining that they did not originally have this meaning at all, but were adapted later to fit into the prevailing eschatological system. In other cases he gives an interpretation which eliminates the apparently futuristic element in the sayings.[34]

Jesus unquestionably spoke about the future. Dodd does not attempt to deny this fact, and he distinguishes between two types of sayings about the future, namely those which foretell coming *historical* events after the manner of classical prophecy, and those which foretell events of an altogether *supernatural* nature, in line with the visions of the apocalyptists. The terminology is not very happy. Actually it is a question of sayings which relate to events up to the Parousia, and those which relate to the Parousia itself and what happens afterwards.[35] The first include the sayings of Jesus about His Passion and death and the afflictions of the disciples. Jesus also foretold the destruction of the Jewish people, its holy

[33] T. F. Glasson, *The Second Advent*, London 1945, denies that Jesus spoke of the Parousia. His teaching on the Kingdom of God reached fulfilment in and with the Resurrection.

[34] *E.g.* Mt. VIII. 11; Mk. XIV. 25. Of the first text, Dodd says: It is an apocalyptic idea to liken life in the coming age to a meal. But because many will sit at table in the Kingdom of God, that is not to say that the Kingdom has not yet come. What has not yet happened but shall happen is that many who are not yet in the Kingdom of God in its earthly form, will enjoy its final revelation in a world beyond this. "The saying does not answer the question whether or not Jesus expected any further 'coming' of the Kingdom of God beyond that which was already taking place in his own ministry" (*Parables of the Kingdom*, p. 55). The Patriarchs live, according to Jewish ideas, in a world beyond this where God is King for ever. The new element in Christianity is that the Kingdom is to be revealed on earth, and this according to Jesus has already happened. "It would, however, be susceptible of the meaning that at some date in the future the present earthly manifestation of the Kingdom of God will yield to a purely transcendent order in which it will be absolute" (*ibid.*). It is rather Dodd's conception of the presence of the Kingdom of God that prevents this, but the Synoptists were evidently not aware of the difficulty.

[35] J. Jeremias, "Eine neue Schau der Zukunftsaussagen Jesu," review of Dodd, *op. cit.*, in *Th. Bl.*, 1941, p. 218.

city and temple. In this He revealed a typical "disaster eschatology." Among the "supernatural events" which relate to the Parousia and what follows, Dodd includes, for example, the Day of the Son of Man, the Resurrection, the Last Judgment, the disciples sitting at table in the Kingdom of God.

Jesus foretold not merely His death but also His resurrection and the ultimate triumph of the cause of God in His person. The "coming in the clouds of heaven" which Jesus foretold (Mk. xiv. 62) is His triumphant revelation in glory, when He takes His seat "on the right hand of power." But the primitive Church, under the influence of its experiences, separated these two events and drew a distinction between (1) the resurrection, (2) *sessio ad dextram*, and (3) the Parousia, which had originally been intimately connected. To Jesus the resurrection after three days was nothing less than the Day of the Son of Man. It follows inevitably that Jesus saw the Day of the Son of Man and the new aeon in immediate proximity, so close, indeed, that one cannot possibly speak here in terms of "future," for what is to happen is the immediate continuation and fulfilment of Jesus' mission. All the various components, therefore, form one single eschatological whole.

Now apart from the Synoptic apocalypse there are four parables, namely the Faithful and Unfaithful Servant (Mt. xxiv. 45-51; Lk. xii. 42-6), the Watching Servant (Mk. xiii. 33-7 *et par.*), the Thief in the Night (Mt. xxiv. 43 f.; Lk. xii. 39 f.) and the Ten Maidens (Mt. xxv. 1-12), all of which have customarily been interpreted from earliest times as meaning that Jesus expected a period of waiting between His death and resurrection on the one hand, and His Parousia on the other. It was natural enough for the primitive Church to relate these parables to the Parousia, applying the various images allegorically to the returning Christ. The parables thus became warnings and exhortations for the period between the death and resurrection of Jesus and His Parousia. But the parables in question originally referred to the situation in the ministry of Jesus. The "crisis" which is already upon them, which is there, and which Jesus precipitated, is about to take an unknown and unexpected turn which demands the utmost watchfulness by the followers of Jesus. The Son of Man is about to be delivered into the hands of sinners. It seems possible, therefore, to apply these purely "eschatological" parables to a given situation in the life of Jesus. "They were intended to enforce His appeal to men to recognise that the Kingdom of God was present in all its momentous consequences and that by their conduct in the presence of this tremendous crisis they would judge themselves as faithful or unfaithful, wise or foolish."[36]

Nowhere, according to Dodd, does the "consistently eschatological" interpretation of the Kingdom of God show itself more strained and artificial than in the attempt to fit the parables of growth (the Sower, the Weeds among the Wheat, the Self-growing Seed and the Grain of Mustard Seed) and the parables of the Net and the Leaven, into the pattern of a purely futuristic Kingdom of God. To interpret the Sower, the Self-growing Seed and the Weeds among the Wheat correctly, one must see in them a clear and consistent reference to the historical situation of Jesus. At the same time one must not lose sight of the fact that, although growth is emphasised so strongly here, that does not necessarily mean that a long period of development is envisaged after the death of Jesus. Under the image of harvest the parables in question illustrate in various ways the coming of the Kingdom of God in the ministry of Jesus.[37] The harvest-time is come and the disciples must go out to bring in the harvest (Mt. ix. 37 f.; Lk. x. 1 ff.). In the words: "Lift up your eyes, and see how the fields are already white for harvest . . ." (Jn. iv. 35-8) the Gospel of St John interprets the tradition that lies behind the Synoptics. The key to the understanding of the parable of the Net Dodd finds in the words Jesus spoke to the fishermen, when He called them to follow Him: "Follow me, and I will make you become fishers of men" (Mk. i. 17). Jesus uses "fish" as a metaphor for the work He and His disciples are to perform. Jesus' call is directed to all, but at the same time a certain selectiveness is apparent in His mission (Lk. ix. 57-62).[38] The parable speaks also of this selective process: by their answer to the call the worthless are separated out from the worthy. It is just this that happens in the ministry of Jesus. "The Kingdom of God, in process of realisation in

---

[36] Dodd, *op. cit.*, p. 174.
[37] The similarity to A. T. Cadoux is striking.
[38] Dodd, cf. Cadoux, *The Parables of Jesus*, pp. 27 ff.

and through that ministry, is like the work of fishing with a drag-net, for the appeal is made to all indiscriminately, and yet in the nature of things it is selective; and, let us recall, this selection *is* the divine judgment, though men pass it upon themselves by their ultimate attitude to the appeal."[39]

But Dodd warns us against reading into the parables of growth a development which begins with the ministry of Jesus and ends with His second Advent. To Jesus there was no such long historical perspective. The *eschaton*, the culmination of history determined by God, is here through an act of God Himself. It comes not through a catastrophe which God sends when He will, but is the harvest which follows after a long period of growth.

Dodd concludes his presentation of the "parables of the Kingdom of God" with the words: "The coming of the Kingdom is indeed a crisis brought by divine intervention; but it is not an unprepared crisis, unrelated to the previous course of history. An obscure process of growth has gone before it, and the fresh act of God which calls the crisis into being is an answer to the work of God in history which has gone before. In Jewish apocalypse, although the metaphor of harvest is used, there is little or no sense of any organic relation between the processes of history and its culmination. The divine event is an unrelated and unconditioned intervention. It is not so in the teaching of Jesus. Having come, however, the Kingdom does call for human effort. The harvest waits for reapers, and it is in this light that Jesus sees His own work and that to which He calls His disciples."[40]

Jesus' historical perspective is short, which by no means means that He believed history would come to an end immediately after His death. The eternal meaning of history is revealed in the "crisis" which came with Jesus. Whether the time that follows is long or short, men live now in a new age, in which the Kingdom of God, His grace and judgment are revealed. So there is room also for ethical instruction in the Gospel. But it is not a question of an interim ethic, but of an ethical ideal for those who have accepted the Kingdom and who live their lives in the judgment and grace which have now finally been revealed.

[39] Dodd, *Parables of the Kingdom*, p. 189.
[40] *Op. cit.*, pp. 193 f.

Let us summarise the most characteristic features of Dodd's interpretation of the Kingdom of God. Jesus expressly declared that the Kingdom of God is come. It is a present "crisis," a fact of the moment, but not in the sense of an ever-present struggle in the world towards righteousness, but in the sense that something has happened which has never happened before.[41] The crisis, which has come through the ministry of Jesus, is the coming of the Kingdom of God.

What, then, is the Kingdom of God to Dodd? Dodd characterises it as a timeless reality.[42] It is the Eternal itself that manifests itself in time, for the inconceivable has happened that history has become the bearer of the Eternal.[43] The Absolute has clothed itself in flesh and blood. The "Ultimate," the Transcendent, has entered into history. In so far as history can contain the timeless entity that is called the Kingdom of God, the Day of the Son of Man, so far these timeless realities are present in the historical crisis which comes with Jesus. Here a meeting takes place between the Eternal and history, in the sense that Jesus' life and work are both history in its decisive moment and an eternal fact. When Dodd goes on to say that the Church in the sacrament of the Communion recapitulates this historical crisis, in which Jesus came, lived, died, and was resurrected, so that the Communion is a re-enactment of this decisive moment in history, it seems clear that the Kingdom of God is to Dodd the Eternal which takes form and manifests itself in history. It is English Incarnation-theology combined with historical philosophy, and through it runs a strong thread of Platonic influence, as a result of which the Biblical conception of time has no place. Futuristic eschatology disappears, and all that is left is "the *eschaton*" as the Eternal.

In order to carry through his interpretation of Jesus' conception of the Kingdom of God Dodd is obliged to disregard certain groups of sayings or to adapt them in accordance with his basic attitude. Dodd admits that Jesus, like the apocalyptists, set the fulfilled Kingdom of God beyond time and space, but he never takes up for real discussion the long series of sayings in which the Kingdom of God is purely futuristically conceived. It is to other sayings, which fall outside this framework, that he attaches decisive importance for Jesus' view of the Kingdom of God.

[41] *Op. cit.*, p. 178.   [42] *Op. cit.*, p. 80.   [43] *Op. cit.*, p. 197.

Here we will only consider and comment upon Dodd's interpretation of two groups of parables, namely the parables of watchfulness and the parables of growth. The watchfulness parables (Mt. XXIV. 45-51; Lk. XII. 42-6; Mk. XIII. 33-7 *et par.*, Mt. XXIV. 43 f.; Lk. XII. 39 f.; Mt. XXV. 1-12) were originally intended to exhort listeners to see and understand the crisis that was now taking place in and through the ministry of Jesus, but the Church has taken them as referring to the Parousia and the watchfulness it demands. A decisive feature in all these parables is that they all speak of a "coming" as the important thing: the master of the house, the bridegroom, the thief, all "come." As W. Kümmel[44] has shown, this ἔρχεσθαι points forward to the Parousia, for to speak of a coming of Jesus when He is already there in the midst of mankind is possible only in the sense of something that is to happen in the future. That in the parable of the Ten Maidens it is the sudden Parousia of the Son of Man that is intended, seems obvious; the whole parable becomes quite inexplicable on any other terms.[45] All the parables in question refer, then, to the Last Judgment and are intended to exhort their hearers to be prepared for its sudden coming.

The interpretation of the parables of growth is based on Dodd's general outlook, with which the material is forced to agree. The parable of the Self-growing Seed (Mk. IV. 26 ff.) provides the key to an understanding of the other parables. Dodd admits that *harvest* is a usual symbol for the Day of the Lord, the Day of Judgment, and that its hearers would have accepted it in this sense even without the quotation from Joel III. 13. Dodd asserts, however, that it is not necessary to bring in this circumstance. In Mt. IX. 37 f.: "Then he said to his disciples, The harvest is plentiful, but the labourers are few; pray therefore the Lord of the harvest, to send out labourers into his harvest," harvest does not refer to what is to come. This saying is to be found in Q as the introduction to Jesus' speech on commissioning the Twelve, and has no reference at all to the Day of Judgment.

Dodd then bases his interpretation of Mk. IV. 26 ff. on the assumption that "harvest" has no futuristic eschatological

<hr />

[44] *Promise and Fulfilment*, pp. 54, 43 ff.

[45] It would seem that "Bridegroom" is intended as a self-designation. Thus Kümmel, *op. cit.*, p. 56, against J. Jeremias, in *Theologisches Wörterbuch zum Neuen Testament*, ed. G. Kittel, henceforth cited as *Th.W.B.N.T.*, VOL. IV, pp. 1094 ff.

meaning here either, saying: "In terms of this parable, there-fore, we must conceive Jesus not as sowing the seed, nor yet as watching the growth and predicting a harvest in the future, but as standing in the presence of the ripe crop, and taking active steps to 'put in the sickle.' *That* is what the Kingdom of God is like. It is the fulfilment of the process."[46] Jesus would thus have regarded His mission as a fulfilment of that of the prophets, and in the success of John the Baptist He saw God's power in action. The parable, therefore, according to Dodd, is intended to point out that the crisis which has now come is the culmination of a long process. The parable says in effect: "Can you not see that the long story of God's dealings with His people has reached its culmination? After the Baptist only one thing remains, namely to grasp the sickle, for the seed is ripe for harvest."

Now it is clearly not the fact that the seed grows that is matter for attention, but that the farmer can do nothing about its growing. The seed grows without his help. The Kingdom of God comes without human effort. The coming of the King-dom of God is likened therefore, to "the certain arrival of the harvest which nothing can influence."[47] Moreover, it is clear from Mt. XI. 12 (*et par.*) that the idea that the Kingdom of God had been in a state of development ever since the days of the prophets, was quite alien to Jesus. The same objection applies also to Dodd's interpretation of the other parables of growth. Dodd reads in modern thoughts. The Kingdom of God which Jesus preached does not grow. It is in process of coming in secret, as those can see who believe in Jesus and follow Him.[48] When Dodd objects that "consistent" escha-tology cannot give any reasonable interpetation of the parables of growth, one can only agree with him, but he himself has hit on an explanation which the contemporaries of Jesus would hardly have been able to understand.[49]

---

[46] *Parables of the Kingdom*, p. 179.

[47] Kümmel, *Promise and Fulfilment*, p. 128. Smith, *The Parables of the Synoptic Gospels*, p. 131: "The lesson is simply that as the farmer waits upon God for the harvest, so should Israel wait upon God for the Kingdom."

[48] Smith, *op. cit.*, p. 120: "The Kingdom which he preached does not grow—it comes; and its coming does not depend upon its acceptance by the world but upon the will of God."

[49] In his criticism of Dodd, Smith says: "The difficulties involved in the interpretation of the teaching of Jesus along the lines of 'consistent eschatology' appear to be negligible in comparison to those involved in such an interpretation,

The fault with Dodd's interpretation is its excessive one-sidedness, brought about by his theological and philosophical attitude. By practically identifying Jesus with the Kingdom of God, he loses sight of the futuristic aspect of the Kingdom. But this does not, of course, in any way prevent recognition of the fact that Dodd (like Rudolf Otto) quite correctly sees, as the new element that came with Jesus, the presence of the Kingdom in and through Jesus. This seems to be fully understandable only in the light of Jesus' exalted claim to be, actually here and now in His earthly ministry, the Son of Man and Consummator of the world, even though in hidden form. So that, even though one rejects Dodd's interpretation, one must agree with him that it is only in the light of Jesus' proclamation that the Kingdom has come through Him and in His acts, that it is possible to understand Jesus' sayings about the future. "The imminent expectation of the Parousia and the *eschata* is not something that had independent existence within the framework of the proclamation of Jesus, but is in the end nothing but the expression of the certainty that *hic et nunc* the hour of fulfilment and the hour of the last absolute word to humanity has struck" (J. Jeremias).[50]

for this would represent him as proclaiming a gospel which, in so far as it would be intelligible to his hearers, must appear to them to be manifestly untrue" (*op. cit.*, p. 78).

[50] J. Jeremias, "Eine neue Schau der Zukunftsaussagen Jesu," p. 222. Kurt Emmerich, "Die formgeschichtliche Betrachtung der Evangelien in der englischen theologischen Literatur," in *Kirchenblatt für die reformierte Schweiz*, 1942, No. 1, declares that Dodd's dogmatic outlook shows the influence of R. Niebuhr. However, R. Niebuhr, in *The Nature and Destiny of Man*; VOL. II, *Human Destiny*, New York and London 1943, p. 50, criticises Dodd: "The modern interpretation of the coming of Christ in the theory of 'realised eschatology,' according to which all symbols of the second coming in the New Testament are without general significance, cannot effectively destroy or obscure either the historic validity or the systematic relevance of the strain of thought in the Gospels embodied in the idea of the 'second coming.' It is indispensable for a gospel interpretation as for a true understanding of the Gospels." See also his *Beyond Tragedy, Essays on the Christian interpretation of history*, New York and London 1938, pp. 21 ff. A. E. J. Rawlinson, *Christ in the Gospels*, London 1944, considers that Dodd's interpretation does not give the whole truth, since he leaves out the futuristic aspect of the Kingdom of God. "It does no kind of justice to the tremendous words of our Lord about the coming of the Son of Man to Judgment, and Consummation of the Age" (p. 49). Under the influence of K. Barth and R. Bultmann, Rawlinson declares that every age is under the judgment of God, and that judgment is near. The return of the Son of Man and the day of fulfilment stand as permanent symbols for knowledge of those things which are beyond time and history: the final victory of God and His righteousness.

The Interpretation of the Kingdom of God
by the "German Christians"

The object of the "German Christian" movement was as far as possible to dissociate Jesus from Judaism. Its attempt to make Jesus an Arian was characteristic. As the futuristic aspect of the Kingdom of God is unquestionably connected with Judaism, it is the presence sayings that determined the German interpretation of Jesus' idea of the Kingdom. The Reports of the Conferences organised in 1940 and 1941 by the "Institute for Investigating the Jewish Influence on German Church Life," actually collections of essays, edited by Walter Grundmann,[51] give a good idea of its theology. Among supporters of the movement may be mentioned, apart from Grundmann himself, Johannes Leipoldt,[52] Rudolf Meyer,[53] Hans Pohlmann[54] and Max-Adolf Wagenführer.[55] Emanuel Hirsch also belonged to the movement during his last theological period.[56] Only Grundmann's interpretation of Jesus will be briefly discussed here.[57]

As a Galilean Jesus was not a Jew. He also failed to observe Jewish forms of devotion and pious practices. When Jesus is represented as having come to fulfil the law (Mt. v. 17), that is the apologia of the early Palestinian Church. The Kingdom

[51] *Christentum und Judentum*, Leipzig 1940, and *Germanentum, Christentum und Judentum*, ed. W. Grundmann, Leipzig 1942.

[52] J. Leipoldt, *Jesu Verhältnis zu Griechen und Juden*, Leipzig 1941, p. 119: "Jesus thus presupposes that the Kingdom is a spiritual entity." Pp. 121 f.: "The Kingdom, then, develops."

[53] R. Meyer, *Der Prophet aus Galiläa, Studie zum Jesusbild der drei ersten Evangelien*, Leipzig 1940, speaks of the distinctiveness of Jesus showing itself, among other things, in the idea of the growth of the Dominion of God as a religious-ethical community (p. 129).

[54] H. Pohlmann, *Der Gottesgedanke Jesu als Gegensatz gegen den israelitisch-jüdischen Gottesgedanken*, Studien zu deutschen Theologie und Frömmigkeit, VOL. IV, Weimar 1939.

[55] M.-A. Wagenführer, "Der Kirchenbegriff des Neuen Testaments" in *Germanentum, Christentum und Judentum*, ed. W. Grundmann, VOL. II, Leipzig 1942, pp. 273-306. M. E. Winkel, *Der Sohn, Die evangelischen Quellen und die Verkündigung Jesu von Nazareth in ihrer ursprünglichen Gestalt und ihre Vermischung mit jüdischem Geist. Nach textlich revidierten kanonischen und ausserkanonisch überlieferten Aussprüchen und Berichten*, Kampen 1935, can best be included in this group.

[56] With regard to Hirsch see below, p. 131, n. 7.

[57] Among Grundmann's works may be mentioned here: *Der Begriff der Kraft in der neutestamentlichen Gedankenwelt*, Stuttgart 1932; *Die Gotteskindschaft in der Geschichte Jesu und ihre religionsgeschichtlichen Voraussetzungen*, Studien zu Deutsche Theologie und Frömmigkeit, VOL. I., Weimar 1938; *Jesus der Galiläer und das Judentum*, Leipzig 1940; *Wer ist Jesus von Nazareth?* Weimar 1940.

of God, which begins here and now, is entirely God's affair.
Jesus and those who believe see in the seed the coming harvest.
The Kingdom is especially active in the hearts of those whose
lives are a fruit of the Kingdom. The heart is the organ of
the Kingdom of God. To Jesus it was not the miracles that
were important, but the teaching. Jesus was the bearer of
good tidings (Is. LII. 7, LXI. I ff.), who sowed the tidings of the
Kingdom of God in the hearts of men. He brought with Him
the Kingdom of God, when He preached peace and salvation
for the poor, freedom for the prisoners and help for the sick.
Thus with Jesus' preaching and works the Kingdom of God
dawns. Jesus is the sign of the Kingdom of God, to which
one must pay attention. "His nature represents the nature
of the Kingdom of God, therefore His Person as bringer of the
Kingdom of God takes the place that was occupied in Palestinian religion by the Law and the other revelatory writings."[58]

   Jesus rejected Jewish Messianic ideas. He was the Servant,
the Son, and both the form He gave to the idea of the Kingdom
of God and His conception of Himself grew out of His relationship with God. Regarding Himself as the Son of God in a
morally religious sense, He felt Himself called to proclaim a
new piety.

   The difference between this interpretation of Jesus and the
liberal interpretation of the turn of the century is extremely
slight. This is an image of Jesus created by wishful thinking.
The fact that the futuristic sayings about the Kingdom of God,
which constitute the majority in the Gospels, are entirely
omitted, reveals its lack of contact with the texts.

[58] *Jesus der Galiläer und das Judentum*, p. 117.

X

Interpretations by Systematic Theology

To scholars who seek, in reverence for the content of the text, whatever it may be, to gain understanding of the unity behind Jesus' idea of the Kingdom of God, it is natural to trace both its conflicts and its unity back to the image of God which Jesus held.

Adolf Schlatter

The long-neglected exegetist and systematic theologian, Adolf Schlatter, who played so large a part in the revival of the "realistic" interpretation of the Bible after the First World War, belongs to the above group. Schlatter tried to see Jesus in the same way as a contemporary who believed in Him as Christ, would have seen Him.[1] Schlatter by no means abandoned this believing attitude in his critical researches, but considered on the contrary that it provides a better and clearer insight into the deeper meaning of the problems than is ever achieved by scholars who believe themselves unprejudiced but are actually entirely bound by (to them) self-evident theological and philosophical preconceptions. Nor can it be denied that Schlatter very often got nearer the heart of the Gospel tradition than the majority of his contemporaries generally did.

In his most important work on Jesus, published in 1921,[2]

---

[1] Cf. K. Bornhäuser's interpretation in terms of contemporary life, *i.e.* his attempt to transport the modern reader back into the conditions of life of a Jew in the days of Jesus.

[2] A. Schlatter, *Die Geschichte des Christus*, Stuttgart 1921, 2nd edn. 1923. Schlatter had already given a resumé of his view of Jesus and His teaching in *Die Theologie*

he presented Jesus not as an outstanding personality, but as the bearer of the Christly office God had given Him. Jesus revealed God in word and deed and carried out His royal will. To Schlatter what we have to do is "so to meditate on the many individual sayings and actions of Jesus that the foundation from which they spring becomes apparent."[3] The mission of Jesus had its basis and its goal in a single-minded purpose which governed Him from His first appearance as a prophet of repentance until His death upon the Cross.[4]

The all-essential to Jesus was the actual idea of God, which He made the central idea of the Kingdom. God was to Jesus the effective kingly will. When Jesus wanted to describe what "the ultimate" means, He did so with the words: Then God shall rule. Schlatter speaks almost invariably of the "Dominion of God," seldom of the "Kingdom of God." The Dominion of God is not the highest good, it is not a value or condition independent of the relationship between God and man; it is not something that is given to man as an enduring possession, but it is the act of God through which God establishes the relationship between mankind and Himself.

Jesus is not merely He who prophesies and preaches the coming of the Dominion of God. By His teaching and His miracles Jesus brought the Kingdom *into the present*. The Dominion of God enters into force through Jesus preaching it. For God and His word constituted to Jesus a unity which nothing can dissolve. God is united with His word. He wills through it and acts through it. The word has power to make mankind pure and holy. Jesus could see the Dominion of God as present already in the preaching of the Baptist, since the word had shown its power. John the Baptist drew a distinction between the time of repentance, which has the character of preparation, and the time of glory, which God will give in

---

des Neuen Testaments; VOL. I, *Das Wort Gottes*, Stuttgart 1909. Much light is thrown on Schlatter's view of the Gospel by his commentaries on Mt., Mk., and Lk. published in 1929, 1935, and 1931. Schlatter's extraordinary insight into the life of the Jews at the time of Jesus plays an important part in his interpretation without being directly apparent.

[3] *Die Geschichte des Christus*, p. 7.

[4] By stressing the unity between the teaching and acts of Jesus, Schlatter avoids the historicism of modern theology. He does not maintain or dispute the historicity of individual sayings, but goes by the meaning of the main body of sayings (cf. J. Schniewind). He is free, too, from psychologising tendencies. Nor does he concern himself at all with literary criticism.

response to the people's conversion. In Jesus these two times are blended firmly together, since He unites conversion and the Kingdom of God. Through conversion man comes to God, and he receives all; he receives eternal life. As a result of his forsaking evil and doing good the Dominion of God and His perfect grace become reality to man.

The preaching of repentance was the offering of the Kingdom; rejection of the word and of Jesus the messenger meant loss of the Kingdom.[5] As the Son and the Christ Jesus had full authority to appeal to God. The word became therefore not merely a promise but the Gospel, which proclaimed what God now did and gave. Conversion therefore also became man's salvation. Jesus saw the ultimate goal in the future, but all His promises contain a pronouncement about the present, for He confronted His hearers with a decision to gain or to lose eternal life *now*.

Not destruction but life is the keyword of Jesus' teaching about the Kingdom. Jesus is the "Evangelist" who proclaims the glad tidings, *i.e.* He speaks of what God does now, that He creates the final perfection. And whoever accepts the tidings has already gained the Dominion of God, which is no longer the object merely of hope.

The affliction of the time meant to Jesus that hostile powers had dominion. When God rules, all that separates from God is taken away through His kingly action. But the destruction of the powers that oppose the Dominion of God will not take place in the present. The present divine dominion is a guarantee that some day it will break through completely and strike down all that stands in its way.

Jesus based His statement that God now revealed Himself as King on His own mission. He who listened had part in the Kingdom and therewith the grace of God and eternal life. He had reached the goal. But this by no means excluded hope, for the office of Christ which Jesus bore did not embrace fulfilment. Fulfilment was something to be hoped for and awaited, so long as the mission of Jesus consisted in preaching repentance, and He therefore Himself was the unknown and rejected. Had Jesus revealed the Dominion of God to all without reservation, that would have meant making His

---

[5] Equivalent terms for the Kingdom of God are the House of God (cf. E. Lohmeyer) and the New Alliance (Schlatter, *Die Geschichte des Christus*, pp. 143 f.).

I

Messianic office public, for the visible Kingdom and the revealed Christ belong together. He who did not see that Christ, the Promised One, had come, did not see either "the presence of the Kingdom of God."

According to Schlatter, Jesus expected the Kingdom to come soon. But that hope would have dissolved completely into uncertainty, if the offering of the Kingdom had had no other basis than the idea that the Kingdom would come soon, so that men would have been reduced to seeking after signs. The basis for saying that the Kingdom, which is now present, will come soon in perfected form, is the fact that he who calls upon the Kingdom is already there.

The unity between the present and final form of the Dominion of God is provided by the *idea of God* which emerges as the decisive central point in the conception of the Kingdom.[6] God is the Gracious God who through Jesus now makes the great offer of grace and shows who is to have part in the Kingdom.

Whereas the eschatology of the contemporaries of Jesus was born of despair over the present and in the feeling of being abandoned by God, Jesus' own eschatology was not a child of despair or of abandonment by God. On the contrary, it was born of certainty in God. The expectation of future perfection derives in Jesus from community with God. It has its roots in nearness to God and not in the want of His grace. Therefore, also, the future with its fulfilment means a revelation and a confirmation of what is taking place now. Schlatter insisted, therefore, as no one else before Otto had done, that the eschatology of Jesus is full of joy.

The Church idea, too, has its place in Schlatter's interpretation of Jesus' conception of the Kingdom of God. The Kingdom of God is not a place or a thing, it is men with whom God deals in a kingly manner. His Church is the Kingdom of God in so far as it is constituted of His sons and servants. Through the community which Christ gathers together the Dominion of God becomes visible. But the group of disciples is not the same as the Kingdom of God, for the disciple can fall and the exhortation to repentance is always equally serious. What

---

[6] "The more the idea of God became the decisive element in the conception of the Kingdom, so that it turned attention from the condition of the people to what they received from the grace of God, the firmer did the unity become between the present and the ultimate form of the Dominion of God" (*op. cit.*, p. 149).

the disciple possesses, he possesses in word and promise, for God works in secret through His word.

Schlatter's interpretation leads him to a magnificent view of Jesus and His mission as a whole, for the Kingdom of God becomes the Dominion of God's grace over all those who now accept the "Bearer of good tidings," through whom God acts and brings His Dominion into the present. What the Jews expected in the future, has already become "present" through Jesus.

Schlatter cannot, however, be entirely cleared of the charge of somewhat overstressing the presence of the Dominion of God in the acts of Christ. No one will deny that the decisive feature of Jesus' conception of the Kingdom of God was His teaching that the Kingdom had become "present" in Himself, His work and word. That is the centre-point of the Gospel. But there is a stronger emphasis on the fact that this presence is soon to be changed into fulfilment than Schlatter seems willing to allow. Otherwise the keen anticipation that prevailed in early Christianity of the fulfilment that was to take place soon, becomes difficult to explain. The day that crowns faith with vision will come soon—that is the united testimony of the New Testament.[7] Schlatter's emphasis on the fact that the Kingdom of God is present in the *word* about the Kingdom is important. This is a circumstance that has received too little attention in the interpretation of the Kingdom of God.

Robert Frick and Gerhard Gloege

The religious-historical school has in general failed to provide a clear answer to the question what it was that made Christianity victorious over the other religions which struggled

---

[7] The influence of Schlatter's interpretation of Jesus is evident in E. Hirsch, *Jesus Christus der Herr, Theologische Vorlesungen*, Göttingen 1926. Hirsch mentions it himself (p. 7). See also M. Dibelius, "Jesus in contemporary German theology," in *J. Rel.*, 1931, p. 210. Hirsch later put forward a definitely liberal interpretation of the Kingdom of God (*Das Wesen des Christentums*, Weimar 1939, and *Frühgeschichte des Evangeliums*; VOL. I, *Das Werden des Markus-evangeliums*; VOL. II, *Die Vorlagen des Lukas und das Sondergut des Matthäus*, Tübingen 1941). The eschatological sayings in the true sense of the word are thrust aside. The Kingdom of God becomes forgiveness and life in God. The Son of Man sayings are thrust aside. Jesus is not the Fulfiller. Jesus is seen primarily as He who fights against the legal hypocrisy of the Pharisees. To Hirsch Jesus becomes "basically nothing more than the ideal theologian of the.twentieth century" (A. Oepke in review of E. Hirsch, *Frühgeschichte des Evangeliums*, 1941, in *Theologisches Literaturblatt*, 1942, p. 142.)

against it. The answer given by Karl Holl[8] has been much discussed. Christianity was victorious because of something that distinguished it from all other religions. This distinguishing feature was its conception of God. Jesus preached a God who is willing to have dealings with sinful man. Jesus foretold the Kingdom of God, which means that judgment waits inescapably at the threshold. Mankind must be judged according to God's own perfection. Against the background of this idea of judgment the preaching of forgiveness acquires a sharpened meaning: that God who in His strictness demands the highest, still does not want mankind to incur His judgment.

Karl Holl's pupil, Robert Frick,[9] tried to apply this line of thought more fully to the Kingdom of God. It is the polarity between power and goodness in Jesus' conception of God that lends the peculiar tension to His certainty of the Kingdom of God. The Kingdom of God occupies a central position in the teaching of Jesus, because here it is exclusively a question of "the exercise of the divine power and the fulfilment of the Fatherly will."[10] The Kingdom of God means that the good and gracious will of God alone rules in human hearts. The strength of Jesus' teaching about the Kingdom of God is due to the fact that He took God seriously both in the matter of His holy wrath and His forgiving grace. The contrast between the call to decisive action (Lk. XII. 49) and the stillness in anticipation of the development of that which has been sown, arises out of the vision of God, for to be in the service of God requires the harnessing of all one's forces; the whole personality has to be involved, but it also means peace, joy, and blessedness. This tension between absolute demand and giving grace can be traced everywhere in Jesus' teaching of the Kingdom. Frick resolves both this tension and that between the presence of the Kingdom of God and its coming, in the light of the "perception of God" ("*Gottesanschauung*"). The Kingdom of God is present wherever the rule of God is absolute and exclusive. Where the will of God is done wholly and without restriction, the Kingdom of God is realised. The

---

[8] K. Holl, *Urchristentum und Religionsgeschichte*, Studien des apologetischen Seminars, No. 10, Gütersloh 1925. Eng. version: *The Distinctive Elements in Christianity*, trans. N. V. Hope, Edinburgh 1937.

[9] R. Frick, *Die Geschichte des Reich-Gottes-Gedankens in der alten Kirche bis zu Origenes und Augustin*, Beihefte z. *Z.N.W.*, No. 6, Giessen 1928.

[10] *Op. cit.*, p. 6.

conclusion which Frick consequently feels justified in drawing is this: Since God rules unrestrictedly in Jesus, the Kingdom of God is present in Him. He is Himself the Kingdom (*auto-basileia*). The presence of the Kingdom in the person of the Servant, which corresponds to the presence of Christ in the same way, points on beyond itself towards the fulfilment. For the idea that the Kingdom of God is revealed in the person of the Servant is paradoxical. It, therefore, necessarily points towards the future, when the Kingdom of God shall show itself in power and with Christ be revealed in glory. The uniting force in all these seemingly conflicting sayings is the idea of God: God is the absolutely holy and the absolutely forgiving. There are traces, however, of another line of thought. The tension in the Gospel is the tension between time and eternity, between God and the world.

Similar ideas come up again in Gerhard Gloege, who published in 1929[11] an interesting contribution to the solution of the problem of the Kingdom of God along the lines of systematic theology. It is consciously under the influence of Adolf Schlatter.

Gloege rendered the Kingdom of God as the "*Dominion of God*" ("*Gottesherrschaft*"). Basic to the Dominion of God is the dynamic conception of God. The Dominion of God meant to Jesus nothing else but God Himself in action. The Kingdom of God was to Jesus, as in the Old Testament, "a living, forward-striving entity merging into the activity of God Himself."[12] In His Messianic activity Jesus by word and deed brought the Dominion of God actually and completely into the present. He who submits to the activity of God has part in the Dominion of God.

Gloege asserts that Jesus' idea of the Kingdom of God was consistent and had an inward unity, just as His idea of God, and in contrast to Judaism. Unlike those who omit or adapt those passages in the Gospel which speak of the presence of the Kingdom of God, he claims unity between present and future in the dynamic conception of the Dominion. If the dynamic conception of God is the basis of the idea of the Dominion of God, it must at once seem suspect to restrict God's kingly

[11] G. Gloege, *Reich Gottes und Kirche im Neuen Testament*, Neutestamentliche Forschungen, ed. O. Schmitz, Ser. II, No. 4, Gütersloh 1929.

[12] *Op. cit.*, p. 56. The parables in both Mt. XIII and Mt. XVIII. 23-35 compare the Kingdom of God to an act someone performs.

action only to the future, and deprive the present altogether of any claims on the Kingdom of God. God acts continuously in all ages, so that the dynamic conception of the Dominion of God makes it impossible to relate this Dominion exclusively to any given age. In the action of Jesus the action of God was involved in all its kingly fullness, and in the fulfilment the same kingly action will be revealed as is present already now in the worldly activity of Jesus.[13]

When one thus consciously makes the idea of God the central point, as the New Testament does, one is released from the false alternative: future or present.[14] Future and present form an organic unity. In the present, in which Jesus is active as the Messiah, the irruption of the future is already implicit, while conversely what is to happen in the future is merely the end of what is happening now. The one is unthinkable without the other, so indissolubly united are they.

Thus, according to Gloege, future and present have merged together into a living organic unit in the activity of Jesus as the Messiah. The Dominion of God, he asserts, is present in the activity of Jesus as the Christ of God, not in His person as such. This close association of the Kingdom of God and the Messiah, so that they are presented as alternative conceptions, was to prove a very fruitful idea, one that would provide the solution to the problem of the Kingdom of God for a number of scholars who wanted to get away from the false alternatives of Schweitzer.[15]

Gloege's interpretation presupposes that the Kingdom of God and God as active force coincide. That God is active in the present is equivalent to saying that the Kingdom is present in the words and acts of Jesus. But with this theological postulate Gloege loses sight of the eschatological nature of the Kingdom of God. When the Kingdom becomes entirely an act of God and not even to the slightest extent a state at the end of the world, the solution has been achieved by an artificial abstraction. There is also a number of sayings about life in the Kingdom of God, which Gloege completely overlooks in his

[13] *Op. cit.*, pp. 110 f.: "In the action of Jesus as the Messiah, which reveals itself equally in word and deed, the Dominion of God, which is also His dominion, becomes manifest actually and completely."

[14] *Op. cit.*, p. 109: "In the New Testament present and future merge completely together in the idea of the Kingdom."

[15] See pp. 75 f.

interpretation. I am thinking of expressions such as to "inherit the Kingdom of God," to "sit at table in the Kingdom of God," to "eat bread in the Kingdom of God," for which Gloege with his dynamic interpretation cannot give any explanation.[16] The same criticism applies to this interpretation of the Kingdom of God as we made of Schlatter: the eschatological fire of expectation has vanished. It seems as though this must always be the result, when the contrast between present and future is smoothed away in order to bring out the unity in God's activity. This continuous, unchanging activity on the part of God is unknown either to the Gospel or the New Testament in general, which on the contrary represent God as acting in a particular way at particular times, and present and future as never quite merging into one another.

Einar Billing

Einar Billing[17] is one of the few Swedish theologians to have combined in one person the systematic and the Biblical theologian, although among German theologians this was not unusual (A. Schlatter, P. Althaus, H.-D. Wendland, A. Oepke, E. Stauffer, and others). Billing asserted that Jesus did not bring a new *teaching*, but that He brought "a lovely and glad *message*, a message such as a herald . . . brings from a king to his subjects: a proclamation."[18] The gospel of Jesus about the Kingdom of God is that the Kingdom has come very close. The hour of the establishment of the Kingdom of God, long awaited in vain, is at last come. Jesus called men to the Kingdom of God, and it is for them to grasp what is at stake, now that promises are about to be fulfilled. Jesus was sent to

[16] Cf. criticism of Gloege in Werner, *Die Entstchung des christlichen Dogmas*, pp. 46 f.

[17] E. Billing's most important contributions to the interpretation of Jesus are: *De etiska tankarna in urkristendomen i deras samband med dess religiösa tro*, VOLS. I-II, Uppsala 1907, 2nd rev. edn. 1936; *Försoningen, Två utvidgade föredrag*, Uppsala 1908, 2nd edn. 1921; and " 'Människosonen' och 'Gudsriket' i Jesu förkunnelse, Två fragment ur ett ofullbordat arbete," in *För tanke och tro, Skrifter tillägnade Oscar Ekman*, Uppsala 1923. The latter essay, which is reprinted in the 2nd edn. of *De etiska tankarna i urkristendomen i deras samband med dess religiösa tro*, 1936, was written at the beginning of the century, according to Billing's own statement in the 1st edn. (p. 242).

[18] *Försoningen, Två utvidgade föredrag*, p. 72.

do the will of God, and was bound by it in all things. In both His preaching and His miracles Jesus did the will of God the Father. The miracles show even more clearly than words that the Kingdom of God is near.

Most of the sayings about the Kingdom of God have, according to Billing, a purely eschatological stamp, *i.e.* they relate entirely to the coming age. The coming of the Kingdom of God means a complete upheaval in every respect, which will come about through a radical break, a creative intervention by God, "an all-embracing catastrophe, in which all spheres of existence, the whole of nature, will be involved."[19] However great the distance may be purely qualitatively between the present and what is to come, purely temporally the distance is slight. The boundary between eschatological sayings and presence sayings is therefore fluid. This is to the advantage of the eschatological interpretation. If one bears in mind the closeness in time, Billing believes that a number of sayings which are usually quoted as evidence of the presence of the Kingdom of God, are just as capable of an eschatological interpretation.[20] The 'Treasure' and the 'Pearl,' for example, express the idea that the time of final decision is irrevocably come. Billing's attitude is seen to be strongly influenced by J. Weiss's purely futuristic interpretation of the Kingdom of God.

Yet Jesus unquestionably spoke of a presence of the Kingdom here and now. Mt. XII. 28 is characterised as "the most unequivocal—the only *absolutely* unequivocal—of Jesus' presence-sayings."[21] The question arises, then, in what sense Jesus could speak of a presence of the Kingdom of God, and where we have to seek it. To Billing the answer lies in the definition of the Kingdom itself. Like G. Dalman, he defines the Kingdom as "rule," "dominion." To Jesus the Dominion of God is God's power and will, which "drives through" and overcomes resistance. So far as this occurs, the Kingdom of

---

[19] *De etiska tankarna i urkristendomen i deras samband med dess religiösa tro*, 2nd edn., p. 417.

[20] The clearest picture of how Jesus saw the question of the coming of the Kingdom of God is given in Lk. XII. 32: "Fear not, little flock, for it is your Father's good pleasure to give you the kingdom." "The *idea* of the Kingdom of God remains purely eschatological: even in 'the parables of the Kingdom of Heaven' the point is this: Take heed, for this, *which belongs to the fulfilment*, is already here" (*op. cit.*, p. 439).

[21] *Op. cit.*, p. 426.

God extends. The Kingdom and the dominating will of God go together.

The Kingdom of God takes its meaning from the idea of God and the coming of the Kingdom means that God's will is done. But since the will of God is one, so the relation between the present and the coming Kingdom of God can only be that what now takes place only at individual points, will in the future take place universally.

In the expressions of God's dominating will and ruling power, in which God subdues to Himself a fresh area of our earth, Jesus saw a presence of the Kingdom of God. In Jesus this Kingdom is already here, but Billing does not see the presence of the Kingdom of God in Jesus as the religious personality or anything of that sort, but in Him as "the bearer of the ruling power and strength of God, which is more powerful than the evil spirits; *so far* as this wins through, so far is the Kingdom of God already here" (Mt. XII. 28).[22] Now is the time of fulfilment. "Now we need wait no longer, now we have only to storm ahead and strike, to become a βιαστής, and we have all that the Kingdom of God has to offer in our hands, we have the 'rule,' we have a power and strength that was still inaccessible to John the Baptist."[23]

The parable of the Figtree (Lk. XIII. 6 ff.) strikes the decisive note in Billing's interpretation of Jesus' view of Himself and His mission. As Son of Man He is the Judge, with all the exaltedness involved in being in God's immediate vicinity, but as Son of Man He adopts here the humble and despised position of servant. But the Judge is not the primary function; Jesus' mission now is to serve the individual. Jesus has come to certainty of this along the path of communion with God. Now He who is to come as Son of Man and hold the Last Judgment has to exercise the humble function of servant and seek out and gather men together. Jesus has the power to break down all obstacles to the Kingdom of God, but He and His Father will not use the method of force.[24] God gives

---

[22] *Op. cit.*, p. 427.   [23] *Op. cit.*, pp. 427 f.

[24] *Op. cit.*, p. 431: "Its power and strength *are* there, active in the teaching and miracles of Jesus; *all* its strength, powerful enough to break down all obstacles. But it strikes against obstacles which Jesus and His Father do not wish to break down with the weapons of power. Therefore the 'little flock' must have patience still and wait in the midst of the old oppression, the old order of things, must still 'wait for the kingdom of God' as they did of old (Lk. XXIII. 51). And yet everyone

Him the new Father-mission, the servant-mission, which God
wants to have executed by Him in the present. Billing does
not attempt to relate these two thoughts to the changing
moods of different moments, "they constitute together the
incomparably calm and unshakable certainty which characterise all His action."[25]   With the divine power which is
vested in Jesus, the Kingdom of God is here, and with the
exercise thereof the Dominion of God moves victoriously
forward.   But the advance of the Kingdom is so greatly obstructed that its presence can be set in question: has Jesus
really the power of God, when so little is done? It requires
faith in Jesus to cling firmly to the knowledge that the power
of God was advanced through the Father-mission, the seeking
out and gathering together, with which He as spiritual guide
was entrusted.   To this faith the parables of the Mustard-
seed and the Leaven and the three Sowing parables testify,
all of which say that here there must be no intervention by
force; we have only to wait and let the forces of the Kingdom
work in secret.

The Kingdom of God and His righteousness belong indissolubly together (Mt. VI. 33), but to Billing it is not the ethical
element that is the essence of the Kingdom in the mind of
Jesus.   The essence is the religious element, the actual communion with God, which is represented as the highest and
central value.   Here the dominant consideration is what the
Kingdom of God gives to the individual.

Jesus' mission to His people meant not judgment but
salvation, not law but gospel.   The nearness of the Kingdom
meant indeed the nearness of the Judgment, for Jesus shared
with John the Baptist the certainty that if the intervention
of God came now, this would mean for the people not salvation
but judgment; but the forces of salvation were active in the
Father-mission Jesus performed as the serving Son of Man.
Jesus stood there as guarantor that he who reaches after the
Kingdom of God shall find it; even if entry into the Kingdom
belongs to the future, it can be received already here and

---

has it already who will only gird up his strength like a βιαστής and gather it to
him, who will understand how to receive like a child what the Father lays in his
lap—he is a υἱὸς τῆς βασιλείας (Mt. VIII. 12, XIII. 38), he has its riches, he has its
authority."
[25] *Ibid.*

now (Mk. x. 15). In Jesus, as Billing represents Him, extreme severity in His demands is combined with an equally unlimited grace. What applies to the conception of God, applies equally to Jesus' conception of the Kingdom of God, where the same tension exists between law and gospel.

XI

Philosophical Modifications of the Kingdom of God

The Interpretation of the Kingdom of God by Dialectical Theology

Albert Schweitzer admitted of no other eschatology in the mind of Jesus than expectation of the, in a purely futuristic sense, imminently impending final miracle and transformation of the world. This "expectation of the imminent end" was doomed to perish, since in the first place it had proved to be a mistake, for the Parousia had not come, and in the second it was so out of date that the modern mind could not accept it. All through the history of Christianity, in fact, a progressive "de-eschatologisation" had been taking place. This had now been brought to its logical conclusion by means of the consistently eschatological interpretation of the Jesus of the New Testament.

But the question now arises: If the Kingdom of God is neither in the human heart (Harnack), nor the goal for the cultural development of all humanity ("Social Gospel," etc.), is one then obliged to regard it, with Schweitzer, as the final miracle in a purely cosmic sense? Is there no fourth alternative? Or, to put it another way: Is there no other solution to the question of an eschatological interpretation of the Kingdom of God than that provided by so-called "consistent" eschatology? To this question, forced upon us by Schweitzer, dialectical theology had a reply which enabled eschatology to come into its own. It argued that, in view of the frequent occurrence of eschatological utterances in early Christianity, it was impossible to regard eschatology as just a troublesome "foreign body." It contained, on the contrary, the heart and core of Christianity. When "crisis" theology emerged at the beginning of the nineteen-twenties, it started off a reaction to de-eschatologisation, and the renaissance of eschatology had begun.

To discuss the causes of this renaissance would take us outside the framework of the present study. So much may, however, be said, that they were not entirely theological in nature but must be sought in a wider field. During the First World War belief in progress had received a mortal blow. Now we met with opinions such as this: "The rise of mankind towards the Kingdom of God, in the sense of moving to higher and ever higher levels, is an idea we do not entertain any longer. At all events, not if we are in our right minds."[1]

New Testament eschatology received new life. Christianity was eschatology. The New Testament was eschatological throughout.[2] Karl Barth declared: "If Christianity be not altogether restless eschatology, there remains in it no relationship whatever with Christ."[3] But what does this eschatological interpretation of Christianity mean to the understanding of the Kingdom of God?

When Barth speaks of the Kingdom "come nigh,"[4] and says that we are dreamers if we believe that the future of the Lord is not immediately outside the threshold,[5] he does not regard the Kingdom of God as the end of time and the coming transformation of the world. He will have nothing to do with any end of time. "The end proclaimed in the New Testament" is not anything temporal; it is wholly unrelated to any historical or cosmic catastrophe. It is "really the *end*, so much the end that the nineteen hundred years mean not merely little but *nothing* at all in relation to its nearness or farness, so much the end that even Abraham saw this day and rejoiced at it."[6]

---

[1] E. Thurneysen, "Christus und seine Zukunft, Ein Beitrag zur Eschatologie," in *Zwischen den Zeiten*, IX (1931), p. 200.

[2] In *Die Letzten Dinge, Entwurf einer christlichen Eschatologie*, Gütersloh 1922, 3rd edn. 1926, P. Althaus says (p. 3): "One reads the New Testament naturally in an eschatological sense." "The New Testament is eschatological through and through," says E. Brunner, *Die Mystik und das Wort, Der Gegensatz zwischen moderner Religionsauffassung und christlichen Glauben dargestellt an der Theologie Schleiermachers*, Tübingen 1924, 2nd edn. 1928, p. 258.

[3] K. Barth, *Der Römerbrief*, 1919; 2nd edn. Munich 1922, p. 298; Eng. version: *The Epistle to the Romans*, trans. E. C. Hoskyns, Oxford 1933, p. 314.

[4] *Op. cit.*, (Eng. trans.), p. 30.

[5] K. Barth, *Das Wort Gottes und die Theologie. Gesammelte Vorträge*, VOL. I. Munich 1925, p. 172.

[6] K. Barth, *Die Auferstehung der Toten. Eine akademische Vorlesung über I. Kor.* 15, Munich 1924, 2nd edn. 1926, p. 59.

"End history" must not be confused with "final history."
Of real "end history" it can be said at any time: The end is
near. The ultimate things are no longer conceived of as the
last. Hope for the future loses its futuristic goal. The Kingdom of God is eternity, before which man stands. To await
the Parousia and the Kingdom of God is to recognise the
seriousness of one's actual position.[7] Eternity becomes the
symbol for the presence of the supra-temporal in the now.
The Kingdom of God is no longer something actually impending in the future. It is always coming and always present.
It is transformed into a symbol for the always urgent relationship with God. Expectation of the closely impending end
serves as the force which impels mankind into existential
seriousness in face of the absolute. Thus mankind lives in the
shadow of the Day of Jesus which, though not yet come, is
endlessly near. "At the *frontier* of all time, before the over-
hanging wall of God, which signifies the *abolition* of all time
and all content of time, stands the man of the 'last hour,'
the man who awaits the Parousia of Jesus Christ."[8]

Eschatological, according to Barth, is that which is " 'related
to the ἔσχατον,' *i.e.* to what from our point of view is still in
arrears for our experience and thought, to the eternal reality
of the divine fulfilment and completion."[9] As Barth has
abandoned the continuous conception of time, this fulfilment
and accomplishment is not conceived as something that lies
along a sequence of time; fulfilment is the relation of the
present moment to eternity. Eternity does not lie at the end
of the time-sequence, but limits and qualifies it all along its
length; it is beyond all time and is the uttermost, fundamental
reality. The statement: the Kingdom of God is near, is not
regarded as indicating time, but the Kingdom is near in the
sense of the eternity which is above all time. The Kingdom
of God is just as near at any time, for every time is the uttermost
time. It is, therefore, true to say of every moment: The
Kingdom of God is near. But this is never understood as a
nearness in time, but "imminent expectation consists to him
(K. Barth) in the transcendental relationship of the now to

---

[7] *Epistle to the Romans*, p. 501.

[8] *Op. cit.*, p. 484.

[9] K. Barth, *Die kirchliche Dogmatik*, VOL. I, PT. I, *Die Lehre vom Worte Gottes.
Prolegomena zur kirchlichen Dogmatik*, Munich 1932, pp. 486 f. Eng. version: *Church
Dogmatics*, VOL. I, PT. I, trans. G. T. Thomson, Edinburgh 1936, pp. 530 f.

its origin in eternity."[10]   The Kingdom of God becomes here
eternity conceived as a metaphysical opposite to time.   The
Kingdom of God cannot then irrupt in time without at the
same time becoming dialectically annulled.   But with this
attitude waiting is also done away with.   The eschatological
tension is dissolved.   "The tense expectancy must be dissipated
and dissolved, when *the Parousia possesses reality merely as a
timeless symbol for the endless and eternal gravity inherent in every
existential situation*—and does not mean the certainty that the
decree of God shall some time in an inevitable future become
definitive, that the period of grace has a fixed temporal limit"
(Folke Holmström).[11]   Barthian theology, in which eternity
can never become time, but always begins where time ceases,
and which therefore does not admit of any, in the temporal
futuristic sense, end of time, possesses indeed an eschatology
but no *future* hope.[12]

What, then, is Jesus' relationship to the Kingdom of God
as Barth sees it?   He says that in Jesus Christ the Kingdom of
God has come as close as it can come, so long as time has not
become eternity.   This does not mean that the Kingdom of
God and its forces are actually present in Jesus, but that Jesus
represents the dividing line between the irreconcilably separated worlds of time and eternity.   "The name Jesus defines
an historical occurrence and marks the point where the unknown world cuts the known world."[13]   But the break-through
of eternity in time is to time merely as the touching of a circle
by a tangent at a single point.   What touches us in Jesus Christ,
when He does not touch us—that is the Kingdom of God.[14]
The Kingdom of God is thus not actually present in Jesus,
but in Jesus we are placed in direct existential relation to the
eternal.   The realism of the Gospel in regarding Jesus as the
Messiah vanishes when Barth regards the Kingdom of God
neither as standing on the threshold in a purely temporal
sense nor as having already come in Jesus Christ, who in
Himself incarnates the Kingdom of God.   Dialectical theology
does not in this way give Jesus the unique position which the

---

[10] Buri, *Die Bedeutung der neutestamentliche Eschatologie*, p. 44.

[11] Holmström, *Eskatologiska motivet*, p. 239.

[12] O. Michel, "Unser Ringen um die Eschatologie," in *Z.Th.K.*, 1932, p. 158.
See also Holmström, *Eskatologiska motivet*, p. 329, n. 2.

[13] Barth, *Epistle to the Romans*, p. 29.

[14] *Op. cit.*, p. 30.

New Testament gives Him. For the Kingdom of God to be present in Jesus does not mean that we are constantly being set face to face over and over again with the eternal, but in the New Testament Christ is the "centre" of history, and we await completion of that which is already on foot, for we await the coming of the Son of Man and the establishment of the Kingdom of God in glory in time. When the New Testament speaks of these things, it does so in temporal realistic terms, but supra-historical eschatology provides a demythologisation and reinterpretation in which their place is taken by timeless abstract ideas. "Eschatological" comes to mean that which has the nature of eternity, but not that which shall some day actually appear in time on the day of fulfilment. "The eschatology of the history of salvation is shattered by the dialectic of the idea of eternity" (H. E. Weber).[15]

It has, of course, been impossible in this brief account to mention the various developments which have taken place in Barth's theological thought. The basic idea would seem, however, to be and remain the same. He has made a serious attempt to work out an eschatological interpretation of Christianity, emphasising the eternal nature of the Kingdom of God, but has lost the eschatological hope for the future.

Karl-Ludwig Schmidt's[16] interpretation of the Kingdom of God is strongly influenced by dialectical theology. The Kingdom of God is defined negatively as "something opposed to everything that is here and now, everything present and earthly, thus something absolutely *miraculous*," and positively as "a *cosmic catastrophe*."[17] The Kingdom of God is the supra-worldly, that which is opposed to everything that belongs to this earth. Its realisation belongs entirely to the future. But man determines this future in his present. The Kingdom of God is "the end of man," but not his death, for when he

[15] Weber, "Die Kirche im Lichte der Eschatologie," p. 326. Weber was a pupil of Martin Kähler, who emphasised the redemptory aspects of the New Testament.

[16] Karl-Ludwig Schmidt's chief contributions to the interpretation of the Kingdom of God are: "Jesus Christus," in *R.G.G.*, 2nd edn. 1929, pp. 110-51; "βασιλεύς" in *Th.W.B.N.T.*, VOL. I, pp. 579-92; "Das überweltliche Reich Gottes in der Verkündigung Jesu," in *Th.Bl.*, 1927, pp. 118-20; *Le Problème du christianisme primitif, Quatre conférences sur la forme et la pensée du Nouveau Testament*, Paris 1938; "Das Christuszeugnis der synoptischen Evangelien," in *Jesus Christus im Zeugnis der Heiligen Schrift und der Kirche*, 1936, pp. 7-33.

[17] Schmidt, "Jesus Christus," pp. 129 f. The definitions of the Kingdom of God are repeated without great variation in all the articles referred to.

follows the call to the Kingdom of God and repents, the Gospel becomes for him the glad tidings. "At the end of man" the Dominion of God is salvation and joy, the glad tidings.

We are told of the heightened relationship between the Kingdom of God and Jesus Himself, but all the decisive sayings about a Kingdom of God present in Jesus as Son of Man (Mt. XII. 28, XI. I ff., and others) are either completely disregarded or else mentioned without any explanation being offered as to how this relationship is understood in the saying in question. The miracles become signs that the Kingdom of God is near and will soon come. But to Schmidt, as to dialectical theology in general, there can be no question of any coming of the Kingdom of God in time, and what was said above about the interpretation of the Kingdom of God by this movement applies again here.

Next to Karl Barth's, the most important name in this new eschatological movement is that of Paul Althaus, author of a monograph which considerably influenced the theological discussion.[18] Even if Althaus is critically disposed towards Barth and differs from him on a number of points, he too is obliged, when it comes to freeing the current belief in eternity from its temporal-historical trappings, to sacrifice everything to do with "end of the world" eschatology. Althaus pays no attention to the fact that what the New Testament expected was a future world transformation. To him the early Christian expectation of the impending end is nothing but a limitation imposed by temporal history. His interpretation of early Christian eschatology is a modification.

Emil Brunner,[19] with his realisation that Jesus saw Himself as the one in whom the Dominion of God, the beyond, "the other," was present, is able to see the coming of the Kingdom of God more in accordance with Bible realism. The old question whether the Kingdom of God is transcendent or immanent is answered in the light of the fact that Jesus, the Messiah, the Son, is the transcendent and coming Kingdom. But in framing his eschatology Brunner nevertheless conceived

[18] Althaus, *Die letzten Dinge*. The various editions of 1922, 1924, 1926, and 1933 show considerable modifications. In the last the playing down of the "end of the world" has been considerably reduced.

[19] E. Brunner, *Der Mittler. Zur besinnungüber den Christusglauben*, Tübingen 1927, 2nd edn. 1930, pp. 381 ff. Eng. version: *The Mediator*, trans. O. Wym, 6th imp., London 1949, pp. 548 ff.

K

the transcendent Kingdom in such a supra-temporal way that the futurist aspect of the Kingdom as coming in time is altogether lost.[20]

Rudolf Bultmann

Among dialectical theologians the most important interpreter of the Kingdom of God, from an exegetic point of view, is Rudolf Bultmann, one of the pioneers of the school of form criticism. He follows the radically critical tradition that runs from Strauss through Wrede, Wellhausen, and Bousset, his study of Jesus published in 1926[21] being perhaps the last publication in this tradition.

Bultmann, who began his theological career as a pupil of Wilhelm Herrmann and E. Troeltsch, was still unable in 1917 to find anything vital to our age in New Testament eschatology. His attitude then was: Even if the Kingdom of God was the centre-point in the mind of Jesus, His significance still does not rest upon the fact that He was an eschatologist.[22] Bultmann's conversion to a new understanding of eschatology took place under the influence of Karl Barth, F. Gogarten, and E. Thurneysen. His philosophical outlook was coloured by the influence of the Marburg school and its Neo-Kantianism (H. Cohen). From 1927 onwards the Existentialist philosopher Martin Heidegger began to determine Bultmann's philosophical attitude. This new influence, however, involved no modification at all in Bultmann's idea of Jesus as it had been revealed in 1921 and 1926,[23] and which remained essentially unchanged. The "dialectical" Christology which Bultmann championed in 1933[24] did not supplant the radical Gospel criticism and the picture of Jesus he gave in his Jesus study, but his aim throughout has been to show that the critical understanding of the Gospel and of the person of Jesus as it is revealed to us there, involves in itself a Christology, even

---

[20] Holmström, *Eskatologiska motivet*, p. 275.

[21] R. Bultmann, *Jesus* (Die Unsterblichen I), Berlin 1926; Eng. version: *Jesus and the Word*, trans. L. Pettibone Smith and E. Huntress, London 1935.

[22] R. Bultmann, "Die Bedeutung der Eschatologie für die Religion des Neuen Testaments," in *Z.Th.K.* xxvii (1917), p. 83.

[23] In *Die Geschichte der synoptischen Tradition*, Forschungen zur Religion und Literatur des Alten und Neuen Testaments, ed. R. Bultmann, N.F. vol. xii, Göttingen 1921, and *Jesus*, 1926.

[24] R. Bultmann, *Glauben und Verstehen, Gesammelte Aufsätze*, Tübingen 1933.

though there may have been no Christ-attitude and no Christ-consciousness in the historical Jesus.[25]

In view of the nature of the sources, says Bultmann, we cannot be too careful when we take upon ourselves to propound the teachings of Jesus, for what the sources give is the teaching of the early congregations about the risen Christ. Admittedly the congregations attributed the sayings to Jesus, but this by no means proves that sayings attributed to Him were actually spoken by Him. During that phase of the tradition which, for linguistic and factual reasons, can only have been formed in the Hellenic Church, the essential material is to be found in the Synoptics, which proves to have been handed down from the Aramaic tradition of the earliest Palestinian congregations. If one sifts out from this all that reveals specific congregational interest or shows signs of advanced development, one comes to the earliest phase, which of course can only be determined with relative certainty. There is no guarantee that the sayings in the earliest phase were actually spoken by Jesus, even though everything may go to show that He was the origin of the tradition. The earliest phase provides no clue to the personality of Jesus or anything of that sort, but it does give us a consistent picture of the *teaching* of Jesus, which is what interests Bultmann.[26] By far the greater part of the material, however, is classified by him as "congregational theology." His presentation of Jesus is now based on a selection of Jesus-Logia, detached from their context, and a number of the parables, whereas the narrative material is left almost entirely out of account. It is, however, not without a certain surprise that one discovers that, in his own book on Jesus, he relies very largely on material which has not passed through the severe purgatorial fires he himself advocates.[27]

Bultmann's account is presented as a "dialogue with

---

[25] After quoting Mt. XII. 6 and Lk. XII. 8 Bultmann says: "Such a call for decision in respect of His own person *implies a Christology*, though admittedly neither as speculation about a Heavenly Being nor as fabrication of a so-called Messiah consciousness" (*op. cit.*, p. 204). Cf. F. Büchsel, *Die Hauptfragen der Synoptikerkritik, Eine Auseinandersetzung mit R. Bultmann, M. Dibelius und ihren Vorgängern*, Beiträge zur Förderung christlicher Theologie, VOL. XL, No. 6, Gütersloh 1939, p. 9.

[26] "The *character* of Jesus, the clear image of His personality, is to us *no longer recognisable*. But what is more important: the content of His teaching, is or becomes ever more clearly recognisable." R. Bultmann, *Die Erforschung der synoptischen Evangelien*, Aus der Welt der Religion, Neutestamentliche Reihe, No. 1, 2nd edn., Giessen 1930, pp. 32 f.

[27] In *Die Geschichte der Synoptischen Tradition*.

history."[28] The exegetist must not merely reflect upon what is said, but try to penetrate through to what is meant, *i.e.* to the actual matter behind the historically coloured words. Bultmann is evidently anxious to free himself of history in order to preserve the spiritual reality. To get at this the student must adopt an attitude of "genuine question" in relation to the text, recognising that his own existence is lived on the same terms as that of the people of the Bible. What he has to do is to transfer the factual matter of the text from the thought-world of the past to that of the present. Here, of course, the exegetist's own philosophic and theological attitude plays an important part. The book on Jesus represents Bultmann's own encounter with history, which he then tries to reproduce in words and ideas. To him the will is the essential part of man, and his attention is therefore concentrated on "what he (Jesus) *purposed* and hence to what in his purpose as a part of history makes a present demand on us."[29] What Jesus *purposed* by His teaching we can find out, but of the person of Jesus we know practically nothing. The book about Jesus is therefore to a large extent a book without Jesus,[30] and brings strongly to mind the liberal interpretation of Jesus. Like Harnack, Bultmann divides the teaching of Jesus into three spheres, each moving round the same central point and all concerned with one and the same thing. These spheres are: (1) The coming of the Dominion of God; (2) The will of God; and (3) The remote and the near God. Jesus is presented throughout as the teacher of the religious faith of the Jews, radically regarded.

Bultmann emphasises strongly that the teaching of Jesus is entirely eschatological, *i.e.* a message that the fulfilment of the promise is at hand. The Dominion of God in the Jewish sense is about to be realised. Like Albert Schweitzer, Bultmann believes that Jesus expected the Dominion of God to begin at His death, for Jesus seems to have gone up to Jerusalem the last time with His group of exalted followers in the certainty that now the Kingdom of God was about to be established. He occupied the Temple with His faithful in order to purify it for the Dominion of God which was to come at any moment.

[28] Bultmann, *Jesus and the Word*, p. 4.

[29] *Op. cit.*, p. 8.

[30] E. Lohmeyer, Review of *Jesus* in *Th. Lz.*, 1927, p. 433: "It is in a certain sense a book about Jesus without Jesus."

To Jesus Himself and His disciples His mission was the sign that this was near. At the eleventh hour Jesus had been sent with the decisive word. God enjoined His claim on mankind, that the power was to be His. " 'For the sake of the Dominion of God' involves complete renunciation, brings every man face to face with the ultimate *Either-Or*. To decide for the Kingdom is to sacrifice for it all things else."[31] (The Treasure, the Pearl, Mt. v. 29 f.). The Kingdom of God is, according to Bultmann, primarily the *Dominion* of God, as the three first petitions of the Lord's Prayer show. The Dominion of God is recognised wherever God's name is hallowed, *i.e.* when God is recognised as God, and His will is done.[32]

When it comes to defining the idea of the Kingdom of God, Bultmann is definitely opposed to the liberal interpretation. It is meaningless, he says, to talk of the Dominion of God as the highest good and so forth. "The Kingdom of God is deliverance for men. It is that *eschatological* deliverance, which ends everything earthly. This deliverance is the only deliverance which can properly be so called."[33] The Kingdom of God is a supra-historical, supernatural entity, it is something miraculous, indeed it is quite simply the miraculous, "the altogether other" (R. Otto). Jesus rejected all apocalyptic speculation about the Kingdom, such as calculation of times and hours and seeking after signs.

But the most important of Bultmann's pronouncements is that the Dominion of God as a state did not interest Jesus at all, but only as the miraculous, supernatural, eschatological fact which for mankind means the great either-or, which *places mankind in the position of decision.*[34] Jesus' call to decision was a call to repentance, for most men cling to this world and do not throw all their energy into the decision for God. The summons to the Dominion of God makes demands on those who are called. They have to set the Kingdom before all else. What is needed is not a sixth sense with which to understand the signs of the end-time, but merely the readiness to hear the words of Jesus and obey them. The essential thing about man is to Bultmann simply this, that he stands at the moment of decision.

[31] Bultmann, *Jesus and the Word*, p. 31.
[32] Bultmann, Review of R. Otto, *Reich Gottes und Menschensohn*, in *Th.R.*, N.F., 1937, p. 9.
[33] Bultmann, *Jesus and the Word*, p. 35.　　　　[34] *Op. cit.*, pp. 40 f.

He now gives his solution to the problem of the future and presence of the Kingdom of God along these same lines. The Dominion of God, according to him, is not something which comes at the end of time, but it is a power which, although entirely future, completely dominates the present because it forces mankind to a decision.[35] Here all chronological considerations vanish. At the point of decision mankind is *always* at the eleventh hour. The Dominion of God makes claims on human existence at the present moment and demands repentance, decision, and radical obedience to the will of God. This element of immediacy, that the Dominion of God is coming *now*, is the only thing that distinguishes Jesus' conception of the Dominion of God from that which was current in Judaism.

Bultmann's interpretation of the Kingdom of God is one-sidedly in terms of will. God is personal will, which has claims on man. God is perceived through will and not through any mysterious intuition. Thus Bultmann can say: "Jesus knows only one attitude toward God—*obedience*. Since he sees man standing at the point of decision, the essential part of man is for him the will, the free act. . . . For on will, on free act, depends man's existence as a unit, as a whole."[36]

It is quite beyond question, Bultmann considers, that Jesus belongs together with the Kingdom of God. But how? By analysis of the Gospel tradition Bultmann believes he is able to distinguish an earliest phase, going right back to Jesus, which does not regard Jesus as the Messiah either in the present or in the future. Jesus did not give Himself out to be the Messiah. Actually, for that matter, it is immaterial whether Jesus regarded Himself as the Messiah or not. If Jesus did regard Himself as the Messiah, that would mean that He subscribed to a contemporary Jewish idea. And in Bultmann's opinion it is of no significance whether Jesus used the Jewish title Messiah—Son of Man to express His mission or not. "Whether He knew Himself as the Messiah or not is of no account. It would merely mean that He made use of a contemporary Jewish idea to express the demand for decision that was the purpose of His mission."[37] The call to decision implies in itself a Christology which is neither metaphysical

---

[35] *Op. cit.*, p. 51.
[36] *Op. cit.*, p. 48.
[37] *Glauben und Verstehen*, pp. 265 f.

speculation over a heavenly being nor a character-sketch of a personality possibly with a Messiah-consciousness, but a Christology which consists in preaching, address.[38]   Jesus formulated no teaching about His person, but He taught that the fact that He was now active was decisive.   Mankind had to make up its mind in face of the message He preached, not of Him Himself.   It was His bringing the prophetic message at the decisive hour that was unprecedented.   Not *what* He preached, but *that* He preached, was crucial.[39]

According to Bultmann Jesus saw Himself as the prophet of the dawning eschatological age.   The eleventh hour had come.   Jesus presented mankind with the final decision before God.   He knew Himself to be the tool of the victorious force of the coming Kingdom, He demanded recognition for Himself and His word, He knew that the spirit was active through and in His mission.   But all this indicates no more than a "prophetic consciousness."   Even where Jesus spoke of the Son of Man, one has to question whether He meant Himself, for in certain sayings it is quite clear that He drew a distinction between His person and the Son of Man (*e.g.* Mk. viii. 38).

Jesus considered the essence of His teaching to be that He assured mankind of the forgiveness of God in the word and only in the word.   Jesus, therefore, wished to be regarded as "bearer of the word," bearer of the word of forgiveness from God.[40]

As already mentioned, Bultmann tried to throw off history in order to concentrate on the spiritual reality.   The concrete religious ideas are contemporary expressions which Jesus used in order to make clear what He actually meant.   The concrete

---

[38] "What, then, is *Christology*?   It is not the theoretical exponent of practical piety, it is not speculation and teaching about the divine Being of Christ, but it is *annunciation, address*" (*op. cit.*, p. 260).

[39] "Jesus of course appeared purely humanly as a prophet and a teacher.   He put forward no teaching about His person, but He said that the fact of His activity was the decisive thing.   His teaching was not new in its thought content; for its content was nothing else but pure Hebraism, pure '*prophetismus.*'   But the fact that He said it *now*, at the final, crucial moment, that was the tremendous thing.   Not the 'What,' but the 'That,' of His teaching was the decisive thing" (*op. cit.*, p. 265). See also *op. cit.*, p. 174.

[40] "Jesus is therefore the bearer of the word, and in the word He assures man of the forgiveness of God" (*Jesus and the Word*, p. 217).   "Jesus put forward no teaching about His person; though He stressed the fact of His person as important, indeed decisive, in so far as He claimed to be the bearer of the decisive word of God at the last hour" (*Glauben und Verstehen*, p. 204).

Bultmann now regards as myth, according to his own definition:[41] "Mythological is used here in the sense in which it is understood in the study of the history of religion. Mythological is the method of presentation whereby the unworldly, the divine is shown as worldly, human, the beyond as of this side."[42] It is no use enquiring after the content of the New Testament ideas, if one wants to arrive at the truth concealed in them, but after "the comprehension of existence expressed in these ideas."[43] In order to achieve this end and bring out clearly this comprehension of existence, Bultmann carries out a demythologisation of Christianity. This demythologisation, a process Bultmann describes in full in the above-mentioned work, he had already applied to the Fourth Gospel in his big commentary, in which the Evangelist himself plays the part of the extraordinarily skilful theologian who had demythologised the basic gnostic myth in order, as a dialectical theologian, to give it dialectical form. The same method is used again in the book on Jesus, where Bultmann divests Jesus' teaching of the Kingdom of God of its historical garb in order to bring out the non-temporal, non-historical meaning in the "myth." This process, according to Bultmann, is necessary because mythological eschatology was invalidated when the hoped-for Parousia failed to appear, but world history went on as before.[44]

Bultmann asserts in his book on Jesus that Jesus' eschatological message, the teaching of the Kingdom of God and the call to repentance can only be properly understood if one bears in mind the conception of man that lies behind it. One must also be prepared to question the current idea of man one holds, *i.e.* the view one holds of oneself, and to measure this according to the interpretation of human existence one finds in Jesus. One must not let oneself be side-tracked by the historical

[41] In "Neues Testament und Mythologie, Das Problem der Entmythologisierung der neutestamentlichen Verkündigung," one of two essays that make up *Offenbarung und Heilgeschehen*, Beiträge zur Evangelischen Theologie, Theologische Abhandlungen, ed. E. Wolf, VOL. VII, Munich 1941.

[42] Bultmann, *op. cit.*, p. 36, n. 20.

[43] *Op. cit.*, p. 36. For criticism of Bultmann's "demythologisation" see R. Prenter, "Evangeliets afmytologisering," in *S.T.K.*, 1946, pp. 89-108; P. Althaus, "Neues Testament und Mythologie. Zu R. Bultmanns Versuch der Entmythologisierung des Neuen Testaments," in *Th.Lz.*, 1942, pp. 337-44; E. Thestrup Pedersen, "Kristendommens Afmytologisering og Forkyndelsen," in *Dansk Teologisk Tidskrift*, VII (1945), pp. 193-222.

[44] Bultmann, *Offenbarung und Heilsgeschehen*, p. 31.

mythology which is merely the outward expression of what Jesus really meant. The mythology falls away from the basic attitude it covers: the conception of man as he stands at the moment of decision in face of God's coming act. Bultmann regards as part of this mythology the expectation of the end coming in time.[45]

This "comprehension of existence" on which Bultmann bases everything is not acquired by an historical analysis of the sources, but arises from philosophical and theological reasoning. The "comprehension of existence" in the New Testament cannot, however, be detached from its "mythological" wrappings and made the essential part of the Gospel without misrepresenting Jesus' idea of the Kingdom of God. Demythologisation is achieved at altogether too high a price: the Kingdom of God is no longer the object of real hope, it ceases to be in any real sense futuristic, and at the same time it loses its quality of being something absolutely unlike anything else.

If expectation of the Kingdom of God is represented as a continual decision, the coming of the Kingdom of God cannot, of course, be an event in time. When Bultmann nevertheless speaks of the Kingdom of God as purely future, this is illogical, for the future stripped of its time character is no future.[46] The coming fulfilment is actually future. It is something coming in time. And when it is said that the Kingdom of God is near, it is not enough to say that it is near as a power which demands decision.

When Bultmann looks for a parallel to what he means when he says that God is the God of the present and at the same time the God of the future, he is driven back on death. The Kingdom of God is to the whole world what death is to the individual. Since death is always coming, it is always already present and throws its shadow over every moment of life. *Media in vita in morte sumus.* But to this we can only reply that death is an actual temporal end to human life, consequently it is not something that remains future to all eternity.[47]

[45] *Jesus and the Word*, pp. 55 f.
[46] O. Cullmann, *Christ and Time*, p. 53, n. 5.
[47] Kümmel, *Promise and Fulfilment*, p. 148, says of Bultmann's "demythologisa-tion": "It would mean that the New Testament message itself is abrogated if a timeless message concerning the present as the time of decision or concerning the

The effect of the sort of demythologisation practised by Bultmann is to replace eschatology by an ethical teaching centred in the demand for a decision. Eschatology becomes nothing more nor less than disguised ethic, and the whole interpretation of Jesus becomes ethicised throughout.[48] The views of Bultmann the dialectician and existential philosopher are not so fundamentally different from those of Bultmann the pupil of Herrmann in 1917. However strongly it may be emphasised that the teaching of Jesus is eschatological, the eschatology disappears if the futuristic aspect is not allowed free play.[49]

Even the idea of man being placed in the moment of decision gives rise to serious objections. It is obvious, of course, that the Kingdom of God demands decision. Man does not dispose over the future. But when Bultmann regards every moment of decision as something essentially new and man as being in absolute uncertainty as to when he has to decide, does not this fragmentation render any ethical action absolutely impossible?[50]

Besides, the Kingdom of God which is the object of decision is emptied of its content and transformed into the eternal or eternity, which rests above time without ever entering into

---

spiritual nearness of God replaces the preaching of the eschatological future and the determination of the present by that future. For this would result in a complete disintegration of Jesus' message that man through Jesus' appearance in the present is placed in a definite situation in the *history* of salvation advancing towards the end, and the figure and activity of Jesus would lose their fundamental character as the *historical* activity of the God who wishes to lead his Kingdom upwards. Therefore it is impossible to eliminate the concept of time and with it the 'futurist' eschatology from the eschatological message of Jesus (and from the New Testament altogether)." Holmström, *Eskatologiska motivet*, p. 432, points out that Bultmann, through the strong emphasis he places on the actual presence of God, throws eschatology into a looser relationship with historical time itself. "The idea of the end becomes merely a symbol for the nearness of God projected into the future." Eschatology here becomes a temporal symbol for the existential earnest.

[48] Th. Siegfried, *Das Wort und die Existenz, Eine Auseinandersetzung mit der dialektischen Theologie*, VOL. II, *Die Theologie der Existenz bei Friedrich Gogarten und Rudolf Bultmann*, Gotha 1933, p. 108, says: "Bultmann's religion is in the most pregnant sense *ethicism*. This ethicism is reflected in Bultmann's basic conception throughout, that of decision."

[49] K. Heim, "Zeit und Ewigkeit, die Hauptfrage der heutigen Eschatologie," in *Z.Th.K.*, N.F. VII (1926), p. 415.

[50] Siegfried, *Das Wort und die Existenz*, p. 140, points out the influence on Bultmann of Hermann Cohen, *Ethik des reinen Willens*, 2nd edn., 1907, p. 386: "Decision in real life, in each individual act. . . . In each individual action there is a new beginning."

time. And apart from that, there are a number of things which have nothing at all to do with the Kingdom of God, about which man also has to make a decision. It is not enough to say that the important thing is *that* Jesus placed mankind in the necessity for a decision, when He preached the Kingdom of God. One can never get away from the actual content of the teaching, *i.e. what* it is that is the object of decision. The essence of this teaching is that the Kingdom of God was present in Jesus, who was thus not only the prophet of the Kingdom of God but had divine authority to bring God's salvation to the world.

Nor is it enough to make Jesus the "Bearer of the word." Bultmann does not, indeed, assert that the decision must be made in face of the word which Jesus preached, but the importance of the person of Jesus is clearly shown when he goes so far as to say: "Whether he was *sent* by God—that is the decision with which the hearer is confronted, and it rests on the words of Jesus: Blessed is he who is not offended in me."[51] When Bultmann, bound by the ideas of his critical predecessors, says that whether or not Jesus possessed a Messiah-consciousness is a question of little moment, which he is mainly inclined to answer along the lines that Jesus did not want to be Messiah, one can only say that he is under the influence of philosophical and theological ideas which have no basis in the Gospels.

Bultmann's interpretation of the Kingdom of God is an attempt to demythologise the Kingdom of God. The demythologisation has turned into a de-eschatologisation. The Kingdom of God becomes the word, which forces decision. The interpretation of Jesus becomes completely legalistic, while the message that the Kingdom of God is primarily gospel comes out too little. The most important criticism of the whole of this interpretation of Jesus would seem, however, to be that the Kingdom of God is never represented as really present in Jesus, and that the truly future character of the Kingdom is not established.[52]

---

[51] *Jesus*, p. 200. Brunner, *The Mediator*, p. 158, comments: "Here there emerges, still undefined, a new conception of 'person,' the Person of Christ, which is still more important than His teaching, because it is itself the Word."
[52] For criticism of Bultmann's theology see H. Eklund, "Theologie der Entscheidung. Zur Analyse und Kritik der 'existentiellen' Denkweise," in *Uppsala Universitets Årsskrift*, 1937, VOL. I, Lund 1937, pp. 101-39.

Ernst Lohmeyer

Between the two World Wars, philosophical ideas began to make themselves felt in exegetic theology in an altogether new way. The two foremost representatives of the school of form criticism, Rudolf Bultmann and Martin Dibelius, by no means despised the apparatus of philosophical ideas. The strongly philosophical element in the interpretation of the Kingdom of God by the dialectical school hardly needs mentioning, it is too well known. Few exegetists, however, have gone in so widely for philosophical speculation as Ernst Lohmeyer.

Lohmeyer would appear in many respects to have been influenced by dialectical theology, though he himself denies any influence by Karl Barth. Although unwilling to give up dualism he tries to feel his way forward to a synthesis. He uses critical idealism, with its conception of such ideas as truth, history, and time, as the instrument of his interpretation of early Christian theology.[53] His philosophical outlook so completely dominates his thought that it is often quite impossible to say where the purely exegetic interpretation ends and the philosophy begins. Philosophy is introduced even into purely philological passages. Lohmeyer also uses philosophical principles to demonstrate how all the images and sayings which Jesus used to preach the Kingdom of God, are necessary expressions of the eschatological situation in which Jesus stood.

Whereas Kant declared that one must act in such a way as to realise the Kingdom of God, which is something infinitely remote, so that a "what should be" requires an infinite succession of actions, Hegel asserted that a "what should be" which is not a "what is" is nothing. The Kingdom of God is therefore a "what is." Lohmeyer now follows up this thought. As an object of faith, says Lohmeyer, the Kingdom of God is a reality. Whatever one is convinced of, is also real. Whereas ordinary knowledge always and in principle remains within the system of "conditions," the very principle of faith is the unconditioned. Faith is the experience of the highest degree of certainty, which is entirely and in principle "unconditioned."

---

[53] F. K. Schumann, *Der Gottesgedanke und der Zerfall der Moderne*, Tübingen 1929, pp. 299 ff. and R. Bultmann, review of E. Lohmeyer, *Vom Begriff der religiösen Gemeinschaft*, in *Th.Bl.*, VI (1927), p. 70.

Faith experiences the unconditioned as the ultimate certainty of a particular kind. So that Lohmeyer can also say: "Faith is possible only *in* the system of conditionality; but it would not be faith, strong and sure of itself, if it could not disregard all conditions, experience God in complete detachment from the world."[54]

How can eternity enter into time, into the conditioned, without itself becoming "material"? It is with this question uppermost in his mind that Lohmeyer approaches the Gospel. He is driven into considerations of the theory of knowledge. How is knowledge of the Kingdom of God, the wholly "Unconditioned," possible at all? The answer is: We have knowledge through Jesus. Jesus and the Kingdom belong together, otherwise Jesus would have had no knowledge of it. But just because in Jesus we have certainty of the Kingdom of God, we have the Kingdom itself. The answer to the question, how can we have knowledge of the Kingdom of God, the Unconditioned, the Eternal, is that the Son of Man enters into time and therewith abolishes time itself.

Actually all the sayings of Jesus speak of "the Kingship and Kingdom of God."[55] Every word and deed of His was inspired by the knowledge: "The Kingdom of God has come near." Jesus, however, never gave any reason for this certainty. He simply said: "I am come." The basis of all His preaching was thus the preacher himself. Faith in its purest form requires this. The bearer of the teaching must at the same time be "the essence of the truth and its historical embodiment."[56] Jesus knew, or more correctly believed, Himself to be He who embodies the faith and the Kingdom of God.[57] Jesus is the religious truth (Mt. XI. 3 ff.). There is never anything to suggest that the message of Jesus would have been possible

[54] E. Lohmeyer, *Vom Begriff der religiösen Gemeinschaft. Eine problemgeschichtliche Untersuchung über die Grundlagen des Urchristentums*, henceforth cited as *Begriff der Gemeinschaft*, Wissenschaftliche Grundfragen, ed. R. Hönigswald, VOL. III, Leipzig and Berlin 1925, p. 23.

[55] E. Lohmeyer, "Vom Sinn der Gleichnisse Jesu," in *Zeitschrift für systematische Theologie*, XV (1938), pp. 328 f.

[56] Lohmeyer, *Begriff der Gemeinschaft*, p. 26. "The prophet remains ever a rabbi, teaching and learning from the holy storehouse of his people, and ever there speaks through him another who has learnt from no one, who in the deeper sense untaught is the absolute authority and the complete content of his own words" "Der Begriff der Erlösung im Urchristentum," in *Deutsche Theologie*; VOL. II, *Der Erlösungsgedanke*, Göttingen 1928, p. 27.

[57] Lohmeyer, *Begriff der Gemeinschaft*, p. 27.

without Him. If that were possible, it would mean that His message was purely theoretical and was included in the system of "conditions of knowledge." He who preaches the Kingdom of God belongs to this Kingdom, is of its nature. Lohmeyer believes that, for knowledge to be possible, there must be an identity between subject and object, *i.e.* here between Jesus and the Kingdom of God. If this Kingdom is "the strangest to man and the most peculiar to God,"[58] then its preacher is also characterised by this divine being. Jesus as a teacher is a rabbi who has learnt and learns from the sacred resources of His people, but there always speaks through His words another who has learnt from no one, who is the absolute authority and who Himself is the whole content of the words He speaks.

Jesus indeed preached the Kingdom of God as an event in time, which His own will see, yet the nearness of the Kingdom of God shall nevertheless put an end to all time and all history. This is expressed paradoxically in the form that the Kingdom of God comes from a sphere which never comprised any time, to a sphere in which time shall no longer be comprised. The content of faith, the very Kingdom of God, is never historical. The Kingdom of God is the complete opposite of all historical life and work. This is to Lohmeyer synonymous with the "end character" of the Kingdom. The Kingdom of God as the Eternal is the "end" of all things, just as in dialectical theology. This "end character" of the Kingdom is most clearly expressed in the idea of the "Son of Manhood" of its bearer.[59] In the Son of Man, to everyone who believes in Him, the Kingdom of God has come. The Kingdom is, as we have already said, according to Lohmeyer, real simply when one believes in it, and in order to believe in the Kingdom, one must believe in the preacher of the Kingdom, as the two belong inseparably together.

That the Kingdom of God is present cannot, from this point of view, mean that it is something "becoming in time," since from the religious point of view there is no "idea of becoming."[60] No, the Kingdom of God is something enduring, something real for all times and therefore also something that is real outside all time. It is timeless.

---

[58] Lohmeyer, "Der Begriff der Erlösung im Urchristentum," p. 26.
[59] *Op. cit.*, p. 29.   [60] *Begriff der Gemeinschaft*, p. 24.

How, then, does Lohmeyer solve the problem of the relationship between the presence and future of the Kingdom of God? Future and present cannot be separated from one another, they are both expressions of the timeless facticity of the idea of the Kingdom of God. To speak of the coming of the Kingdom of God involves speaking of its presence and vice versa. "'The Kingdom of God' is always here and always near. For this duality of its time relationship is the necessary expression of a religiously determined timelessness, which is inherent in the idea of it."[61] Thus the eschatological character of the Kingdom of God means that it relates to two different spheres of time, which are comprehended in a religious unity, but also that it is the "end" of time. That future definitions preponderate with Jesus is due not merely to a number of specific historical circumstances, but chiefly to the fact that "this futurity is rooted in the idea of working for the Kingdom."[62]

Because time and eternity are thought of as absolutely opposed metaphysical spheres, there is an unbridgeable gulf between the Kingdom of God and the world. The ultimate reason for the opposition between the historically conditioned and the divine kingdom lies in the natural quality of human existence, or to express it mythically, in the demoniac dependence of existence.[63] When the Kingdom of God comes, the power of the demons will be crushed. But He who overcomes them must have metaphysical forces at His disposal, forces which are not historically comprehensible but divinely incomprehensible. He who hurls Satan from heaven is the Son of Man, who is of heaven but at the same time not of it, but is He who lives among His people as a rabbi, who takes to Himself the poor and heavy-burdened. Starting from this basis Lohmeyer proceeds, both in his commentary on St Mark and again in his last work,[64] to determine the two Messianic traditions which on the one hand found expression in the concept of the Son of Man, on the other in that of the Servant of God and Son of David. So far as I can understand, here again the contrast between the conditioned and the unconditioned forms the basis of the interpretation.

---

[61] *Op. cit.*, p. 31.
[62] *Op. cit.*, p. 30.
[63] "Der Begriff der Erlösung im Urchristentum," p. 27.
[64] *Das Evangelium des Markus* (Meyers Kommentar), VOL. I, 10th edn., Göttingen 1937, and *Gottesknecht und Davidsohn*, Symbolae Bibl., Ups. 5, Västervik 1945.

How, then, is the eternal to be realised? The answer, as
Lohmeyer gives it, is that this is done in the cultus, through
which the Kingdom of God is saved from being transformed
into merely a timeless idea. The very essence of the Gospel
is concentrated in Jesus' Last Supper with the disciples.[65]
Lohmeyer is not content with this, however, but sets out to
investigate the attitude of Jesus towards the cultus, in Judaism
and in relation to the Kingdom of God. The work he published in 1942[66] sets forth his view on these questions in their
entirety.

The way he translates ἡ βασιλεία τοῦ Θεοῦ always provides
a certain clue to a scholar's affiliations. Lohmeyer has no
fixed practice. In his earlier writings he often translates
the term as "Reich Gottes" ("Kingdom of God"); in the Mark
commentary he changes his translation at Mk. ix. 1. Up to
that point he uses "Königtum Gottes," but from then on consistently "Reich Gottes"; while in 1942 he states that "Gottesreich" is the best translation.[67] In his last work he returns to
"Königtum." He is against the translation "Gottesherrschaft"
("Dominion, sovereignty, of God,") for whatever may have been
the case with the Aramaic word, the Greek word βασιλεία
implies an entity determined in space and time and not a
function of God, as is shown beyond doubt by such expressions
as: enter into the Kingdom of God, be cast out or shut out
from, sit at table in, the Kingdom of God, the giving of the
keys of the Kingdom of Heaven to Peter. The Kingdom of
God is thus "the House or the City of God"[68] and its opposite
pole is the house or city of Satan (Mt. x. 25). This emphasis
on the Kingdom of God being the house or city of God inevitably also establishes the cultic nature of the Kingdom.

In Israel the expression "City of God" or "House of God"
was connected with the Temple, which was the place of God's
kingly power, where His accession to the throne was celebrated

---

[65] Lohmeyer has gone deeply into the question of the Communion. See, for
example, "Vom urchristlichen Abendmahl," in Th. R., n.f. ix (1937), pp. 168-227,
273-312, and Th.R., x (1938), pp. 81-99, 218-22. A short summary is given in
S.T.K., xiv (1938), pp. 302-10. With regard to Jesus and the cult see "Die
Reinigung des Tempels," in Th.Bl., xx (1941), pp. 257-64, and "Das Gleichnis
von den bösen Weingärtnern," in Zeitschrift für systematische Theologie, xviii (1941),
pp. 243-59.

[66] Kultus und Evangelium, Göttingen 1942. Eng. version: Lord of the Temple,
trans. Stuart Todd, Edinburgh 1961.

[67] Op. cit.   [68] Op. cit., p. 63.

in hope of His eschatological Dominion some day.   The cultic
thoroth d'entrée which appeared in the Temple were the models
for Jesus' sayings about entering into the Kingdom of God.
But the restriction to Israel is abandoned.   People stream from
all quarters to the House of God of which Jesus speaks.   To
the objection that this is only a figure of speech, Lohmeyer
gives his usual reply, that in the case of an eschatological
message figures and parables are the only possible form.

As the Temple in the Old Testament was the House in which
God rules and judges and where He is served, so the Kingdom
of God in the New Testament is also that house.   But whereas
the House of God in the Old Testament is associated with
a definite place, the Kingdom of God is the eternal place
where God shall dwell with His faithful.   Here all historical
frontiers are down.   Another decisive difference is that the
priestly function is lacking here.   In God's eschatological
House and Kingdom there is no need for priests, *i.e.* inter-
mediaries between God and man, for there man can behold
God without any mediator; the elect are called the sons of
God; Master, disciples and the nations of the earth shall sit
together in the Kingdom of God.   The eschatological community is a Temple which the Master shall erect (Mk. xiv. 58;
Mt. xvi. 18 f.).   "The difference is striking and profound:
in Jerusalem a temple which is a building of stone embellished
with the costliest materials the earth can boast, here the temple
. . . built up of men, burdened with all the earth's cares and
infirmities; in Jerusalem a ceaseless sacrifice of animals on
holy altars, here a meal shared with the Master 'in his Father's
Kingdom'; in Jerusalem in all divine service the exercise
of ecclesiastical authority over men, here the Master Himself
in the midst of His own 'as one who serves' (Lk. xxii. 27).
Nor should one be surprised that God's *basileia* and the Master's
ekklesia share the same metaphor.   Already in the Old Testament the close relationship between the two is adumbrated
and certainly here they belong together even more closely.
Basileia means from God's point of view that which *ekklesia*
describes from the Master's point of view.   In view of this
relationship the temple metaphor becomes the point of coinci-
dence which reveals their essential identity.   Those that
are oppressed with care and want, poverty and guilt, whom
the Master calls to Himself, are of the Kingdom of God.

L

And because He calls them to His Father's holy House, He builds the temple where God reigns eternally, and destroys the other, which formerly presumed to be the place of God's kingly rule."[69] For membership of this new Temple what is demanded is not cultic purity and holiness but compassionate love, which is greater than all sacrifices. The group of disciples is the kernel of this community of the Kingdom of God, and the disciples have been granted the priestly and cultic function of loosing and binding.

Unlike Bultmann's interpretation of Jesus, Lohmeyer's is definitely anti-ethicistic.

If then we ask in conclusion: What is the Kingdom of God to Lohmeyer? only one answer seems possible. *The Kingdom of God is the unconditioned, the timeless, the supra-worldly, which enters into time and is the "end" of all time. The Kingdom of God is the eternal which we learn to know in the Son of Man and His teaching of the Kingdom of God.* The eschatology of the Gospels is interpreted here on the Greek dualistic pattern: time-eternity, nature-spirit, etc. One can only agree with Rudolf Bultmann when he says in a review of Lohmeyer that the latter resolves eschatology in Platonism.[70] The "end character" of the Kingdom of God is not only a definition of quality but also a definition of time: the Kingdom of God, the eschaton, comes actually in time. Even though Lohmeyer makes some extraordinarily penetrating observations on the text, which help us to understand Jesus and His teachings to some extent in a new way, he is so fixed in certain philosophical ways of thought that Biblical realism is in danger of being altogether lost, or forced into a mould that is alien to its whole nature.[71]

[69] *Op. cit.*, p. 67.

[70] Bultmann, Review of E. Lohmeyer, *Die Offenbarung des Johannes*, 1926, in *Th.Lz.*, 1930, p. 510.

[71] Schumann, *Der Gottesgedanke und der Zerfall der Moderne*, gives as his final criticism of Lohmeyer's interpretation of the idea of the Christian community some comments which might also apply to his later writings: "Critical-idealistic basic conceptions have gained the preponderance with Lohmeyer over New Testament ideas and set the tone of his understanding of these; the all-prevailing idealistic concept of consciousness leads to an interpretation of the community concept in which there is no room left for the distinctive characteristics of the Christian community—with the *same* necessity with which it leads to the purely speculative concept of God (the "Unconditioned"), which has nothing in common with the Christian idea of God. Again, the impossibility of understanding the Christian community from an idealistic standpoint, demonstrates the impossibility of entertaining the Christian idea of God in these same circumstances" (pp. 303 f.).

Martin Dibelius

Martin Dibelius, who stands with Bultmann at the head of the school of form criticism, has made the Gospels and the question of Jesus his main study.[72] We cannot here discuss his view of the tradition in any detail. We will only say that he regards the message of Jesus as being preserved homogeneously and in a comparatively uncorrupted form in the Synoptic Gospels, but that the scholar must take the *whole* mass of tradition into account and not build too much on individual sayings of Jesus, where these deviate from the tradition in general.

That the Kingdom of God is eschatological seems to Dibelius quite obvious. Every Jew who spoke of the Kingdom of God meant the Dominion of God at the end of time. There is not one saying in which Jesus gave any other interpretation of the expression in question. Jesus spoke of the coming of the Kingdom of God, and that God sent it. When exegetic criticism first recognised the eschatological nature of the Kingdom of God, it fell into a serious dilemma. It seemed as though the greater part of Jesus' spiritual world had proved to be a mistake, since the Kingdom of God which Jesus expected did not come. Many tried to get round the difficulty by saying that the teaching of the eschatological Kingdom of God was not important to Jesus. Dibelius, with the respect for the Synoptic material that is characteristic of him, could not take that course. The Kingdom of God occupies the forefront of the teaching of Jesus and there is no way past. The difficulty is due to overstressing the importance of Jesus' outlook on the world. His idea of the Kingdom of God was undoubtedly associated with a world outlook that has since been abandoned. His expectation of an imminent cosmic catastrophe proved false. But that does not dispose of Jesus' "end belief," neither has it been proved unimportant. For Jesus' "end belief" contains not merely ideas about the eschatological hope which He had taken over and developed, but in its capacity of faith it contains something other than a mere

---

[72] Among the works of Dibelius may be mentioned: *Die Formgeschichte des Evangeliums*, Tübingen 1919, 2nd edn. 1933 (Eng. version: *From Tradition to Gospel*, trans. B. L. Woolf, London 1934); *Geschichtliche und übergeschichtliche Religion im Christentum*, Göttingen 1925, 2nd edn., 1929, *Evangelium und Welt*; *Jesus* (Sammlung Göschen, No. 1130), Berlin 1939; *The Sermon on the Mount*, New York 1940. No change in basic attitude is noticeable in these works.

world outlook and high-pitched expectations which proved to be illusions. It contains the driving element of the whole Gospel, for it is only "end belief" that can explain why Jesus appeared at just that moment of time, and why He spoke and acted as He did. "The Gospel undergoes a *topical intensification*, from which the Jewish hope was far removed. But the topicalisation extends merely to the motive, not to the goal. For what Jesus brought is more than time-conditioned word and world-conditioned act. Eschatological faith gives us precisely the key to interpret word and act correctly. Within the framework of eschatological faith even what is most time-bound appears in the light of the eternal, and what is most worldly in the perspective of a great world distance. *The raising into the unconditioned* is the second factor, besides this topical intensification, through which eschatological faith distinguishes the message of Jesus from other teachings, philosophies and doctrines."[73]

Dibelius is thus trying to find a way to preserve the essential content of Jesus' eschatological faith, without being bound by the form of which eschatology avails itself. He believes this to be possible, since to him the historical is merely the form, even though necessary form, for the supra-historical content. In "end belief" time is raised to eternity, and the Gospel is no longer historically conditioned. "End belief," which itself is historically conditioned, is nevertheless the historical form for supra-history. Eschatological faith is not destroyed as faith with the destruction of the outlook it contains. For there is something in this faith which is quite independent of changes in conceptions related to this world: that the human soul, human life, human destiny are set face to face with the reality of God, that everything human is measured by His yardstick, the judgment of eternity on time.[74] What Dibelius is trying to get at in the Gospel is the unconditioned, the supra-historical and the timeless, for to him it is only this that can have eternal validity.[75]

Before going on to discuss what Dibelius meant by this "supra-historical," we will give a brief account of his interpretation of Jesus' teaching of the Kingdom of God.

---

[73] *Geschichtliche und übergeschichtliche Religion im Christentum*, p. 41.
[74] *Op. cit.*, p. 65.
[75] "Die Zeitlosigkeit der Botschaft Jesu," in *Christliche Welt*, 1927, p. 546.

Dibelius sees Jesus as opposed to everything in the nature of the religion of law. He also represents Jesus and His faith as being consistently anti-rationalistic.[76]

Jesus always saw the Kingdom of God as something coming, which we should pray for, and He never said that it had come. Nor did He ever speak of the slow growth of the Kingdom or anything of that sort. The parable of the Self-growing Seed does not mean that the Kingdom of God is like a seed which will bear fruit. "For what is compared is not the fruit, but the harvest," and the exhortation is an exhortation to wait.[77] The time is accomplished *now*. The Kingdom of God stands at the threshold; nothing can stop its coming. What grips the hearers and the disciples is just this topical intensification which characterises the teaching about the Kingdom. But even though the Kingdom is imminently close, so that one can hear, as it were, the murmur of it, it has not yet appeared. The *signs*, however, are visible and testify that the Kingdom is in process of coming. The Kingdom, which is entirely opposed to the world, is purely to come, but it is in process of coming. We cannot, says Dibelius, understand the mission of Jesus at all, if we do not bear clearly in mind that everything Jesus said and did lies between these two poles.[78]

The end of the present age comes suddenly and unexpectedly. But if men are as God wishes them to be, they will be able to interpret the time and its signs. They find then that the time is ripe. Jesus, who in word and deed testifies to the Kingdom of God, the group of disciples He gathers, the movement among the people, all these things should open their eyes. Just as Jonah was a sign to Nineveh, so Jesus Himself is the sign of the Kingdom of God. "The kingdom of God is not coming with signs to be observed; nor will they say, 'Lo, here

[76] In *Geschichtliche und übergeschichtliche Religion im Christentum* it is said of Jesus (p. 37): "Here a stream of life works itself out, sure of itself, in need of no direction, and it is not a clarification, but a falsification, to rationalise this life by raising it into consciousness."

[77] Dibelius, *Jesus*, pp. 56 f.

[78] *Op. cit.*, p. 58. "It is impossible to understand the mission of Jesus unless one keeps in mind these two poles, between which everything that He said and did lies. The one pole is the conviction that the Kingdom of God is to come and is completely opposed to this world. The other pole is the consciousness that this Kingdom is already in process of coming and has already been set in motion; its approach can no longer be stopped. The popular movement that Jesus unleashed moves from the time of unfulfilment to the time of fulfilment; but it exists in time between these times."

it is' or 'There!' for behold, the kingdom of God is in the midst of you" (Lk. XVII. 21). It is, according to Dibelius, a mis-interpretation to suppose that these words deny that the King-dom of God is something coming. What is rejected is the customary technique of making observations about its coming, *e.g.* by the stars. The signs are not to be detected here and there, for the signs are in the midst of you, Jesus means. Jesus, His message, His acts are the only sign.[79] What is important above all else is therefore that we should recognise in Jesus and His activity, the coming Kingdom of God.

Jesus casts out evil spirits. So the Kingdom of God has already made itself known (Mt. XII. 28). Even if we translate this saying as "So the Kingdom of God has already come to you," this does not mean either that the Kingdom of God is already here, but "that in the abundance of such marvellous events its nearness is made known."[80] Thus the exorcisms are signs of the coming Kingdom. Similarly the healing miracles are not an anticipation of the Kingdom of God—no one knows when God will send it—but they *proclaim* the Kingdom, are promises of the Kingdom and prove that it is on its way, and that God already allows the glory of the Kingdom to shine forth through Him whom He has sent. The forces of the Kingdom are already here; not as power, which is to transform the world, but as force, which streams forth from the only one who knows the Kingdom and mediates it. He who mediates signs of the Kingdom through His teaching and His acts is Himself the sign of the last time, indeed the only sign of the Kingdom of God in the fullness of time.

To Dibelius the Kingdom of God is not, as it is to Otto, a territory in which the power of God is active and brings Christ with it. The active importance of Jesus to the Kingdom is emphasised in a quite different way. Dibelius also stresses that one cannot separate the message and acts of Jesus from His person. It is precisely in the person of Jesus that the

---

[79] Dibelius gives this interpretation, *op. cit.*, pp. 62 f. In *Geschichtliche und übergeschichtliche Religion im Christentum*, p. 40, he puts forward another interpreta-tion of Lk. XVII. 20 f.: "The Kingdom of God is in the midst of you." "Kingdom" stands here for "sign of the nearness of the Kingdom." Jesus meant that it is in their hearts that men must find the certainty that the Kingdom is near. The sign is within them, in the experience of Jesus and His works.

[80] *Jesus*, p. 66. The interpretation is clearly dictated by Dibelius's basic view, which does not allow the idea of the actual presence of the Kingdom in the acts of Jesus.

Kingdom of God breaks through.   The important thing is
not what one calls Jesus, but that, when one sees how "the
blind receive their sight, and the lame walk, lepers are cleansed
and the deaf hear, and the dead are raised up, and the poor
have the good news preached to them" (Mt. xi. 5), one should
recognise the forces of the Kingdom of God and not take
offence at Jesus.   The decisive thing for man is a right attitude
in face of the overwhelming nearness of God.   It is to this
inner attitude towards the near God that the Lord's Prayer in
the form in which it appears in Luke, and the Beatitudes,
testify.   The child who gratefully accepts what is given it, has
this preparedness for the Kingdom of God.   This new way of
being before God, Jesus preached.   All His concrete commands
are expressions of and a constant variation upon this ethos,
this "new being," which Jesus did not teach but brought and
revealed.   Jesus never taught a new ethic in the sense of giving
a collection of new commands.   He merely gave examples
as occasion offered.   The demands of Jesus are fundamentally
not: This is how you shall act, but: This is how you must be.
"This being is released by the critical momentum of the world
turning-point, by the knowledge of the nearness of God, but
it is itself independent of time and world, because it is based
in that other, supra-temporal world which we call eternity.
All the demands of Jesus, whether they took the form of
practicable rules or of sharp imperatives, aim fundamentally
at one thing only, to awaken this new being.   Thus every
commandment of Jesus, from the apparently everyday to the
strangest and most difficult, is based on the ever newly-
testifying and all-embracing end faith: God is near, now all
considerations and conditions are at an end, now only one
thing matters, now be, live, act in view of one thing only!
What fills the hearer of Jesus, then, is not a new outlook on the
world, a new principle, a newly revealed wisdom, but it is
the emotion released by the overwhelming nearness of God,
which now modifies, ennobles and widens other emotions."[81]
Dibelius believes, in other words, that fundamentally the
sayings of Jesus spring from a timeless basis: the consciousness
of the nearness of God, in comparison with which all that is
important in the eyes of the world becomes unimportant.   The
sayings have also a timeless objective: to create men who can

---

[81] *Geschichtliche und übergeschichtliche Religion im Christentum*, p. 60.

live in this nearness to God on the frontier between time and eternity with a new attitude of life, a new ethos.

Dibelius answers in the affirmative the question whether there was any Messianic element in Jesus' consciousness of His mission. Even taking into account the strong Messianic colouring which the tradition later acquired, there still remains ample evidence that the Messianic dignity occupied its place in the thoughts of Jesus. When Jesus went up to Jerusalem for the last time, He went not as an ordinary Galilean pilgrim, but seeking a settlement. Crucified as the Pretender to the throne, He must have raised claims to be the Anointed of God. Jesus entered the Holy City as the Messiah chosen by God for the future, and was acclaimed the King of Peace; in the Temple He behaved as its Lord.

When it comes to considering more fully the meaning of the title Son of Man, Dibelius points out that Jesus applied the notion of the hiddenness of the heavenly man to His own life and mission. "The heavenly man" who is to be revealed at the end of time, must first be hidden for a while. Jesus' earthly life with its suffering was just such a hidden, disregarded, and unknown life. But He is to return at the Parousia as the revealed Son of Man. The saying in Mt. VIII. 20: "Foxes have holes, and birds of the air have nests; but the Son of man has nowhere to lay his head," may have been spoken by Jesus and indicates the contrast and yet the connexion between the hiddenness of Jesus' earthly life in poverty and the glory of the heavenly man. Jesus may even have connected the Passion idea with the Messiah idea. To Jesus, however, the whole Messiah question was of secondary importance and was not a condition for salvation. What Jesus demanded is that one should recognise in His mission the coming of God with His Kingdom, for He is the decisive sign at the last hour. So that He, who does not require recognition of Himself as the Messiah but refers the revelation of His dignity to the future, nevertheless practically identifies Himself with His mission.

Whereas the Church idea, according to Bultmann, fell completely outside Jesus' range of vision, Dibelius makes a definite attempt to combine the idea of the Church with the idea of the Kingdom of God. The group of disciples forms the "kernel community of the future people of God,"[82]

---

[82] *Jesus*, p. 49. Cf. *Geschichtliche und übergeschichtliche Religion im Christentum*, p. 78.

which is to be gathered together from among the old people. This new people is to be prepared for the coming Kingdom.

When Dibelius tries to penetrate behind the contemporary form in which Jesus' teaching of the coming Kingdom of God was presented, he employs the terms "historical" and "supra-historical." In so doing he associates himself with a line of thought that can be traced back to rationalism.[83] Unlike that school, to which the supra-historical meant supra-temporal teachings and eternal rational truths, it is clear to Dibelius that Jesus did not bring any new general truths. On the other hand the ethos from which spring the sayings of Jesus, spoken under the gravity of the approaching Kingdom of God, is "supremely supra-temporal." This ethos is not affected by any of the conditions involved in the given temporal-historical circumstances.

Dibelius denies absolutely that it was the peculiar personality of Jesus that provided the essence of Christianity and the force that worked through history. This supra-temporal, supra-historical, unconditioned is the actual life basis (*"Lebensgrund"*) of the teaching of Jesus, which is independent of the world and raised above it. This timeless basis, from which the sayings of Jesus spring, is the consciousness of the nearness of God, which makes everything in this world essentially inessential. The timeless goal is to create men who live in this nearness to God directly and naturally like children. Dibelius can therefore say of the sayings of Jesus: "They are spoken out of eternity into eternity, over and beyond time as it was then."[84] Jesus showed men the signs of the Kingdom of God and confronted them with the Kingdom, not in order to bring forth anything in this world, but to create among mankind the right attitude to God. What He commands will then spring from this attitude. The concrete commands are impulses which are to bring forth this attitude, this new "being," they are constant variations on the same theme. This attitude, too, is characterised as "supra-temporal" and independent of the world. Through this one comes into contact with the "life basis," which is characterised as the "testifying basis." This new, supra-temporal "being," which

[83] Bultmann, *Glauben und Verstehen*, p. 65.
[84] *Geschichtliche und übergeschichtliche Religion im Christentum*, p. 45.

is called "creative being" or "creative life,"[85] is "an ultimate, an innermost, for which there is no adequate expression."[86] Words can only imply it. More important, however, than characterising and describing it is to grasp this fruitful, creative basis and this new "being" in the symbol through which the eternal becomes visible. Jesus Himself found the symbol in the ways of a child, its directness and simplicity. This new manner of being stems from the creative-subconscious level.[87] The task of the Christian is not to imitate, but to create anew. Faith gives to him who creates receptiveness and the possibility of living this new life, through the impulses and emotions which arise from the deepest life basis.

The Kingdom of God as revealed by Jesus is thus, according to Dibelius, a radiation of the eternal into time. It is a supra-historical, timeless quality, a life in the nearness of God, which is not controlled by any exterior command but flows forth freely, spontaneously and creatively, and whose outward form is determined from within its own being without any other objective than the realisation of itself.

Martin Dibelius's eschatological ideas are dependent on Karl Barth. Like Barth, he asserts the unconditioned gravity of eternity for which eschatology stands, and interprets the "end belief" of Christianity as the actualisation of the gospel and its transposition up into the sphere of the unconditioned, supra-historical.[88] But when it comes to defining what the supra-historical in Jesus' teaching of the Kingdom of God actually was, Dibelius shows himself to be under the influence of that expressionism and irrationalism which played such a large part in Germany after the First World War.[89] Dibelius's interpretation of Jesus reveals striking similarities to Johannes Müller's.[90] Similarities could also be pointed out to Ludwig

[85] The various terms and expressions occur in a number of places in the last-named work.

[86] Op. cit., p. 60.

[87] Op. cit., p. 102.

[88] Holmström, Eskatologiska motivet, p. 251.

[89] See E. Bernheim, Einleitung in die Geschichtswissenschaft, (Sammlung Göschen, No. 270), 3rd and 4th edns., Berlin 1926, pp. 34-43. Note in particular p. 37. History is expression, sign, the embodied life of the soul. What we need to grasp is, not the tangible facts of history, but what these facts stand for.

[90] According to J. Müller the Sermon on the Mount is not commands but simply impulses sent out by Jesus to bring the hidden forces in mankind into vital and creative development, in order to bring about that condition of the soul that gives form and stature to our life. See also pp. 14 f.

Klages, who exerted a strong influence on certain circles, and Arthur Bonus.[91] Dibelius himself says he was greatly influenced by Friedrich Naumann.[92]

Man can reach the "life basis" and acquire the new "being" that is spoken of without revelation. It is a question here of something eternal, something timeless, which can only make itself felt in the world and in time in the form of symbols and signs. Thus it cannot in the real sense come near at the appointed time, as the Kingdom does in the teaching of Jesus. This Platonic-Greek conception of time that dominates Dibelius's thought and that sees time and eternity as qualitatively opposed to one another, necessarily involves a modification of Jesus' teaching of the Kingdom of God, in which the New Testament doctrine of redemption is thrust to one side. The Kingdom of God becomes eternity, which "hangs" for ever above time and history but can never enter into history. The futuristic aspect of the Kingdom of God is in process of disappearing and the topical view of the ultimate replaces the conception of the Kingdom of God as actually present. Its actual presence can be claimed only if one sees the Kingdom of God as present in Jesus and in His teaching and work in a different way from Dibelius. Then it would also no longer be necessary to provide the far-fetched explanation Dibelius gives of the "hiddenness" of the Son of Man, which is without support in the Gospels. If Jesus saw the Kingdom of God as near in His teaching and actions, He certainly did not refer the revelation of His dignity as the Son of Man entirely to the future.[93] Lack of faith has not seen it, but God has revealed it to faith.

Finally it must be pointed out that the Kingdom of God requires not a new attitude, but conversion, *metanoia*. God's forgiveness of sins opens the door to the Kingdom of God. When Jesus cited the child as a model, it is not the child's simplicity He was thinking of. On the contrary, He was

---

[91] Ludwig Klages is a strong anti-rationalist. The life of man must be led back to its original depths. A. Bonus, *Religion als Wille, Grundlegendes zur neuen Frömmigkeit*, Jena 1915, speaks of the real, active life that man possesses, but must discover anew.

[92] M. Dibelius, in *Die Religionswissenschaft der Gegenwart in Selbstdarstellungen*, ed. D. Erich Stange, VOL. v., *Martin Dibelius*, 1929, p. 27. Naumann discovered the problem of our culture, "the soul of the machine age." Dibelius found him "a synthetic personality" (p. 28).

[93] A. Fridrichsen, review of M. Dibelius, *Jesus*, in *Th.Lz.*, 1939, p. 448.

emphasising the necessity for conversion. "To become like a child" then means quite simply "to begin again."

The final verdict on Dibelius's interpretation of Jesus must therefore be that, when he represents the Kingdom of God as the nearness of God, in the presence of which men must learn to live, he is foreshortening the early Christian perspective, and is modifying the eschatological tension and expectation of the coming Kingdom, however much he may maintain that Jesus expected the coming of the Kingdom.

Rudolf Otto

The gifted and many-sided Rudolf Otto published works on practically every aspect of theology, and discussed the problem of Jesus in a number of connexions. The book he published in 1901 on the life and work of Jesus[94] kept entirely to current lines of thought and won the whole-hearted approval of H. J. Holtzmann.[95] Jesus, whom Otto characterised as "a person who unquestionably possessed the highest power and the supremest worth, and who left a most lasting impression upon a community of disciples,"[96] had been conscious, ever since He received His mission, of being the Messiah. He abstained altogether from ambitious political dreams and expected the longed-for Kingdom to come exclusively through the intervention of God. To recognise Him as the Messiah meant to bow down before and confess the ideal of morality and piety that was embodied in Him. His piety, "faith in God the Father" (Bousset), was the consummation of the piety of Isaiah and Deutero-Isaiah. Jesus embraced the view of His day, that the Kingdom of Heaven which stands at the threshold is an external ideal condition. He thus shared in the Utopia of His time. But Otto pointed out two important differences.

In comparison with the often fantastic speculations of His age, all the eschatological utterances of Jesus were surprisingly bare, scanty, and meagre.[97] What previously had been of the first importance became now merely the external shell. Otto was in complete agreement with the fashionable theology of his time when he said: "Large portions of his teaching were given up to the removal of matter pertaining to the Kingdom

[94] Otto, *Life and Ministry.*
[96] Otto, *Life and Ministry*, p. 3.
[95] *D.L.Z.*, 1902, p. 2319.
[97] *Op. cit.*, p. 54.

of God, matter which had no further general validity. And there was much else which was closely connected with the 'preaching of the Kingdom,' but which could be so removed as to inflict no injury upon the subject under discussion. Under the covering of the 'preaching of the Kingdom' he became the great curé and shepherd of his people and of his community, planting a spiritual life, that is, an inwardness possessing absolutely peculiar worth."[98]   Here we have what was characteristic and essential in Jesus. The teaching that the Kingdom of God was near does not distinguish Jesus in any way from His contemporaries. But by right of the new piety He aroused and the new righteousness He demanded, He was the light that shines into the world. This new piety involves having always the most vivid sense of God and His nearness, and feeling one's whole life upborne by this sense of His nearness. This piety is itself salvation. The prospect of a coming salvation is immaterial. "The external world was brought into the midst of life as a subject of experience and even of possession; it penetrated with its light and its warmth into the hearts of men."[99]   In this higher atmosphere the new righteousness develops as moral character through and through.

The conception of the Kingdom of God acquired with Jesus a wider significance. The Kingdom of God was no longer merely an other-worldly, coming entity; but Jesus modified the conception so that it came to mean an internal condition, a fortune already possessed, a rule of God and service toward Him, a community with the other redeemed ones.[100]   Admittedly the new meaning of the conception was incomplete. Mk. IV. 26 speaks of the quiet growth of the inner man, which develops according to the laws necessary to it. In this interpretation of Otto's the eschatological character of the Kingdom of God is, of course, completely lost. He represents the standard theology of the turn of the century, to which eschatology was something that has to be overcome. In principle, of course, according to this theology, it is already overcome by Jesus.

[98] *Op. cit.*, pp. 55 f.
[99] *Op. cit.*, pp. 62 f. Of the teaching and works of Jesus Otto says: "Its centre and well-spring was the new piety, the consciousness of divine sonship, of union with God, and this as a restful, permanent, and blessed possession of life. In this union with God was given at once the strong foundation and the constant source of supply of its free, pure and deep morality" (p. 71).
[100] *Op. cit.*, p. 74.

When Rudolf Otto published his main work in 1917,[101] his attitude was completely changed. Now he attacked the current, all too plausible representation of Jesus' faith in God the Father, which does not correspond to the atmosphere of the early communities. Jesus' teaching was from beginning to end the gospel of the Kingdom of God. In accordance with the most up-to-date research, Otto defines the Kingdom of God as "just greatness and marvel absolute, the 'wholly other' 'heavenly thing,' set in contrast to the world of here and now, 'the mysterious' itself in its dual character as awe-compelling yet all-attracting, glimmering in an atmosphere of genuine 'religious awe'."[102] This Kingdom of God sheds a colour upon everything that stands in relation to it: the men who proclaim it, the life and practice that are its precondition, and the congregation of those who await it. All becomes numinous.

This insight he had thus acquired, Otto applied in his last great work,[103] which is both the sum and the crown of his whole lifetime of religious research, and which he dedicated to the theological faculty at Uppsala in acknowledgement of an honorary doctor's degree.

We will first give an account of Otto's interpretation of the Kingdom of God, which we will then discuss and criticise, and finally try to discover the philosophical and theological principles that underlie his interpretation.

Jesus' idea of the Kingdom of God had a long prehistory which Otto sets himself to try to trace to its earliest roots. Although Jesus' teaching of the Kingdom of God belonged to the world of late Judaism, His idea of the Kingdom was not purely Jewish, and its non-Jewish origins are to be sought in the religion of Zarathustra and its later manifestation in Avesta. But the real source lies still farther back, namely in the ancient Asura religion, which was practised among the Arians before

---

[101] R. Otto, *Das Heilige. Über das Irrationale in der Idee des Göttlichen und sein Verhältnis zum Rationalen*, Breslau 1917, 7th edn., 1922. Eng. version: *The Idea of the Holy. An Inquiry into the non-rational factor in the Idea of the Divine and its Relation to the Rational*, trans J. W. Harvey, henceforth cited as *Idea of the Holy*, London and New York 1923, 1950.

[102] *Op. cit.*, p. 85.

[103] R. Otto, *Das Reich Gottes und Menschensohn, Ein religionsgeschichtlicher Versuch*, Munich 1954, 2nd rev. edn. 1940; Eng. version: *The Kingdom of God and the Son of Man, a study in the History of Religion*, henceforth cited as *Kingdom of God*, trans. F. V. Filson and B. L. Woolf, London 1938.

they separated into Indians and Iranians. Varuna, who is called rājā, king, possessed all divinity, wisdom and glory. He possessed numinous force and power. Varuna was king because he ruled through divine right and order. He had a kingdom, *kshatram*. This word signified originally something like "sovereignty in the sense of being lord, prince or king."[104] This ruler, however, also implied an area over which his *kshatra* extended, in which his power was active and his sovereign will prevailed.[105]

Through Zarathustra the old Asura religion triumphed on Iranian soil. But important differences arose, namely the idea of God's warfare against His enemy (dualism), and the beginnings of eschatology. The whole cosmic drama became a battle between evil and good, in which mankind is called upon to join the fight against God's enemy. At the end comes the great final battle with the destruction of God's enemy, the resurrection of the dead, the final judgment, and lastly the "wondrous new creation" of the world. With all this came the *kshatra* of the Lord, which here accordingly meant the ultimate state in a transfigured world, in which purity, truth and righteousness prevail, *i.e.* the Kingdom of God. Purely etymologically *kshatra* means the dignity, power, and function of lordship even in Persian, but the idea of the Kingdom as a territory ruled over is also to be found already in ancient Persian. The final kingdom of Ahura was conceived as an imperial sphere when it was spoken of as the house of Ahura. When it was spoken of as the sunny kingdom, "there is undoubtedly present the idea of a redemptive whole, in which the primitive root of *chshathra* has long since lost the narrowness of its first concept and has been enlarged to embrace various connotations and to signify the final state of a transfigured paradise and divine world."[106]

What Otto is obviously trying to discover is not merely the etymological meaning of *kshatra*, but also the associations attached to the idea. "Kingdom" can sometimes mean "area of sovereignty," and with it is associated a *dynamis* working against demons and all evil.

[104] *Op. cit.*, p. 25.

[105] "Where a *kshatra*, a *malkut*, a *basileia* is meant, where it is to come or to be realised or is real, there also an empire or 'kingdom' in the sense of a province is necessarily implied" (*op. cit.*, p. 26).

[106] *Op. cit.*, p. 32.

As to how the Iranian ideas influenced the religion of the Bible, Otto gives no full account. What interests him, here again, is to show what associations are connected with the idea of the "kingdom" and to note the extensions and modifications of meaning which occur in the course of its development.

When it says in the Psalms (xcIII, xcvII, and others): The Lord reigns, this is almost a stereotyped formula of praise-giving to Jahweh as the highest and mightiest. The *malkuth* that belongs to Jahweh is synonymous with the dignity and power that characterise him who is Lord. The associations which the word arouses, Otto finds all assembled together in 1 Chron. xxix. 11 f.: "Thine, O Lord, is the greatness, and the power, and the glory, and the victory, and the majesty; for all that is in the heavens and in the earth is thine; thine is the kingdom, O Lord (*melakah*) . . . thou rulest over all. In thy hand are power and might." To the kingship, then, is attached by association the territory or sphere over which Jahweh rules, which here is heaven and earth, which are "the Kingdom" to which the kingship relates.

The idea of kingship acquires a certain eschatological quality in connexion with the Old Testament expectations of the end of the world. Although Jahweh is always king, it is still said that he shall become so (*e.g.* Is. xxiv. 23, xxxIII, 22; Zeph. II. 15; Zach. xiv. 16). It is worthy of note that in such passages the term *malkuth* is not used, which is clearly due to the fact that the term is not distinctly and emphatically eschatological. A definitely eschatological term *basileia*, as we find it in the teaching of Jesus, could hardly therefore have its origin merely in the conception that Jahweh will one day become king. It is the sharp apocalyptic distinction between the present and the coming age (in Daniel) that first gives the idea definite shape. But Daniel's thought-world looks towards Persia. Otto, therefore, feels justified in asserting that the Kingdom of God first became an eschatological term in the real meaning of the word under Eastern influence. The first time the Kingdom is characterised as a transcendent, miraculous world into which the elect may gaze is in Wis. x. 10, where it is said of Jacob's vision of the heavenly ladder: "He led the righteous . . . and ἔδειξεν αὐτῷ βασιλείαν Θεοῦ." Here the old meaning of "Kingdom" is forgotten, for

Jacob does not see "the royal sovereignty, the function of God's rule, but the *world* in which He rules, the world above, especially as the world of angels."[107]

When the righteous man hears, then, that the Kingdom of Heaven is coming, he does not merely know that the time is near when God's claims to be King are to be fulfilled, but he knows too that this Kingdom is to descend from above, and that the world will undergo a marvellous transformation. Such expectations form, according to Otto, the inevitable connotations surrounding all preaching of the coming of the Kingdom of God and every prayer for it. Thus, too, the Kingdom is presented in the second and third petitions of the Lord's Prayer as a pure miracle coming from heaven which transforms the earth, so that the will of God is now done by men.

The new elements in late Jewish apocalyptic were far from being absolutely and radically alien to ancient Israelite religious feeling. Rather they worked upon germinal ideas which were found even in ancient Israel. What apocalyptic gives is the sharp dualism between that which is not God's world and the sphere in which His will is done. Otto leaves it an open question whether the division into an earthly sphere and a heavenly one is due to Iranian influence, but wherever the idea of a divine conflict is to be found, Iranian influence is clear. Traces of it are to be seen in the apocalyptic literature.

How the eschatological ideas handed down from Persia link up with the Israelite we can see best in the Book of Enoch. The Eastern influence was strong in Galilee, through which the Eastern Jews had to pass on their journeys of pilgrimage. Otto asserts that Jesus as a Galilean encountered Judaism in a syncretistic form, in which the Iranian influence had made itself felt, and that the speculations of the Enoch circle were known to Jesus.

The Kingdom of God, appearing already during the lifetime of Jesus, is victorious over the kingdom of Satan, and the vanquished enemies of God are flung down from Heaven. The Iranian influence is seen most clearly in the tremendous power which the idea of Satan had gained over men's minds. That being so, we realise that the message: "The Kingdom

[107] *Op. cit.*, pp. 36 f.

M

of God has come," is something other than a call for a decision. It is a gospel for the generation in which the power of Satan is great. All interpretations of the Kingdom of God in the mind of Jesus which do not incorporate in a massive and realistic way the idea of a *dynamis* before which the kingdom of Satan crumbles, are false.

This is perhaps a suitable point at which to insert a few critical comments. Otto's purpose was to trace the associations linked up with the idea of the Kingdom of God. He was trying to determine the passages in which the Kingdom of God has the meaning "area of sovereignty" (*"Herrschaftsbereich"*). The evidence in support of his view is not very strong. The value of Wis. x. 10 is slight. This book is generally believed to have been compiled in Egypt between 150 B.C. and A.D. 40, so that other influences than those that affected Palestinian Judaism may have entered in.

In the Old Testament and in late Judaism *malkuth Jahweh* means the kingship of God.[108] It seems also to be not entirely without significance for the understanding of Jesus' idea of the Kingdom of God, that among the rabbis the Kingdom of Heaven never meant the territory ruled over by God, but always "the kingly being, the sovereignty of God."[109] The term thus indicates the fact that God is King. If the basic meaning of the Kingdom of God is the kingship of God, the sovereignty of God, this does not rule out the possibility of a gradual shift in meaning in the direction of the sphere ruled over. The basic meaning, however, continued to form the kernel of the conception of the Kingdom of God, round which new and other ideas eventually became associated, an inevitable result being that the Kingdom of God is primarily *God's* Kingdom. But for Biblical interpretation God is and remains primarily personal will. The element of will in the idea of the Kingdom of God must therefore be strongly emphasised, and is of vital importance for the understanding of Jesus.

[108] G. von Rad, "βασιλεύς," in *Th.W.B. N.T.*, VOL. I, p. 569: "Best translated as '*Königtum*' (kingship)."

[109] K. G. Kuhn, "βασιλεύς" in *Th.W.B. N.T.*, VOL. I, p. 570. See also Dalman *The Words of Jesus*, p. 94: "Kingly rule, not kingdom" (*Königsregiment, nicht Königsreich*), and W. Bousset and H. Gressman, *Die Religion des Judentums im späthellenistischen Zeitalter*, 3rd edn., Tübingen 1926, p. 214: The Kingdom of God is in the first place "the rule of God, in the second place at most . . . a territory ruled over."

Even the Iranian influence does not all point in the same direction. It seems to me to be a warning not to stress the Iranian influence too strongly, that the Jewish apocalyptic books, in which the influence of Iranian eschatology is most marked, with rare exceptions (Ass. Mos. x. 1; Baruch LXXIII. 1) do not use the term Kingdom of God. One need not therefore go so far as to assert that the eschatological idea of the Kingdom of God evolved entirely on Israelitic-Jewish ground from the Hebraic conception under the influence of the teaching of the prophets and of outward events.[110] The Iranian influence seems incontestable. Dualism—God-Satan, and the opposition between the present and the coming age, unquestionably have Iranian roots. But however much these ideas may have influenced the idea of the Kingdom of God, the conception that God is King and shall be King, nevertheless injects an element of will into the Kingdom of God, such that it can never become a merely numinous sphere of power or anything of that sort.[111]

Any interpretation of the teaching of Jesus necessarily pre-supposes critical study of the sources, *i.e.* the Synoptic Gospel tradition. Otto believes that there existed before our Gospels, in addition to one or more collections of the sayings of Jesus, also an anonymous writing giving a narrative account of Jesus as the eschatological Redeemer. He considers it certain that the earliest missionary teaching was not based on a loose collection of logia and scattered accounts but on a "gospel," or perhaps more correctly "an embryo gospel."[112] This gospel, which he calls "*Stammschrift*," parent document, is the common source of our Synoptic versions. Luke goes back to an earlier and shorter form of this source, while Mark has preserved the original construction better. On the basis of this modified two-source hypothesis, Otto regards Luke as the more reliable source.[113]

[110] See *e.g.* Dodd, *The Parables of the Kingdom*, p. 39.

[111] In opposition to the view that almost everything that is new and important in later Israelite-Jewish religious developments is of foreign, principally Iranian, origin (von Gall), possibly modified by Babylonian cosmology (Gressmann), the tendency now is to limit the importance of this influence. (H. H. Schraeder, H. Ödeberg, *S.T.K.*, XVII (1941), p. 316).

[112] Otto, *Kingdom of God*, p. 82.

[113] On the question of the mutual relationship between the Synoptic Gospels Otto follows the hypothesis put forward by W. Bussmann, *Synoptische Studien*, VOL. I, *Zur Geschichtsquelle*; VOL. II, *Zur Redenquelle*; VOL. III, *Zu den Sonderquellen*, Halle

He maintains the reliability of the tradition and even ascribes great value to the narrative account. He believes, in the face of general scepticism, that it is possible to trace a certain development in the life of Jesus from these sources.

The difference between this more simple and summary theory of the Jesus tradition and the view of the school of so-called form criticism is striking. But are we justified in assuming the existence of any such *"Stammschrift"* for the missionary teaching? To this the main object was to preach redemption through Jesus Christ. Stories from the life of Jesus provide to a certain extent support for the preaching of salvation, but do *not* provide its content. Probably the early Christian missionaries had at their disposal a not too strictly defined collection of stories and logia which they used as a basis for their preaching of the Christ-*kerygma*. The various pericopes existed side by side without being linked together. Only the story of the Passion provided a connected unit from the very beginning. We must therefore regard the different pericopes as independent units, whose connexion with other closely associated pericopes is secondary. It is clear that Mark has retained most of the original pericope framework, whereas Luke, so to speak, more or less spills over and loses the dividing lines between the various sections. Many things are to be found in the Gospel of Luke in better context and more concrete form than in the other Synoptics. But this quality, which appeals to the modern man, is an expression of Luke's historical sense and literary skill, and testifies to his editorial gifts rather than to the originality of the material. When Otto prefers Luke he is thus the victim of false reasoning.[114]

It is important for an understanding of Otto's view of the Gospel tradition to realise the strong emphasis he places on the fact that the earliest Jesus tradition had been ecclesiasticised. The idea that the Kingdom of God is a present entity once occupied the forefront in a quite different way from now, but is has become submerged so that only traces remain of what was once a far greater factor. The later ecclesiastical Christology, too, covers over the old ideas like a veil. The original

---

1925-31. Bussmann's hypothesis is rejected by M. Dibelius, R. Bultmann, and others. See in particular K. Grobel, *Formgeschichte und synoptische Quellenanalyse*, Göttingen 1938.

[114] M. Dibelius, review of R. Otto, *Reich Gottes und Menschensohn*, in *Göttingische Gelehrte Anzeigen*, cxcvii (1936), p. 212.

message of Jesus has faded away. What still remains stands out like the peaks of a mountain-chain that has sunk into the sea, revealing the presence of the submerged mass beneath the surface of the water. But what still remains enables us to know what Jesus meant by that which is to come, and how He saw it Himself.

Even if Otto's source criticism is untenable,[115] which it is, it must still be clearly borne in mind that his theories on the origin of the Synoptics are of only secondary importance as compared with the interpretation he reached by other means, which is of a more intuitive nature. Otto brings out the inner relationships far more clearly than those who concentrate on hair-splitting detailed criticism. As a counterbalance to this sort of negative criticism, Otto's last work is of great value.

Otto's exposition of Jesus' teaching of the Kingdom of God is arranged as follows. First he gives an account of the basic features of Jesus' teaching of the Kingdom of God and determines its eschatological type, then he works out what is distinctive to Jesus by a comparison between Jesus and John the Baptist, and finally he examines in a mainly exegetic section Jesus' teaching that the Kingdom has already begun.

[115] The following example may be quoted of Otto's source criticism. According to Otto the present parables of the Sower and the Self-growing Seed originally formed one single parable, which comprised Mk. IV. 3-8, 26-9, "the finest of all the parables of Jesus" (*Kingdom of God*, p. 118), the point of which is vss. 26-9, which taken by themselves are only fragmentary. The introductory οὕτως refers back to the preceding verses: "So" means "in this way." *i.e.* as described in vss. 3-8. The original parable has been split by a later interpolation (vss. 10-25). But Otto's procedure is purely arbitrary. οὕτως does not refer back, but forward to what is to come: "So is the kingdom of God, as if a man . . . ." Mk. IV, 26-9 is not a fragment but a completed whole and as such completely understandable. The parable of the Sower is also a completed whole with its own particular point, which is the fact that not everything that is sown bears fruit, which is completely lost in Otto's interpretation. In the parable of the Net Otto excludes vss. 48-50 as being "detailed allegorical explanation by way of commentary" (*Kingdom of God*, p. 127). It is possible that the application of the parable is secondary, but in any case vs. 48 is part of the original parable, the object of which must clearly be, to any unbiased mind, to convey the teaching that the separation of good from evil does not take place now, but on Judgment Day. Otto is so completely blinded by his all-engrossing idea, that the Kingdom of God "seizes, carries with it, 'brings together,' the unwilling and varied elements into a unity" (*op. cit.*, p. 128) that he alters the text to make it fit his theory. Most hazardous of all is perhaps his literary commentary on the subject of the earliest Communion pericope, which cannot be discussed here. For criticism of Otto's source criticism see above all R. Bultmann, review in *Th.R.*, IX (1937), pp. 3 ff., and L. Brun, "Guds rike og Menneskesønnen," review of R. Otto, *Reich Gottes und Menschensohn*, in *Norsk Teologisk Tidskrift*, pp. 112 ff.

According to Otto Jesus was not an Apocalyptic but a "consistent eschatologist." Consequently His teaching necessarily contains the following two basic elements. One is the conception of the Kingdom of God as supernatural, supramundane, a complete "*mirum*," which is to come when the "transfiguration," the "transformation," the "wondrous new creation," occurs. The Kingdom of God is the new, sanctified existence that is to be, in contrast to the present existence. The second idea is the actual coming of the *eschaton* in time. "Consistent eschatology" involves a strictly temporal contrast between a now and a then. As against Bultmann's assertion that the coming of the Kingdom of God is not something chronological but means that mankind is confronted with a decision, Otto vigorously insists that "the eschatological order 'comes.' It comes according to the original conception, as something which breaks in upon the final generation universally."[116] Here it is a question of an actual temporal advent and Parousia.

Since the Kingdom of God is not a homogeneous conception but covers a complex of associations, it is no use asking for a definition of the Kingdom of God, but one has to ask instead: What does the expression bring to mind? The answer, of course, always has to do with a time when God shall really be King, and His character as king will be openly and fully maintained. But to translate ἡ βασιλεία τοῦ Θεοῦ as "royal sovereignty" instead of as "the Kingdom of God" is altogether too narrow and limited. One should rather say "realm of God's sovereignty."[117] The Kingdom of God is a divine realm which reveals itself on earth among men. It would be going too far if one were to say frankly "a new world which descends from above," but undoubtedly the idea lies along this line. Because the Kingdom is a realm, one can enter into it, which, if it were a *basileia*, that is simply the divine king's function, dignity or title to sovereignty, would be a meaningless expression. It can begin on a small scale and grow and expand its confines. This realm has the attributes of the heavenly world, because it actually is the heavenly world: the heavenly Son of Man, the angels of God, the heavenly banquet, the children of the Kingdom, etc.

[116] Otto, *Kingdom of God*, p. 52.
[117] *Op. cit.*, p. 53.

Behind the term "Kingdom of God" lies the idea of a new ideal for human conduct and mode of life. But above all there is associated with the concept of the inbreaking "realm of heavenly sovereignty" the idea of a *dynamis*, a *supernatural power, wonderful, coercive and operative from above*. Both Jesus' teaching about the Kingdom and His charismatic activity— to Otto Jesus is the "Ur"-charismatist—express with all possible clarity this idea of a *field of power*, which expands and gains ground, working with forces which overcome the kingdom of Satan, as the stronger overcomes the strong.

Also associated with the Kingdom of God is the idea of a supernatural end to the whole course of the world. With the preaching of the Kingdom goes the *preaching of the approaching judgment*. But the Kingdom itself is *not judgment* but "the consolation of Israel," the blessed final time of consummation, for which the "quiet in the land" waited. It is a domain of salvation of an absolute kind, "*an absolute domain of salvation*, indefinable and undefined as are all 'domains of salvation',"[118] and its highest content is to see God.

And this Kingdom is near, indeed it is here. It is palpably near, "already dawning." It is approaching and its arrival is imminent, indeed it has come. It is secret and hidden, yet nevertheless visible to the eyes of the blessed.

The associations which the concept of the Kingdom of God arouses and the whole complex of ideas which it embraces, are summarised by Otto as follows: "Divine dignity and glory, sovereign claim and demand that the will of the Lord be effective; realm of sovereignty and heavenly realm; heavenly world, coming into the world; miraculous power and coercion of the devil; healing and performance of miracle; charismatic preaching and seeking of the lost; consciousness of mission as the secret Son of Man; divine judgment and sternest call to repentance, new righteousness with strongest tension of will, and yet the praise of a childlike attitude which no will can create and no man can confer; transcendental domain of salvation, which does not harass the will by threatening but draws it out by attraction; purely a coming and future reality, and precisely as such on the point of breaking in, indeed already in the process of breaking in, mysterious, imperceptible, but visible to 'blessed' eyes; an operative and penetrating

[118] *Op. cit.*, p. 56.

power—all this is meant and included when the Kingdom of God is preached."[119]

The Kingdom of God is thus to Otto an indefinable mystery, but one that is observable in its effects; it is pure *"mirum,"* "pure miracle."[120]

Where, then, do we find the *distinctive* element in Jesus' teaching of the Kingdom of God, when many of the associations which, according to Otto, are connected with the Kingdom of God, have either Israelitic-Jewish or ancient Arian or Iranian parallels? First and foremost there are no national hopes connected with the Kingdom of God. The second distinction is the rejection of all speculation as to when the Kingdom will come and the extreme reticence in filling in the details of the eschatological drama. But that is not all. Otto tries to attain a deeper understanding of the individual quality of Jesus' idea of the Kingdom of God by a comparison between Jesus and John the Baptist. Both reflect the strongly eschatological temper of the time. In contrast to John the Baptist, the preacher of repentance, Jesus stands out as the charismatic "Evangelist" who is also exorcist. Otto formulates the difference under two theses: (1) in place of the gospel of a threatening "day of Jahweh," Jesus offers the gospel of the "Kingdom of God"; (2) in place of the magical *dynamis* of an eschatological baptism by water, Jesus preaches the spiritual *dynamis* of the *eschaton* in the "approaching dawn" of the Kingdom.

Jesus' gospel of the Kingdom is thus the preaching of the fulfilment of the promise to all the lost members of the "house of Israel," to those who awaited "the consolation of Israel." In spite of the radical demands the Kingdom makes, the gospel is "a preaching the quintessence of which is a gospel of *salvation.*"[121] In the circle around Jesus it is wedding-joy that prevails and not fear. The preaching of John the Baptist was: Repent and receive the eschatological baptism by water. Jesus preaches: Repent and believe the glad tidings (*besorah*). So it is not through a magical sacrament, but through glad tidings, that the salvation of the *eschaton* comes, and which it is necessary to accept in faith, as a child accepts a gift that is given to it.

All this is ultimately due to the fact that the Kingdom is approaching *actively.* The disciples of John the Baptist knew

[119] *Op. cit.,* p. 57.   [120] *Op. cit.,* p. 72.   [121] *Op. cit.,* p. 71.

nothing of the Spirit, but Jesus possesses this supra-worldly and divine *dynamis*, which is of the end-time. The spirit is thus ἀρραβών, a pledge, and ἀπαρχή, *i.e.* the first dawning of the supra-mundane future salvation itself. The Spirit is "the eschatological order itself as *dynamis*, in its anticipatory first dawning.[122] This *dynamis* is active in Jesus Himself and vanquishes the Kingdom of Satan and deprives it of its prey. Jesus is Himself a part of the approaching, redeeming realm of power and as such the saving eschatological Redeemer-figure. "In Christ's person and message the eschatological order itself came, its energy was operative and it drew men into its saving realm of power."[123]

That the ultimate has already appeared in Jesus, in His gospel and mission is, however, a mystery which not everyone discovers, but blessed are the eyes that see it. Jesus, by his preaching and His acts of power, is to open the eyes of men to this marvel, renewing and redeeming, which is the Kingdom of God, so that they receive it gladly and thankfully like children. To him who has eyes to see and ears to hear and who uses them aright, the secret that the Kingdom is already appearing and its quiet growth "of itself" shall be apparent. He finds the Treasure and the Pearl of Value. He sees the dynamic reality of the Kingdom of God, and something new enters into life. As the Grain of Mustard Seed grows (Mk. IV. 31 ff.), so does the Kingdom of God expand as the suddenly appearing eschatological "sphere of salvation," begins as something small, grows and increases in a miraculous, mysterious way. It gains ground more and more and becomes a movement which begins to win the people. The Leaven (Mt. XIII. 33 and Lk. XIII. 21) refers not merely to the growth but also to the transformation, which begins *partim* and ends *totaliter*. In Otto's interpretation of the Kingdom of God the parable of the Self-growing Seed and the sayings in Mt. XI. 12 and Lk. XVII. 21 have a quite special importance, so that we will pause here to consider these more fully.

As we have already seen, to Otto the parables of the Sower and the Self-growing Seed were originally one single parable, the deepest of all the parables. Here there is nothing to allegorise, nothing to psychologise. One simple, single

[122] *Op. cit.*, p. 80.
[123] *Ibid.*

meaning underlies it all. Two processes are compared, the one something everyday, well-known, repeated every year, the other a spiritual process, the peculiar quality of which is to be brought home to the hearers. Both are connected with growth. When the sower has completed his task he goes away, sleeps and wakes and does nothing. The seed is left to itself. Much of it is lost in various ways, but some falls into good ground and grows quietly and unnoticed, "first the blade, then the ear, then the full grain in the ear." It grows "of itself," αὐτομάτη, no one knows how. It is a hidden mystery. It is a miracle that happens. So does the Kingdom of God grow, quietly, in silence, unnoticed by weak eyes, grows by the power of God, not by human action. Ever since the days of John the Baptist this secret miracle has been going on. Incessantly, irresistibly it exerts its power; comes as in heaven, so on earth and extends its boundaries. And this is the great mystery of the Kingdom of God, whose secret is revealed to him who receives the Kingdom as a child.

Jesus says in the Beelzebub speech: "But if it is by the Spirit of God (Luke has "the finger of God") that I cast out demons, then the Kingdom of God has come upon you" (Mt. xii. 28; Lk. xi. 20). Here the Kingdom of God is as a victorious, compelling area of power struggling against the kingdom of Satan and making conquests from the devil (Mt. xii. 29; Lk. xi. 22; cf. also Mk. iii. 27). According to Otto, however, ἔφθασεν ἡ βασιλεία could just as well have been expressed: ἤδη βιάζεται ἡ βασιλεία.

In Mt. xi. 12: ἀπὸ τῶν ἡμερῶν Ἰωάννου τοῦ βαπτιστοῦ ἕως ἄρτι ἡ βασιλεία τῶν οὐρανῶν βιάζεται, καὶ βιασταὶ ἁρπάζουσιν αὐτήν, the verb βιάζεται may be in the passive. The Kingdom of Heaven is stormed, is seized by force. But the Kingdom of which Jesus speaks in the Beelzebub passage does not "suffer" violence but "exercises" violence. As βιασταί in the second half of the verse are not exposed to violence but themselves exercise violence, it is the same also with βιάζεται. The word corresponds to the Hebrew פּזק in Hiphael, which means to be strong, to become strong, to increase, to become powerful and even to "get the upper hand" (Dom. i. 28). Thus βιάζεται is here the middle voice. Ἡ βασιλεία βιάζεται, seizes and overpowers. The Kingdom is not already here completely fulfilled, but it is detectable in its effects. It was not yet present itself, but it was

"present as a power effective in advance."[124] And this characterises the very time from the days of John the Baptist. The second
half of the sentence Otto translates: "And those who exercise
force capture it."[125] The Law and the prophets could prophesy
about it, the Baptist could prepare the way, but now one can
wrest it to oneself as booty. Luke says therefore πᾶς εἰς αὐτὴν
βιάζεται (Lk. XVI. 16). When one conquers a kingdom, one
presses into it; when one presses into it, one conquers it. A
new age has come: the Kingdom is no longer at rest in a
distant heaven but "exercises its force," and mankind no
longer needs to wait but to storm into the kingdom which
has come near.[126]

The parable of the Net says the same as Mt. XI. 12. Its
original form was: "The kingdom of heaven is like a net which
was thrown into the sea and gathered fish of every kind"
(Mt. XIII. 47). Jesus speaks not of the good and the evil and
their fate at the judgment, but of the present miracle of the
power of God which "spread, took hold, carried with it, and

---

[124] Op. cit., p. 109.

[125] Op. cit., p. 108.

[126] Whether βιάζεται in Matthew is middle or passive voice is a debatable
point. But the arguments seem mostly in favour of its being passive. It certainly
seems more natural to render βιασταί as raptores mali and not boni. These exercise
force against the Kingdom, which is resisted, obstructed, attacked by militant
opponents (cf. G. Schrenk, "βιάζομαι" in Th.W.B. N.T., VOL. I, pp. 608-13).
According to M. Dibelius, Die urchristliche Überlieferung von Johannes dem Täufer,
Forschungen zur Religion und Literatur der Alten und Neuen Testaments,
VOL. XV, Göttingen 1911, what is meant here is not zealots or anything of that sort,
but "the invisible rulers to which this world is subject, the Pauline ἄρχοντες τοῦ
αἰῶνος τούτου (I Cor. II. 6-8), the spiritual powers (p. 26). Dibelius accordingly
translates: "From the days of John the Baptist until this time violence has been
done to the Kingdom of God and rulers of violence seek to seize it" (Jesus, p. 57).
A. Fridrichsen, "Jesu kamp mot de urene ånder," in S.T.K., 1929, p. 306, agrees
with this interpretation. The appearance of John the Baptist is a warning to the
kingdom of Satan that the time of reckoning is at hand. He does his utmost to
snatch the Kingdom to himself and so thwart the teaching of John the Baptist
and of Jesus. It seems, on the other hand, that Lk. XVI. 16 should be interpreted
as Otto does. βιάζεται is middle voice and means "penetrate in" (F. Hauck,
Das Evangelium des Lukas, Theologischer Handkommentar zum Neuen Testament,
edd. P. Althaus, O. Bauernfeind et al., Leipzig 1934, p. 207). The Lukan text
is obviously simplified and cut and shows a typical Lukan missionary tendency
(Schrenk, Hauck). According to Wellhagen, Anden och Riket, the intended
parallelism between εὐαγγελίζεσθαι and βιάζεσθαι would seem to show that the
latter is passive. "The paradox lies for Luke in the fact that εὐαγγελίζεσθαι is
at the same time a βιάζειν (p. 118). Should all be forced into the Kingdom by
the preaching? Is not rather an active penetration into the Kingdom intended,
as in Lk. XIII. 24: "Strive to enter by the narrow door"? Mt. VII. 13 means something quite different.

brought together 'of every kind'."[127]   Here again the Kingdom is a realm, but the important thing is that it βιάζεται, visibly exercises its power.

When the Pharisees asked when the Kingdom was to come, Jesus replied: "The kingdom of God is not coming with signs to be observed; nor will they say, 'Lo, here it is!', or, 'There!' for behold, the kingdom of God is *in the midst of you*" (Lk. XVII. 20 f.).   Many have translated: "The kingdom of God shall (suddenly, all at once) be in the midst of you" (Bultmann, Wrede, and others).   To translate the passage in this way is, according to Otto, to insert one's own meaning into the words, not to explain their meaning.   Here again it is its quality of mystery, *mirum*, that is decisive for the Kingdom.   The wholly transcendent Kingdom of God descends with its *dynamis* and breaks into this "world sphere,"[128] and so is "in the midst of you."   The original purpose of the saying is to startle and say something paradoxical, and in that way to "shatter the dogmatism of a finished eschatology and burst its too narrow limits."[129]

According to Otto, the saying that the Kingdom of God is to come ἐν δυνάμει, "with power" (. . . "before they see the kingdom of God come *with power*," Mk. IX. 1), proves that the Kingdom has already come, but concealed and "without power."   There is a similar strange logic again in the saying: "For there is nothing hid, except to be made manifest; nor is anything secret, except to come to light" (Mk. IV. 22), which is often regarded as secondary.   What was the object of this sentence?   "It would have had none at all, if not that of making an inference from something already present to something coming.   In the present case it meant that one should infer from the existence of the Kingdom of God, which was already perceived by the seeing eye, that its full revelation was in prospect."[130]   The saying is a prophecy about the future, the correctness of which is based on what has already been experienced.

Jesus knew Himself called to preach this Kingdom of God to Israel, to preach the gospel, *besorah*, salvation, redemption, and to call men to repentance, which however is not the same thing as to make a decision in a given situation, but involves

---

[127] Otto, *Kingdom of God*, p. 126.
[129] *Op. cit.*, p. 136.

[128] *Op. cit.*, p. 137.
[130] *Op. cit.*, p. 148.

conversion to the very depths of the heart. He only can rightly believe the Gospel of the Kingdom who receives it as a child. Jesus through his utterances and His charismatic acts mediated contact with the miracle of the transcendental.

It is, however, according to Otto altogether erroneous to represent the relationship between Jesus and the Kingdom as being that Jesus brings the Kingdom—such an idea is entirely alien to him—no, on the contrary, it is the *Kingdom* that *brings Jesus with it*. The Kingdom exists, but it is not yet here and now the Kingdom of *Jesus*: He is to inherit it some day. For God, in consideration of Jesus' obedience in suffering, is to give Him the Kingdom after He has passed through death. Not even when the kingdom of Satan recoils before the victorious power of God does Jesus regard this as His own work. He knows about the victory, for He has seen it. "I saw Satan fall like lightning from heaven" (Lk. x. 18). *Jesus bar Joseph* "knew Himself to be the Messianic King, inasmuch as He was the claimant to the throne of the kingdom of heaven."[131] What is distinctive in Jesus' relationship to the Kingdom of God that is even now appearing is, then, this, that He does not bring with Him, create or establish the Kingdom, but that the Kingdom of God, coming "of itself" ($a\dot{v}\tau o\mu\acute{a}\tau\omega s$), brings with it Christ as "*Christus designatus.*" After the death of Jesus a change takes place in this conception Jesus had of Himself. To the community, in the tradition, His life and activity becomes a Christophany.

Jesus expected the imminent end and destruction of this age, and the coming of the Kingdom of God in glory and splendour. But we must not lose sight of the fact that there are elements in His teaching which indicate that He did not expect the period of time before this happened to be so very short. For Jesus, in accordance with the dogma of the time, also reckoned with the Messianic agonies, with temptations, suffering, and oppression for the faithful, before the great final cataclysm and transformation came. The fact that He developed a new ethic and was able to say: "I will destroy this temple that is made with hands, and in three days I will build another, not made with hands" (Mk. xiv. 58; cf. Mt. xxvi. 61; Jn. ii. 19), which according to Otto implies that one must almost speak of a new religion in place of the old, points in the same direction.

---

[131] *Op. cit.*, p. 150.

Jesus rejected all chronological calculations with regard to eschatological events and observed strict reticence in depicting the details of the eschatological drama. But it is evident nevertheless that the Kingdom of God was and remained to Jesus the strictly eschatologically conceived, coming Kingdom of the end-time. Jesus could therefore say: "There are some standing here, who will not taste death before they see the kingdom of God come with power" (Mk. ix. 1; cf. Mk. xiii. 30 *et par.*).

But Jesus was not exclusively an "eschatologist of the end" and therefore did *not* see His mission *only* in the light of the *coming* Kingdom of God. The time is ripe, and the Kingdom of God is perceptibly near at hand, indeed it has come, and is in the midst of men. The Kingdom of God is here "in its preliminary dawning," "with mighty preparations."[132] The supra-mundane, coming Kingdom of God intervenes already here and now as saving *dynamis*, as the sphere of power and "area of salvation," in this inbreaking the signs of which have already begun to appear. Jesus lived in the already present miracle of the end-time, He saw the Kingdom grow of itself and drive back the kingdom of Satan, and knew Himself in His teaching and His works to be upborne by the forces of the Kingdom already appearing as ἀπαρχή. Otto points out emphatically that this presence of the Kingdom in present time is a *temporal* advent. The great secret, which blessed eyes may see, is that the Kingdom of God has already come, temporally, actually.

The entirely futuristic, transcendental Kingdom of God is active at this moment in Israel, but the transformation and transfiguration of the world, the "wondrous new creation," as Otto loves to call it, is something to come, even though the *dynamis* of the Kingdom of God drives on with irresistible force towards it. An eschatology in which future and present stand together as with Jesus in a meaningful, paradoxical entity, Otto calls "consistent" or even preferably "genuine" eschatology.

In answer to the question how the Kingdom can be at the same time both coming and present, Otto replies that this is possible because it is pure miracle, *mirum*, *mysterium*. "Ordinary things can be either future or already present. Purely future

---

[132] *Op. cit.*, p. 105.

things cannot sally forth from their future and be operative here and now." Marvels can be both and do both. That is the very reason that they are marvels—*mysteria*. Thus with Jesus the conception of a purely and strictly future thing passes over into that of something working even now, "in your midst."[133]

Otto thus finds the answer to the question of the present or future time of the Kingdom of God in the numinous category. The Kingdom is present as the already active "miraculous present."

Unfortunately Otto did not live to give us any detailed study of the ethic of Jesus. In *Reich Gottes und Menschensohn*, however, we find a number of statements which make it possible for us to trace, at least in main outline, his conception of the relationship between eschatology and ethic in the teaching of Jesus.

There is a strong eschatological tension in the teaching of Jesus. The end is near. But equally we find there the preaching of a new righteousness, which surpasses that of the Pharisees, a new ideal of human conduct, which requires love towards one's neighbour "as a lasting attitude of the disposition," and which therefore presupposes "a variety of enduring and changing circumstances of life."[134] These demands cannot be deduced from the idea that "the end" is near. Otto sees in Jesus a peculiar double-sidedness, which appears paradoxical: on the one hand the liveliest feeling of the immediate inbreaking of the supra-mundane future, on the other a religious and moral teaching which presupposes a continuance in time and is concerned with what happens during this time. This paradox is, however, according to Otto, very frequently to be found in conjunction with a keen eschatological feeling, and is characteristic of such divergent figures as Zarathustra, Mohammed, St Francis and Luther. It is "the irrationality of the genuine and typical eschatological attitude."[135] So that, in order to explain the relationship between eschatology and ethic, Otto falls back on the "numinous" category, which contains in itself the elements of the mysterious, the irrational. This tendency towards mysticism is a characteristic feature of what is essentially and in the first place a theology of *mirum*, in which opposites unite.

[133] *Op. cit.*, p. 73.   [134] *Op. cit.*, p. 61.   [135] *Op. cit.*, p. 62.

But on this principle practically any irreconcilables can be brought together, without one's being able to detect the slightest "internal logic."

What is it that is new in this righteousness that Jesus preached? Otto replies: It is not any new commands that Jesus brings, for God's commands are always basically the same. The command: "Thou shalt love God with all thy heart and thy neighbour as thyself" is not valid merely because the Kingdom of God is coming, and cannot be intensified by the eschatological situation. The in itself holy command of God is absolute and therefore cannot be intensified. The Sermon on the Mount cannot add to the demand that is enjoined on us in Lev. XIX. 2, but it reiterates it and drives it into the depths of the soul. Nor is the demand for a radical decision anything new over and above the Law and the prophets.

The newness lies, according to Otto, in the new possibility of fulfilling the demands, which the presence of the Kingdom of God provides. To him who receives the Kingdom like a child, immediately and without reflexion, it reveals its inmost nature; it is the saving, redeeming power of God, which even now is active, concealed and secret. The Kingdom of God demands radical conversion, but a radical change of heart is as such "beyond all capacity of the will," [136] and is bestowed on him who enters into the domain of salvation of the Kingdom of God. Here the demand is fulfilled αὐτομάτως, and what no decision of will can achieve is brought about. Of especial significance in Otto's conception of this question are the parables of the Treasure in the Field and the Pearl of Value. What these are designed to represent is, as always, that the Kingdom is the radical demand, but *first and foremost* that the Kingdom is "the blessing of salvation, the blessing pure and simple, and purely and simply a blessing." But "a blessing does not demand, it does not work through *command* on the will."[137] What the parables mentioned above describe is "what happens spontaneously as soon as this blessing comes home to the mind, viz. strongest effort in utter surrender owing to the *interest* that has been set alight, an interest which as such needs no command; indeed, being an interest it cannot be

---

[136] *Kingdom of God*, p. 56.
[137] *Op. cit.*, pp. 128 f.

given by command."[138] The Kingdom of God becomes here clearly entirely grace.

To Rudolf Otto it is perfectly clear that the community did not create the Messiah belief, but that the community was itself created by this belief, and would never have come into being without it. Even if we leave out of account obviously Messianic sayings and acts, it is still perfectly clear that Jesus knew Himself to have been sent by God on a quite special mission. In Jesus' exorcistic acts is fulfilled the victory of the stronger over the strong. Never had any prophet spoken as He did, or emphasised His own authority as He did (Mt. v). Jesus demanded to be followed in His own person and to receive devotion in His own person, with sacrifice of house and home. The whole figure, appearance, speech, and acts of Jesus were surrounded by a numinous nimbus. He aroused surprise, fear, consternation.[139] Jesus revealed Himself as having power to forgive sins. Here we are in the presence of a power and an authority far beyond anything that any prophet ever possessed. He is in possession of the Spirit (Mt. xii. 24 ff.; Lk. iv. 16 ff.), even more than Jonah (Mt. xii. 40), and He speaks in the name of wisdom, indeed He is Himself wisdom.

It is of the utmost importance to Otto to emphasise the charismatic element in Jesus. He classifies Him under a religious-historical "heading," He is a wonder, a holy man, a θεῖος ἄνθρωπος.

Jesus preached the coming of the Son of Man, and He associated the ideas connected with the Son of Man with Himself. The Messiah-Son of Man belongs to the Kingdom and is as transcendental as it. Just as the Kingdom, although purely transcendental and to come, already "throws its shadow forward into the present,"[140] so also with the Son of Man. Jesus' consciousness of His mission is clearly connected with the theology of the Book of Enoch.[141] Jesus must have known

---

[138] Op. cit., p. 129.

[139] Typical in this connexion is Lk. v. 26: "And ἔκστασις seized them all, and they glorified God, and were filled with awe (φόβου), saying, 'We have seen παράδοξα today'." [140] Kingdom of God, p. 161.

[141] On the question of Enoch and the Son of Man see S. Mowinckel, "Henok og 'Menneskesønnen'," in Norsk Teologisk Tidskrift, 1944, pp. 57-69, and "Opphavet til den senjødiske forestilling om Menneskesønnen" in Norsk Teologisk Tidskrift, 1944, pp. 189-244; also E. Sjöberg, Der Menschensohn im äthiopischen Henochbuch, Skrifter utgivna av Kungl. Humanistiska Vetenskapssamfundet i Lund, vol. xli, Lund 1946.

Himself destined to be the Son of Man and have acted already here and now as He who is destined to be Son of Man, "as personal representative of that Son of Man,"[142] but He did not teach about Himself as the Son of Man. Just as the Kingdom is altogether to come and yet casts its shadow over the present moment, is there not *with* power but *before* its power, so also with the Son of Man. The Kingdom of God brings the Son of Man with it *now* as "*Christus designatus.*"

With the dogma of the Son of Man Jesus associated the idea that the Son of Man must suffer, which is characterised as a new Messianic teaching. Here Otto bases his interpretation mainly on the saying in Mk. x. 45: "For the Son of Man also came not to be served, but to serve, and to give his life as a ransom for many," and the saying about the succession (Mk. VIII. 27-37 *et par.*).

To Otto the Kingdom of God in the sayings and acts of Jesus is an indefinable mystery, but one that can be observed and experienced in its effects and which the eyes of the blessed see, for it makes itself felt already now as a redeeming sphere of power, as *dynamis*, which compels, conquers, and expands.

One can only agree with Otto when he says that it is impossible to define the Kingdom of God briefly. One does not get at what the Kingdom of God is by an etymological derivation of βασιλεία and its Jewish antecedents, one can only let oneself be guided by the emotionally-coloured associations which the thought and idea "Kingdom of God" aroused among Jesus' contemporaries. But doubts arise when Otto characterises the Kingdom of God as "*Königherrschafts-Bereich,*" as the sphere or area ruled over, and especially emphasises the charismatic features. The Kingdom of God becomes somehow impersonal. It is not sufficiently emphasised that the Kingdom is primarily *God's* Kingdom, where God is conceived as personal will. The Kingdom of God is not an impersonal force of will, which is effective within a certain area. The first three petitions of the Lord's Prayer show that the element of will is present in Jesus' idea of the Kingdom of God in a more personal way. When God's name is hallowed, *i.e.* when God is recognised as God, and when His will is done, this is closely connected with the coming of the Kingdom. The many associations in the image of the Kingdom of God are not disconnected and orderless,

[142] Otto, *Kingdom of God*, pp. 219, 227.

they are all gathered around a central point, around God, conceived as commanding will. In defining the Kingdom of God as "*Wunderding*" and so forth, there is a danger that the whole image may dissolve away in a diffuse, impersonal mysticism which has nothing to do with the Gospel.

Indissolubly connected with the Kingdom of God, says Otto, is the idea of a *dynamis*, a supernaturally operative power which is victorious over the kingdom of Satan and causes the Kingdom to grow "of itself, no one knows how." Jesus is the "Ur"-charismatist, and it is impossible to understand Him unless one realises how important this characteristic is. The Kingdom is the "*Wunderding*," active though hidden.

Jesus belongs to the sphere that now enters in, as part of it. But according to the Gospel Jesus' relationship with the Kingdom is far more personal. How otherwise is one to explain that to accept Jesus, not to take offence at Him, to follow Him, etc., means the same thing as to receive the Kingdom? When Otto says that Jesus *lives in* the marvel of the end-time, he might say with more justification that Jesus *is* the marvel of the end-time. Because the Son of Man is here, the Kingdom is here. He is the only decisive evidence that the Kingdom of God is present. The crucial point, therefore, is not that the Kingdom is present as a sphere of power, but that the Lord of the Kingdom is here and, with His disciples, possesses this *dynamis* as a gift from God. Thus Jesus in His teaching and in His acts brings the Kingdom of God close to mankind.

Otto finds the solution of the question of the relationship between the present and the coming Kingdom in the numinous category. As a marvel, as a pure *mirum*, it can be both. It is present as a "miraculous presence." If Otto means by his interpretation that Jesus' contemporaries found no great difficulty in picturing the forces of the Kingdom as present in the immediate moment, one can only agree with him. That, however, is of minor importance; the decisive question, on the other hand, might be formulated as follows: Why was it possible for *Jesus* in particular to announce that the future Kingdom had come? Otto just hints at the answer when he says that Jesus drew a sharp distinction between the time that is now come, when fulfilment begins, and all previous time. The question is answered if one bears firmly in mind that with

Jesus a decisive turning-point had been reached in history. He is the fulfilment of all expectations. In Him the Kingdom of God is near. The Kingdom of God is here, because the Son of Man is here. But both are hidden.

Otto's interpretation brings out to the full the evangelical tone of the teaching of Jesus. To Jesus, the Kingdom of God is redeeming power and gift, wedding joy and blessedness. But the fact that the Kingdom is a gift does not prevent its making the very strongest demand for a decision. This demand, however, Otto underestimates.

It is not enough to see the Kingdom present as miraculous power. Even he who sees the miracles is obliged to make a decision for or against Jesus. His enemies say that it is the work of Beelzebub (Mk. III. 22). The invitation to the Kingdom is always a call for decision (Mt. XXII. 1-14; Lk. XIV. 12-24).

A sort of "esoteric searching"[143] is of little help to him who would enter into the Kingdom. He must take the decisive step in full consciousness of what it involves (Lk. XIV. 28-32). It can only be due to Otto's whole underlying attitude that such sayings as Mt. V. 29, VIII. 22, XI. 20 ff.; Mk. VIII. 34; Lk. IX. 62, XIV. 26 f., hardly find any place in his exposition.

In saying that Jesus saw Himself as the *Messias designatus*, Otto seems not to have done full justice to the fact that He saw Himself as the Son of Man. If Jesus during His earthly life was not yet the Messiah-Son of Man, then neither can His activities and His sufferings have been Messianic. The Gospel tradition gives no adequate support for the view that Jesus toiled and suffered as the representative or functionary of the Son of Man. Otto's thesis that Jesus saw Himself as the "latent Son of Man" corresponds with the tradition better. But then "latent" must be given some definite meaning. Any suggestion that Jesus was a "claimant" to be the Son of Man must be quite unacceptable, for we are bound to admit that Jesus brought the Messiah-Son of Man into the present in His lifetime in the same way as the Kingdom of God.

The lasting value of Otto's interpretation of Jesus is that it shows how vital the proclamation in word and deed of the present Kingdom of God was to Jesus, and that it so clearly brings out that the Kingdom of God is above all things gospel. Whether, on the other hand, the numinous category is really

[143] *Op. cit.*, p. 105.

calculated to express clearly what the Kingdom of God meant to Jesus, appears highly doubtful. Otto seems to have forced his own conception of the true religion into the image of the Kingdom of God. To gain clarity on this point we shall have to investigate to some extent Otto's own theological and philosophical beliefs.

It has been pointed out how extremely complicated Otto's own mental background was.[144] He began as a pupil of Albrecht Ritschl, and retained from this period a strong apologetic interest which colours all his later work. He was convinced that Christianity is the highest religion, and that Christ is the highest point of revelation. But he never embraced any Incarnation theology, but held that what is deepest in humanity and what is deepest in religion are one and the same.

Otto's great concern was to discover the distinctive element in religion. This aim was already noticeable in his dissertation,[145] in which the encounter between God and man in the experience of grace is the object of his deepest interest. In later works[146] his religious philosophy appears fully developed. The philosophy which he takes as his basis is that of S. A. Fries, which he adopts without reservation and from which he never departs. This means that Otto accepts the principles of critical idealism, *i.e.* that the rational mind may make use of both the "rational" confession of faith and the "irrational" sensing of the eternal through emotion.

What particularly interests Otto is the relationship between the irrational and the rational in the idea of the divine. The irrational here is not that which cannot be grasped by thought, but that of which one gains knowledge through other means than the rational. The divine is not identical with the numinous. The divine can find expression even in wholly rational affirmations. But the rational elements need to be supplemented by the irrational. In the development of religion there has to be a union between the irrational-numinous and the rational. Here is revealed one of the inner

---

[144] H. Eklund, "Die religiöse Qualität und die Sittlichkeit, Eine Untersuchung in heutiger Religionsphilosophie," in *Acta Acad. Aboensis Humaniora*, VOL. XIV, No. 9, Åbo 1942, p. 26: "His investigation of the holy is not a phenomenology of religion, but a whole philosophical system."

[145] *Geist und Wort nach Luther*, Diss. theol., Göttingen 1898.

[146] In *Idea of the Holy* and the following writings: *Aufsätze, das Numinöse betreffend*, Munich 1923; *Sünde und Urschuld*, Munich 1929.

secrets of development of "the holy," which "yields us the complex category of 'holy' itself, richly charged and complete and in its fullest meaning."[147] Otto uses here the term schematisation. There are also, according to Otto, other ways by which the said union of different elements may come about. Schematisation takes place by inner necessity. Real schematisation is distinguishable from merely incidental by the fact that, with the further development of the religious sense of truth, it does not disintegrate but grows ever more strongly together. The history of the holy is a development in a definite direction. The incidental is sifted out, and the holy is expressed more and more through genuine, *i.e.* firm and definite, schematisation. "In the gospel of Jesus is perfected that movement towards the rationalisation, moralisation and humanisation of the idea of God, which had been active from earliest times and outstandingly in the prophets and psalms, and in which the numinous is revealed ever more fully and completely through the affirmation of clear and deep rational emotional values."[148] So Christianity becomes to Otto the highest religion. In Jesus' Kingdom of God we find the perfect union of rational and irrational-numinous elements.

The Kingdom of God is a mystery which does not merely appear now but has always been, and which is to be found in other religions, too. Otto makes similar statements about *atman* and *ruach* as about the Kingdom of God. The most important difference is the idea of grace in the Gospel. The essence of the Kingdom of God, according to Otto, is the overwhelming experience of the numinous as grace, which occurs in connexion with the Gospel. The experience of the grace of God as a tremendous force which sweeps men with it, which forces them into the Kingdom, which liberates from every care, which demands the utmost effort of strength, all this Otto has objectivised. One could also express it in this way: the Kingdom of God as taught by Jesus is a "mytho-logisation" of the holy, of "*numinosum*."

One grasps the holy through divination. Christ is the subject of divination, He is the prophet. But what is more important is that He is also its object. He is "the holy" in its revelation. He is "*numen praesens*." He is the charismatist whose doctrine

---

[147] *Idea of the Holy*, p. 46.
[148] *Op. cit.*, p. 85.

of forgiveness in itself has redeeming power. But in addition, Jesus represents and realises in His person what He preaches: the Kingdom is in process of entering in. But the distinctive element cannot be expressed by saying that Jesus is a charismatist, for His disciples are actually just as much charismatists as Jesus Himself. Besides which, many of the passages in the Gospel which emphasise the charismatic element in Jesus and which Otto uses for his interpretation, are secondary.[149]

Jesus preached the inmost reality, which the eyes of the blessed can see. It exists already and existed before Jesus, for actually the miraculous has always existed. The Kingdom of God becomes unqualified when Otto's general religious ideas are applied to the New Testament material.

Vilhelm Grønbech

Grønbech portrays Jesus throughout his study[150] as the severe and merciless critic of Jewry, who set Himself to break down its faith and mode of life, indeed its whole culture. Jesus found Himself confronted by a people bogged down in moralism. In contrast to this, Jesus represents the truly human; no hard and fast rules of morals or conduct are to be derived from His sayings. As they stand, they are the speech of life itself. He who listens to the sayings cannot fail, says Grønbech, to see behind them the face of Jesus with its unforgettable smile. In this interpretation of Jesus, personality and message blend into one.

The Kingdom of God is represented as something purely of this world and spiritual: "The kingdom of God is within you." God and the Kingdom of God are to be found at the roots of life. The Kingdom is self-obvious and natural, it is *Life* quite simply, and therefore true humanity. It is to be poor and free from everything that mankind counts as essential: honour, power, virtue, piety, etc. It is defined as faith, but faith seen not as a relationship to God but as a state of directness and devotion. The Kingdom of God enters into a man when the whole agglomeration of commands, statutes, systems, and strivings for perfection, in a word, all the "Jewishness," is stripped away.

[149] Bultmann, review in *Th.R.*, N.F. IX (1937), p. 33.
[150] V. Grønbech, *Jesus Menneskesønnen*, Copenhagen 1935.

The whole teaching of Jesus is eschatological. The day of judgment is in the midst of the people, for Jesus set a dividing line between the living and the dead, He is the judgment, because He has *Life* within Him. It is for man to follow Jesus, give up the world, deny it, escape within himself, where he is free from the march of destiny.

In this interpretation of Jesus the Kingdom of God is represented as sheer inwardness. The relationship of Jesus to the Kingdom is that of the messenger, He is the spokesman of life, foretelling a new age. He is the mystic of life. Dead, says Grønbech, is he who has not courage to live the strong, direct, natural life. Everyone has a possibility of *Life*, for everyone has something in him of the creative genius.

Grønbech makes Jesus the ultra-individualist, without real contact with inherited tradition. This involves doing violence to the texts. The Gospels tell of a connexion between Jesus and John the Baptist, and Jesus characterised Himself as the fulfiller of the law and the prophets (Mt. v. 17 f.). The true objection to Grønbech, however, is that Jesus never departed from the massive realism of eschatology. To depict all the eschatological ideas as merely symbols of the life that exists deep in each individual, is a modification and modernisation, for the Kingdom of God is and remains a transcendent reality. The Kingdom of God demands faith and obedience, but faith is not a self-obvious quality. To Jesus it was not for every man to believe; faith is τὸ σκάνδαλον. To turn obedience into obedience to life is to abandon every possibility of judging an action from an ethical viewpoint.

No one has ever represented Jesus so consistently as an anti-moralist as Grønbech. It is unquestionably a merit that he helps us to see what is radical in Jesus and forces us to consider what is new in Him. Nor can anyone deny that Grønbech has shed a new light on a number of individual Bible sayings.

Grønbech has much in common with Johannes Müller. There are also striking similarities to Hans Hartmann,[151] to whom the distinctive element in Jesus is "life saturated through with eternity."[152] To Hartmann, too, Jesus was an anti-moralist.

[151] H. Hartmann, *Jesus, das Dämonische und die Ethik*, Berlin 1923.
[152] *Op. cit.*, p. 64.

XII

Interpretations of the Kingdom of God
on the Basis of Bible Realism

Comparing the theology of the period 1920-45 with that of the turn of the century, one is struck by the fact that the great majority of theologians during the latter period adopt an eschatological interpretation of Christianity. This fact must be placed to the credit of Albert Schweitzer and Karl Barth. But at the same time the interpretations of Jesus' idea of the Kingdom of God given by these two pioneers were not found altogether satisfactory. It was felt to be useless to try to deny that Jesus did not see the Kingdom of God only futuristically, but also preached the presence of this Kingdom in word and deed. The question arose, how sayings of the present and future fit together in Jesus, and furthermore how the presence of the Kingdom of God is to be understood. A number of scholars, striving after a realistic interpretation of the texts without rejecting sayings which prove difficult to fit into the pattern as a whole, show an increasing tendency to maintain that the Kingdom of God is near in the very teaching and work of Jesus, Son of Man. This emphasis on the close connexion between Jesus and the Kingdom is far from being anything new, but they try to go somewhat farther than a mere naked statement of the fact. So, for example, K. L. Schmidt.

Julius Kaftan,[1] the follower of Ritschl, declared in his old age that the Kingdom of God reveals itself in Jesus, His acts and deeds. The Kingdom of God and the Messiah belong indissolubly together: if the Messiah is here, then the Kingdom of God is also here. Gerhard Kittel asserts in various connexions that the Kingdom of God, which is entirely the work

[1] J. Kaftan, *Neutestamentliche Theologie, im Abriss dargestellt*, Berlin 1927.

of God, entered into the world and into time with Jesus, in the presence of His person (Lk. xvii. 21; Mt. xii. 28).[2] In Him the power and authority of the second aeon has been revealed. The presence in the world and in time of the Kingdom in Jesus is the presence of the other world, is "present eschatology." Side by side with the Parousia sayings are sayings which spring from a "consciousness of the presence of the αὐτοβασιλεία"[3] (Lk. iv. 21, "today," and Mt. xi. 5), thus an eschatology effective in time, and effective beyond time rub shoulders together. The key word is αὐτοβασιλεία. (P. Feine,[4] G. Holstein,[5] R. Frick,[6] and others).

It is not possible to give a full account here of all the shades of difference between the views of the various scholars. We should, however, mention, in addition to those already given, the names of H. Greeven,[7] H. Lietzmann,[8] E. Seeberg,[9] J. Hempel,[10] E. Stauffer,[11] J. Schneider,[12] J. Jeremias,[13] H.

---

[2] G. Kittel, "Das innerweltliche Reich Gottes in der Verkündigung Jesu," in *Th.Bl.*, 1927, pp. 122 f.; "'Ιησοῦς ὁ διδάσκαλος καὶ προφήτης," in *Th.Bl.*, 1928, pp. 249 f.: "All New Testament eschatology is fulfilled in the person of Jesus as present eschatology in the historical presence of His person (Mt. ix. 15; Lk. xvii. 21), as future eschatology in the Parousia of the Son of Man, as ἀπαρχή in His πνεῦμα (ii Cor. v. 5, iii. 17)." See also *id.*, *Die Problem des palästinischen Spätjudentums und das Urchristentum*, Beiträge zur Wissenschaft von Alten und Neuen Testament, iii, pt. i, Stuttgart 1926, p. 130.

[3] With reference to αὐτοβασιλεία see *Th.W.B. N.T.*, vol. i, p. 591.

[4] P. Feine, *Theologie des Neuen Testaments*, 7th edn., Leipzig 1936, p. 80.

[5] G. Holstein, *Die Grundlagen des evangelischen Kirchenrechts*, Tübingen 1928, p. 24.

[6] See pp. 132 f.

[7] H. Greeven, *Gebet und Eschatologie im Neuen Testament*, Neutestamentliche Forschungen, ed. O. Schmitz, Ser. iii, No. 1, Gütersloh 1931.

[8] H. Lietzmann, *Geschichte der alten Kirche*; vol. i, *Die Anfänge*, Berlin and Leipzig 1932, pp. 34-51.

[9] E. Seeberg, *Wer ist Christus?* Sammlung gemeinverständ. Vorträge, No. 183, Tübingen 1937.

[10] J. Hempel, "Der synoptische Jesus und das Alte Testament," in *Zeitschrift für alttestamentliche Wissenschaft*, n.f. xv (1938), pp. 25 f.

[11] E. Stauffer, *Die Theologie des Neuen Testaments*, Theologische Wissenschaft, Stuttgart and Berlin 1941. Eng. version, *New Testament Theology*, trans. J. March, London 1955, p. 123: "Jesus claimed the title of Son of Man for Himself. He proclaimed the advent of the Kingdom of God (Mt. iv. 17, xi. 12). He joined both together and declared: The Kingdom of God comes in and with and as the coming of the Son of Man. 'For behold, *the kingdom of God is in the midst of you*' (Lk. xvii. 21). It is already there, in His person and in His works."

[12] J. Schneider, "Die biblische Botschaft vom Reiche Gottes," in *Das kommende Reich, Stimmen aus der deutschen christlichen Studentbewegung*, No. 78, Leipzig 1933, pp. 5-26, and *Der Sinn der Bergpredigt. Von der Grundordnung christlichen Lebens*, Berlin n.d.

[13] J. Jeremias, *Jesus als Weltvollender*.

Preisker,[14] F. Büchsel,[15] J. Schniewind, the Englishman
R. N. Flew,[16] and above all H.-D. Wendland.[17]

All of them see a close connexion between the Kingdom of
God and Jesus. It is not to be denied that, even among these
scholars, philosophical and theological preconceptions play
their part, but the fear of giving a free rein to Biblical realism
is no longer dominant.

Following F. Kattenbusch's contention in 1921[18] that the
Messianic office of Jesus necessarily brought with it the
Messianic community and that Jesus with the Last Supper
expressly founded the Church, there were many who believed
that the beginning of the Kingdom of God was to be found
not merely in the person and work of Jesus but also in
the circle of disciples which He gathered around Him,
and which constitutes the *ekklesion* founded by Him (G.
Gloege,[19] H.-D. Wendland, J. Schneider, R. N. Flew, and
others).

The question of the conditions for entering into the Kingdom
of God led naturally on to the question of the ethic of Jesus.
The ethic of the Sermon on the Mount is presented as the
ethic of the Kingdom of God (H.-D. Wendland, J. Schneider,
H. Preisker). It is not possible, declares this group, to pick
out certain passages of the teaching of Jesus as uneschatological; all His sayings and actions are bound up with the fact
that the Kingdom of God, which shall some day be revealed in
glory, is already present now in the person of Jesus. The idea
of the Kingdom of God, the conception of the Messiah, the
idea of the Church and of ethic are all eschatological and form
an unbroken unit.

We will consider three of these writers more at length,
namely Jeremias, Wendland, and Preisker. These three should
suffice to illustrate the position of exegetic interpretation

---

[14] H. Preisker, *Die urchristliche Botschaft von der Liebe Gottes im Lichte der vergleichenden Religionsgeschichte*, Aus der Welt der Religion, Bibl. Reihe, No. 5, Giessen 1930,
and *Geist und Leben, Das Telos-Ethos des Urchristentums*, Gütersloh 1933.

[15] F. Büchsel, *Theologie des Neuen Testaments, Geschichte des Wortes Gottes im Neuen
Testament*, Gütersloh 1933, 2nd edn., 1933.

[16] R. N. Flew, *Jesus and His Church.*

[17] H.-D. Wendland, *Die Eschatologie des Reiches Gottes bei Jesus. Eine Studie über
den Zusammenhang von Eschatologie, Ethik und Kirchenproblem*, Gütersloh 1931.

[18] F. Kattenbusch, "Der Quellort der Kirchenidee" in *Festgabe für A. Harnack*,
Tübingen 1921, pp. 143-72.

[19] G. Gloege, *Reich Gottes und Kirche im neuen Testament.*

of the Kingdom of God at the beginning of the nineteen-thirties.

Joachim Jeremias

After a discussion of the New Testament idea of time, in which he makes use of the term "cycle," now first introduced into Bible studies, Jeremias puts forward the thesis that Jesus claimed to be He at whose coming world fulfilment was set in motion. Jesus claimed that in Him, as bearer and bestower of the Spirit of God, the re-creation, the fulfilment of the world had begun. God's year of grace had started. When Jesus characterised Himself as the bestower of the Spirit, as the "Bridegroom," the Son of Man ("the new man"), when He entered Jerusalem for enthronement and the purification of the Temple, He did so in the knowledge that He brought with him the great revolution in the life of the world, world transformation and the time of salvation. It is in a world that is under the rule of Satan that all this occurs. The exorcisms of demons by Jesus are "manifestations of the future dominion of God in the present."[20] Satan falls like lightning from heaven (Lk. x. 18), the sick become whole, evil spirits flee before Jesus the bearer of the gospel. The power of evil is broken.

But world fulfilment is not yet visible. Satan is conquered but not destroyed. Jesus appears in humility, and so long as He does that, He is as world perfecter visible only to faith, as Mt. xvi. 18 f. shows. The community is safe from the powers of the underworld. Membership of the community opens the way to the kingly Dominion of God. But a day will come when it shall be revealed that Satan has been bound. Then the transfiguration of the world will take place. The state of the transfigured world is described by Jesus in ancient images and figures, of which the most important are: the meal of the holy, perfected community and the new Temple, of which He is the keystone which brings the building to completion.

Jeremias's account shows how consistently eschatological are the words and acts of Jesus. With Jesus salvation has come, He has gathered the community of the last days about Him and exercises towards it His office of Saviour. "World fulfilment is present in time."[21]

---

[20] Jeremias, *Jesus als Weltvollender*, p. 60.   [21] *Op. cit.*, p. 35.

Heinz-Dietrich Wendland

A typical example of the interpretation of the Kingdom of God at the beginning of the nineteen-thirties is Heinz-Dietrich Wendland's study[22] published in 1931. He tried to break away from the old, unprofitable questions of the immanence or transcendence of the Kingdom of God, largely along the lines of systematic theology. His dependence on the interpretation of the Kingdom of God provided by dialectical theology and in particular by Bultmann is evident, but the main influence on him is that of Schlatter, just then at the height of his fame, as is shown by the dedication in 1933 of the *Theologisches Wörterbuch*[23] to "Adolf Schlatter the Octogenarian."

The first chapter-heading of Wendland's book: "The idea of God and the Dominion of God," indicates in itself his general line of approach. One can only understand the teaching of Jesus through His idea of God, and His gospel of the Kingdom of God is an expression of His faith in God. Jesus' idea of God is most clearly revealed in His idea of the Kingdom of God. The idea of God's Dominion is the Biblical form of the idea of God. Whether one believes with Holl that Jesus brought a new idea of God, or with Bultmann that this idea is entirely derived from Judaism but conceived, of course, with purity and consistency, one must still agree that the decisive element is Jesus' conception of sin and grace, with which He completes the prophetic line. It is important to remember all the time that Jesus' idea of the Kingdom of God is as consistent as His idea of God.

The Kingdom of God is the Dominion of God. "The coming Kingdom is the Dominion of God. The Dominion of God is His kingly, unconditioned action, through which He shows Himself as Lord. . . . The βασιλεία τοῦ Θεοῦ signifies therefore the fulfilment and accomplishment of divine dominion over the world. . . . The Kingdom of God is an event, indeed an act, a deed of God's. In it God shows Himself as Lord. It is the accomplishment of His will. Behind the word of the Kingdom of God lies the perception of God as *personal, creative, active and all-powerful will.*"[24] The Kingdom of God has therefore at the same time a personal and a dynamic

---

[22] Wendland, *Die Eschatologie des Reiches Gottes bei Jesus.*
[23] *Th.W.B.N.T.*, vol. i, Stuttgart 1933.
[24] Wendland, *Die Eschatologie des Reiches Gottes bei Jesus*, pp. 15 f.

character. In the parables of the Kingdom of God it is just this activity of the King that is often emphasised.

Since the activity of God is twofold—judgment and grace, so also is the gospel of the Kingdom, at the same time as it is a call to repentance and also a gospel of salvation (Mk. 1. 15). This dual activity is represented in the image of God as the Father and the King. The call to repentance is a summons to the Kingdom of God. It is based on the fact that the Kingdom is near, for the coming salvation requires conversion.

When the Kingdom of God comes, it means the entry into the existing age, which is hostile to God, of the world to come, which will bring not merely catastrophe but also world fulfilment. The struggle of the Dominion of God against evil is waged through personal decision, but for that reason it is not allowable to individualise the teaching of the Kingdom, in such a way that the universally eschatological perspective of Jesus would be lost. Even nature shall be transformed.

In discussion of the question of the presence and future of the Kingdom of God, immanence has often been taken as presence and transcendence as future. So long as the Kingdom of God was regarded as an immanent, personally-ethical entity, the idea of the presence of the Kingdom predominated. With the discovery of the eschatology of Jesus, more emphasis came to be laid on the transcendence, and with it the purely futuristic character, of the Kingdom (Johannes Weiss, Albert Schweitzer). The vital question to Wendland is whether eschatology is merely a conception of time which applies to the future, or whether the future in an eschatological sense has a deeper meaning. As against the interpretation of the Kingdom as a community of this world or a moral-spiritual gift which is bestowed on the individual, the strictly eschatological view is right. For if the activity of God is the most important thing in Jesus' image of God, and the Kingdom of God is His Dominion, then the Dominion belongs to God alone. Everything is the gift of God. But that does not answer the question whether the eschatological view of the Kingdom of God absolutely excludes its present character. The decisive question is whether we are to consider the present nature of the Kingdom from the angle of man, or from that of God's activity in the present moment. Then only that conception of the present would be possible which is entirely determined by what God does at the moment. The decisive element is the emphasis on the Kingdom as something qualitatively different from everything that belongs to this age.

The Kingdom of God is not merely the coming Kingdom but also at the same time the *eternal* Kingdom, that has existed since the beginning of the world (Mt. xxv. 41 ff.). But this Kingdom that has existed from eternity is only given at the end-time as a gift of the Father to His blessed ones. "So the eternal Kingdom is at the same time a future Kingdom, the future Kingdom at the same time an eternal. The eschatological idea of the Kingdom of God combines the qualities of being *beyond* time and at the *end* of time."[25] But the question then arises whether this combination is necessary. According to Wendland it is, because the Last Judgment has not yet taken place, and the present state of the world has not yet been abolished. So long as this aeon continues, the eternal Kingdom must be revealed as a future Kingdom.[26] "The eternal Kingdom is in fact 'here' in the sense of its eternal being, its supra-temporality."[27] The eternity of the Kingdom of God follows from its futurity, and its futuristic character follows from its eternity. This relationship between future and eternity Wendland calls "the *theonomous idea of the future.*"[28]

From mankind's point of view the future is indeterminate and indeterminable, something over which we have no control. We fill it with our dreams and hopes but also with our fears and our anxieties. But to Jesus the future is controlled by God. "*The to-come means the coming-to-us of God.*"[29] In this view of the future the now is not the point that divides the past from the future in the unbroken stream of time through which we have to live, but it is the moment of decision, an eschatologically determined now, qualified by the fact that God is coming to us.

On going through the Synoptics Wendland finds a number of sayings in which the Kingdom of God is seen in the light of future eschatology. The coming of the Kingdom involves the coming final catastrophe and the end of all time. But since the Kingdom does not merely belong to the end-time but is at the same time supra-temporally eternal, so the "end-time

[25] *Op. cit.*, p. 33.
[26] Cf. Bultmann, *Glauben und Verstehen*, p. 80.
[27] Wendland, *Die Eschatologie des Reiches Gottes bei Jesus*, p. 33.
[28] *Op. cit.*, p. 34.
[29] *Ibid.*

quality" of the Kingdom necessitates a definite present-time quality. Through its supra-temporal, eternal quality the Kingdom is present and near. In order to understand this question of the presence of the Kingdom of God, it is necessary to pause and consider the disputed passages which refer to the Kingdom as present. Mt. xII. 28 testifies to the fact that in God's activity through Christ, in His conquest over the demons, the Kingdom of God has been revealed. Through His victory over the evil spirits the end-time has appeared. The presence of the Kingdom is the beginning of the end-time and the overthrow of the existing order. Mt. xI. 4-6 belongs together in subject matter with Mt. xII. 28, even though here the reference to the miraculous cures takes the place of the victory over the demons.

Thus the Synoptic material shows us the Kingdom of God as future as well as present. But how are these opposites to be reconciled? Wendland rejects a number of attempts at interpretation. It is not possible to start from the presence of the Kingdom now and look for the future to bring the development and completion of something that already exists, for that would destroy the whole force of the basically eschatological element in the teaching of Jesus. But neither can we start from the futurity of the Kingdom and then interpret all sayings of its presence as psychological and proleptic, which would mean dismissing them altogether. The terms ideal and reality take us nowhere, for the Kingdom of God is to Jesus no ideal but reality itself, which dominates and renews the world. Modern research no longer allows the eschatological sayings to be brushed on one side, as though they were merely a contemporary form which Jesus adopted in His preaching. To Wendland only one solution remains. "We must start, as the eschatological movement does, from the Kingdom being future or at the end of time, but at the same time grasp the inner polarity of the idea of the Kingdom as belonging to the end-time and being supra-temporal and see the presence of the Kingdom as actually in principle founded in that, so that we also avoid interpreting its presence as psychological anticipation. The coming Kingdom of God places man and the world in a κρίσις τοῦ κόσμου" (Jn. xII. 31).[30] But the Kingdom of God is not present merely as a

[30] *Op. cit.*, pp. 51 f.

claim and a demand or as a threat of judgment, but in the crisis which is now upon us, if the Kingdom is *actually active* in the casting out of demons and acts of healing, even though it is visible only to those who have already seen the coming of God in Jesus and have not taken offence at Him. The presence of the Kingdom is based in the dynamically creative realism of the idea of the Dominion of God. As the characteristic of Jesus' idea of God is grace, so also does He see the Kingdom of God as grace, which gives life. The problem of the presence of the Kingdom of God is consequently not solved by pointing to the passages which speak of its presence, for the question can only be answered if one takes into consideration the fact that the Kingdom gives forgiveness and eternal life. But the presence of the Kingdom, which shows itself in the fact that it demands a decision, that it expresses itself as divine, active power, that it is a divine gift, is all linked up with the fact that the messenger of the Kingdom is present. The last word on the presence of the Kingdom must therefore always be Christological.

It is definitely to Wendland's credit that he, like Schlatter, recognises that the demands of the Kingdom apply to the generation which is called to be the people of God, and that he develops the evangelical nature of the Kingdom. The Kingdom of God is the forgiveness of sins, it is the Fatherhood of God and it is eternal life. To the extreme futuristic interpretation of the Kingdom of God it was impossible to think of the ethic of Jesus otherwise than as interim ethic. But to present the ethic of Jesus as interim ethic is not enough, for all Christian ethic is interim ethic. As the Kingdom of God unites in itself the qualities of being above time and at the end of time, the ethic of Jesus combines in itself absoluteness and eschatology. Indeed, these two are one and the same, and say both that the will of God, when it comes to us, drives us to repentance, demands new righteousness, but also gives forgiveness and gives new righteousness. That the ethic of Jesus can be at the same time absolute ethic and eschatological ethic is due ultimately to His idea of God. "That God who summons and conditions us in the present time of here and now, who has created and supported us, as He has the world, from the very beginning, is the coming God whose holy will can and will fulfil itself, because He is eternal power."[31] Wendland is

---

[31] *Op. cit.*, p. 106.

O

thus able to reject all exegetic hypotheses which divide the ethic of Jesus into two distinct spheres of thought. He declares, largely in opposition to Windisch, that with the abolition of a factual unity between ethic and eschatology there is no longer any compelling need to divide the teaching of Jesus into the rabbinical teaching of wisdom and a prophetic preaching of judgment and salvation, nor to divide His ethic into a "human-religious" and a "heroic-eschatological" morality. Even in ethic, the God of Jesus appears as the God of love. The demanding will and giving will of God are one. The teaching of salvation, the gift of God, makes it possible to fulfil the commands of God. Wendland declares himself in agreement with Gerhard Kittel's thesis, that perform-ance is not the condition for, but the effect of, God's gift.

Under the purely futuristic interpretation of the Kingdom of God it has always been extremely difficult to set the King-dom of God and the Church in a positive relationship to one another. Jesus began His activity by calling together disciples. He who calls is the bearer of the Kingdom of God. What constitutes the community of disciples is the coming of the Dominion of God. But the Kingdom of God and the com-munity of disciples cannot be identified, for the Kingdom of God is an entirely new, all-embracing reality. The com-munity of disciples is not a demonstration or presentation of the Kingdom of God but a group of men who, in following Jesus, place themselves in the service of the Kingdom that is to come.

To discuss the attitude of Jesus towards the Church would take us outside our present framework. The outcome of the debate is clearly summarised in the closing words of the chapter entitled: "The Kingdom of God as Community": "A community does not bring forth the Kingdom as product, but the Kingdom creates the community."[32]

The weakness of Wendland's interpretation of the Kingdom of God lies in too great a dependence on philosophical terms such as supra-temporality, etc., and also in the fact that the terms are often dialectically determined. The effect of this survival from dialectical theology is to obscure the historical perspective of salvation. Wendland emphasises later that the

[32] *Op. cit.*, p. 199.

Kingdom of God comes *in* history.[33] God intervenes in a certain *kairos* and brings about a decisive change. With this the end-time begins, which is at the same time the time of salvation. God enters into the midst of time and transforms it into the time of fulfilment. The Dominion of God is Jesus. Only in Him has the Kingdom come near. In His activity and teaching the Kingdom of God, the time of salvation, becomes present in history. Eschatology is inseparably united with history.

Herbert Preisker

The whole of Christianity is united, according to Preisker, by one and the same article of faith: the expectation of the coming Kingdom of God as the revelation of God's love. This applies also to Jesus, who however saw the Kingdom of God as already present on earth in Himself and the dynamic creative force He possessed. The coming Kingdom is, in other words, an actually present force in Jesus. The Kingdom of God has value as present only as part of the future, which brings with it the revelation of the Dominion of God, and the future is bound by the present. This mixture of future and present Preisker calls "the dynamic of the present-future Kingdom of God."[34]

Behind the Sermon on the Mount lies the power of the coming Kingdom, because He who brings the gospel is the beginning of the Dominion of God on earth. The Kingdom of God is above all action, it is God's assault on mankind, but it is also grace, for the inconceivable power of this Kingdom removes human sin. It is the idea of this power-filled Kingdom now breaking through that dominates all Jesus' rules of life. His teaching is homogeneous. The early Christian ethos is the ethos of eschatological certainty and of eschatological possession, called by Preisker *telos-ethos*. This stupendous thing that Jesus demands, man cannot fulfil of himself, but only in so far as he is possessed by the tremendous power of the Kingdom of God. The love which Jesus demands is a creation

---

[33] See Wendland, *Geschichtsanschauung und Geschichtsbewusstsein im Neuen Testament*, Göttingen 1938, and "The Kingdom of God and History," in *Church, Community and State*, VOL. III, London 1938.

[34] Preisker, *Geist und Leben, Das Telos-Ethos des Urchristentums*, p. 14.

of God's own power of love. The human time- and earth-
bound will and ability is overwhelmed by the power of the
Kingdom of God. God Himself is love activity.[35]

The strong emphasis on the actively dynamic character
of the Kingdom of God and the assertion that the Kingdom in
its innermost essence is love, recalls Rudolf Otto's interpretation of the Kingdom of God, but with Preisker the ethic is
unquestionably more firmly welded to the idea of the Kingdom
of God.

Werner Georg Kümmel

Many students of the Gospel have entertained strong preconceived philosophical and theological ideas, whose correctness they have usually not sufficiently examined. The remedy
for this state of affairs is a closer adherence to the actual Bible
text and what it really says. That was the way the eschatological interpretation of Jesus originally broke through with
Johannes Weiss and Albert Schweitzer. After the long succession of philosophical adaptations of the Kingdom of God
it is refreshing to come to Werner Georg Kümmel,[36] who keeps
closely to the text and does not try to remove by critical
procedure sayings which do not fit in with his ideas as a whole.
In such cases he prefers to leave the question open.

Kümmel takes as his starting-point the sayings of Jesus that
the Kingdom of God is at hand (Mk. i. 15; Mt. x. 7 [Q]).[37]
A number of passages in the Bible represent the Kingdom of
God as a future entity in time, and the coming of the Kingdom
as connected with the Parousia of the Son of Man and the

---

[35] Jewish ethics are directed towards the perfection of mankind in the coming
aeon, when comfort is expected. Jesus and the New Testament do not merely
turn men's eyes toward the new world to come, but they do so for the reason that
mankind is involved in and determined by the coming perfection. "It is not a
question of the will of the moral individual, but of action through involvement
in the ultimate reality of the coming Kingdom of God; that is the Telos-dynamic
of early Christianity" (op. cit., p. 37).

[36] Kümmel, Promise and Fulfilment. In Kirchenbegriff und Geschichtsbewusstsein in
der Urgemeinde und bei Jesus, Symbolae Bibl. Ups. VOL. I, Lund 1943, Kümmel
asserts that the ecclesiastical ideas of the early congregation had no direct connexion
with Jesus. Among his other works may be mentioned "Jesus und der jüdische
Traditionsgedanke," in Z.N.W., 1934, pp. 105-30, and "Die Eschatologie der
Evangelien, ihre Geschichte und ihr Sinn," in Th.Bl., 1926, pp. 225-41.

[37] Kümmel argues, in opposition to Dodd, that ἤγγικεν (Mk. i. 15) cannot
mean "has come," but "has come near."

Judgment (Mk. XIV. 62, x. 17; to "inherit eternal life," the entry sayings, etc.).

As regards the length of time that is to elapse before the coming of the Kingdom, there are two different traditions. On the one hand are the sayings that some of those who stand around Jesus shall not taste death before they see the Kingdom of God come with power (Mk. IX. 1), that this generation will not pass away before the Kingdom comes (Mk. XIII. 30), that the disciples will not have gone through all the towns of Israel before the Son of Man comes (Mt. x. 23), which mean that the Kingdom is to be expected in a very short time. On the other hand it is said that no one but the Father knows when the "day" shall come, whose coming coincides with the establishment of the Kingdom of God (Lk. XVII. 24; Mt. XXV. 13; and most of all Mk. XIII. 32). Jesus thus rejected all apocalyptic calculation of the length of time until the expected eschatological fulfilment. But there is no getting away from the fact that Jesus expected the Kingdom in His own generation. The many sayings about watchfulness emphasise this. The parable of the Absent Master (Lk. XII. 36-8), which compares the coming of the Son of Man with that of the thief, emphasises that the length of time until the Parousia is unknown, but therefore also at the same time that the *eschaton* is imminently near.

If Jesus hoped that the Kingdom of God would come in His own generation, then one must, of course, ask whether He expected an interval of time between His death and Parousia. Even if the formulation of the prophecies of the Passion (Mk. VIII. 31 f., IX. 30 ff., x. 32 ff. *et par.*) is the work of tradition, still the reply to the request of the sons of Zebedee that they should have places of honour in the coming glory (Mk. x. 35-40), as also Lk. XII. 50 and XVII. 25, show that Jesus, at any rate during the latter part of His life, expected a violent death, after which His resurrection would follow.

Kümmel finds no support in the texts for any connexion in time between the resurrection and the Parousia, which a number of scholars has favoured. On the contrary, Mk. II. 18 ff.: "Can the wedding guests fast while the bridegroom is with them? as long as they have the bridegroom with them, they cannot fast. The day will come, when the bridegroom is taken away from them and then they will fast in that day," and Mk. xiv. 28, show that Jesus reckoned with a considerable passage of time between His resurrection and Parousia.[38]

When Jesus says: "For whoever is ashamed of me and of my words in this adulterous and sinful generation, of him will the Son of man also be ashamed, when he comes in the glory of his Father with the holy angels" (Mk. viii. 38 *et par.* in Q; Mt. x. 32 f.; Lk. xii. 8 f.), the meaning is clear, even though the exact wording of the text is difficult to trace: whoever publicly takes sides for or against Jesus, shall receive a fate corresponding to his attitude, when the Son of Man comes in His glory to hold judgment.   Jesus has thus connected the *eschaton* with the present time in a new way.   "The present is not only, as the present *always* is, the time in which man decides in advance by his actions the sentence to be passed on him at the final judgment, but the presence of Jesus is in itself already an eschatological hour of decision, because in *this* present Jesus has appeared who confronts men with denial or confession; by their action they determine in advance the sentence of the 'Son of Man' at the final judgment."[39]

Just as there is no question but that Jesus expected the Kingdom of God in the near future, so also is it impossible to get away from the fact that Jesus was conscious of the *eschaton* as active in His own person.   Jesus says: "The kingdom of God has come upon you" (Mt. xii. 28).[40]   Satan is strong, but Jesus is the stronger, who snatches from Satan those whom he has overpowered (Mk. iii. 27).   As it was expected in Judaism that Satan would be bound, when the end-time came (Ass. Mos. x. 1), so Jesus believed that the Messiah was already active and that the Dominion of God had already begun.   In a vision He saw Satan fall from heaven (Lk. x. 18).   The Messianic works (Mt. xi. 2-6; Lk. vii. 18-23) show that in the person of Jesus and in His acts the future is realised already now, so that the real meaning of the eschatological teaching is to point out that He who brings salvation at the end of time,

---

[38] Also Mk. xiii. 2 and xiv. 25 show that one cannot assume any early connexion between the death of Jesus and the Parousia, but "the expectation of a considerable interval between resurrection and Parousia is evident here" (Kümmel, *Promise and Fulfilment*, p. 77).

[39] *Op. cit.*, pp. 46 f. See also Mt. xix. 28 and Lk. xxii. 30.

[40] *Op. cit.*, p. 107. "It is thus exegetically untenable to assimilate the prediction Mt. xii. 28 simply to Jesus' proclamation about the proximity of the Kingdom of God, which is indeed likewise attested with complete certainty."

is already present. The presence of the Messianic fulfilment of salvation in the acts and sayings of Jesus is revealed in calling the disciples blessed in seeing what prophets and righteous men have longed to see and have not seen (Mt. XIII. 16 f.; Lk. x. 23 f.). The time of the law and the prophets is now past (Lk. XVI. 16). The time is come when the present Kingdom of God is fought for by violent men who try to snatch it away from mankind, but their time is limited (Mt. XI. 12 f.). Jesus not merely claimed to replace the Old Testament revelation with one that is new and perfect, but He preached that the eschatological fulfilment prepares the end of the old aeon even in the present time.

As against Dodd and others, who tried to read some of the parables of the Kingdom of God as showing the growth of the Kingdom (Mk. IV. 26 ff., 30 ff.; Mt. XIII. 24 ff., 33, 47 ff.), Kümmel maintains that the purpose of the parables of the Seed, the Leaven, and the Grain of Mustard Seed is to give comfort and encouragement. The Kingdom of God comes surely without our being able either to prevent or hasten it, and the fact that it is now hidden ought not to have any effect on that certainty. The parables of the Weeds among the Wheat and the Net show, on the other hand, that a sifting is taking place at the present time, the result of which will only be revealed at the coming Judgment. Kümmel emphasises strongly that Jesus saw the presence of the Kingdom of God only in His own person and work; He spoke also of a community of those who gather round Him as the coming Messiah but never of a Church, for the saying in Mt. XVI. 18 f. does not go back to Jesus.

Examination of the actual text leads Kümmel to the decisive question, which he formulates as follows: What is the meaning of the time element in Jesus' eschatological teaching, when we find side by side the expectation of the imminent Kingdom of God, the expectation of the Kingdom within Jesus' own generation, the emphasis on the time of the coming of the Kingdom being unknown, and the presence of the expected future?[41]

He quite rightly considers it out of the question to eliminate the truly future character of the eschatological fulfilment as seen by Jesus. Was Jesus mistaken, when He expected the Kingdom in the near future? Kümmel replies that Jesus was mistaken in this particular, but at the same time he points out

---

[41] *Op. cit.*, p. 141.

that too much must not be made of the fact that the ideas of Jesus in this instance were set in a contemporary mould which has since proved to be erroneous. For on the question of the moment of the coming of the Kingdom of God, there are two groups of opposing statements: firstly those which speak of a definite period, secondly those which say that the period is indeed short, but at the same time point out that the actual moment is unknown to anyone except the Father. Those in the first group are relatively few (Mt. x. 23; Mk. ix. 1, xiii. 30), which seems to support the conclusion "that this idea did not receive much emphasis in Jesus' message."[42] Passages in support of the second attitude are very much in the majority. It is clear, however, that neither group can be eliminated by critical procedure, by psychological explanations, or by referring them to different periods in the life of Jesus, so that the question must be left open.[43]

Nor is the question actually one of primary importance, for Jesus regarded the question of "the appointed time of the dominion of God" as secondary (Lk. xvii. 20 f.). As a prophet Jesus preached the present Kingdom of God, so that the apocalyptic fixing of the moment of time is naturally not to be looked for. Jesus merely makes clear to man that he is now at the eleventh hour, and that the fulfilment of salvation cannot be long delayed. In His preaching He persistently turns men's minds towards that end of history which God has set as its goal. The awaiting of God's future eschatological action is thus indissolubly united with Jesus' eschatological teaching, since the certainty that God's redeeming will strives for the appearance of the Kingdom of God in all its reality, can only be given in that form. Jesus speaks of the *nearness* of the Kingdom of God, "in order to clothe in living words the certainty of God's redemptive action directed towards the consummation,"[44] and of its *futurity*, since only so is it possible to establish that the redeeming act of God is *historical*.

Jesus linked the future and the coming of the Kingdom of God very closely together with the present, whose centre He

---

[42] *Op. cit.*, p. 149. "It must be frankly confessed that we do not know how to strike a balance between these two sets of assertions, yet this only means that we can gain no clear insight into one particular aspect of the *forms in which Jesus conceived* His eschatological message." (p. 151).

[43] *Op. cit.*, p. 150.

[44] *Op. cit.*, p. 152.

Himself was. "The Kingdom of God is in the midst of you."
Man's attitude to Him at the present moment decides the
judgment that will be passed on him at the Last Day. But more
than that, the Kingdom of God is present in the person of
Jesus, in His teaching and works. The sayings about the
present Kingdom of God provide the key to the understanding
of Jesus' teaching about the future. Since Jesus Himself, who
is the bringer of the Kingdom of God, is already here and the
forces of the new age have begun to be effective, He is in a
position to preach the coming Dominion of God with unique
authority, and to call for a decision for or against this Kingdom. The hope that the Dominion of God will appear in its
fullness is born of the certainty of God's redeeming action in
the present. Attaching oneself to Jesus means attaching
oneself to "the coming Kingdom of God at work in advance
already in the present."[45] The presence sayings do not invali-
date the future sayings, but on the contrary make the latter
really convincing and inevitable. For the presence of the
coming Kingdom of God guarantees that the end of the world
will surely come, that the eleventh hour has dawned which is
to bring in the end.

In Jesus as Son of Man men see the present Kingdom of God.
Through faith in Him they gain the Kingdom and the guarantee of its appearance. The certainty and distinctiveness of the
promise of Jesus is that it is to find fulfilment in Him Himself.
Promise and fulfilment are therefore indissolubly united. The
object of Jesus' teaching is not to impart knowledge of near-at-
hand apocalyptic events, or to give the present an eschatological meaning. Kümmel says: "On the contrary the
inseparable union of hope and present experience demonstrate
the fact that the true meaning of Jesus' eschatological message
is to be found in its reference to God's action in Jesus Himself,
that the essential content of Jesus' preaching about the Kingdom of God is the news of the divine authority of Jesus, who
has appeared on earth and is awaited in the last days as the
one who effects the divine purpose of mercy. So for the
believer the question is not whether he will accept the correctness of an apocalyptic prediction or an interpretation referring
to the present of that which relates to the beyond, but whether
he will respond to the divine mission of *that* Jesus who could

[45] *Op. cit.*, p. 154.

promise us the reign of God, because it was already being fulfilled in Him."[46]

Even though to Kümmel it is beyond question that Jesus claimed to be, and in certain of His sayings confessed Himself to be, the Son of Man and the Messiah, that is by no means to say that He must have regarded Himself as the *Messias praesens*. Both the fact that the Jewish Messianic expectations invariably saw the Messiah as a figure of the future, whose appearance was connected with the renewal of the world, and also the fact that Jesus adopted the eschatological expectation of the Son of Man, show that He expected to receive His Messianic office in its full reality only at the end of time, even though He characterised Himself proleptically even during His earthly life as the "Man." Kümmel summarises his views as follows: "However much Jesus may have seen the Dominion of God and with that His Messianic dignity as already active in His works, His teaching and His person, however much His dignity might in the present remain hidden, He was still *destined* to be the Messiah."[47]

One cannot, therefore, conclude from Jesus' Messiah-consciousness that He *must* have gathered around Him the men of the last generation. In following Him, who was destined to be the Messiah, the little group was formed of those who were promised the Dominion of God. Any other conclusions from the connexion between the Messiah and the community of the end-time would be unjustified.

Kümmel's account of Jesus' attitude towards the Son of Man and the Church does not seem to accord with the conclusions he reached in his analysis of the Kingdom of God in the mind of Jesus. If Jesus saw the Kingdom of God as actually present in His person, that is not the Jewish apocalyptic hope. Why, then, could He not have given the Messianic conception a new meaning also in the question of the Son of Man? He could have seen Himself as the *Messias praesens* and not merely as the *Messias futurus*, since the Kingdom of God was present in His person and actions. When Jesus says, speaking of Himself, that the Son of Man has power on earth to forgive sins (Mk. II. 10), that the Son of Man is Lord even of the

---

[46] *Op. cit.*, p. 155.
[47] Kümmel, *Kirchenbegriff und Geschichtsbewusstsein in der Urgemeinde und bei Jesus*, p. 35.

sabbath (Mk. ii. 28), and that the Son of Man came to give His life as a ransom for many (Mk. x. 45), when Jesus rides into Jerusalem as Prince of Peace and purges the Temple, it is not enough to say that He is speaking and acting as the one destined to be Son of Man and the Messiah. He is more than He who gives faith in the Kingdom. He is the surety of its coming. Even though His real rank is never revealed except to those who have faith, He is even in the present the Son of Man.

To the Kingdom of God and its King belong the people of God; to the Son of Man belongs the community of the Messiah. If one accepts this statement, that is not to derive the idea of the Church from the *idea* of the Son of Man; even from the days of Jesus there is support for the connexion between individual and people in the idea of the Son of Man.[48] Kümmel has shown that Jesus expected an interval between His death and His Parousia. But an interval between death and Parousia is synonymous with Church. Kümmel has thus not drawn the right conclusions from his own arguments.[49]

We have seen how the introduction of Greek ideas on the relationship between time and eternity has often resulted in interpretations alien to the Biblical conception of time. It was therefore felt desirable to form a clearer picture of the New Testament conception of time. Important contributions to this problem have been made by H.-D. Wendland,[50] G. Delling,[51] and above all by O. Cullmann,[52] author of one of the foremost theological works of the last few decades.

[48] A. V. Ström, *Vetekornet. Studier över individ och kollektiv i Nya Testamentet*, Stockholm 1944, p. 224. Examples pp. 136-9.

[49] M. Barth, *Der Augenzeuge. Eine Untersuchung über die Wahrnehmung des Menschensohnes durch die Apostel*, Zollikon-Zürich 1946, interprets the sayings to the effect that the Son of Man would be revealed already to Jesus' own generation as applying only to a few chosen people, *i.e.* the Twelve and possibly a few more, to whom Jesus revealed Himself after His Resurrection. They were witnesses to the revelation of the presence of the Kingdom of God, and so to the fulfilment of the "Naherwartung." Whether this literal interpretation of Mk. ix. 1 really reproduces the meaning of the text seems highly doubtful. The whole mass of Parousia sayings would then have to be interpreted in accordance with this single saying.

[50] Wendland, *Geschichtsanschauung und Geschichtsbewusstsein im Neuen Testament*.

[51] G. Delling, *Das Zeitverständnis des Neuen Testaments*, Gütersloh 1940.

[52] Cullmann, *Christ and Time*. E. von Dobschütz, "Zeit und Raum in Denken des Urchristentums," in *Journal of Biblical Literature*, XLI (1922), pp. 212-23, points out that expressions such as ἤγγικεν ἡ βασιλεία τοῦ Θεοῦ and αἰών represent a transition from a spatial to a temporal scheme. With regard to literature see Cullmann, *Christ and Time*, p. 51, n.1.

Gerhard Delling

To Delling there is a decisive difference not only between the Greek or Hellenistic conception of time on the one hand and the Biblical on the other, but also between the Jewish and Christian conceptions. To the Jews time was never felt as a problem at all, whereas to the Greeks it was an insoluble problem. Christianity differs from both, in so far as it has overcome time through knowledge of the entry into time of eternity.

In Mk. 1. 15 καιρός signifies not just time in general but a decisive point in time. The use of the term is, according to Delling, formally purely Greek, but it has acquired an entirely new meaning. Prophetic understanding of what takes place involves knowledge of God's plan: in the presence of Jesus the purposeful activity of God is fulfilled in the utmost intensity. "It is directed in absolute concentration on *one* point (which admittedly cannot be mathematically isolated), on one solitary event, which shines out throughout the entire extent of creation and of history."[53] This "Christ-event" is characterised as πλήρωμα. In Christ, with whom *pleroma* entered into the world, time has been overcome. The Christian is upraised above time, if he stands under *pleroma*. He has part in eternal life.

But *pleroma* presses on with inward dynamism towards τέλος, the goal and end. That *pleroma* and *telos* should be temporally close to each other is a heritage from Jewish apocalypse. Jesus Himself gave the answer to the relationship between them. He saw the decisive fulfilment already in His activity on earth, but *pleroma* is not yet the real fulfilment, the achievement of *telos*, but merely the guarantee of *telos*. The new religious reality moves towards its full realisation, which gives liberation from cosmos and temporality.

The New Testament conception of time is principally determined by fulfilment. In Jesus Christ *pleroma* and *telos* coincide. In that way the *telos* idea receives its full strength and the *pleroma* idea its full depth. The decisive thing to Jesus is not when the final fulfilment will come. It is in process of coming. The Kingdom of God is an entity that grows. It reveals itself in the present moment and stretches out into the

[53] Delling, *Das Zeitverständnis des Neuen Testaments*, p. 88.

future. The two systems of thought, the present and the future kingdom, are not mutually exclusive. The parables of the growing Kingdom of God point out beyond the present time towards an end, an accomplishment, which does not comprise finality but fulfilment. With this, Jesus has given a new conception of time. "In the growth of the Kingdom of God eternity reaches into time, penetrates and overpowers it, until in some final event time will be swallowed up by eternity."[54] What is new in Jesus is the gospel of the present Kingdom of God, which however loses something essential when hope of ultimate fulfilment is lost.

Jesus thus detaches His work and His teaching from Jewish eschatology. He is interested neither in the "when" nor the "how" of the final events. The "Christ-event" means an entirely new interpretation of the conception "fulfilment of God." It means the entry of eternity into time, and with that the removal of the opposition between time and eternity.

We will not attempt any criticism of Delling here. Cullmann gives that. It must be reckoned to his credit that with him considerations of salvation come into their own, and that his solution to the problem of present and future in the Kingdom of God is made on the assumption that fulfilment entered into the world with Jesus Christ.

Oscar Cullmann

Delling's view, that in early Christianity time was regarded as a problem, is opposed by Oscar Cullmann. Time is not regarded as something that is against God and has to be overcome. Eternity is not an opposite to time. What Delling calls the entry of eternity into time, is actually something quite different, a new *division* of time brought about by the mission of Jesus. What is new in Christianity is, according to Cullmann, not the actual conception of time, which is Jewish, but the *division* of time. Early Christianity did not think in terms of the opposites—Here-Beyond, but in terms of the temporal difference between before, now, and afterwards. Time is regarded as a line. The New Testament emphasises the temporal character of all statements of faith. Eternity is

[54] *Op. cit.*, p. 132.

never the same as timelessness.[55] All such philosophical processes of thought are alien to the New Testament. The
difference between the present and the coming aeon is temporal.

The terms which best illustrate the New Testament conception of time are καιρός and αἰών. *Kairos* is a certain
definite *moment of time*, whereas *aion* is a limited or unlimited
space of time. The divine plan of salvation is bound up with
moments of time, *kairoi*, selected by God, which constitute the
history of salvation. There are divine *kairoi* in past time,
present time, and future time. The decisive moment is the
coming of Jesus with the Gospel of the Kingdom of God.

The time symbol of early Christianity is the rising line, not
the circle. The Biblical history of revelation has "the linear
conception of time."[56] Whereas the Greek conception of
blessedness is determined by the contrast Here-Beyond and is
therefore spatial, the idea of salvation, in accordance with the
Bible's linear conception of time, is temporal. The Kingdom
of God comes in time. The coming fulfilment is really future.
Owing to this linear conception of time, time in early Christianity can provide the framework for the divine acts of revelation and salvation, for these *kairoi* which God in His infinite
power has determined, and also for the aeons, into which the
whole process is divided. Since time is thought of as a rising
line, something can be "fulfilled," a divine plan can be put
into execution, the goal that shines out at the end of the line
can bend the whole course of the line towards itself, the Christ-
mission can point the way for all events before and after it.

Time is only spoken of in the New Testament in connexion
with the history of salvation,[57] as is shown by the expressions
πλήρωμα and πληροῦσθαι. To allow the early Christian idea
of the history of salvation to become lost in metaphysics is to
Cullmann the root of all heresy, in so far as heresy means

---

[55] Cullmann, *Christ and Time*, p. 49. "In the New Testament we find this word
for 'time' used in concrete reference to the redemptive history; it may have the
meaning of 'season' or of 'age,' or it may simply signify some space of time that
is to elapse. Thus even the well-known passage in Rev. x. 6, where it is said that
there will be no more *chronos*, it is not to be understood as if the era of timelessness
were meant; rather on the analogy of Hab. ii. 3. and Heb. x. 37, we must translate:
'There will be no more *delay*.' "

[56] *Op. cit.*, p. 52.

[57] The so-called "*Heilsgeschichte* school" of the nineteenth century, with names
such as Joh. Tobias Beck, Joh. Chr. K. von Hofmann, Carl Aug. Auberlen, and
Martin Kähler, must be regarded as the forerunner of Cullmann.

departure from early Christianity. This appears most clearly
in Gnosticism, in which, for example, the early Christian
expectation of the end with its characteristic temporal distinction between the present and the coming aeon, was replaced
by the Greek metaphysical distinction between "Here" and
"Beyond." The linear time of the history of salvation is
preserved throughout the whole of the New Testament, and in
the second century is to be seen particularly clearly in Irenaeus.

The difference between the Old and New Testament
division of time lies in the fact that the "centre of time" is
differently placed. Biblical time consists actually of three
aeons: (1) that which lies before creation, when the process
of revelation is determined by divine predestination; (2) the
period between the creation and the end, the "present" aeon;
and (3) the "coming" aeon, in which the final event will
take place. The chronologically distinctive feature of
early Christian faith is that, after the resurrection of Jesus,
the "centre" no longer lies in the future, in the coming of the
Messiah, but in something that is already past, namely the
already completed, historical life-work of Jesus. To Judaism
the centre lies at the Parousia, but to early Christianity the
second aeon, that between the creation and Parousia, is
divided by the mission of Christ, so that the period immediately
after the centre-point already belongs to the new aeon, even
though the third period, *i.e.* the end-time, that begins with the
Parousia, has not yet begun.[58] Even to the Synoptists, the
"centre of time" no longer lay in the future. It was identified
with "the present for Jesus and the apostles."[59] Jesus Himself

[58] Cullmann shows this diagrammatically as follows (*Christ and Time*, p. 82):

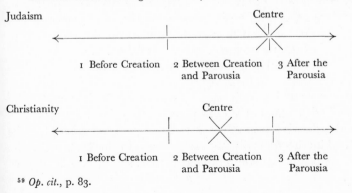

[59] *Op. cit.*, p. 83.

took the same view. "For Him, too, His coming signifies that the mid-point has already been reached in His lifetime. Therefore He sees Satan already fallen from heaven, He already expels demons 'by the finger of God,' He heals the sick, He checks the power of death, He forgives sins and explains that the Kingdom of God has already come, although He holds fast on the other hand to the future character of this Kingdom."[60] Hope remains, but is no longer the centre of historical salvation. That lies in an historic event, "the Christ-event." The centre has been reached, but the end remains. Cullmann illustrates this in terms of warfare. The decisive battle may be fought at a relatively early stage in a war, but the war continues. Even though not everyone admits the decisive importance of this battle, it still means that victory is already won, even though the war continues until "victory day." The centre-point is the overwhelming event which Jesus Himself sees enacted in the fulfilment of His mission: "The blind receive their sight and the lame walk, lepers are cleansed and the deaf hear, and the dead are raised up, and the poor have the good news preached to them" (Mt. xi. 5). To the early community the decisive battle was fought in and with the death and resurrection of Jesus.

Cullmann maintains that anyone to whom the early Christian rearrangement of the time pattern does not stand out as the radically new element in the New Testament, cannot really understand Christianity. It can be to him nothing more than a Jewish sect. The New Testament hope is something other than the Jewish hope. This hope has just as great intensity as the Jewish, indeed even greater, although to the early community future hopes were not of central importance. Intensity and central position must not, however, be confused. The intensity of the Christian hope rests on the fact that an historical event has become the centre of time. The hope of the *final* victory is all the more intensive, that the conviction is firmly held that the decisive battle has already taken place.

In the teaching that the Kingdom of God is near, the chronological element may be predominant, but the knowledge that the decisive battle has already taken place also plays its part. The theologically important point in the teaching of the nearness of the Kingdom of God is that, since Christ, we have

[60] *Ibid.*

entered into a new sector of time and have therefore come closer to the end. The idea that the Kingdom might have come a decade or so after Jesus Cullmann calls an "error of perspective." Its psychological explanation is the same as for a too-early expectation of the end of a war, once the decisive battle has been fought. Determination and limitation of date are secondary, whereas division of time is primary, and this is not altered by the fact that the interval of time between Jesus and the Parousia has come to be milennia instead of decades.

When Jesus expected an interval of time, as Kümmel has clearly shown that He did, Cullmann asserts that He was thinking of the position and task of His disciples during that time, as is also shown by the Church saying in Mt. xvi. 18, the genuineness of which there is no reason to doubt, least of all if one goes back to the Aramaic equivalent of ἐκκλησία.

Were Cullmann's interpretation of the important questions relating to the New Testament conception of time in the light of historical salvation to win general acceptance, we should be justified in assuming that a corrective has been applied to the philosophical adaptations of Jesus' idea of the Kingdom of God, and that a realistic interpretation of the Kingdom of God according to the Bible will gain ground and win new respect in the light of the New Testament sayings. One great merit of Cullmann is that, like E. Stauffer, H. Preisker, A. Fridrichsen, and others, he clearly recognises the unity of the New Testament. "The eschatological view of the Kingdom of God which was Jesus' own and was established by Him in the Church, welds together the different parts of the New Testament in a firm inward unity. We live in the last days. Judgment and salvation lie ahead of us now. The situation is crucial and craves a decision. But this situation, full of τὸ ἔσχατον, is concentrated in one person, in *Jesus*" (A. Fridrichsen).[61]

Scandinavian Exegetists

Johannes Lindblom defines the Kingdom of God in a popular book[62] as a metaphysical, transcendental world which shall be

---

[61] A. Fridrichsen, "Nya Testamentets enhet," in *Svensk Exegetisk Årsbok*, 1941, p. 45.

[62] J. Lindblom, *Guds rike, En biblisk studie*, Stockholm 1919.

P

brought about by the creation of God at the end of time. "Now when Jesus from time to time speaks of this world as of something that is already present, He does so because He already sees the *beginnings of this divine world realised in the midst of this earthly world*. Even now is enacted what might be regarded as a prelude to what is to come. Those forces which will one day constitute the coming world of the Kingdom of God are already showing signs of activity."[63] The Kingdom of God is in process of coming. Jesus possesses the Spirit and is therefore "the bearer of the power of the Kingdom of God."[64] Jesus is bearer of the nature of the Kingdom of God. He represents the Kingdom of God on earth, and in Him the forces of the Kingdom of God are active already now in an initial form. In later works Lindblom emphasises the connexion between Jesus and the new people of God.[65]

Unfortunately Anton Fridrichsen has not left any full exposition of the teaching of Jesus on the Kingdom of God. A number of minor writings and articles, however, present an interpretation of Jesus based on Biblical realism.[66]

The historical background to Jesus' teaching of the Kingdom of God was the radical pessimism and supra-worldly hope of apocalyptic pietism, which Jesus encountered in John the Baptist and inherited from him. But Jesus is distinguished from this pietistic movement by His awareness of His task of preaching the gospel. He is the bearer of the glad tidings. The Kingdom of God in the mouth of Jesus is not merely the coming judgment and blessedness, but something that man encounters here and now. "The necessary condition for this gospel is once again that Jesus is convinced that He brings fulfilment, in other words He is convinced that He is the Messiah of God. Only if Jesus knew Himself chosen to preach the Kingdom of God as its Messiah could He preach it as a

---

[63] Lindblom, *op. cit.*, p. 117. [64] *Op. cit.*, p. 118.

[65] J. Lindblom, *Ekklesia. En biblisk studie till belysning av kyrkoproblemet*, Uppsala 1943.

[66] Among A. Fridrichsen's writings may be mentioned: *Le Problème du miracle dans le christianisme primitif*, E.H.P.R., VOL. XII, Strasbourg 1925; "Jesu kamp mot de urene ånder," in *S.T.K.*, 1929, pp. 297-314; *Vem ville Jesus vara?*, Verdandis småskrifter, No. 346, Stockholm 1931; "Omkring Jesu Gudsrikestanke," in *S.T.K.*, 1932, pp. 41-9; "Kyrka och sakrament i Nya Testamentet," in *S.T.K.*, 1936, pp. 301-17; "Människosonen och Israel," in *Till Gustaf Aulén*, Lund 1939, pp. 100-16; "Älska, hata, förneka (försaka)," in *Svensk Exegetisk Årsbok*, 1940, pp. 152-62; "Messias och kyrkan," in *En bok om kyrkan*, Lund 1942, pp. 26-45.

'gospel,' as a redeeming, liberating, saving message. For through the Messiah the supra-worldly reality has entered the world, the Kingdom of God has become the sphere of the Messiah, and whoever enters this sphere, enters the community of the Messiah, belongs already to the Kingdom of God and is upborne and interpenetrated by its forces."[67]

Fridrichsen finds support for his belief that this was the basic view of Jesus Himself in the fact that the best traditional material, the figurative sayings and parables, represent the Kingdom of God in this way. In the parables of the Treasure in the Field and the Pearl of Value, it is certainly not just the sure expectation of sharing in the coming Kingdom of God that inspires the enthusiastic joy which is willing to sacrifice everything in order to gain its desire, but the joy of having *found* the treasure and the pearl is first and foremost the joy of having *found* and gained the Kingdom of God through following Jesus. It is the joy in the "Bridegroom" that is the secret of the joy in the Kingdom of God (Mk. II. 19). He is the Treasure and the Pearl, for which everything must be sacrificed. The secret of Jesus' idea of the Kingdom of God lies precisely in the way in which Jesus regarded the personal relationship between Himself and the Kingdom.

The parables of the Mustard Seed, the Leaven, and the Self-growing Seed allow us a glimpse of the way Jesus saw the Kingdom of God. The Kingdom is a mystery that fulfils itself in secret. We can only catch glimpses of it, but we can hope for it with complete assurance. When Jesus uses images from plant life, He means to bring home to us that as surely as we count upon the miracles of nature, so surely can we count upon the Kingdom of God. If the miraculous result in nature corresponds to the fully revealed Kingdom of God, then it is Jesus Himself, His teaching, His miracles and His identity with the Messiah, that correspond to the preparatory stages. These "signs" give us certainty of the coming fulfilment. Just as surely as the grain of mustard seed grows into a tree and the wheat shoots up of itself above the ground, no man knows how, so surely shall that which is now taking place when the forces of the Kingdom of God are active in Jesus, one day burst forth in the final fulfilment. But all that occurs here in and with the appearance of Jesus is a mystery which

[67] "Omkring Jesu Gudsrikestanke," p. 45.

only he who possesses the inner qualifications can detect and interpret aright.

The counterpart to the mystery of the Kingdom of God is the mystery of evil. Just as in the life of nature there are not only creative forces at work, but also destructive and obstructive forces (the parables of the Sower and the Weeds among the Wheat), so is it also with the life of man. A demoniac power is at work. The establishment of the Kingdom of God means that this power is vanquished and destroyed. When Jesus casts out evil spirits, that is the most glorious revelation of the Kingdom of God through the Messiah. Until Judgment Day, however, the Kingdom of God and the kingdom of Satan shall exist side by side and struggle against one another in secret. For what remains of the present age, the words of the parable of the Weeds among the Wheat shall apply: "Let both grow together." But what has already taken place strengthens our certainty of the coming of the Kingdom of God.

Present and future go together in Jesus' idea of the Kingdom of God. What holds them together is the miracle which is characteristic of the Messianic age. This miracle is that the Kingdom of God constantly breaks through at individual points, thus heralding the great breakthrough that will come at the final fulfilment, when all shall be united with God's own revelation in heavenly splendour and glory.

Fridrichsen emphasises strongly how the Kingdom of God was concentrated in Jesus, in His words and acts. "The mystery of the Kingdom of God was one with Him Himself."[68] This insistence on the fact that the Kingdom of God with its irresistible penetrating force is a mystery, foreshadows Rudolf Otto's interpretation of Jesus. But Fridrichsen emphasises in a quite different way from Otto that the beholding of the Kingdom of God in "esoteric searching" is not enough; the Kingdom is won through faith and repentance. It is part of the secret of the Kingdom of God that the Son of Man shall give His life for mankind. The way to the blessedness of the Kingdom lies through suffering as a follower of the Son of

[68] *Vem ville Jesus vara*, p. 44. "Människosonen och Israel," p. 104: "Ultimately 'The Kingdom of God is near, believe the gospel' means this: Understand who I am; believe in me! This is implicit in the message of Jesus, which contains a reference to Jesus Himself. But a hidden reference." Jesus is "the bearer of the great universal mystery of the Kingdom of God" (*op. cit.*, p. 113).

Man. Fridrichsen can therefore assert that the exhortation: "Repent and believe the gospel" actually means the same thing as the invitation: "Follow me." "Repentance, *metanoia*, is the same thing as to abandon the world in faith in the Son of Man and to enter into His circle, to become one of 'the Bridegroom's friends'—and to take the consequences."[69] Among these is also righteousness, as expressed in the Sermon on the Mount: "You therefore, must be perfect, as your heavenly Father is perfect" (Mt. v. 48).

It is further characteristic of this interpretation of the Kingdom of God that it sees the power of the Kingdom of God concentrated not only in the Messiah-Son of Man but also in His community. As Jesus in His mission is not merely the prophet who preaches the word of the Kingdom, faith and repentance, but is also the Messiah, He has also the task of gathering together and sanctifying Israel at the end of time. The people of God is the *ekklesia* of the Son of Man, which He has made bearer of the new covenant, and which is to share in His glory. The path to glory lies, for the people of God as for the Son of Man, through persecution and suffering. Anton Fridrichsen sums up his views on the question of the Kingdom of God and the Church as follows: "Thus Jesus laid the foundation of the New Testament idea of the Church. This is coloured throughout by His eschatology, which, in that it links the Kingdom of God with the Son of Man, comprises a people of God of the end-time, in the world but not of the world, an *ekklesia* of the new covenant, which is one with the Son of Man in faith and follows Him. The forces of the Kingdom of God, its grace, righteousness and miraculous power, are active in this *ekklesia*, which is the centre of the world and heir to the coming world, always threatened by the powers of destruction, but in possession of the promise that 'the powers of death shall not prevail against it.'"[70]

The Kingdom of God is, according to this interpretation, a transcendent miracle, which Jesus has proclaimed as present; it has come (Mt. xii. 28), is within reach, but only for him who repents and believes the gospel: "The Kingdom of God is at hand." The Kingdom of God is an actual reality in and through the word of the Kingdom. The Kingdom is real in

[69] "Messias och kyrkan," p. 39.
[70] *Op. cit.*, p. 40.

the word of the Kingdom. "The transcendent reality is in *the prophetic word*, it accompanies this and works through it."[71] But it has, nevertheless, an independent existence. In itself the Kingdom of God is a secret, a *mysterion*, which only he can see who first has it in his heart, in faith. Then he sees also glimpses of the power of the Kingdom of God in the miracles Jesus performs, and he feels its joy and blessedness when he is close to the "Bridegroom," who feasts with his wedding-guests, and with the Messiah-Son of Man, who takes them into the new covenant at the farewell Supper on the last evening.

Lyder Brun[72] sees the unity between present and future in Jesus' Kingdom of God in the fact that in both cases it is a question of God's kingly rule. What is brought into the present through the activities of Jesus in the power of God is precisely the Kingdom of God, which is the object of hope and salvation. That is also the reason why the first, apparently insignificant beginnings have the glory of fulfilment about them; future and present belong together. But to him who stands outside it is a secret. It is only revealed to faith.[73]

In Denmark H. Mosbech, who should probably be regarded mainly as a liberal theologian, clearly recognises in his interpretation of the Kingdom of God[74] that, even though most of the sayings in the Synoptic versions represent the Kingdom of God as future, there still remain a number of sayings which speak of a beginning of the Kingdom already here in time (Lk. XVII. 20 f.; Mt. XII. 28, XI. 5, XIII. 16 f.; the parables of the Mustard Seed, the Leaven, the Weeds among the Wheat, the Net, the Self-growing Seed). The eschatological Kingdom of God for which the Jews longed has begun with the appearance and activity of Jesus and with the little group of disciples who gathered round Him. Here, according to Mosbech, we have the beginnings of a new way of looking at the Kingdom of God. As Jesus felt Himself to be the Servant of the Lord,

[71] *Op. cit.*, p. 38.

[72] L. Brun, *Jesu evangelium, En historisk framställning av Jesu förkunnelse*, 1917, 2nd edn., Oslo 1926; *id.*, "Der Name und die Königsherrschaft im Vaterunser," in *Harnack-Ehrung*, Leipzig 1921, pp. 22-31.

[73] N. A. Dahl, *Das Volk Gottes, Eine Untersuchung zum Kirchenbewusstsein des Urchristentums*, Skrifter utg. av Det Norske Videnskabs-Akademi, Hist. filos., II Kl., 1941, No. 2, Oslo 1941, strongly stresses the connexion between the Kingdom of God and the Son of Man.

[74] H. Mosbech, "Jesu Forkyndelse efter de tre Første Evangelier," in *Haandbog i Kristendomskundskab*; VOL. III, *Det Nye Testamente*, pp. 309-18.

the Kingdom of God must necessarily be connected with His appearance. His exorcisms, His healings, His preaching of the gospel, and the group of disciples are the insignificant beginnings, the seed, that is to become a great tree, just as it is said of the present humble position of the Messiah that it shall some day be changed to glory.[75]

[75] Two particularly valuable contributions to the study of Jesus appeared in the English language during the nineteen-forties, namely: in England, R. W. G. Tasker, *The Nature and Purpose of the Gospels*, London 1944; and in America, A. T. Olmstead, *Jesus in the Light of History*, New York 1942. In a review in *Journal of Near Eastern Studies*, II (1943), pp. 124 f., T. J. Meek characterises Olmstead's work as follows: "All in all this life of Jesus is a much more conservative treatment and more positive in its results than we should have expected from a professional historian" (p. 125).

XIII

Conclusion

To try to establish the meaning of ἡ βασιλεία τοῦ Θεοῦ in the teaching of Jesus by means of a definition of the term itself takes us nowhere. The expression "Dominion of God," customary since Gustaf Dalman, has too often been given such a wide meaning that it can be made to include almost anything. It can be used to mean the kingly rule of God, exercised in time past, present or future. The strong emphasis on the demands made by God's kingly will has sometimes resulted in the Kingdom of God becoming more law than gospel.

The Kingdom of God is a transcendental miraculous world, the whole meaning of which cannot be covered by a brief formula. Even though one cannot share Rudolf Otto's views in every particular, one can only agree with him when he says that the phrase "Kingdom of God" aroused in those who heard the preaching of Jesus a number of ideas connected with the heavenly Kingdom and its coming. But the Kingdom is *God's* Kingdom; everything is concentrated in the King of the Kingdom, who is one with the Kingdom. The personal-theocentric character of the Kingdom of God must therefore not be lost sight of.

The lasting value of the work of Johannes Weiss and Albert Schweitzer is shown by the fact that, since their time, very few scholars have denied the eschatological nature of the Kingdom of God. The Kingdom of God is not a community of Christians nor an inner life of the soul, nor yet an earthly paradise which mankind is bringing into being and which is in process of development. The Kingdom of God is absolutely eschatological. It is a Kingdom which is not of this world. It is

God's work. It appears at the end-time. Lest the coming of the Kingdom of God should be lost sight of in all manner of philosophical speculations in which eternity becomes the same as timelessness, it is of the utmost importance that the purely future quality of the Kingdom should be clearly emphasised. The Kingdom of God comes *in* time, at that καιρός which He who is lord over time determines.

Jesus looked forward to the imminent end of the present age. It was not to be long before the Kingdom of God came "with power." But He did not wish to force on the Parousia by His death, nor did He expect it immediately after His death. An undefined period of time was to elapse between the resurrection and the final revelation of the Son of Man.

But Jesus was not a "consistent" eschatologist. He did not see the Kingdom of God which he preached as belonging exclusively to the future. He preached it as being present in the present time. The most important supporting texts are: Lk. xi. 20 (Mt. xii. 28): "It is by the finger (Spirit) of God that I cast out demons, then the kingdom of God has come upon you." The finger of God was active at the Creation (Ps. viii. 3). It was said of the miracles of Moses: "This is the finger of God" (Ex. viii. 19). If Jesus had the finger of God, He was a new Moses. Jesus had at His disposal the creative power of God, and a new age had begun with Him.—Mk. iii. 27: "No one can enter a strong man's house and plunder his goods, unless he first binds the strong man; then indeed he may plunder his house." The stronger, the Messiah, has thus already entered into activity, and the Kingdom of God has begun.—Lk. xvii. 21: "The kingdom of God is in the midst of you."—Mt. xi. 2-6 (Lk. vii. 18-23), where the disciples of John the Baptist, in answer to their question: "Are you he who is to come, or shall we look for another?" are told by Jesus: "Go out and tell John what you hear and see: The blind receive their sight and the lame walk, lepers are cleansed and the deaf hear, and the dead are raised up, and the poor have the good news preached to them. And blessed is he who takes no offence at me."—Mt. xiii. 16 (Lk. x. 23 f.): "Blessed are your eyes, for they see; and your ears, for they hear."—Lk. x. 18, where Jesus says: "I saw Satan fall like lightning from heaven." There is also that difficult passage in Mt. xi. 12: "From the days of John the Baptist until now the kingdom of heaven has suffered violence, and men of violence take it by force,"[1] where, even if βιάζεται is middle voice, the presence of the Kingdom of God is meant. Besides this there are a number of parables of the Kingdom of God, which refer not merely to the coming but also to the present Kingdom, namely the Leaven, the Mustard Seed, the Self-growing Seed. Even the Weeds among the Wheat and the Net in the Sea may refer to the present Kingdom. The parables of the Treasure in the Field and the Pearl of Value, which are often regarded as neutral in the matter of future or present, would seem rather to imply the presence of the Kingdom of God, as they describe the joy over what one *has*, not over what one *is to have*.

Jesus taught that the time was fulfilled. The Kingdom of God was approaching. It already made itself known and was perceptibly close. At certain points it was already victorious and revealed itself as present, namely in the miracles of Jesus and in the glad tidings: "The Kingdom of God is at hand." Its break-through at individual points makes clear to him who has rightly understood what is happening that the coming of the Kingdom in glory cannot be long delayed. What takes place during the present time while Jesus is active, leads onwards towards the fulfilment with the Last Judgment and the glory of the heavenly Kingdom. What is new about Jesus is that He preached the purely eschatological Kingdom which is to come in the future as being already present.

The parable of the Self-growing Seed shows us to some extent how Jesus saw the Kingdom of God in the present. What is said there about the seed that is cast into the earth and then shoots up above it, so that the earth bears fruit of itself, applies also to something else that is happening here and now. He who has eyes to see, understands the secret of God. He sees with the very eyes of the teller of the parable. He discovers the mystery. The heavenly Kingdom of God has really come to earth and its force is active, hidden but just as real as the miracle that takes place when the seed grows and bears fruit. When the grain is ripe, the sower "puts in the sickle, because the harvest has come." So also do present

---

[1] The parallel passage in Lk. xvi. 16 runs: "The law and the prophets were until John; since then the good news of the kingdom of God is preached, and every one enters it violently."

events lead on towards fulfilment. The present Kingdom of God is a mystery, a miracle, which it is not for every man to grasp and understand.

It is important to emphasise that the Kingdom of God is present in the word, in the preaching of the Gospel by Jesus. That God is in His word, is one with His word and works through His word, is a thoroughly Biblical thought which we find, for example, in Is. LV. 10 f. The Kingdom of God is incarnated in the gospel of the Kingdom.

The present Kingdom is concentrated in Jesus, the Son of Man and Servant of the Lord, who is to give His life as a ransom for many. Jesus is thus not merely the prophet who preaches the Kingdom of God. He surpasses everything that is meant by the word prophet. He gives God's forgiveness, which to the Jews was blasphemy (Mk. II. 7). As the Stronger he binds the Strong, who holds mankind in his bonds. As the time that is left to the demoniac powers is short, it is full of violent activity on the part of Satan. But Jesus can use the finger of God like a second Moses (Ex. VIII. 19), and when He casts out the evil spirits with it, then the Messianic time has come. The Kingdom of God has come.

Jesus already in the present is Son of Man. His appearance in Israel is the decisive moment in history. The time of fulfilment has come, with all that that involves. But that Jesus already in the present is Messiah-Son of Man is a mystery, just as the presence of the Kingdom of God is a mystery, which only they can understand to whom God has revealed it (Mt. XVI. 17).

The Son of Man includes within Himself a collective, humanity, the people, the "Remnant." The community of the Son of Man, the kernel of the new people of God, belongs together with the Son of Man. The mystery of the Kingdom of God and the mystery of the Son of Man are revealed to those who belong to the people of the new covenant, to the House of God. To them it is given to celebrate the Messianic feast with Jesus.

Jesus says that he who denies himself, abandons the whole of his life and follows Him in suffering, shall gain his life. He who confesses Jesus before men, him shall Jesus confess before His Father which is in heaven. Does this mean that he who acts upon his belief in Jesus as He who is to come by following Him and confessing Him before men, is already now in the Kingdom of God? So far as the author can understand, the answer to this question must be no. To him who repents and believes the gospel: "The kingdom of God is at hand," which is the same thing as believing in Jesus, the mystery of the Kingdom of God may be revealed. But that is not to say that he has entered into the Kingdom. All the sayings about entering into the Kingdom refer to the coming Kingdom, which is often characterised as Life. Between the present and the future Kingdom of God lies the Last Judgment, at which all must answer for what they have done and what they have failed to do (Mt. xxv. 31-46).

The saying of Jesus: "Unless your righteousness exceeds that of the scribes and Pharisees, you will never enter the kingdom of heaven" (Mt. v. 20), shows us the demand He placed upon His disciples: to do the will of God. The demand for righteousness is raised to the highest imaginable point: "You, therefore, must be perfect, as your heavenly Father is perfect" (Mt. v. 48). As God is "whole" in His actions, so also must the Christian be. In the better righteousness which Jesus demands of His followers, there is no talk of harder or greater achievements, merely of whole-hearted devotion to God and to one's neighbour, a loving service without limit or end. However high the demand may be set, no one is asked to do the impossible, but the disciple must consider, when he accepts the challenge, what it is going to cost. For this cost will include suffering and persecution: "Whoever would save his life will lose it; and whoever loses his life for my sake and the gospel's, will save it" (Mk. viii. 35).

It is important to bear in mind that the burden of Jesus' teaching is primarily not an imperative but an indicative: "The Kingdom of God is at hand"—"The kingdom of God has come"—"The kingdom of God is in the midst of you." The exhortation "Repent!" is followed by a "For the kingdom of God is at hand." The dominant note is joy that the time of fulfilment has come, that the "Bridegroom" is among his guests, that the Kingdom of God is demonstrating its presence in words and miracles of various kinds. Life in the community of the Son of Man is described as a King's feast for His people, a wedding feast, a feast that fills life at once with joy and strength.

There are, however, other notes intermingled which give us to understand that, according to Jesus, it is by no means everyone who will "inherit the kingdom of God." It is hard to enter there (Mk. x. 24), for some it is beyond the limits of possibility: "Enter by the narrow gate; for the gate is wide, and the way is easy, that leads to destruction, and those who enter by it are many. For the gate is narrow and the way is hard that leads to life, and those who find it are few" (Mt. vii. 13 f.). This, then, is the doctrine of *selection* that we find in the teaching of Jesus, which distinguishes between *the many* who are called and *the few* who are chosen. There are men who cannot find the way as it "winds ahead like an almost invisible track" (Anton Fridrichsen),[2] nor are they attracted by the narrow little gate in the wall. They do not see it because it looks so insignificant. In the same way the masses of mankind do not see the Son of Man in the unassuming figure of Jesus, and do not perceive in His simple parables, which are concerned with everyday events of life, God's great message to humanity. It is invisible to their eyes like the path that leads through ground covered with stones and tussocks of grass, or like the gate in the wall that has neither splendour nor magnificence. Only those who have been gifted with the power of faith to see the great in the small, belong to the chosen of the Kingdom. They are the elect, οἱ ἐκλεκτοί (Mt. xxii. 14), they belong to οἱ σῳζόμενοι (Lk. xiii. 23). Yet the fact of being chosen of God does not at all mean that the elect must not, throughout the whole of their earthly life and exerting the full strength of their souls, *seek* the way and *fight* to enter in through the gate to the Kingdom of God. If we turn to the parable of the Sower (Mk. iv. 3 ff. *et par.*), we learn more about the nature of Jesus' doctrine of election and also the explanation why He speaks of many who are called, but only few who are chosen to share in the Kingdom. The "Sower" is Jesus the Messiah Himself, who while sowing the seed of the word had just the same experience as the farmer, that the fate of the seed is determined by the nature of the ground it falls on. Much seed never bears any fruit. Only that which falls "into good soil" does. That which falls among thorns and thistles is lost. It is destined to destruction. What Jesus meant by this cannot be interpreted as "an expression of a biological-deterministic

[2] Fridrichsen, "Nya Testamentets enhet," p. 52.

outlook" (Fridrichsen). It is not "psychological characteristics" which determine whether the individual is to belong
to the *few* or to the *many*, and is to have part in or be excluded
from the Kingdom of God. The fate of the individual rests
upon whether he is open or closed to the word, in which resides
the "*dynamis*" of God which creates faith and its fruits.

To Jesus the present and the coming Kingdom of God
stood side by side. Neither can be explained away or assume
a dominating position at the expense of the other. What
unites them is the Son of Man. "The new age" exists after
the coming of Jesus in "the old age." The Kingdom of God
has come and is active in the sayings and miracles of Jesus.
Satan is overcome and πτωχοὶ εὐαγγελίζονται (Mt. xi. 5).
Only faith sees what is afoot, but at the Last Day the power
and glory of the Kingdom shall be revealed to all.

XIV

Postscript

The purpose of this book, as it was originally published in 1947, was to trace the history of research into the Kingdom of God from the eighteen-nineties down to the middle of the nineteen-forties. The present chapter brings this account up to date with a brief survey of the debate as it has continued during the past fifteen years. It will again inevitably largely take the form of a resumé of the books published during these years. The author continues to hold in the main the views expressed in the previous chapter.

The arrangement is as follows. An introductory account of the renewal of research into the life of Jesus will be followed by a discussion firstly of the purely futuristic interpretation of the Kingdom of God, secondly, of criticism of "realised eschatology" and of recent attempts to de-eschatologise Jesus. The last section of the chapter will be devoted to books on Jesus' idea of the Kingdom of God in which an attempt is made to do justice to both the future and present aspects of the Kingdom of God (S. H. Hooke, N. A. Dahl, Günther Bornkamm, and Rudolf Schnackenburg).

Albert Schweitzer's book on the study of the life of Jesus rendered it absolutely impossible for any New Testament scholar to write a scientifically based biography of Jesus, though this did not prevent numbers of popular lives of Jesus being written, more particularly in the Anglo-Saxon world. In the middle of the nineteen-twenties, Ernst von Dobschütz[1] remarked that the flood of presentations of the life of Jesus had completely dried up after the appearance of Schweitzer's

---

[1] E. von Dobschütz, *Die evangelische Theologie, ihr jetziger Stand und ihre Aufgaben*, Das Neue Testament, VOL. II, Halle 1927, pp. 26 f.

book. No one dared any longer write a "Life of Jesus," the most they dared undertake was certain problems connected with His life. But von Dobschütz was convinced that a time would come when some theological writer would venture once again on a comprehensive study of the life and work of Jesus. In the meantime, scholars concerned themselves primarily with the message of Jesus. The theology of the life of Jesus gave way to a *kerygma*-theology which left "the historical Jesus" altogether out of account.

It was not until the nineteen-fifties that the problem of "the historical Jesus" again became the subject of serious discussion. Hans von Campenhausen[2] wrote then, in connexion with the stories of the resurrection: "It seems to me . . . that, in comparison with the innumerable investigations into the history of literature, the history of tradition, the history of motive and the history of form, the question of the simply historical has fallen far too much into the background, *i.e.* the question of the historical kernel of these things which tradition presents as historical." A number of articles appeared in periodicals. I will mention the names of only Professor Ernst Käsemann[3] of Göttingen, the Norwegian N. A. Dahl,[4] and the Englishman T. W. Manson.[5] It is characteristic of the new outlook that Günther Bornkamm should have opened his book, *Jesus von Nazareth*,[6] with a chapter on faith and history in the Gospels. In this he states that we do not possess one single saying of Jesus or story of Him, however genuine it may be, that is not also at the same time a confession of faith of the early community. But the tradition is not a creation of the imagination, but a response to the figure and mission of Jesus. The *kerygma* (teaching)

---

[2] H. von Campenhausen, "Der Ablauf der Osterereignisse und das leere Grab," in *Sitzungsberichte der Heidelberger Akademie der Wissenschaften, Philosophisch-historische Klasse*, 1952, PT. 4, Heidelberg 1952, p. 7.

[3] E. Käsemann, "Das Problem des historischen Jesus," in *Z.Th.K.*, LI (1954), pp. 125-53.

[4] N. A. Dahl, "Der historischen Jesu als geschichtswissenschaftliches und theologisches Problem," in *Kerygma und Dogma*, I (1955), pp. 104-32.

[5] T. W. Manson, "The Life of Jesus: some tendencies in present-day research," in *The Background of the New Testament and its Eschatology*, Cambridge 1956, pp. 211-21. The author has not been able to obtain a copy of J. M. Robinson, *A New Quest of the Historical Jesus*, London 1959.

[6] Günther Bornkamm, *Jesus von Nazareth*, Stuttgart 1956; Eng. version: *Jesus of Nazareth*, trans. I. and F. McLuskey and J. M. Robinson, London and New York 1960.

of the Gospels confirms His historicity and the reality of His resurrection. An intensive study of the origin of the Gospel tradition according to new methods,[7] a deeper insight into the life and thought of late Judaism, and not least the discovery of the Dead Sea Scrolls, have compelled scholars to consider afresh the question of the historical Jesus. Ethelbert Stauffer went so far as to appeal for a resumption of the study of the life of Jesus,[8] and himself published in 1957[9] a critical reconstruction of Jesus' self-revelation in history.[10] The same tendency is apparent in Joachim Jeremias,[11] who is no longer satisfied with the earliest available traditional forms, but tries to get right back to *ipsissima verba Jesu*. And in principle, this is no longer regarded as impossible or unreliable.

Any trace of a new understanding of the Kingdom of God in the teaching of Jesus is, however, hard to find in the debate of the past fifteen years. Attitudes seem fixed and set. Thoughts are bound by preconceived ideas which are never put to the test. These ideas may be either theological or philosophical. As many times in the past, however, renewed study of the Old Testament seems to bring deeper insight into the Gospels. The effect of taking seriously the idea that God is King on one's understanding of Jesus' idea of the Kingdom of God may be seen in two, in many respects such different books as those of John Bright[12] and Rudolf Schnackenburg.[13] Mention should, of course, also be made of S. Mowinkel's work.[14]

I

In his Gifford Lectures of 1955, on the subject of "History and Eschatology," Rudolf Bultmann emphasised that the New

[7] See H. Riesenfeld, *The Gospel Tradition and its Beginnings. A study in the Limits of "Formgeschichte,"* London 1957.

[8] E. Stauffer, "Der Stand der neutestamentlichen Forschung," in *Theologie und Liturgie*, ed. L. Henning, Kassel 1952, pp. 35-105.

[9] E. Stauffer, *Jesus, Gestalt und Geschichte*, Berne 1957; Eng. version: *Jesus and His Story*, trans. D. M. Barton, London 1960.

[10] E. Stauffer, *Jesus, Paulus und wir*, Hamburg 1961.

[11] J. Jeremias, *Die Gleichnisse Jesu*, 4th edn., Zürich 1956; Eng. version: *The Parables of Jesus*, trans. S. M. Hooke, London 1954.

[12] J. Bright, *The Kingdom of God in Bible and Church*, London 1955. Also New York 1958 under the title, *The Kingdom of God. The Biblical Concept and its Meaning for the Church*.

[13] R. Schnackenburg, *Gottes Herrschaft und Reich. Eine biblisch-theologische Studie*, Freiburg 1959.

[14] S. Mowinkel, *He that cometh*, Oxford 1956.

Q

Testament preserves both the Old Testament and apocalyptic views of history, though the apocalyptic view predominates. He summarised the present state of research as follows: "Today it is commonly accepted that the reign of God which Jesus proclaimed is the eschatological reign. The only point in dispute is whether Jesus thought that the reign of God was immediately imminent, indeed already dawning in His exorcisms, or whether He thought that it was already present in His person—what today is called 'realised eschatology.' With this is connected the question of what He thought about His own person. But it is not disputed that Jesus understood His time as the time of decision, and that He thought that men's attitude to Himself and His message was decisive for them. The time has now arrived in which the old promises and hopes will be fulfilled."

Bultmann holds firm to his earlier view of Jesus' teaching of the Kingdom of God in word and deed. He emphasises[15] that what is new and individual in Jesus' idea of the future is the certainty with which He says: "The time is come! The Dominion of God (*Gottesherrschaft*) is appearing! The end is here!" The rule of Satan is over, for "I saw Satan fall like lightning from heaven" (Lk. x. 18). The sign that the end is at hand is Jesus Himself, His appearance and activity, His preaching (Mt. xi. 5 *par.*). Jesus saw the Dominion of God already coming in His miracles (Lk. xi. 20 *par.*).

All this that is taking place does not mean that the Dominion of God is already present; but it means that it is in process of coming. The Dominion of God is breaking through ("*im Anbruch*"). All that men can do is to hold themselves in readiness. Now is the time of decision. The voice of Jesus is a voice crying out for decision. It is Jesus Himself in His own person who is the sign of the times. He Himself in His own person means the demand for decision, in so far as His words are God's last words before the end. Men must be ready to sacrifice everything for the Kingdom of God (Mt. xiii. 44-6). In face of the Kingdom of God, man must become like a child, waiting to be given some great gift.[16]

English New Testament scholars have generally adopted

---

[15] R. Bultmann, *Theologie des Neuen Testaments*, 1953; Eng. version: *Theology of the New Testament*, trans. K. Grobel, London 1952-5.

[16] Bultmann, *op. cit.*, (Eng. trans.), pp. 9 f.

a critical attitude towards the radical results reached by the form critics. William Manson's thoroughgoing conclusions with form criticism in his *Jesus the Messiah*[17] form no exception. Reginald H. Fuller subjects Bultmann's interpretation of Jesus to penetrating criticism in *The Mission and Achievement of Jesus*.[18] Bultmann, Fuller says, has failed to give a consistent explanation of the death of Jesus and "one which stands in organic relation with his proclamation: 'The Kingdom of God is at hand.'"[19] Jesus was an eschatological prophet "who announced the impending of the reign of God, and his own person and activity as the signs of its coming."[20] Here he is in agreement with Bultmann. But more emphasis must be laid on the fact that Jesus saw God as already active in Him in a way which belongs organically together with that which is to come. The forces of the Kingdom of God are proleptically operative in Jesus. But the chief fault is that Bultmann does not go farther than the first part of Jesus' ministry, and as a representative of radical form criticism he cannot do otherwise. There is no bridge between Jesus' preaching in Galilee and the closely impending arrival of the Kingdom of God and Jesus' death in Jerusalem. Jesus went up to Jerusalem in fulfilment of His mission as the Suffering Servant of the Lord. His death was to be the decisive event in the coming of the Kingdom.

Fuller asserts that the eucharistic sayings in the Markan tradition are as early as *c.* A.D. 33. The Last Supper was an anticipated passover, at which Jesus says: "Truly I say to you, I shall not drink again of the fruit of the vine until that day when I drink it new in the kingdom of God" (Mk. XIV. 25). Jesus abstains from the wine. "Either he intends his abstention as an expression of his total consecration to the Father's will, in manner which recalls Jn. IV. 34: 'My meat is to do the will of him that sent me, and accomplish his work.' Or, alternatively, it is an expression of his resolve to drink that other cup (ποτήριον, Mk. XIV. 36), the cup of suffering, to the dregs. It is precisely this consecration to the Father's will, as expressed in his abstention from the cup at Supper, which will make it possible for him to drink 'it new in the kingdom of God' (Mk. XIV. 25*b*), which will inaugurate the coming of the Kingdom

[17] W. Manson, *Jesus the Messiah*, London 1943.
[18] R. H. Fuller, *The Mission and Achievement of Jesus*, London 1954.
[19] Fuller, *op. cit.*, p. 78, n. 1.   [20] *Op. cit.*, p. 50.

(Lk. xxii. 18*b*, cf. vs. 16*b*). In other words, this saying is an additional proof that Jesus regards his death as the decisive event in and through which God will inaugurate the End. That is to say, between Jesus as he sits at Supper and the coming of the Kingdom, there stands the crucial event of the cross."[21] Jesus has not come merely to preach the coming of the Reign of God, but to carry out the decisive work through which God is to inaugurate this Reign.

The majority of German scholars accept the strongly futuristic aspect of the Kingdom of God and reject the idea that the Kingdom was regarded by Jesus as being present in His person. Hans Conzelmann may be quoted as an example. In his book, *Die Mitte der Zeit*,[22] he tries to bring out the theology of Luke himself. The Kingdom of God retains its transcendental character with Luke, indeed this is intensified. The Kingdom is shown as something far away in a meta-physical distance. Its realisation in the future is not denied, but it is hidden. What primarily interests Luke is the nature of the Kingdom, not its futurity. Only Lk. xvii. 20 and xxii. 18 speak of the coming of the Kingdom.

Conzelmann's interpretation of Lk. xvii. 20 ff. is illuminating. According to the futuristic interpretation it is not the Kingdom that is present, but its signs. What are present are the Mes-sianic signs (Lk. iv. 18 ff.) and the message of the Kingdom, which is distinct from the Kingdom itself. All calculation of when the Kingdom of God is to come must be striven against. So long as I concern myself with "When," I show by so doing that I have not understood the call.

What, then, is the connexion between the Kingdom of God and the person of Jesus Himself? "How is the relationship understood here between present (which in the person of Jesus is qualified as the atoning presence) and future (the Kingdom of God)?"[23] In the parable of the Weeds among the Wheat the Kingdom of God is to come. But the connexion with Jesus is clear. He refuses to make a visible distinction now between men. Other parables such as the Net (Mt. xiii. 47 ff.) and the Marriage Feast (Mt. xxii. 1 ff. *par.*) set the Kingdom in

---

[21] *Op. cit.*, pp. 76 f.

[22] H. Conzelmann, *Die Mitte der Zeit, Studien zur Theologie des Lukas*, Tübingen 1954. Eng. version: *The Theology of St Luke*, trans G. Buswell, London and New York 1960.

[23] Conzelmann, *op. cit.*, p. 284.

relation to Jesus, but the coming of the Kingdom is never questioned. Jesus is the preacher of the Kingdom of God, but He did not see Himself as the Son of Man. Conzelmann declares, in conformity with P. Vielhauer,[24] that nowhere in the teaching of Jesus is any connexion established between the Kingdom of God and the Son of Man. The two cannot be reconciled with one another. The Son of Man sayings are secondary. But it is clear that Jesus saw Himself as inseparably connected with the Kingdom of God and its coming.[25]

In 1953 Albert Schweitzer entered the debate with an article in a Swiss periodical.[26] In this he takes as his starting-point the statement that the eternal truth of the Gospel must always reveal itself differently through different outlooks on the world. We cannot, as earlier generations could, cling to the faith that the Kingdom of God would come of itself at the end of time. Schweitzer regards as a falsification of the truth any attempt to escape recognition of the fact that Jesus held an idea about the Kingdom of God and its imminent coming which was not fulfilled and which cannot be adopted by us today.

But mankind has the choice of realising the Kingdom of God or of going under. If the Kingdom of God is not in our hearts, however, it cannot come in the world. We must struggle to make the Kingdom-of-God mentality prevail in our thoughts and deeds.

The essence of the message of Jesus is non-Jewish, and its kernel is not eschatological. This makes it possible for us to retain the actual substance, even though we cannot accept the form in which it is presented to us.[27]

Joachim Jeremias renews the purely futuristic interpretation of the Kingdom of God. After C. H. Dodd's book, *The Parables of the Kingdom*, which Jeremias considered introduced a new

[24] P. Vielhauer, "Gottesreich und Menschensohn in der Verkündigung Jesu," in *Festschrift für Günther Dehn*, ed. W. Schneemelcher, Neukirchen 1957, pp. 51-79.

[25] Mention should also be made of Erich Grässer, *Das Problem der Parusieverzögerung in den synoptischen Evangelien und in der Apostelgeschichte*, Beihefte z. *Z.N.W.*, No. 48, Berlin 1957. Jesus expected the Kingdom in the future, and that it would come very soon. "What Jesus left His followers as their heritage is the heightened and *well-founded* hope of the imminent coming of the Kingdom of God" (p. 15).

[26] A. Schweitzer, "Die Idee des Reiches Gottes im Verlaufe der Umbildung des Eschatologischen Glaubens in den uneschatologischen," in *Schweitzerische Theologische Umschau*, 1953.

[27] See Hermann Schuster, "Die konsequente Eschatologie in der Interpretation des Neuen Testaments, kritisch betrachtet," in *Z.N.W.*, XLVII (1956), pp. 1-25.

epoch in the study of the parables, he felt encouraged to
continue along the same path. Jeremias's own book on the
parables appeared first in 1947, and has been followed by a
number of revised editions.[28]

Jeremias's objective is to work back to the earliest form of the
parables of Jesus. To do this, it is necessary to find the concrete
situation in the life of Jesus which gave birth to the parable.
For the original historical location of the parables is always
the activity of Jesus in a definite concrete situation. After
that, the parables lived their life in the early Church and
underwent changes there. The laws that govern this transformation are so many aids in finding the original meaning.
Just a few words about the most important of these laws. The
parables which, in the teaching of Jesus, were directed towards
His opponents or the populace, are applied in the early
Church to the community. This often involves a transfer of
stress from the eschatological to the parenetic. The parables
are altered by being treated as though they referred to the
mission of Jesus and the Parousia that failed to appear. The
form becomes more and more allegorical. Investigation along
these lines produces "a strange result."[29] All the material
of the Synoptic versions and of John reveals allegorical interpretations with one single exception, namely the special
material of Luke. From this result Jeremias feels justified in
drawing the conclusion: "The whole parabolic material was
originally as free from allegorizing interpretations as is the
special Lucan material."[30]

How, then, does Jeremias see the actual face of the Son
of Man, *ipsissima vox Iesu*, behind the words of the Gospels?

Jesus, according to Jeremias, proclaimed "the presence of
salvation," for: "The blind receive their sight and the lame
walk, lepers are cleansed and the deaf hear, and the dead are
raised up and the poor have the good news preached to them"
(Mt. XI. 5, 6; Lk. VII. 22). This is not intended to be a cata-
logue of the miracles of Jesus. It is rather an outburst of
exultation, in which Jesus makes use of ancient images for the
time of salvation. The hour has come when Paradise shall
return. The perfection of the world has begun, and is made

---

[28] J. Jeremias, *Die Gleichnisse Jesu*, 1947. All quotations and references are to
the English version, translated from the 3rd German edn., 1954.
[29] Jeremias, *op. cit.*, p. 69.   [30] *Ibid.*

manifest in the words and deeds of Jesus. The fields are white
for harvest (Jn. IV. 35). The budding and bursting into leaf
of the fig-tree foretells the summer. "As soon as its branch
becomes tender and puts forth its leaves, you know that summer
is near; so also, when you see these things taking place, you
know that he is near, at the very gates" (Mk. XIII. 28, 29).
This saying referred originally, not to the terrible events of the
end-time, but to the time of salvation. The fig-tree, unlike
other trees, loses its leaves in the winter. When it buds and
grows green, this is a testimony to the return of life and a
presage of summer. In the same way, Jesus means, the Messiah
has his forerunner. Winter is past, summer is at the door, the
last fulfilment is just about to appear. The time of salvation
is here, because the Saviour is here. The signs of his presence
are God's gifts of salvation: the sick become whole, death has
lost its power, the message of joy is preached to the poor. Sins
are forgiven (Mk. II. 5). Satan is overcome, the evil spirits
flee before the spirit of God (Mt. XII. 28).

Jesus looked towards the future with great confidence.
We see this in the parables of the Kingdom of God about the
Grain of Mustard Seed, the Leaven, the Sower, and the
Self-growing Seed (called by Jeremias the Patient Farmer).
These parables are parables of contrast: the Dominion of God
corresponds with the final stage in the parables. From the
small beginning God creates His " Kingly Dominion" ("*Königsherrschaft*"). As surely as the harvest comes after long waiting,
so surely will God, when the hour is come, let final Judgment
and the Kingly Dominion come. And the Kingly Dominion
is seen by Jesus entirely eschatologically.

But Jesus preached not merely salvation but also judgment,
not merely "*Heil*" but "*Unheil*." He set men in the moment
of decision before judgment. The seriousness of the hour
demanded preparedness. The exhortation ran: "Watch
therefore" (Mk. XIII. 35), "Let your loins be girded and your
lamps burning" (Lk. XII. 35), have on "a wedding garment"
(Mt. XXII. 11). Jeremias insists particularly on the element
of joy in the teaching of Jesus. Conversion according to him
is to have festive garments on and heads anointed (Mt. VI. 17),
it is the joy of the returning son, which must be combined with
the renewal of life. But he who did not accept the call of Jesus
placed himself outside the Kingdom of God.

For him who was seized and overwhelmed by the joyful message, it is obvious that in his great joy he would do anything to acquire the Pearl of Value. "The effect of the joyful news is overpowering; it fills the heart with gladness; it makes life's whole aim the consummation of the divine community and produces the most whole-hearted self-sacrifice."[31] The life of him who allows himself to be overwhelmed becomes a life in the imitation of Jesus, the most important characteristic of which is just its joy. The disciple rests secure in the hand of God. The gift of God impels him to labour as a fisher of men and a harvester.

When Jesus spoke of the final perfection, He always spoke in figurative terms. Judgment was to be held over the living and the dead (Mt. XII. 44 f.). Everything would be changed. Evil would be no more. Debts would be forgiven and God give repayment. God is King and would be worshipped in the new Temple, where the transfigured community would stand before His throne. The heathen would come to the Kingdom of God and assemble on the Mountain of the Lord. In another work,[32] Jeremias develops these ideas on the basis of Mt. VIII. 11 f.: "Many will come from east and west and sit at table with Abraham, Isaac, and Jacob, in the kingdom of heaven, while the sons of the kingdom will be thrown into the outer darkness; there men will weep and gnash their teeth." The promise given by the prophets of the eschatological flowing of the nations to the mountain of the Lord (Is. II. 2 f.; Mic. IV. 1 f.), will be fulfilled. "Thus we see that the incorporation of the Gentiles in the Kingdom of God promised by the prophets, was expected and announced by Jesus as God's *eschatological act of power, as the great final manifestation of God's free grace.* For the last time God brings life out of death, creates children to Abraham out of stones, when in the hour of final revelation He summons the nations to Zion and by constituting the universal people of God from Jews and Gentiles abolishes all earthly distinctions."[33]

Jeremias never ceases to emphasise that Jesus preached "the coming of God" ("*der Einbruch Gottes*"). He summarises

---

[31] *Op. cit.*, p. 140.

[32] Jeremias, *Jesu Verheissung für die Völker*, Stuttgart 1956. Eng. version: *Jesus' Promise to the Nations*, trans. S. H. Hooke, London 1958.

[33] *Op. cit.*, (Eng. trans.), pp. 70 f.

the teaching of Jesus thus: "Jesus preaches the turning-point in time in word and deed. This message is unfolded under six headings. God stands at the door. The redeemed spirit returns. World perfection dawns. Forgiveness is preached to the poor. The power of Satan is broken. The call for belief goes out. The message of Jesus is sent forth in the face of catastrophe."[34]

Jeremias thus defends the purely futuristic interpretation of the Kingdom of God. The Dominion of God is to Jesus, he says,[35] entirely eschatological. Jesus sets mankind face to face with the coming catastrophe, *God's hour is coming*. This is not "realised eschatology," but "eschatology in process of realisation" (*eine sich realisierende Eschatologie*).

Emphatically, then, as Jeremias declares the futuristically eschatological character of the Kingdom of God, he is equally anxious to emphasise that the time of salvation has come with Jesus. The Messiah has come, the time of salvation is therefore here. That is the message of the Gospels.

He denies that Jesus regarded the Kingdom of God as in any way present. To do this, he has to disregard certain of the utterances in his presentation. Sayings such as Mt. XII. 28 and others about the casting out of demons are left out of account. This gives rise undeniably to a certain inner inconsistency in Jeremias's interpretation. Can one really speak of the presence of the Messiah-Son of Man without involving the idea that the Kingdom of God is in some way present? The Messiah and the Kingdom of God must be kept separate. The Messiah sets mankind face to face with the coming Kingdom of God. Jeremias clearly cannot envisage the Kingdom of God as entering into conditions of time, in accordance with the old saying: *Finitum non capax infiniti*.[36]

[34] From the synopsis of the lectures Jeremias gave in Uppsala in the spring of 1959 on the subject of "*Die Botschaft Jesu.*"

[35] *Parables of Jesus*, p. 92.

[36] See Ernst Percy, *Die Botschaft Jesu, Eine traditionskritische und exegetische Untersuchung*, Lunds universitets årsskrift, N.F., Ser. I, VOL. XLIX, No. 5, Lund 1953, whose views on the Kingdom of God show a striking resemblance to those of Jeremias. He asserts that "the Kingdom of God according to Jesus is something which, in its perfected form, is still to come, but on the other hand it has already begun to come in His acts and in His message, in the latter case in the sense that mankind is confronted, through the teaching of Jesus, with the Kingdom of God as a gift of salvation" (p. 223). Jesus is the bearer of the Kingdom of God and of a new and perfect communion with God, as perfect as it can be within the limits of earthly life.

2

C. H. Dodd's view that Jesus even during His lifetime proclaimed a "realised eschatology" has won general recognition and acceptance in England. The eschatological Dominion of God entered into history with Jesus, the Kingdom of God has come. The futurist apocalyptic imagery of the Gospels is thrust aside as "an accommodation of language."

In his four broadcast addresses published in 1951[37] Dodd seems to emphasise more strongly than ever before the tension between realisation and expectation. The Kingdom is still to come, but yet it is present. But in the interpretation of what is to come, decisive importance must be attached to this fact that Christ has come. The prophecies of His coming in history are counterbalanced by those that speak of a "coming beyond history."[38] It is thus not a question of any coming event in history, nor even of a last such event. This seems to imply that Dodd is again guilty of the same sort of distortions of the New Testament idea of time as we discovered in him before.[39]

In 1953[40] Dodd spoke of the term "realised eschatology" as that "not altogether felicitous term."[41]

Reginald H. Fuller demonstrates in an extraordinarily clear and convincing manner that Dodd's theory is, for both linguistic and other reasons, not tenable. He subjects the four principal texts, which Dodd used as his basis, to exhaustive criticism. Dodd translates Mk. 1. 15: "The Kingdom of God has come." In LXX, ἐγγίζω normally means "to draw nigh," though it may also sometimes mean "reached," which

---

[37] C. H. Dodd, *The Coming of Christ*, Cambridge 1951.

[38] Dodd, *op. cit.*, p. 17.   [39] See p. 121.

[40] Dodd, *The Interpretation of the Fourth Gospel*, Cambridge 1953, p. 447, n. 1.

[41] It has been suggested from various quarters that the term "realised eschatology" should be changed to "inaugurated eschatology" (Georges Florovsky), or "eschatology in process of realisation (*sich realisierende Eschatologie*) (Joachim Jeremias). The former term is used, for example, by J. A. T. Robinson, *Jesus and His Coming, The Emergence of a Doctrine*, London 1957, who asserts that Jesus did not look forward to a second advent of the Son of Man "beyond and separate from the culmination of the ministry which He came to fulfil" (p. 82). "As in glory, so in visitation, we must speak, not of a realised, but of an inaugurated eschatology, of the Son of Man 'coming to His own' in all the power of God, till the kingdoms of this world shall have become the Kingdom of God and His Christ" (p. 81). Alan Richardson follows Jeremias and speaks of "an eschatology that is in process of realisation" (*An Introduction to the Theology of the New Testament*, London 1958, p. 86, n. 1).

is then clearly shown by the context. Wherever this verb
occurs in the New Testament without having ἡ βασιλεία
τοῦ Θεοῦ (τῶν οὐρανῶν) as subject, it is used of events which
have not yet happened but which lie in the immediate future.
"The phrase ἤγγικεν ἡ βασιλεία τοῦ Θεοῦ speaks of an event
which, *though near, still lies in the future.*"[42] The background to
the use of this verb in the Synoptics is to found be in Deutero-
Isaiah, where the victories of Cyrus are signs of restoration.
A longer quotation will make Fuller's meaning clear. He says:
"With the emergence of Jesus, God is already at work, as He
was at work in the preliminary victories of Cyrus, preparing
to inaugurate His eschatological Reign. The signs of the
coming Kingdom, concentrated in the person and activity of
Jesus, are already there. Yet the decisive event itself has not
yet taken place, any more than the return from exile had taken
place at the time of the proclamation of Deutero-Isaiah.
The Kingdom of God has not yet come, but it is near, so near
that it is already operative in advance. This may not look, on
the face of it, so very different from 'realised eschatology.' But
there is in fact an all-important difference. 'Realised eschatology' asserts that the decisive event has already occurred.
The view outlined here on the other hand seeks to give full,
though not exaggerated, emphasis to what is already happening
in the ministry of Jesus, yet at the same time to place the decisive event in the future."[43] Dodd translates Mt. XII. 28; Lk.
XI. 20: "The Kingdom of God has arrived upon you," which
Fuller considers to be an adequate translation, but it does not
necessarily involve a "realised eschatology." Jesus sometimes
uses the prophetic method of speaking of what is to come as
though it were already present. In Mk. IX. 1 the Kingdom
must be something in the future, and in Lk. XVII. 21 the
meaning is that the eschatological Kingdom "is dawning,"
and signs of its coming are apparent in Jesus. To deny the
futurist aspect of, for example, Mk. XIV. 25; Mt. VIII. 11, VI. 10
or Lk. XII. 32, would be impossible. "The attempt of Dr Dodd
to explain the obvious future reference of these sayings, especially when he relegates Mk. XIV. 25 to 'the transcendent order
beyond space and time' (a wholly nonbiblical, Platonic
conception!) is singularly unconvincing."[44]

[42] R. Fuller, *The Mission and Achievement of Jesus*, p. 24.
[43] *Op. cit.*, p. 25.   [44] *Op. cit.*, p. 33.

Fuller points out that it has become fashionable to interpret the miracles of Jesus as signs of a realised eschatology. With the healings and the teaching of Jesus a new age is dawning, but it has not yet come but belongs to the future.

What is correct in "realised eschatology" is, according to Fuller, that something crucial happened in the ministry of Jesus, that God was already active in the words and acts of Jesus, so that what took place may be described as "proleptic instalments of the final blessings of the End."[45] But the future aspect cannot be dismissed as some sort of "accommodation of language." To refer what is decisive either to the past or to the present is to do violence to what Jesus says of the Kingdom of God. The tension between present and future which runs through the whole Gospel vanishes, and above all such an interpretation "destroys the cruciality of the cross."[46]

Fuller quite correctly insists in his criticism on the futurist eschatology of Jesus, but he overlooks the fact that, at the same time, the Kingdom of God is active among mankind in the teaching and miracles of Jesus. He shows a certain tendency to regard such sayings as: "The Kingdom of God is in the midst of you" (Lk. XVII. 21) or "Blessed are the eyes which see what you see" (Lk. X. 23), as prophetic utterances. But Lk. X. 17 ff. cannot be treated as representative of the whole material. Fuller underestimates the presence sayings.

R. Morgenthaler gives a full account and critique of C. H. Dodd in his *Kommendes Reich*.[47] He asserts that Dodd demythologises the Gospels. His aim is fundamentally the same as Bultmann's, but the result is something quite different. Dodd's interpretation of the Kingdom of God rests basically on one of the fundamental ideas of consistent eschatology, namely the thesis that there is in the New Testament an "imminent expectation."[48] But the difference between Schweitzer and Dodd is that the latter ascribes this expectation to the early community.

This expectation is to be found in the Synoptics side by side with a fulfilled expectation. In Jesus' casting out of the demons the Kingdom of God is already present. Morgenthaler illustrates this by an image from present-day life. In the last

---

[45] *Op. cit.*, p. 48.   [46] *Op. cit.*, p. 49.
[47] R. Morgenthaler, *Kommendes Reich*, Zürich 1952.
[48] *Op. cit.*, p. 63.

World War, the Allied armies were already present on the Continent when small groups of commandos landed on the coasts. In the same way "the Kingdom of God *has already come to you*" (Mt. XII. 28). *Φθάνειν* expresses this, whereas *ἐγγείζειν* in the New Testament never means "to come" but rather "to come near." The Kingdom of God has thus swept into the immediate vicinity but has not become actually present. The Kingdom is present in Jesus. A realised eschatology does exist. Its name is Jesus Christ.[49]

Even though it is principally among English exegetists that one finds any strong emphasis on the doctrine that the Kingdom of God is primarily present in Jesus, one does encounter, even on the Continent, criticism of the radically eschatological interpretation of the message of Jesus. The most militant of such critics is unquestionably Professor Ethelbert Stauffer of Erlangen, whose book on New Testament theology,[50] written in 1938 though not published until three years later, leads the attack on the accepted lines of thought. The sayings that may most confidently be regarded as *ipsissima verba Jesu* are the Son of Man sayings. The Son of Man and the Kingdom of God belong together even in Dan. VII. Jesus uses the term, Son of Man, of Himself and proclaims the coming of the Kingdom of God. In, with, and through the coming of the Son of Man, comes the reign of God. "For behold, the kingdom of God is in the midst of you" (Lk. XVII. 21). It is already here, in the person and activity of Jesus. The reign of God is here, the reign of the antagonist is over.

Since then, Stauffer has devoted himself almost exclusively to the study of Jesus. He believes that the original Jesus-tradition has undergone a severe "re-Judaisation." Many of the sayings of Jesus in the Gospels, which have always been regarded as genuine because they sound as though they must have originated in the Palestine of the time of Jesus, do not actually spring from Him. The texts have undergone a "re-Judaisation" and a "re-Qumranisation." What we have to do now is to get behind this distortion to what Jesus really taught.

Stauffer holds that Jesus was not one of those who preached an imminent end to the world. The proofs he brings forward

---

[49] *Op. cit.*, p. 60.
[50] E. Stauffer, *Die Theologie des Neuen Testaments*, Berlin 1941.

are: (1) In the Logia source there is not a single word about the imminent end of the world. And this source is in all probability the earliest book about Jesus in Christendom; (2) In the Jewish polemics against Jesus, it is never said that He preached the imminent end of everything. If that had been so, the Jews would not have failed to criticise Jesus when His hopes turned out to be false; (3) Apocalyptists and oracles were common in Palestine during New Testament times. Jesus broke with the apocalyptists.

Jesus is shown as being far less a child of His time and His people than has been commonly supposed. "He is far more alone, far more militant, far more revolutionary, than has hitherto been recognised."

In the earliest of the Gospels we find the saying: "The time ($\kappa\alpha\iota\rho\delta s$) is fulfilled" (Mk. I. 15). Not the future, but the present, is decisive in the teaching of Jesus. His message is a message of the present. The Kingdom of God is in the midst of you (Lk. XI. 20). When the malefactor on the Cross prays: "Lord, remember me when you come in your kingly power" (Lk. XXIII. 42 f.), that is the ordinary apocalyptic eschatology. But Jesus corrects this eschatology without criticism. His reply says nothing of a coming kingdom of the Messiah, but speaks merely of "today," merely of Paradise.[51]

3

When the celebrated Old Testament scholar, S. H. Hooke, gave his popularly written book on the Kingdom of God the title, *The Kingdom of God in the Experience of Jesus*,[52] this in itself gave a clue to the basic idea set forth in the book. For according to Hooke, Jesus passed through a creative experience which cannot be explained by the influence of apocalyptic literature, and through this experience of His was born an entirely new conception of the Kingdom of God. "In His experience the question of the reality and meaning of the Kingdom of God was brought to a focus for all time and for eternity, and our present concern is to examine afresh the Gospel records in order to find out what the reality of the Kingdom of God meant for Him. Nor is it merely a matter of setting out and arranging His sayings and teaching about the

[51] Stauffer, *Jesu, Gestalt und Geschichte*, (Eng. trans.), p. 113.
[52] S. H. Hooke, *The Kingdom of God in the Experience of Jesus*, London 1949.

Kingdom of God, but much more a question of discovering the creative force of His experience which gave to the Kingdom of God a new character, revealed as something new, something which many prophets and righteous men had desired to see but had not seen."[53]

Of decisive importance was the experience Jesus had—we may assume, recounted by Himself—when He came up out of the baptismal waters. The Old Testament prophets had had moments of deep experience of God; such an experience Jesus had now. According to Mark He saw "the heavens opened." We find the same prayer in Is. LXIII. 15-LXIV. 12: "Oh that thou wouldest rend the heavens, and come down." Jesus identified Himself with the cry of longing and received His answer: "he *saw* the heavens opened." And He saw the Spirit like a dove descending. The Spirit is the Lord Himself in action. The words at the baptism are taken from Is. XLIII. 1. "For Him (Jesus) the pattern of the Kingdom had become the yoke of that willing service which only a Son could render."[54]

Hooke argues, then, that the baptismal vision "was in reality the impact, overwhelming in its intensity, of the Kingdom of God upon the mind and will of Jesus."[55] From the beginning of His public mission Jesus was fully aware of the responsibility that was laid upon Him; He was the Son and the Servant, to do the will of the Father with regard to the Kingdom which was about to come.

Following Matthew, Hooke then distinguishes different stages in the teaching of Jesus about the Kingdom of God. He ascribes to the earliest stage the conditions for entry into the Kingdom; then come new laws of the Kingdom, the character of the children of the Kingdom, and finally the nature of the Father. Beside the teaching there were the miracles. Jesus saw how through Him God broke victorious into the dominion of Satan and challenged the powers of evil to the last battle that was at hand. It is important that to Jesus the coming of the Kingdom of God was God's act, and that the coming of the Son of Man was directly connected with the coming of the Kingdom.

Mt. x. describes the commissioning of the Twelve and how Jesus says to them: "For truly I say to you, you will not have gone through all the towns of Israel, before the Son of man

---

[53] Hooke, *op. cit.*, pp. 16 f.   [54] *Op. cit.*, p. 32.   [55] *Op. cit.*, p. 33.

comes" (vs. 23). Hooke considers this to be an authentic saying, which gives us insight into the setting for the crisis that is developing. Jesus felt that the hour when God was to intervene was near, and accordingly He sent out His chosen Twelve. But they were to be prepared for the coming of the Son of Man even before they returned.

But what Jesus expected did not happen. "He was forced to realise that some obstacle lay in the way of the coming of the Kingdom; something had prevented God from intervening in the decisive action which He was expecting."[56] In Mt. xi. 13 we are able to follow the process of "learning" which Jesus had to undergo. He came to realise that His work during the first period of His activity had produced no results. The people had not repented. The last words of Mt. xi show how Jesus accepted the situation. He thanked the Father. "I thank thee, Father, Lord of heaven and earth, that thou hast hidden these things from the wise and understanding, and revealed them to babes; Yea, Father, for such was thy gracious will" (Mt. xi. 25 f.). Jesus accepted the Father's ordering that only the little band of simple men saw in Him what was hidden from the leaders of the people. More clearly than anything else, however, the parables of the Kingdom of God revealed the effect of the crisis on Jesus and the changed point of view He gained on the Kingdom of God and the actions of God.

The parable of the Sower is an account in symbolic form of the experience Jesus had had during His mission. Jesus accepted the facts and saw the situation as an expression of the Father's intentions. Those who have to do with the Kingdom of God must learn the lesson of the husbandman, to await "the mysterious death and rebirth of the seed." The parable of the Self-growing Seed shows that Jesus recognised the necessity of waiting, but there was no question but that the harvest— the Day of the Lord—would come. The two parables of the Grain of Mustard Seed and the Leaven (Mt. xiii. 31 ff.) have often been misinterpreted as referring to the growth of the Church or the spreading of the gospel. The meaning of these parables is to be found in the experience of Jesus. According to Gen. 1 there are three types of vegetation: grass, herbs, and trees, each type having its appointed place in the divine order, and according to Jewish ideas this order is a part of the Kingdom

[56] *Op. cit.*, p. 75.

of God. The grain of mustard seed, which is the smallest of all seeds, breaks out of this order and becomes something which God had not intended: it grows into a tree. When it has become a tree, the birds of the air come and build their nests there, and the birds here, as in the parable of the Sower, are symbols of "the demoniac and hostile activity."[57] Jesus warns His disciples against seeking greatness. Instead He puts forward a little child as pattern. The condition for entering into the Kingdom of God was to become as a little child. "And it is in the light of this insistence upon the littleness, the lowness, the servant's place, as the order of the Kingdom, that this parable must be seen."[58] This interpretation seems too far-fetched. It is inspired by the author's idea of the crisis which he believed Jesus had reached. But where is all this to be found in the actual text? As to the Leaven, this Hooke believes must have a bad sense, as it does so everywhere else in the Old and New Testament. Jesus is warning His disciples against the insidious infection of unreality and falseness.

The three following parables in Mt. XIII have a common motive, "the principle of value depending on knowledge."[59] Jesus reveals the mystery of the Kingdom, which it is a privilege to know and to possess. In the parable of the Net it is the gathering together that is important. The little band that Jesus had gathered round Him constituted the nucleus of God's family, the Church the future pattern of which Jesus foresaw. Jesus saw the gathering as the true task of the Servant of the Kingdom.

The solution of the crisis into which Jesus was drawn when the Kingdom of God failed to appear after the preaching of the Twelve, comes after the death of John the Baptist. In this Jesus sees the act of God and God's indication of the way He was to go. The Forerunner had shown the way He had to take. So, too, must the Son of Man suffer. When Simon made the Messiah confession at Caesarea Philippi, Jesus saw this as the Father's work and saw the situation in Is. XXVIII. 14-16 repeated in His own experience. "The religious leaders of the people were united in resistance to the purpose of God; the shadow of death lay ahead, but Jesus held fast to the same conviction which supported the prophet, namely, that God had

---

[57] *Op. cit.*, p. 90. [58] *Op. cit.*, p. 91. [59] *Op. cit.*, p. 94.

R

laid the unshakable foundation for the Kingdom, against which death could not prevail. As in Is. xxvIII. 16, where the prophet connects God's foundation with the faith which cannot be shaken, 'he that believeth shall not be moved,' so here, Jesus finds in the response of Peter's faith, rudimentary though it was, something which even Messiah's death could not overthrow, and upon this divine certainty, Jesus felt that His new community, His *ekklesia*, could be built; as a pledge of this, and following the Old Testament custom, Jesus changed Peter's Jewish name of Simon to one which bore witness to the fact that Peter's act of faith stamped him with the rocklike quality of the foundation which God had laid."[60]

During the last weeks, Jesus was preoccupied with the question of forgiveness. He tried to turn the minds of the disciples towards the inward character of the Kingdom and towards the only condition for participating in the Kingdom of God, namely infinite forgiveness.

When Jesus accepted the rejection and death of the Messiah as expressions of the will of God, He destroyed all known conditions and patterns for the coming of the Kingdom. His faith reached out to the other side of the Cross. The death of the Messiah was not merely an end, but also a beginning. In His death the old order died. The eschatological conditions were destroyed, and with them the old conceptions of the Kingdom of God. To Jesus, the coming of the Kingdom was indissolubly connected with His resurrection.

It has not been possible in this brief account to discuss the Old Testament parallels to which Hooke often points. There lies the strength of his thesis. But its weakness is also obvious. Is it really possible to draw the conclusions he does about the course of development of Jesus' view of the Kingdom of God, simply from the arrangement of the account in Matthew? Is this not placing a greater burden on the texts than they can bear? In spite of the emphasis on eschatology, too little is made of the eschatological tension. In the chapter entitled: "The manner of the Kingdom's coming," Hooke says: "In one sense the Kingdom of God was always there, always a reality for experience, as it is still; it has never ceased to be true that 'the Lord reigneth.' It was in this sense that Jesus could say 'the Kingdom of God is among you.'"[61] But that

[60] *Op. cit.*, p. 104.　　　[61] *Op. cit.*, p. 56.

is not the message of the Gospel. The peculiarity of that is that the Kingdom is here and is in process of coming, because Jesus Son of Man is here.

Nils Alstrup Dahl's careful analysis of the parables of growth[62] leads him to a somewhat different conclusion from that of Jeremias. His view of Jesus' idea of the Kingdom of God is also different. In relation to Dodd's present eschatology and Jeremias's revival of an earlier, futurist eschatology, Dahl's position lies somewhere between the two.

Dahl argues that the idea of organic growth was nothing strange to the peoples of antiquity. To both Jews and Christians it represented "the other side of what was essentially the creative work of God who alone gives growth."[63] This view of organic life applies also to human history. History is not an immanent development. All its stages are governed by God, or by the struggle between God and the powers of evil.

The parable of the Fig Tree (Mk. xiii) may originally have related to what took place in the ministry of Jesus: the signs of the coming of the Kingdom of God could be seen by those who had eyes to see. The basis of the parable is the idea of an eschatological event which corresponds with the growth of the tree in spring. The coming of the Kingdom is preceded by events which foretell its nearness. "To the growth which God in accordance with His own established order gives in the sphere of organic life, corresponds the series of events by which God in accordance with His plan of salvation leads history towards the end of the world and the beginning of the new aeon."[64] But this is not to say that we should seek the point of the parables in this idea of growth.

The parables of growth are also parables of contrast. The point of the parable of the Mustard Seed is that the mustard plant is a tree under the shadow of which the birds find shelter, even though the seed from which it sprang is very, very small. So it is with the Kingdom of God. "The first appearance of the coming, glorious Kingdom of God could seem to be quite little and insignificant. But in spite of the contrast there is identity. The lesson of the parable is, thus, not so

---

[62] N. A. Dahl, "The Parables of Growth," in *Studia Theologica*, v, No. 2 (1952), pp. 132-66.

[63] Dahl, *op. cit.*, p. 143.   [64] *Op. cit.*, p. 146.

much the great results of the work of Jesus, as it is the 'organic unity' between His ministry in Israel and the future Kingdom of God."[65] The parable provides the answer to the burning question in the circles surrounding Jesus. Israel expected a glorious Kingdom of God. Nothing of this was to be seen in the ministry of Jesus. Could what was happening really be the beginning of God's establishment of the Kingdom? Yes, look at the mustard seed. For all its littleness it grows into a tree. "The apparent smallness and insignificance of what is happening does not exclude the secret presence of the coming Kingdom—in the seed-stage, so to say."[66]

Israel expected that the Kingdom of God would bring with it a complete change in everything. But nothing of this was to be seen in the ministry of Jesus. The parable of the Leaven supplies the answer. Nothing is to be seen when the leaven is placed in the dough, yet nevertheless it leavens all the dough. It is the same with the Kingdom of God. The proclamation of the Kingdom of God and the signs which take place relate to "the hidden presence of the Kingdom of God."[67] God has already taken the decisive step which is the beginning of the series of eschatological events which lead up to the coming of the Kingdom and the transformation of the world. The parable of the Self-growing Seed says the same. "The events of the final era have already begun to happen, the forces of the Kingdom are at work; when the time is ripe, at the end of the world, God will certainly establish his Kingdom in glory."[68] The ministry of Jesus in Israel was the condition for and the beginning realisation of the coming of the Kingdom of God. "The Kingdom of God has not yet come in glory, but its powers are at work, its seed has been sown," is what Jesus meant by the parable of the Sower.

The parables of growth thus proclaim the presence of salvation. The forces of salvation and of the Kingdom are here, in spite of everything that speaks against it. This hidden presence of the Kingdom is a period in the "history" of the Kingdom, and its revelation in glory is a period to come. The secret, hidden presence of the Kingdom was revealed in the preaching and healings of the Son of Man. Dahl claims that the Kingdom of God was present in the Son of Man. The

[65] *Op. cit.*, p. 148.   [66] *Ibid.*
[67] *Op. cit.*, p. 149.   [68] *Op. cit.*, p. 150.

parables of growth were originally, in his opinion, more "Christological" than the Synoptics give us to understand.

When God finally assumes complete power, He shall be revealed as King of all the world. He will then also have about Him a community, the eschatological assembly. But it is extremely improbable that Jesus would have spoken of the presence of the Kingdom unless He had also reckoned with "a secret, proleptic presence of the eschatological assembly."[69] The choosing of the Twelve and their commissioning, the sayings about the disciples as fellows and followers of the Son of Man in humiliation and future glory, and not least the significance of the meals taken in common, including the Lord's Supper, as anticipations of sitting at table together in the Kingdom of God, all testify to this.

"The parables of growth speak of the coming of the Kingdom, but even in them it is clear that the Kingdom is thought to bring the pure, great and glorious Messianic community. The present facts which they have in view, accordingly, must be not only the person of Jesus, but also the humble community of disciples, tax collectors, and sinners gathered around Him. This should, however, not be taken to mean that the growth of which the parables are speaking, is to be identified with the inward and outward growth of the Church, or of the community of disciples, until the day when it is made perfect in the Kingdom of God. The subject of the parables is the Kingdom, not the Church, and, as we have seen, what corresponds to the growth is the acts of God by which He, according to His plan, leads the process of eschatological events until the day comes which He has determined. The growth of the Church can come in here at all only in so far as it is the result of this activity of God, and is seen in close correlation to it. But under these conditions, we will have the right to say that the calling and gathering of men who are to enter the Kingdom of God, belongs to those events which must precede the coming of the Kingdom in power. Where eschatology is 'in process of realisation,' the Church is in process of formation, or, rather, the eschatological assembly is in the state of being gathered in."[70] Dahl also applies his view of the present and future character of the Kingdom of God to the Church. "Like the Kingdom of God, so also the Church properly belongs to

[69] *Op. cit.*, p. 160.　　　　[70] *Ibid.*

the eschatological future. But as the Kingdom at the same time is present in a mysterious, dynamic way, like the mustard seed or like growing grain, so the Church has a similar kind of presence: the rock is found, the building can begin."[71]

Thus according to Dahl, Jesus reckoned both with a proleptic and hidden as well as with a future and glorious coming of the Kingdom. Both these stages include the gathering of a Messianic community. "A series of events, ordered by God, connects the initial and proleptic realisation of eschatology with its future and final realisation."[72]

There is always room for a book that will give a combined account of the life and teaching of Jesus. Such of these as have had any scientific aspirations have usually restricted themselves to the teaching of Jesus in word and deed. Ethelbert Stauffer is the great exception; and Günther Bornkamm in his *Jesus von Nazareth*[73] follows in Stauffer's footsteps. If one is to understand Jesus in the light of contemporary Jewish categories it must be as a prophet and rabbi. But He differs from these on essential points, chiefly through the sovereignty that characterises His teaching and actions.

Jesus did not have a Messianic consciousness, He did not see Himself as the Son of Man. Jesus, Bornkamm asserts, was the prophet of the coming Kingdom of God. He was at the same time a rabbi who preached God's law, taught in the synagogues, gathered disciples about Him and argued with the scribes.

The essence of Jesus' message was that the Kingdom of God was near. The Kingdom of God means the victory and triumph of God over the power of Satan, and with that a turning-point in the life of the world. God shall reign. The turning-point of the age is already there in the sayings and acts of Jesus. It is for mankind to see this and not take offence at it (Mt. xi. 6). The parables of Jesus speak of the mystery of the Kingdom of God. This is nothing else but the hidden coming of the Kingdom of God into the midst of a world where the ordinary eye does not see or understand what is taking place in secret. Bornkamm, like Dahl, warns us against carrying the idea of contrast too far in interpreting such parables as the Grain of Mustard Seed or the Leaven.

---

[71] *Op. cit.*, pp. 160 f.　　　　　　　　　　[72] *Op. cit.*, p. 166.
[73] G. Bornkamm, *Jesus von Nazareth*, (Eng. trans.).

Jesus' hearers knew that a wonderful end came of a small beginning: the fruit from the seed, the leavened bread from the leaven. What matters is to see the Kingdom of God in its hidden form in the present and not demand signs and proofs. The parables are the reply to the charge that Jesus had not proved His identity. The Kingdom comes of its own inner power. It is a miracle for which one must wait patiently. It is the Self-growing seed. But God's new world is already active in the midst of the present world.

Jesus' task was to gather together, not a "Sacred Remnant," not some limited group like the Pharisees or the "children of light," but the publicans and sinners. Jesus was their friend (Mt. XI. 19). He was to gather together "the lost sheep of the house of Israel" (Mt. XV. 24). Just these Jesus gathered together to eat with Him. This is an image of the community with God and the joyous Messianic age. There can therefore be no question but that this eating together was part of the teaching of the Kingdom of God that was to come. What the parables of the Wedding Feast, the Lost Sheep, the Lost Talent, the Prodigal Son, say in words, the sitting at table together says in concrete action. What was spoken of in the parables, took place when Jesus sat at supper with His followers. God's love became reality in the words and acts of Jesus.

On the much-debated question of present and future in Jesus' idea of the Kingdom of God, Bornkamm tries to avoid giving a one-sided answer. The sayings about the Kingdom of God as belonging to the future and the sayings about its appearance now, stand side by side. Neither group can possibly be left out of account. Attempts at a solution have often been made from false premises. One must bear in mind that Jesus said: "The kingdom of God is not coming with signs to be observed" (Lk. XVII. 20). So that when one enquires what is taking place now and what is to take place later, what is growing out of the beginnings and how the fulfilment will appear, there is implicit in the very nature of the questions a temptation to treat the Kingdom of God as something that belongs to this world, as a phenomenon of this world, which can be observed and made the object of calculations. The decisive objection to singling out either the presence sayings or the future sayings is that these are so closely dependent on one another and so intimately connected in the teaching of

Jesus. "The present dawn of the Kingdom of God is always spoken of so as to show that the present reveals the future as salvation and judgment, and therefore does not anticipate it. Again, the future is always spoken of as unlocking and lighting up the present, and therefore revealing today as the day of decision. . . . The future of God is *salvation* to the man who apprehends the present as God's present, and as the hour of salvation. The future of God is *judgment* for the man who does not accept the "now" of God but clings to his own present, his own past and also to his own dreams of the future. We might say with Schiller: 'What we have denied the moment, eternity will never give back.' Only here it applies in a new and fulfilled sense. In this acceptance of the present as the present of God . . . pardon and conversion are one in the works of Jesus. God's future is God's call to the present, and the present is the time of decision in the light of God's future."[74]

Jesus' message of the nearness of the Kingdom of God and His teaching of God's will are not to be separated. They form a unity. The task of the disciples was to live "in the presence of God and in the expectation of His future,"[75] as the children of the heavenly Father. That is the blessedness which is promised in the Beatitudes, and the same blessedness is in the message of Jesus. Beatification and demand form a unity.

Jesus chose disciples who were to follow after Him. They were to be fishers of men and to preach the nearness of the Kingdom of God and to heal the sick. The disciples were not merely recipients of the forces of salvation present in the Kingdom of God that was appearing in the words and acts of Jesus, they were actively engaged in the service of the Kingdom of God. The selection of the Twelve goes back to Jesus. The number twelve symbolises the twelve tribes of Israel (Mt. xix. 28; Lk. xxii. 30). The disciples are thus the new God's people of the End-time. But they are no "Sacred Remnant"; they are the lost sheep of the house of Israel (Mt. x. 6, xv. 24).

In his interpretation of Jesus, Bornkamm reveals himself as the definite opponent of an extreme futurist conception of the Kingdom of God. The Sermon on the Mount is not "interim ethic" (A. Schweitzer), *i.e.* exceptional laws for the last time down to the end of the world which is just at the threshold.

---

[74] Bornkamm, *op. cit.*, pp. 92 f.   [75] *Op. cit.*, p. 108.

The Sermon on the Mount contains a hidden eschatology. Jesus' demands bear in themselves the ultimate things. But at the same time, the sayings about the presence of the Kingdom of God are not clear. Jesus is in His word, has entered entirely into His word. That is true. But He who speaks is not merely a prophet and rabbi. It is not enough to say that. He who spoke was He who was to come. He was the Son of Man. Where He was, there the Kingdom was present, in a hidden yet real sense. It was in process of breaking through. What happened through Jesus and His disciples testified, to Him who had eyes to see and did not take offence at Jesus, to the hidden presence of the Kingdom.

When a professor of Hebrew and Old Testament scholar such as John Bright publishes a book on the Kingdom of God,[76] one takes it for granted that the main emphasis will be on the Kingdom of God as it appears in the Old Testament, and that the New Testament will be dealt with more summarily. Such is indeed the case. And the idea of the Kingdom of God in the Old Testament is outside our task.

As regards Jesus, Bright says that He never gave any definition of the Kingdom of God, because this was completely unnecessary. All who heard Him knew what the Kingdom of God was, and longed for it. In both the Old and New Testaments we find "the dynamic concept of the rule of God."[77] The difference between them is that, whereas the Old Testament always sees the victory of God as "a future thing," the New Testament always uses the present tense: the Kingdom is here. This is something quite new. The gospel is the glad message, the good news that God *has* acted. He has sent the Messiah, and Jesus saw Himself as the Messiah, "the Suffering Servant of God, the Messiah of the Remnant."[78]

Bright then links up the Kingdom of God as closely as possible with the Messiah. For to proclaim anyone as the Messiah is the same as to proclaim the coming of the Kingdom of God, since the task of the Messiah is to establish the Kingdom. The Messiah without the Kingdom would be nothing less than a complete anomaly.[79]

[76] J. Bright, *The Kingdom of God in Bible and Church*. References are to the Eng. edn., followed in brackets by the American.

[77] Bright, *op. cit.*, p. 200 (197).   [78] *Op. cit.*, p. 218 (214).

[79] "To acclaim anyone as Messiah is to announce in Him the coming of the Kingdom of God, for it is precisely the business of the Messiah to establish the

In what sense, then, has the Kingdom come? Bright replies that in the person and activity of Jesus the Kingdom of God is already active as a force in the world. And Jesus in His teaching confronted those He called with radical decision for or against the Kingdom. "And those who heed it have entered the Kingdom, nay, *are* the Kingdom."[80]

"The New Testament, then, speaks of the Kingdom of God as if it were in a real sense a present thing. Christ, it declares, is the promised Messiah who has come to establish his Kingdom among men; in Him and in His Church is all hope of Israel for a true Remnant and a New Covenant made actual. The New Testament faith is, therefore, a triumphant faith. Yet it was inevitable that with that shift of tense with which the New Testament speaks of the Kingdom of God there should enter a severe tension. For on the one hand, that Kingdom is at present a victorious reality; on the other hand, it is a thing of the future and far from victorious."[81]

A well-balanced account, which tries to do justice to the various aspects of Jesus' teaching of the Kingdom of God without one-sidedly stressing certain sayings at the cost of others, is that of Rudolf Schnackenburg, the Roman Catholic exegetist.[82] This book also provides an account of the scientific debate on the Kingdom of God in the teaching of Jesus, and a "discussion" with other scholars.

Schnackenburg follows the history of the idea of the Kingdom of God from the Old Testament through Jesus on to early Christianity as we find it in the books of the New Testament. The main emphasis is naturally on the Kingdom of God in the teaching and activity of Jesus.[83]

Kingdom. Messiah cannot be separated from Kingdom. . . . A Messiah who had come to set up no Kingdom would have been an anomaly indeed. If Jesus, therefore, is in any sense the Messiah, then He has come to make actual the victorious rule of God over His people which Israel's faith had long awaited. And this, the New Testament declares, Jesus has done." *Op. cit.*, p. 219 (pp. 215 f.).

[80] *Op. cit.*, p. 224 (220).

[81] *Op. cit.*, p. 235 (pp. 230 f.).

[82] R. Schnackenburg, *Gottes Herrschaft und Reich.*

[83] Schnackenburg says that in general it is correct to speak of *"Gottesherrschaft"* (the Dominion of God) or *"Königsherrschaft Gottes"* (the Kingly Dominion of God) and not of *"Gottesreich"* (the Kingdom of God). Only in certain figurative expressions is the translation *"Gottesreich"* the only possible one, as in "to enter into the Kingdom of God," "to sit at table in the Kingdom of God." Where the perfected, cosmic *basileia* is meant, he prefers *"Gottesreich."* But this translation

The idea that God is King has various roots. Israel experienced the "Kingship" of Jahweh in God's acts in history. Jahweh *rules* as King. This idea dominates the whole development of the *basileia* idea. "Not passive strength, but exerted power, not the office, but the function, not the title, but the deed, characterise the kingship of God in the Bible."[84] God rules over creation, over Israel, His covenanted people, and over the nations. To Him alone is full and completely kingly honour due; but His power is not everywhere recognised. But Jahweh shall one day be victorious and establish His kingly rule. And thereafter shall follow the manifestation that He is King. He will show Himself as King and take His Kingdom in possession. In Israel's hope for the future, the kingly Dominion of Jahweh is always the fundamental idea. The origin of Israel's hope for the future and of salvation is shrouded in darkness. But it is clear that, as a result of the severe catastrophes which overtook Israel—the fall of the kingdoms, the Babylonian captivity and the developments that followed, which did not restore to the people the national freedom and independence that they had hoped for—the Messianic ideas and the eschatological hopes grew. By the time of Jesus they were widespread and stronger than ever before.

It is above all Deutero-Isaiah that deals with the ideas of the Kingdom of God. Here we find all the essential features which we encounter later with Jesus: the joyful message of the Kingdom of God, a new age when God will rule to the great joy of those who belong to Him, the universality which ensures that other peoples will not be excluded, and a purified religious conception of the Kingdom of God. One day God's eschatological Dominion shall prevail completely over mankind, yes, over the whole of creation. But the idea that God should have an earthly regent is completely absent. Instead of this, the "Servant of God" is of decisive importance. Jesus took up this prophecy. However dependent Jesus may be on Deutero-Isaiah, the message He brings can never be completely explained by this contact. One cannot understand Jesus' teaching of the Kingdom of God without taking into account

---

should never be used in speaking of the present character of the *basileia*. The translation "*Königtum Gottes*" (Kingship or Kingdom of God) is admirable with reference to the Old Testament sayings that Jahweh is King, but " 'es komme dein *Königtum*' sounds somewhat strange" (*op. cit.*, p. 247). [84] *Op. cit.*, p. 3.

developments within late Judaism. In late Judaism "national" eschatology forced its way right down to the broad masses of the people. Everyone expected that God would send the Messiah, the King, "the Son of David," to re-establish the Kingdom. In times of hardship and struggle, the longing that the Kingdom of God should be revealed in glory and power quickly, yes, even in the very days through which they were living, grew to passionate prayer. Side by side with this expectation we find the rabbinical teaching of the now hidden Dominion of God, to be revealed some time in the future, and the apocalyptic expectation of the cosmic-universal Dominion of God. In this latter, cosmic-eschatological expectation, the idea of the kingly Dominion of God becomes increasingly spiritualised and supra-worldly. The idea of individual salvation replaces the idea of the people and of belonging to the people.

When it comes to characterising Jesus' teaching of the Kingdom of God, Schnackenburg emphasises strongly that this always relates to God's eschatological "*Königtum*." He says: "It cannot be said too definitely that the *idea* of the '*Gottesherrschaft*' in his (Jesus') mouth always means the eschatological '*Königtum*' of God, even though the *thought* of the everlasting divine world government is also to Him familiar and irrefutable. But Jesus does not speak of this, when He speaks of the '*Königsherrschaft Gottes*'; where this expression comes, it means invariably the eschatological Kingdom ('*Königtum*') of God and the texts should not be interpreted uneschatologically" ("blunted").[85] The Kingdom of God which Jesus preached does not mean God's power over the universe or His Dominion over Israel (even though this is presupposed), but God's "fully realised, fully effective, end of time, definitive *Königtum*."[86] The Kingdom of God is something which comes to men, something which is offered to them, but not something over which they dispose, which they can force or defy their way to. It is also important to keep clearly in mind that the Kingdom of God was always connected by Jesus with verbs in which the temporal element is essential. The Kingdom of God was thus to Jesus something entirely eschatological and wholly supernatural.

Jesus never spoke of revenge. He offered and enjoined on

[85] *Op. cit.*, p. 52.   [86] *Op. cit.*, p. 53.

men the salvation of God. His preaching was the preaching
of salvation. Schnackenburg speaks of "the salvationary
character of the Kingdom of God."[87] Jesus taught of salvation
as being present and active already now, even though it is not
yet full and complete. Jesus' time was the time of salvation,
for the gospel was preached and God had mercy on mankind.
God's mercy came close to them in the activity of Jesus. He
forgave sins. He healed the sick and cast out evil spirits. He
required an answer to the divine offer of grace.

Jesus preached of the present time that it was the time
of salvation. But of the time to come He preached salvation
and judgment, according to the attitude men adopted and how
they decided in face of His message. The preaching of salvation
by Jesus has a quite peculiar quality. We will let Schnackenburg speak for himself: "The present revelation of God's love
for sinners as the sign of His eschatological Dominion, the
forgiving of all without exception who believe Jesus' message
of salvation and repent, the joy of God in forgiving and in
bestowing the gifts of His salvation: that is an absolutely
unique and incomparable feature of the *basileia* message of
Jesus. There is also yet another feature which, in comparison
with late Jewish testimony, must be regarded as the distinctive
expression of His thinking and as the peculiar content of His
preaching: He raised the Kingdom of God into an inclusive
term for all salvation, the pinnacle of all expectation of
salvation."[88] This must be regarded as something peculiar to
Jesus.

Further, all earthly national and religious-political elements
are lacking in Jesus' idea of the Kingdom of God. He rejected
any attempt to calculate when the Kingdom of God shall be
established in glory. Neither did He give any real description
of the Kingdom of God. He used traditional images. These
were not to Him a description of what the Kingdom is like,
but He used this language of religious symbolism which men
have used in all ages when they wanted to express eternal
things, the heavenly reality and the fact that fulfilment is
quite otherwise. When, for example, He used the image of
the supper, He did so to express perfect communion with God
and between those who have part in salvation.

Jesus' message of salvation was addressed to the whole of

[87] *Op. cit.*, p. 56.   [88] *Op. cit.*, p. 60.

Israel. The idea of a "Sacred Remnant" which He should gather from the whole of Israel, was quite alien to Him. When Jesus did not win the whole of Israel, but only a small part of it, a "little flock" (Lk. xii. 32) remained, this was a development in the history of salvation that by no means corresponds to the universality of His message. "He does not create a special community of the saved, but a community of the faithful as the future members of salvation, a community which lives in the mercy of God."[89]

Jesus demanded *metanoia*. He called for a higher righteousness. He who regards the uncompromising commands of the Sermon on the Mount as a programme for a new order of things in this world has misunderstood them fundamentally. For Jesus was not trying to bring about a social revolution or a progressive evolution towards an earthly kingdom of peace, but a revolution within man himself to enable him to have part in the coming Kingdom of God. It is also a misconception to see the morality He demanded simply as the ideal order in a coming world. For there no imperatives will be needed, there man will have the law of God written in his heart (Jer. xxxi. 33, xxxii. 40) and will be led by the Spirit of God (Ezek. xxxvi. 26 f.). No, the demands Jesus made are related to conditions in the world still existing, are directed to those who desire to be present in the coming Kingdom, and exhort them to decision. Nor is it a question of any interim ethic, applicable to the short time until the end of the world. All Jesus' commands are contained in the one master command: to love God with all your heart, all your soul, all your mind, and all your strength, and to love your neighbour as yourself (Mk. xii. 29-31 *par.*). This radical demand and the message of salvation are combined in a synthesis for those who believe in Jesus as the bringer of salvation.

God's absolute demands upon man were exemplified in a special way by the fact that Jesus required to be followed in His person. "This binding to His person is one of the new and incomparable elements in the message and demands of Jesus."[90]

The strangest thing about Jesus' *basileia* picture is this: that the message that the time is fulfilled and the Kingdom of God near has its basis in the fact that God's special messenger, the eschatological herald, has raised His voice. The actual kernel

[89] *Op. cit.*, p. 66.   [90] *Op. cit.*, p. 73.

of the problem is the relationship between the Kingdom of God Jesus preached, and His person and activity. This is the greatest mystery in Jesus' image of the Kingdom of God.

Schnackenburg poses the question thus: What importance does Jesus attach to Himself and His activity in the coming of the Kingdom of God? Is He merely its prophet and preacher, or is it making its appearance with Him, and if so, in what way?

According to Schnackenburg, Jesus claimed to be the Messiah. This indeed He did secretly, in order that He should not be misunderstood, but still clearly enough for all who wished to understand. Those who had ears to hear and eyes to see could discover who He was. His teaching cannot be separated from His person. Even if it were possible to separate His teaching from His person and to regard that as a prophetic mission from God, it would be quite impossible in the case of His miracles. This is shown with all possible clarity by the reply to John the Baptist: "Go and tell John what you hear and see: the blind receive their sight and the lame walk, lepers are cleansed and the deaf hear, and the dead are raised up, and the poor have the good news preached to them" (Mt. xi. 4 f.; Lk. vii. 22 f.). By using words from the Scriptures, from the prophet Isaiah, Jesus showed who He believed Himself to be. To Him, teaching and miracles were closely associated. It is above all His miracles, the healing of the sick and the forgiveness of sins, that reveal the coming of the Kingdom of God. "Here salvation comes to pass, here in this particular way the Kingdom of God breaks through; one might call the miracles 'the Kingdom of God in action'."[91] In the very fact that Jesus is there lies the blessedness of the age (Lk. x. 23; Mt. xii. 16).

Rather than give a resumé, I think it is better to quote what Schnackenburg himself says on one of the principal sayings about the Kingdom of God, namely Mt. xii. 28; Lk. xi. 20: "If it is by the Spirit of God (the finger of God, Lk.) that I cast out demons, then the kingdom of God has come upon you." "Jesus' teaching of the Kingdom of God and His work of salvation do not stand independently side by side, but fuse into a unity and testify together to the eschatological event

---

[91] *Op. cit.*, p. 82. Schnackenburg quotes here L. de Grandmaison, *Jésus Christ, Sa personne, son message, ses preuves*, VOL. II, Paris 1929, p. 366.

that took place in Jesus. But over and above this, there is also an old logion that sets the acts of Jesus in direct relationship with the dawning Kingdom of God; it refers to His casting out of demons: If it is by the finger of God (Mt. by the Spirit of God), that I cast out demons, then the kingdom of God has come upon you (Lk. xi. 20; Mt. xii. 28). The following features of this incontestable saying of Jesus are important: (1) The verb φθάνειν in the aorist tense cannot be understood in any other sense than as meaning 'it has come'; any weakening of this sense of completed time would be unjustified. (2) This presence of the Kingdom of God is *recognisable* in the casting out of the demons by Jesus; the conditional clause provides the basis for recognition and proof (cf. ἄρα). (3) The casting out of the demons is an actual event, a demonstration of power with concrete results; accordingly the Kingdom of God is regarded here as being an effective power (not as a 'kingdom,' an institution, but also not as a purely inward entity). (4) This entering into effect of the Kingdom of God is brought about through *Jesus*; He plays a part in it that can only be played by Him. The power of God, or the Holy Ghost, is vested in Him in order that He may break the power of the demons. . . .

"It may be concluded, then, from this logion: that Jesus is aware that divine authority has been vested in Him, and that through it the eschatological Kingdom of God breaks through in His works. This is not, of course, the cosmic 'appearance' of the Kingdom of God, though it is more than just a premonition or promise, and also something different from a purely inward or completely hidden presence. The *basileia* is essentially a revelation of the power of God, even though it is not yet the complete revelation of His glory."[92]

On the subject of the "presence sayings" on the Kingdom of God, it is important to recognise clearly the limits within which one has to keep. Schnackenburg defines these as follows: It would be too *little* to regard the teaching of Jesus, His healings and exorcisms, as merely a *presage* of the coming Kingdom of God.[93] They are rather *signs* of its presence. On the other hand, it would be too *much* to speak of this present

---

[92] *Op. cit.*, pp. 84 f.

[93] As J. Weiss, *Die Predigt Jesu vom Reiche Gottes*, p. 70, and Fuller, *The Mission and Achievement of Jesus*, pp. 35-43.

Kingdom of God as something completed or even actually institutional. By its very nature it indicates the coming perfected Kingdom of God, makes it certain, demands it. On the first assumption, Jesus becomes fundamentally a prophet; on the second, the present world-perfecter. Both conflict with Jesus' message and testimony about Himself. Schnackenburg cautiously formulates his own view as follows: "The Kingdom of God as present in Jesus and His works is 'precursory,' because and in so far as it paves the way for what is to come, and is not something complete or finished in itself. It may be spoken of as 'hidden,' but only relatively hidden, namely in comparison with the future revelation in glory, as on the other hand it is manifest in the words and miracles of Jesus. The expression that it has come 'in weakness' is to be deprecated, since this is incompatible with the nature of the Kingdom of God. Jesus was here to proclaim God's powerful and perceptible eschatological offer of salvation."[94]

The nearness of the Kingdom of God is "dynamic" in the real sense of the word, *i.e.* the Kingdom of God is here as an active Kingdom. The part played by Jesus in the coming of this Kingdom is not merely passive. His person is important for the present breaking through of the Kingdom of God. His coming coincides with its coming as the forerunner of the perfected Kingdom. It is perceptible only through His teaching and works.

We cannot here discuss in detail Schnackenburg's commentary on a number of debated passages such as Mt. XI. 12 f.; Lk. XVI. 16; Lk. VII. 28; Mt. XI. 11; Lk. XVII. 20 f. and Mk. I. 15. All of them reveal the peculiar eschatological consciousness that Jesus had: the time is come when the prophetic sayings about the End-time shall enter into fulfilment, but the fulfilment is not yet come. But the time that is come gives certainty that the perfected Kingdom of God stands at the door.

The parables of growth have always played a decisive part in the understanding of Jesus' idea of the Kingdom of God. Interpretations have varied extremely. Schnackenburg's discussion with exponents of various interpretations cannot be dealt with here. But we will briefly summarise his own view on these parables. The parable of the Sower (Mk. IV. 1-9 *par.*) is according to him a *basileia* parable, which belongs

---

[94] Schnackenburg, *Gottes Herrschaft und Reich*, pp. 87 f.

S

to the last period of Jesus' activity in Galilee, when a large part
of the people had turned their backs on Him or were on the
point of leaving Him. Even so, Jesus is saying, the beginning
has been made, and the coming Kingdom approaches. God
will bring His work to a conclusion whatever happens. Even
though only few accept the message, it is enough to be certain
of the Kingdom. The fact that many fall away does not
destroy God's plan. The figure of the Sower himself is not
given prominence. Jesus may have meant that He Himself
was the Sower.

The parable of the Self-growing seed (Mk. IV. 26-9) teaches
that man can do nothing to bring about growth. It is God's
creative activity that causes growth. Jesus rejects such false
human activity as was expected of a political Messiah. The
sower waits calmly, for he knows that the harvest will come.
The very words καρποφορεῖ (vs. 28), ὁ καρπός and ὁ θερισμός
(vs. 29), show that attention is focused on the harvest. The
parable is thus intended to illustrate the supernatural nature
of the Kingdom of God, which constantly draws near.

The parables of the Grain of Mustard Seed (Mk. IV. 30-2
par.) and the Leaven (Lk. XIII. 20 f.; Mt. XIII. 33), are concerned, not with the power of development of the Kingdom
of God, but with a comparison between the beginning and the
end. In spite of the slight beginning, the glorious end is
certain. "God in His power lets the inconsiderable beginning
be followed by the glorious end; He gives the promise and
guarantee that His Kingdom comes. Here again the presence
of the Kingdom of God in the words and acts of Jesus is taken
for granted, as is also the continuity between its beginning and
its future perfection, a continuity which corresponds to that
between sowing and harvesting: *because* the power and reality
of the Kingdom of God is already revealed and perceptible,
its cosmic revelation is certain."[95]

In the parables of the Weeds among the Wheat and of the
Net (Mt. XIII. 24-30, 47 f.), Jesus reveals what is the
characteristic element of His *basileia* teaching, namely that
the coming of the Kingdom now applies only to salvation,
whereas judgment belongs to the perfected Kingdom.

The parables of growth cannot, then, be regarded as one-
sided evidence for either the future or present conception of the

[95] *Op. cit.*, p. 107.

Kingdom of God. They testify to the tension between beginning and end, between the insignificance of the Kingdom of God now and its revealed glory in the future. But there is a continuity between Jesus' teaching of salvation and acts of salvation now, and the triumph of the Kingdom of God in glory in time to come.

What constitutes the present character of the Kingdom of God, Schnackenburg summarises in the following words: "The present character of the Kingdom of God may be described, however, briefly as follows: Jesus preaches the eschatological Kingdom of God as a near and approaching Kingdom, one effective and perceptible, connected with His person and His works, and calling His hearers to an inescapable decision. In this sense it is present already in Him, His words and acts."[96]

Even if Jesus saw the Kingdom of God as present in His teaching and His miracles, the main emphasis lies with Him on the fact that it is to come some time in the future. There is no place in the Gospels where the verb "to come" ($\check{\epsilon}\rho\chi\epsilon\sigma\theta\alpha\iota$) is connected with the Kingdom of God now breaking through. The sayings about "entering into the Kingdom of God" and cognate expressions are associated with the future Kingdom of God. Figurative terms such as supper and harvest belong also to the same category.

The question now arises: Did Jesus attach importance to His person in respect also of the coming, perfected Kingdom of God? To answer this, Schnackenburg examines the sayings about the coming Son of Man, and comes to the conclusion that the perfected Kingdom of God is to come through God's sovereign will, when the Son of Man comes in power. And this Son of Man is Jesus Himself, who now completes His Messianic task on earth in humility and to a certain extent in secret, but who shall be revealed to all the world as the bearer of kingly dignity and divine power to establish God's perfect, cosmic-universal Kingdom of God.

The results of Jesus' teaching were negative. Large groups of the people did not believe the message. Only a small, limited circle accepted the revelation of the Kingdom of God. The passage in Mk. IV. 11 f.: "To you has been given the secret of the kingdom of God, but for those outside everything

[96] *Op. cit.*, p. 109.

is in parables; so that they may indeed see but not perceive, and may indeed hear, but not understand; lest they should turn again, and be forgiven," was originally not a defence of Jesus' way of teaching in parables, but may have applied to His message of the Kingdom of God in general, in this new situation which arose when the majority rejected His message. Jesus said then that the secret was revealed only to a narrow circle, whereas it was hidden from the mass of the people. Behind this lay a divine plan, according to which only a few were chosen to receive Jesus' message. The "secret" was the hidden presence of the Kingdom of God in the activity of Jesus, which was to be followed by the revelation of the Kingdom of God in glory in the future.

After Simon Peter's confession at Caesarea Philippi we have sayings which connect the coming of the perfected Kingdom of God with the expiatory death of Jesus. The most important of these is what Jesus said at the Last Supper, and which Mark reproduces as follows: "Truly, I say to you, I shall not drink again of the fruit of the vine until that day when I drink it new in the kingdom of God" (Mk. xiv. 25). If He said this before the institution of the Last Supper, as Lk. xxii. 16, 18, indicates, then new light is thrown on the saying by the sacramental words in which Jesus ascribes to His death a vicarious atonement. Jesus said that He would not eat passover any more on earth until it was fulfilled in the coming Kingdom of God. His death was the condition for the disciples having part in the coming passover in the Kingdom of God. To Jesus, God's plan of salvation was unfolding: "His perfected Kingdom will not come, in spite of the rejection of His last messenger, as universal, annihilating judgment, but on the basis of the atoning death of His faithful Servant, God will offer to all mankind, even to the hitherto unbelieving Jews, yet another opportunity of salvation. . . . The gospel sounds on, the eschatological Kingdom of God remains the source of joy and salvation for all who repent and believe."[97]

On the much-debated question of whether Jesus expected the Kingdom of God in the very near future ("*Die Frage der Naherwartung*"), Schnackenburg adopts, as on other questions, a cautious, intermediate standpoint. There exists, indeed, a broad stream of tradition that Jesus expected the coming of

[97] *Op. cit.*, p. 135.

the Kingdom of God in the near future, but He expressly avoided any closer definition of time. There are a few sayings about the coming of the Kingdom of God during the present generation. It is impossible to establish definitely the position of these sayings in the teaching of Jesus. The early Church failed to incorporate these awkward fragments of tradition in the eschatological teaching of Jesus, yet they kept eschatological expectation alive. And that Jesus might have been mistaken was not an idea that the early Church would admit. Nor need we admit it either, Schnackenburg believes, if we keep the whole tradition in mind and concentrate on the meaning and purpose of the teaching of Jesus.

What is the relationship of the group of disciples Jesus gathered round Him to the eschatological community in the perfected Kingdom of God? Is the band of disciples merely a group of men awaiting the Kingdom of God, or an anticipation of the fulfilled community of the blessed? Is any trace of the emergent Kingdom of God to be seen in the existence and activity of this group of disciples? Schnackenburg starts with the assumption that the Church saying to Simon Peter (Mt. XVI. 13-19) is a saying of Jesus. He sees the relationship between the Kingdom of God and the Church as follows:

1. The Kingdom of God and Jesus' earthly community are not identical, but not without relationship to one another. The community that Jesus founded has part through Him in the present salvationary forces of the Kingdom of God and in the promise for the future.

2. The congregation shall some day become the community of the perfected Kingdom of God. The *ekklesia* is the community of those in expectation of the Kingdom of God.

3. The forces of the present Kingdom of God are active in the community as they were in the teaching and acts of Jesus.

4. The gates of hell, *i.e.* the powers of death, shall not overcome the community founded by Jesus. This shall therefore endure until God reveals the cosmic Kingdom of God. But in this existence it lives in constant struggle against the powers of evil and is an *ecclesia militans et pressa*, an *ecclesia crucis*.

5. Membership of this *ekklesia* on earth is no guarantee of belonging to the coming Kingdom.

6. It is the conception of the eschatological people of God that unites present and future. The people of God is still

being gathered together, but it is nevertheless God's people, over whom God rules. The *ekklesia* is the place where the elect are gathered together under the Messianic shepherd, Jesus.[98]

Schnackenburg's book on the Kingdom of God stands out as an important contribution to research on the Kingdom of God, not least through its moderation and its carefully balanced attitude on controversial questions. It also throws light on the prevalent ecumenical attitude among Bible scholars who have their spiritual home in widely different Churches.

To express any general verdict on the debate on the Kingdom of God in the past fifteen years is not easy. But it seems obvious that no such epoch-making work has appeared during this brief period as Rudolf Otto's *Reich Gottes und Menschensohn*, or C. H. Dodd's *The Parables of the Kingdom*. The most important contribution seems to me to be Schnackenburg's *Gottes Herrschaft und Reich*, chiefly because of the author's determination to understand Jesus' teaching about the Kingdom of God as we find it in the Synoptics, without suppressing either the futuristic sayings or the presence sayings. To this must be added his firm Christocentric anchorage, which he has in common with S. H. Hooke, Günther Bornkamm, J. Bright, and above all N. A. Dahl. In this respect Dahl is a worthy follower of a strong tradition among Scandinavian Bible scholars.

[98] As exponents of the views of Roman Catholic exegetists on the question of the Kingdom of God may be mentioned: F. Gils, "Jésus prophète d'après les Évangiles synoptiques," in *Orientalia et Biblica Lovaniensia*, VOL. II, Louvain 1957, who considers that the Kingdom of God according to Jesus is "already mysteriously present on earth" (p. 98); and J. Schildenberger, "Verheissung und Erfüllung," in *Biblica*, XXIV (1943), pp. 107-24, 205-30, who says that in Mt. x. 23 = Mk. IX. 1, Jesus obviously means His contemporaries. The Parousia was to come during the generation then living, but no one could know the day. Some of those present should see the Son of Man come in kingly glory and see the Kingdom of God in power (Mt. XVI. 28). The Kingdom of God was already present in the person of Jesus (Mt. XII. 28). In Mk. I. 15 he translates ἤγγικεν by "has arrived, is there" (p. 225).

J. Bonsirven, *Le Règne de Dieu*, Théologie, VOL. XXXVII, Paris 1957, gives an elegantly written, popular account. The Kingdom has already made "its appearance in Jesus" (p. 48).

An excellent survey of the position of research and a detailed discussion is given by A. Feuillet, "Le Règne de Dieu et la personne de Jésus d'après les évangiles synoptiques," in A. Robert and A. Feuillet, *Introduction à la Bible*: VOL. II, *Nouveau Testament*, Tourrnai 1959, pp. 771-818.

Bibliography

ALEXANDER, A. B. D. "The Kingdom of God and the Ethics of Jesus," in *Exp.T.*, 1928-29, pp. 73-7.

ALTHAUS, P. *Die letzten Dinge. Entwurf einer christlichen Eschatologie.* Gütersloh 1922; 3rd edn. 1926.

——"Neues Testament und Mythologie. Zu R. Bultmanns Versuch der Entmythologisierung des Neuen Testaments," in *Th.Lz.*, 1942, pp. 337-44.

AULÉN, G. *Den kristna gudsbilden genom seklerna och i nutiden. En konturteckning.* Stockholm 1927.

BALDENSPERGER, W. *Das Selbstbewusstsein Jesu im Lichte der messianischen Hoffnungen seiner Zeit.* Strassburg 1888.

BARTH, K. *Das Wort Gottes und die Theologie. Gesammelte Vorträge*, VOL I, Munich 1923. Eng. version: *The Word of God and the Word of Man*, trans. D. Horton, New York and London 1928.

——*Der Römerbrief.* Munich 1919, 2nd edn. 1922. Eng. version: *The Epistle to the Romans*, trans. E. C. Hoskyns. Oxford 1933.

——*Die Auferstehung der Toten. Eine akademische Vorlesung über I Kor. 15.* Munich 1924, 2nd edn. 1926. Eng. version: *The Resurrection of the Dead*, trans. H. J. Stenning. London 1933.

——*Die kirchliche Dogmatik*, VOL. I, PT. 1; *Die Lehre vom Worte Gottes, Prolegomena zur kirchlichen Dogmatik.* Munich 1932. Eng. version: *Church Dogmatics*, VOL. I, PT. I, trans. G. T. Thomson, Edinbrugh 1936.

BARTH, M. *Der Augenzeuge. Eine Untersuchung über die Wahrnehmung des Menschensohnes durch die Apostel.* Zollikon-Zürich 1946.

BELL, G. K. A. and A. DEISSMANN, eds. *Mysterium Christi. Christological Studies by British and German theologians.* London 1930.

BERNHEIM, E. *Einleitung in die Geschichtswissenschaft.* Sammlung Göschen, No. 270, 3rd and 4th edn. Berlin 1926.

BEYSCHLAG, W. *Neutestamentliche Theologie oder Darstellung des Lebens Jesu und des Urchristentums nach den neutestamentlichen Quellen.* 2 vols. Halle 1891-92. Eng. version: *New Testament Theology: Or Historical Account of the Teaching of Jesus and of Primitive Christianity according to the New Testament Sources*, trans. N. Buchanan. 2 vols. Edinburgh 1895.

BILLING, E. *De etiska tankarna i urkristendomen i deras samband med dess religiösa tro.* 2 vols. Uppsala 1907; 2nd rev. edn. 1936.

——*Försoningen. Två utvidgade föredrag.* Uppsala 1908; 2nd edn. 1921.

——" 'Människosonen' och 'Gudsriket' i Jesu förkunnelse; Två fragment ur ett ofullbordat arbete," in *För tanke och tro, Skrifter, tillägnade Oscar Ekman.* Uppsala 1923.

BLUMHARDT, Ch. *Ihr Menschen seid Gottes.* Erlenbach-Zürich and Leipzig 1936.

BLUMHARDT, Ch. *Predigten und Andachten aus dem Jahre 1888 bis 1896.* Erlenbach-Zürich and Leipzig 1925.

——*Vom Reiche Gottes.* Berlin 1925.

BOHLIN, T. *Den kristna Gudsrikestanken under 1800-talet och i nutiden.* Lund 1928.

—— "Die Reich-Gottes-Idée im letzten halben Jahrhundert," in *Z.Th.K.*, N.F. x (1929), pp. 1-27.

BONSIRVEN, J. *Le Règne de Dieu.* Théologie, VOL. XXXVII. Paris 1957.

BONUS, A. *Religion als Wille. Grundlegendes zur neuen Frömmigkeit.* Jena 1915.

BORNKAMM, G. *Jesus von Nazareth.* Stuttgart 1956. Eng. version: *Jesus of Nazareth,* trans. I. and F. McLuskey and J. M. Robinson. London and New York 1960.

BOSWORTH, E. I. *The Life and Teaching of Jesus. According to the First Three Gospels.* New York 1924.

BOUSSET, W. "Das Reich Gottes in der Predigt Jesu," in *Th.R.*, v (1902), pp. 397-407, 437-49.

——*Die Religion des Judentums im neutestamentlichen Zeitalter.* Berlin 1903; 2nd edn. 1906.

——*Jesus.* Religionsgeschichtliche Volksbücher, 1 : 2-3. Tübingen 1904: 4th edn. with intro. by Professor K. L. Schmidt, 1922. Eng. version: *Jesus,* trans. J. P. Trevelyan, ed. W. D. Morrison. London and New York 1906.

——*Jesu Predigt in ihrem Gegensatz zum Judentum. Ein religionsgeschichtlicher Vergleich.* Göttingen 1892.

—— "Kantisch-Friessche Religionsphilosophie und ihre Anwendung auf die Theologie," in *Th.R.*, XII (1909), pp. 419-36, 471-88.

——*Kyrios Christos. Geschichte des Christusglaubens von den Anfängen des Christentums bis Irenäus.* Forschungen zur Religion und Literatur des Alten und Neuen Testaments, ed. R. Bultmann, N.F. VOL. IV. Göttingen 1913; 3rd edn. 1926.

—— "J. Weiss, *Die Predigt Jesu vom Reiche Gottes*" (review), in *Th. Lz.*, 1901, pp. 563-8.

——and GRESSMAN, H. *Die Religion des Judentums im späthellenistischen Zeitalter.* 3rd edn. Tübingen 1926.

BRIGHT, J. *The Kingdom of God in Bible and Church.* London 1955. American edn., *The Kingdom of God. The Biblical Concept and its Meaning for the Church.* New York 1958.

BRUN, L. "Der Name und die Königsherrschaft im Vaterunser," in *Harnack-Ehrung.* Leipzig 1921, pp. 22-31.

—— "Guds rike og Menneskesønnen" (review of R. Otto, *Reich Gottes und Menschensohn*), in *Norsk Teologisk Tidskrift,* 1937, pp. 105-25.

——*Jesu evangelium. En historisk framställning av Jesu förkunnelse,* 1917; 2nd rev. edn. Oslo 1926.

BRUNNER, E. *Der Mittler. Zur Besinnung über den Christusglauben.* Tübingen 1927; 2nd edn. 1930. Eng. version: *The Mediator,* trans. O. Wym. London 1934; 6th imp. 1949.

——*Die Mystik und das Wort. Der Gegensatz zwischen moderner Religionsauffassung und christlichem Glauben dargestellt an der Theologie Schleiermachers.* Tübingen 1924; 2nd edn. 1928.

BÜCHSEL, F. *Die Hauptfragen der Synoptikerkritik. Eine Auseinandersetzung mit R. Bultmann, M. Dibelius und ihren Vorgängern.* Beiträge zur Förderung christlicher Theologie, VOL. XL, No. 6. Gütersloh 1939.

——*Theologie des Neuen Testaments. Geschichte des Wortes Gottes im Neuen Testament.* Gütersloh 1933 ; 2nd edn. 1933.

BULTMANN, R. "Die Bedeutung der Eschatologie für die Religion des Neuen Testaments," in *Z.Th.K.*, XXVII (1917), pp. 76-87.

——*Die Erforschung der synoptischen Evangelien.* Aus der Welt der Religion. Neutestamentliche Reihe, No. 1. 2nd edn. Giessen 1930.

——*Die Geschichte der synoptischen Tradition.* Forschungen zur Religion und Literatur des Alten und Neuen Testaments, N.F. VOL. XII. Göttingen 1921; 2nd edn. 1931.

——*Glauben und Verstehen. Gesammelte Aufsätze,* VOL. I. Tübingen 1933.

——*Jesus.* Die Unsterblichen VOL. I. Berlin 1926. Eng. version: *Jesus and the Word,* trans. L. Pettibone Smith and E. Huntress. London 1934.

——*Offenbarung und Heilsgeschehen.* Beiträge zur Evangelischen Theologie. Theologische Abhandlungen, ed. E. Wolff. VOL. VII. Munich 1941.

——*Theologie des Neuen Testaments,* 1953. Eng. version: *Theology of the New Testament,* trans K. Grobel, 2 vols. London 1952-5.

——"E. Lohmeyer, *Vom Begriff der religiösen Gemeinschaft*" (review), in *Th.Bl.*, VI (1927), pp. 66-73.

——"E. Lohmeyer, *Die Offenbarung des Johannes,* 1926" (review), in *Th.Lz.*, 1930, pp. 505-12.

——"R. Otto, *Reich Gottes und Menschensohn*" (review), in *Th.R.*, N.F. IX (1937), pp. 1-35.

BURI, F. *Die Bedeutung der neutestamentlichen Eschatologie für die neuere protestantische Theologie.* Diss. Berne. Zürich 1934.

BURKITT, F. C. *Jesus Christ. An historical outline.* London 1932.

——"The Eschatological Idea in the Gospels," in *Essays on some Biblical questions of the day, by members of the University of Cambridge,* ed. H. B. Sweete. London 1909, pp. 193-213.

——"The Parables of the Kingdom of Heaven," in *The Interpreter,* 1910-11, pp. 131-48, 353-8.

BUSSMANN, W. *Synoptische Studien.* VOL. I, *Zur Geschichtsquelle*; VOL. II, *Zur Redenquelle*; VOL. III, *Zu den Sonderquellen.* Halle 1925-31.

CADBURY, H. J. *The Peril of Modernizing Jesus.* New York 1937.

CADOUX, A. T. *The Parables of Jesus. Their art and use.* London 1930.

——*The Theology of Jesus.* London 1940.

CADOUX, C. J. *The Historic Mission of Jesus. A constructive re-examination of the eschatological teaching in the Synoptic Gospels.* London 1941.

CAMPENHAUSEN, H. von. "Der Ablauf der Osterereignisse und das leere Grab," in *Sitzungsberichte der Heidelberger Akademie der Wissenschaften, Philosophisch-historische Klasse,* 1952, No. 4, p. 7.

CASE, S. J. *Experience with the Supernatural in Early Christian Times.* New York 1929.

——*Jesus. A New Biography.* Chicago 1927.

——*Jesus through the Centuries.* Chicago 1932.

——*The Evolution of Early Christianity.* Chicago 1914.

Case, S. J. *The Historicity of Jesus.* Chicago 1912.
——"The Life of Jesus during the last Quarter-Century," in *J.Rel.*, v (1925), pp. 56-73.
——*The Social Origins of Christianity.* Chicago 1923.
Charles, R. H. *A Critical History of the Doctrine of a Future Life in Israel, in Judaism, and in Christianity: Or Hebrew, Jewish, and Christian Eschatology from pre-Prophetic times till the close of the New Testament canon. Being the Jowett Lectures for 1898-99.* London 1899.
Clavier, H. *L'Accès au Royaume de Dieu,* E.H.P.R., No. 40. Paris 1944.
——*La Notion de Dieu dans l'enseignement de Jésus.* Études théologiques et religieuses. Montpellier 1932.
Cohen, H. *Ethik des reinen Willens.* 2nd edn. 1907.
Colani, T. *Jésus-Christ et les croyances messianiques de son temps.* Strasbourg 1864.
Conzelmann, H. *Die Mitte der Zeit. Studien zur Theologie des Lukas,* Tübingen 1954. Eng. version: *The Theology of St Luke,* trans. G. Buswell. London and New York 1960.
Cullmann, O. *Christus und die Zeit. Die urchristliche Zeit- und Geschichtsauffassung.* Zürich 1946. Eng. version: *Christ and Time,* trans. F. G. Filson. London 1951.
——*Königsherrschaft Christi und Kirche im Neuen Testament.* Theologische Studien, ed. Karl Barth, vol. x. Zollikon-Zürich 1941.
——*Le Retour du Christ, Espérance de l'Eglise, selon le Nouveau Testament.* Cahiers théologiques de l'actualité protestante, vol. i. Neuchâtel 1943.
Dahl, N. A. *Das Volk Gottes. Eine Untersuchung zum Kirchenbewusstsein des Urchristentums.* Skrifter utg. av Det Norske Videnskaps-Akademi, Hist. filos. ii. Kl., 1941. No. 2. Oslo 1941.
——"Der historische Jesu als geschichtswissenschaftliches und theologisches Problem," in *Kerygma und Dogma,* i, (1955), pp. 104-32.
——"The Parables of Growth," in *Studie Theologica,* v, No. 2 (1952), pp. 132-66.
Dalman, G. *Die Worte Jesu. Mit Berücksichtigung des nachkanonischen jüdischen Schrifttums und der aramäischen Sprache.* Leipzig 1898; 2nd edn. 1930. Eng. version: *The Words of Jesus, Considered in the Light of Post-Biblical Jewish Writings and the Aramaic Language,* trans. D. M. Kay. Edinburgh 1902.
De Grandmaison, L. *Jésus Christ, Sa personne, son message, ses preuves,* vol. ii. Paris 1929.
Delling, G. *Das Zeitverständnis des Neuen Testaments.* Gütersloh 1940.
Dewick, E. C. *Primitive Christian Eschatology.* Cambridge 1912.
Dibelius, M. *Die Formgeschichte des Evangeliums.* Tübingen 1919; 2nd edn. 1933. Eng. version: *From Tradition to Gospel,* trans. B. L. Woolf. London 1934.
——*Die Religionswissenschaft der Gegenwart in Selbstdarstellungen,* ed. Erich Stange; vol. v, *Martin Dibelius,* 1929.
——"Die Unbedingtheit des Evangeliums und die Bedingtheit der Ethik," in *Christliche Welt,* 1926, pp. 1103-20.

DIBELIUS, M. *Die urchristliche Überlieferung von Johannes dem Täufer.* Forschungen zur Religion und Literatur des Alten und Neuen Testaments, VOL. XV. Göttingen 1911.

—— "Die Zeitlosigkeit der Botschaft Jesu," in *Christliche Welt*, 1927, pp. 546-52.

—— *Geschichtliche und übergeschichtliche Religion im Christentum.* Göttingen 1925; 2nd edn., 1929, *Evangelium und Welt.*

—— *Jesus.* Sammlung Göschen, No. 1130. Berlin 1939.

—— "Jesus in contemporary German theology," in *J.Rel.*, 1931, pp. 179-221.

—— *The Sermon on the Mount.* New York 1940.

—— "R. Otto, *Reich Gottes und Menschensohn*" (review), in *Göttingischer Gelehrte Anzeiger*, CXCVII (1935), pp. 209-21.

DOBSCHÜTZ, E. VON. "Der heutige Stand der Leben-Jesu-Forschung," in *Z.Th.K.*, N.F. V (1924), pp. 64-84.

—— *Die evangelische Theologie, ihr jetziger Stand und ihre Aufgaben.* Das Neue Testament, VOL. II. Halle 1927.

—— "The Eschatology of the Gospels," in *Exp.*, Ser. VII, No. 9, 1910, pp. 97-113, 193-209, 333-47, 398-417; also in book form. London 1910.

—— "Zeit und Raum im Denken des Urchristentums," in *Journal of Biblical Literature*, XLI (1922), pp. 212-23.

—— "Zur Eschatologie der Evangelien," in *Theologische Studien und Kritiken*, 1911, pp. 1-20.

DODD, C. H. *History and the Gospel.* New York 1938.

—— *The Apostolic Preaching and its Developments. Three Lectures with an Appendix on Eschatology and History.* London 1936.

—— *The Coming of Christ.* Cambridge 1951.

—— *The Gospel as History: a Reconsideration.* Manchester 1938.

—— *The Interpretation of the Fourth Gospel.* Cambridge 1953.

—— "The Kingdom of God and History," in *Church, Community and State*, VOL. III. London 1938, pp. 11-36.

—— "The Kingdom of God has come," in *Exp.T.*, XLVIII (1936), pp. 138-42.

—— *The Parables of the Kingdom.* London 1935; 3rd edn. 1936.

DOR, P. *Le Royaume de Jésus et la passion selon M. Guignebert.* Paris 1939.

DU BOSE, W. P. *The Gospel in the Gospels.* London and New York 1906.

DUHM, B. *Das kommende Reich Gottes.* Tübingen 1910. Eng. version: *The Ever-Coming Kingdom of God*, trans. A. Duff. London 1911.

DU PASQUIER, R. *Le Royaume de Dieu dans la prédication de Jésus.* Lausanne 1906.

EASTON, B. S. *Christ in the Gospels.* New York 1930.

EDERSHEIM, A. *Life and Times of Jesus, the Messiah.* London 1883.

EDWARDS, D. *The Shining Mystery of Jesus.* London 1928.

EISLER, R. 'Ιησοῦς βασιλεὺς οὐ βασιλεύσας. *Die messianische Unabhängigkeitsbewegung vom Auftreten Johannes des Täufers bis zum Untergang Jacobs des Gerechten nach der neuerschlossenen Eroberung von Jerusalem des Flavius Josephus und den christlichen Quellen.* 2 vols. Rel. wiss. Bibliothek. Heidelberg 1929-30. Eng. version: *The Messiah Jesus and John the Baptist, according to Flavius Josephus' recently rediscovered 'Capture of Jerusalem' and the other Jewish and Christian Sources*, trans. A. H. Krappe. London 1931.

EKLUND, H. "Die religiöse Qualität und die Sittlichkeit. Eine Untersuchung in heutiger Religionsphilosophie," in *Acta Acad. Aboensis Humaniora*, VOL. XIV, No. 9. Åbo 1942.

——"Theologie der Entscheidung. Zur Analyse und Kritik der 'existentiellen' Denkweise," in *Uppsala Universitets Årsskrift*, 1937, VOL. I. Lund 1937.

EMMERICH, K. "Die formgeschichtliche Betrachtung der Evangelien in der englischen theologischen Literatur," in *Kirchenblatt für die reformierte Schweiz*, 1942, No. 1.

EMMET, C. *The Eschatological Question in the Gospels*. Edinburgh 1911.

FEIGEL, F. *"Das Heilige." Kritische Abhandlung über Rudolf Otto's gleichnamiges Buch*. Verhandelingen rakende den Natuurlijken en Geopenbaarden Godsdients uitgeven door Teyler's Godgeleerd Genootschap. N.F., PT. XXIII. Haarlem 1929.

FEINE, P. "Die konsequente Eschatologie," in *Neutestamentliche Studien Georg Heinrice zu seinem 70. Geburtstag . . . dargebracht*. Untersuchungen zum Neuen Testament, ed. H. Windisch, No. 6. Leipzig 1914.

——*Jesus*. Gütersloh 1914.

——*Theologie des Neuen Testaments*. 7th edn. Leipzig 1936.

FEUILLET, A. "Le Règne de Dieu et la personne de Jésus d'après les évangiles synoptiques," in A. Robert and A. Feuillet, *Introduction à la Bible*; VOL. II, *Nouveau Testament*. Tourrnai 1959, pp. 771-818.

FLEW, R. N. *Jesus and His Church. A study in the idea of the Ecclesia in the New Testament*. London 1938.

FRICK, H. *Das Reich Gottes in amerikanischer und in deutscher Theologie der Gegenwart*. Vorträge der theologischen Konferenz zu Giessen, No. 43. Giessen 1926.

FRICK, R. *Die Geschichte des Reich-Gottes-Gedankens in der alten Kirche bis zu Origenes und Augustin*. Beihefte z. *Z.N.W.*, No. 6. Giessen 1929.

FRIDRICHSEN, A. "Älska, hata, förneka (försaka)," in *Svensk Exegetisk Årsbok*, 1940, pp. 152-62.

——"Jesu kamp mot de urene ånder," in *S.T.K.*, 1929, pp. 297-314.

——"Kyrka och sakrament i Nya Testamentet," in *S.T.K.*, 1936, pp. 301-17.

——*Le Problème du miracle dans le christianisme primitif*. E.H.P.R., VOL. XII. Strasbourg 1925.

——"Människosonen och Israel," in *Till Gustaf Aulén*. Lund 1939, pp. 100-16.

——"Messias och kyrkan," in *En bok om kyrkan*. Lund 1942, p. 26-45.

——"Nya Testamentets enhet," in *Svensk Exegetisk Årsbok*, 1941, pp. 43-54.

——"Omkring Jesu Gudsrikestanke," in *S.T.K.*, 1932, pp. 41-9.

——"Söderbloms Jesustolkning. En forskningsuppgift," in *Religion och Bibel*, I (1942), pp. 58-63.

——*Vem ville Jesus vara?* Verdandis småskrifter, No. 346. Stockholm 1931.

——"M. Dibelius, *Jesus*" (review), in *Th.Lz.*, 1939, pp. 446-50.

FRIES, S. A. *Guds rike*. Stockholm 1910.

FOERSTER, E. "Rudolf Bultmanns Jesusbuch," in *Z.Th.K.*, N.F., IX (1928), pp. 28-50.

FULLER, R. H. *The Mission and Achievement of Jesus*. London 1954.

GALL, A. FREIHERR VON. *BASILEIA TOU THEOU*. *Eine religionsgeschichtliche Studie zur vorkirchlichen Eschatologie*. Religionswissenschaftliche Bibliotek, VOL. VII. Heidelberg 1926.

GARDNER, P. "The Present and the Future Kingdom in the Gospels," in *Exp.T.*, XXI (1909-10), pp. 535-8.

GILS, F. "Jésus prophète d'après les Évangiles synoptiques," in *Orientalia et Biblica Lovaniensia*, VOL. II. Louvain 1957.

GLASSON, T. F. *The Second Advent*. London 1945.

GLOEGE, G. *Reich Gottes und Kirche im Neuen Testament*. Neutestamentliche Forschungen, ed. O. Schmitz, Ser. II, No. 4. Gütersloh 1929.

GOGUEL, M. "Eschatologie et apocalyptique dans le christianisme primitif," in *Revue de l'histoire des religions*, CV-CVI, pp. 380-434, 489-524.

——*La Vie de Jésus*. Paris 1932.

GRANT, F. C. *The Gospel of the Kingdom*. New York 1940.

GRÄSSER, E. *Das Problem der Parusieverzögerung in den synoptischen Evangelien und in der Apostelgeschichte*. Beihefte z. *Z.N.W.*, No. 48. Berlin 1957.

GREEVEN, H. *Gebet und Eschatologie im Neuen Testament*. Neutestamentliche Forschungen, ed. O. Schmitz, Ser. III, No. 1. Gütersloh 1931.

GROBEL, K. *Formgeschichte und synoptische Quellenanalyse*. Göttingen 1937.

GRØNBECH, V. *Jesus Menneskesønnen*. Copenhagen 1935.

——*Kampen för en ny själ*. 2nd edn. Stockholm 1940.

GRUNDMANN, W. *Der Begriff der Kraft in der neutestamentlichen Gedankenwelt*. Stuttgart 1932.

——*Die Gotteskindschaft in der Geschichte Jesu und ihre religionsgeschichtlichen Voraussetzungen*. Studien zu Deutschen Theologie und Frömmigkeit, VOL. I. Weimar 1938.

——*Jesus der Galiläer und das Judentum*. Leipzig 1940.

——*Wer ist Jesus von Nazareth?* Weimar 1940.

——(ed.) *Christentum und Judentum. Studien zur Erforschung ihres gegenseitigen Verhältnisses*. Leipzig 1940.

——(ed.) *Germanentum, Christentum und Judentum*. VOL. II, *Studien zur Erforschung ihres gegenseitigen Verhältnisses*. Leipzig 1942.

GUIGNEBERT, CH. *Jésus*. L'Évolution de l'humanité. Synthèse collective, XXXIV. Paris 1933. Eng. version: *Jesus*, trans. S. H. Hooke. London 1935.

GUNKEL, H. "Issel, E., Schmoller, O., Weiss, J.: Die Lehre vom Reiche Gottes" (review), in *Th.Lz.*, 1893, pp. 39-45.

HAMMAR, G. *Christian realism in contemporary American theology. A study of Reinhold Niebuhr, W. M. Horton and H. P. van Dusen*. Diss. Uppsala 1940.

HARNACK, A. *Das Wesen des Christentums*. Leipzig 1900, 1927. Eng. version: *What is Christianity?*, trans T. B. Saunders. London and New York 1901.

——*Dogmengeschichte*. Grundriss der Theol. Wissenschaften, VOL. IV, PT. 3, 4th edn. Tübingen 1905.

——*Lehrbuch der Dogmengeschichte*. Samml. theol. Lehrbücher, VOL. I. Freiburg i. B. 1886; 2nd edn. 1888; 4th edn. 1909.

HARTMANN, H. *Jesus, das Dämonische und die Ethik*. Berlin 1923.

HAUBOLD, W. *Die Bedeutung der Religions-Geschichte für die Theologie Rudolf Ottos.* Leipzig 1940.

HAUCK, F. *Das Evangelium des Lukas.* Theologischer Hand Kommentar zum Neuen Testament, VOL. III. Leipzig 1934.

——*Das Evangelium des Markus.* Theologische Hand Kommentar zum Neuen Testament, VOL. II. Leipzig 1931.

HAUPT, E. *Zum Verständnis der eschatologischen Aussagen Jesu in den synoptischen Evangelien.* Berlin 1895.

HEADLAM, A. C. *The Life and Teaching of Jesus the Christ.* 3rd edn. London 1936.

HEIM, K. "Zeit und Ewigkeit, die Hauptfragen der heutigen Eschatologie," in *Z.Th.K.*, 1926, pp. 403-29.

HEITMÜLLER, W. *Jesus.* Tübingen 1913.

HEMPEL, J. "Der synoptische Jesus und das Alte Testament," in *Zeitschrift für die alttestamentliche Wissenschaft*, N.F., XV (1938), pp. 1-34.

HERING, A. "Die Idee Jesu vom Reiche Gottes und ihre Bedeutung für die Gegenwart," in *Z.Th.K.*, 1890, pp. 472-513.

HERING, J. *Le Royaume de Dieu et sa venue, object de l'espérance de Jésus et de S. Paul.* Thèse, Strasbourg. E.H.P.R., No. 35. Paris 1937.

HERRMANN, W. *Christlich-protestantische Dogmatik.* Kultur der Gegenwart, VOL. I, PT. IV. 2. 2nd edn. Berlin and Leipzig 1909.

——*Dogmatik. Mit einer Gedächtnisrede auf Wilhelm Herrmann von M. Rade.* Gotha 1925. Eng. version: *Systematic Theology*, trans. N. Micklem and K. A. Saunders. London 1927.

——*Ethik.* Tübingen 1901; 6th edn. 1921.

HIRSCH, E. *Das Wesen des Christentums.* Weimar 1939.

——*Frühgeschichte des Evangeliums; VOL. I, Das Werden des Markus-evangeliums; VOL. II, Die Vorlagen des Lukas und das Sondergut des Matthäus.* Tübingen 1941.

——*Jesus Christus der Herr. Theologische Vorlesungen.* Göttingen 1926.

HOLL, K. *Urchristentum und Religionsgeschichte.* Studien des apologetischen Seminars No. 10. Gütersloh 1925. Eng. version: *The Distinctive Elements in Christianity*, trans. N. V. Hope. Edinburgh 1937.

HOLMSTRÖM, F. *Det eskatologiska motivet i nutida teologi. Tre etapper i 1900-talets teologiska tankeutveckling.* Stockholm 1933.

HOLSTEIN, G. *Die Grundlagen des evangelischen Kirchenrechts.* Tübingen 1928.

HOLTZMANN, H. J. "Der gegenwärtige Stand der Leben-Jesu-Forschung," in *D.L.Z.*, 1906, pp. 2357-64, 2413-22, 2477-83, 2541-46.

——*Lehrbuch der neutestamentlichen Theologie.* 2 vols. Freiburg 1897; 2nd edn. Tübingen 1911.

HOLTZMANN, O. *Christus.* Leipzig 1907; 2nd edn. 1914.

——*Leben Jesu.* Tübingen and Leipzig 1901. Eng. version: *The Life of Jesus*, trans. J. T. Bealby and M. A. Canney. London 1904.

HOOKE, S. H. *The Kingdom of God in the Experience of Jesus.* London 1949.

HOPKINS, C. H. *The Rise of the Social Gospel in American Protestantism 1865-1915.* New Haven 1940.

HOSKYNS, E. and F. N. DAVEY. *The Riddle of the New Testament.* London 1931.

INGE, W. R. "W. Sanday, *Christologies Ancient and Modern*, 1910" (review) in *Journal of Theological Studies*, IX (1909-10), pp. 584-6.

ISSEL, E. *Die Lehre vom Reiche Gottes im Neuen Testament.* Leiden 1891.

JACKSON, H. L. *The Eschatology of Jesus.* London 1913.

JEREMIAS, J. "Eine neue Schau der Zukunftsaussagen Jesu" (review of C. H. Dodd, *The Parables of the Kingdom*), in *Th.Bl.*, 1941, pp. 216-22.

——*Die Gleichnisse Jesu.* 4th edn. Zürich 1956. Eng. version: *The Parables of Jesus*, trans. S. H. Hooke. London 1954.

——*Jesus als Weltvollender.* Beiträge zur Förderung christlicher Theologie, VOL. XXXIII, No. 4. Gütersloh 1930.

——*Jesu Verheissung für die Völker.* Stuttgart 1956. Eng. version: *Jesus' Promise to the Nations*, trans. S. H. Hooke. London 1958.

——"νύμφη," in *Th.W.B. N.T.*, VOL. IV, pp. 1092 ff.

JONES, M. *The New Testament in the Twentieth Century. A survey of recent Christological and historical criticism of the New Testament.* London 1914.

JÜLICHER, A. *Die Gleichnisreden Jesu.* 2 vols. Tübingen 1888-89; 2nd edn. 1910.

——"Die Religion Jesu und die Anfänge des Christentums," in *Die Kultur der Gegenwart*, VOL. I, PT. 4. Berlin and Leipzig 1906; 2nd edn. 1909, pp. 42-131.

——*Neue Linien in der Kritik der evangelischen Überlieferung.* Giessen 1906.

KAFTAN, J. *Das Wesen der christlichen Religion.* Basle 1881; 2nd edn. 1888.

——*Neutestamentliche Theologie, im Abriss dargestellt.* Berlin 1927.

KANT, I. *Die Religion innerhalb der Grenzen der blossen Vernunft.* Reklam.

KÄSEMANN, E. "Das Problem des historischen Jesus," in *Z.Th.K.*, LI (1954), pp. 125-53.

KATTENBUSCH, F. "Der Quellort der Kirchenidee," in *Festgabe für A. Harnack.* Tübingen 1921, pp. 143-72.

KING, H. C. *Ethics of Jesus.* New York 1910.

KITTEL, G. "Das innerweltliche Reich Gottes in der Verkündigung Jesu," in *Th.Bl.*, 1927, pp. 122 ff.

——*Die Problem des palästinischen Spätjudentums und das Urchristentum.* Beiträge zur Wissenschaft von Alten und Neuen Testament, VOL. III, No. 1. Stuttgart 1926.

——"Ἰησοῦς ὁ διδάσκαλος καὶ προφήτης," in *Th.Bl.*, 1928, pp. 249 f.

——(ed.) *Theologisches Wörterbuch zum Neuen Testament.* Stuttgart 1930-60.

KLÖPPER, A. "Das gegenwärtige und zukünftige Gottesreich in der Lehre Jesu bei den Synoptikern," in *Zeitschrift für wissenschaftliche Theologie*, 1897, pp. 355-410.

KÖSTLIN, J. "Die Idee des Reiches Gottes," in *Theologische Studien und Kritiken*, 1892, pp. 401-73.

KROP, F. *La Pensée de Jésus sur le Royaume de Dieu.* Paris 1897.

KUHN, K. G. "βασιλεύς," in *Th.W.B. N.T.*, VOL. I, pp. 570-3.

KÜMMEL, W. G. " Die Eschatologie der Evangelien. Ihre Geschichte und ihr Sinn," in *Th.Bl.*, 1936, pp. 225-41.

——"Jesus und der jüdische Traditionsgedanke," in *Z.N.W.*, 1934, pp. 105-30.

——*Kirchenbegriff und Geschichtsbewusstsein in der Urgemeinde und bei Jesus.* Symbolae Bibl. Ups., VOL. I. Lund 1943.

KÜMMEL, W. G. *Verheissung und Erfüllung. Untersuchungen zur eschatologischen Verkündigung Jesu.* Abhandlungen zur Theologie des Alten und Neuen Testaments, edd. W. Eichrodt and O. Cullmann, VOL. VI. Basle 1945. Eng. version: *Promise and Fulfilment. The Eschatological Message of Jesus,* trans. D. M. Barton. London 1957.

LEIPOLDT, J. *Jesu Verhältnis zu Griechen und Jüden.* Leipzig 1941.

LIETZMANN, H. *Geschichte der alten Kirche*; VOL. I, *Die Anfänge.* Berlin and Leipzig 1932.

LINDBLOM, J. *Ekklesia. En biblisk studie till belysning av kyrkoproblemet.* Uppsala 1943.

——*Guds rike. En biblisk studie.* Stockholm 1919.

LINDROTH, Hj. "Det kristna dogmat och kristendomens aveskatologisering," in *S.T.K.,* 1943, pp. 82-93.

LINTON, O. "Eskatologien som exegetisk och systematisk problem," in *S.T.K.,* 1942, pp. 298-319.

LOHMEYER, E. *Das Evangelium des Markus.* Meyers Kommentar, VOL. I, 10th edn. Göttingen 1937.

——"Das Gleichnis von den bösen Weingärtnern," in *Zeitschrift für systematische Theologie,* XVIII (1941), pp. 243-59.

——"Das Gleichnis von der Saat," in *Deutsche Theologie, Monatsschrift für die Deutsche Evangelische Kirche,* 1943, pp. 20-39.

——"Der Begriff der Erlösung im Urchristentum," in *Deutsche Theologie*; VOL. II, *Der Erlösungsgedanke,* Göttingen 1928.

——"Die Reinigung des Tempels," in *Th.Bl.,* XX (1941), pp. 257-64.

——*Gottesknecht und Davidsohn.* Symbolae Bibl. Ups. Vol. V. Västervik 1945.

——*Kultus und Evangelium.* Göttingen 1942. Eng. version: *Lord of the Temple,* trans. Stuart Todd. Edinburgh 1961.

——"Om nattvarden i Nya Testamentet," in *S.T.K.,* 1938, pp. 333-45.

——*Vom Begriff der religiösen Gemeinschaft. Eine problemgeschichtliche Untersuchung über die Grundlagen des Urchristentums.* Wissenschaftliche Grundfragen, ed. R. Hönigswald, VOL. III. Leipzig and Berlin 1925.

——"Vom Sinn der Gleichnisse Jesu," in *Zeitschrift für systematische Theologie.* XV (1938), pp. 319-46.

——"Vom urchristlichen Abendmahl," in *Th.R.,* N.F. IX (1937), pp. 168-227, 273-312; X (1938), pp. 81-99, 218-22.

LOISY, A. *Autour d'un petit livre.* Paris 1903.

——*Les Evangiles synoptiques.* 2 vols. Cheffonds 1907-8.

——*L'Evangile et l'Eglise.* Cheffonds 1892. Eng. version: *The Gospel and the Church,* trans. C. Hume. London 1908.

——*Mémoires pour servir a l'histoire religieuse de notre temps.* VOL. III, *1908-27.* Paris 1931.

LOOFS, F. *Wer ist Jesus Christus?* Halle 1916.

LÜHR, K. "Das Bild Jesu bei den Eschatologen," in *Protestantische Monatshefte,* 1903, pp. 64-78.

LÜTGERT, W. *Das Reich Gottes nach den synoptischen Evangelien. Eine untersuchung zur neutestamentlichen Theologie.* Gütersloh 1895.

McCOWN, C. C. *The Promise of His Coming. A historical interpretation of the idea of Second Advent.* New York 1921.

McCOWN, C. C. *The Search for the Real Jesus: a century of historical study.* New York 1940.

MACKINTOSH, H. R. "The Eschatology of Jesus," in *Exp.*, Ser. VIII, No. 10, 1915, pp. 97-116.

MAJOR, H. D. A., T. W. MANSON and C. J. WRIGHT. *The Mission and Message of Jesus. An exposition of the Gospels in the light of modern research.* London 1937.

MANSON, T. W. *Christ's View of the Kingdom of God. A study in Jewish apocalyptic in the mind of Jesus Christ.* London 1918.

——"The Life of Jesus—some tendencies in present-day research," in *The Background of the New Testament and its Eschatology.* Cambridge 1956, pp. 211-21.

——*The Servant-Messiah. A study of the Public Ministry of Jesus.* Cambridge 1953.

——*The Teaching of Jesus. Studies of its form and content.* Cambridge 1931; 2nd edn. 1935; repr. 1943.

MANSON, W. *Jesus the Messiah.* London 1943.

MATHEWS, S. *Jesus on Social Institutions.* New York 1928.

——"The Development of Social Christianity in America during the past twenty-five years," in *J.Rel.*, VII (1927), pp. 376 ff.

——*The Messianic Hope in the New Testament.* Chicago 1905.

——*The Social Teaching of Jesus.* New York 1897.

MAURENBRECHER, M. *Von Nazareth nach Golgatha. Untersuchungen über die weltgeschichtlichen Zusammenhänge.* Berlin-Schöneberg 1909.

METZGER, P. *Der Begriff des Reiches Gottes im Neuen Testament.* Strassburg 1910.

MEYENBERG, A. *Leben-Jesu-Werk.* 3 vols. Lucerne 1922-32.

MEYER, R. *Der Prophet aus Galiläa. Studie zum Jesusbild der drei ersten Evangelien.* Leipzig 1940.

MICHAELIS, W. *Das hochzeitliche Kleid. Eine Einführung in die Gleichnisse Jesu über die rechte Jüngerschaft.* Berlin 1939.

——*Der Herr verzieht nicht die Verheissung. Die Aussagen Jesu über die Nähe des Jüngsten Tages.* Berne 1942.

——*Es ging ein Sämann aus, zu säen. Eine Einführung in die Gleichnisse Jesu über das Reich Gottes und die Kirche.* Berlin 1938.

——*Reich Gottes und Geist Gottes nach dem Neuen Testament.* Basle 1931.

——*Täufer, Jesus, Urgemeinde. Die Predigt Jesu vom Reiche Gottes vor und nach Pfingsten.* Neutestamentliche Forschungen, ed. O. Schmitz, Ser. II, No. 3. Gütersloh 1928.

——*Zur Engelchristologie im Urchristentum. Abbau der Konstruktion Martin Werners.* Gegenwartsfragen biblischer Theologie, VOL. I. Basle 1942.

——"Zur Frage der Äonenwende," in *Th.Bl.*, 1939, pp. 113-8.

MICHEL, O. "Unser Ringen um die Eschatologie," in *Z.Th.K.*, 1932, pp. 154-74.

MONNIER, H. *La Mission historique de Jésus.* Paris 1906; 2nd edn. 1914.

MORGENTHALER, R. *Kommendes Reich.* Zürich 1952.

MOSBECH, H. "Jesu Forkyndelse efter de tre Første Evangelier," in *Haandbog i Kristendomskundskab*; VOL. III, *Det Nye Testamente, pp.* 309-18.

MOWINCKEL, S. "Henok og 'Menneskesønnen'," in *Norsk Teologisk Tidskrift*, 1944, pp. 57-69.

T

Mowinckel, S. *He that Cometh.* Oxford 1956.
——"Opphavet til den senjødiske forestilling om Menneskesønnen," in *Norsk Teologisk Tidskrift*, 1944, pp. 189-244.
Müller, J. *Die Bergpredigt, verdeutscht und vergegenwärtigt.* Munich 1906; 5th edn. 1919.
——*Von den Quellen des Lebens. Sieben Aufsätze.* 4th edn. Munich 1914.
Niebuhr, H. R. *The Kingdom of God in America.* Chicago and New York 1937.
Niebuhr, R. *Beyond Tragedy. Essays on the Christian interpretation of History.* New York and London 1938.
——*The Nature and Destiny of Man;* vol. ii, *Human Destiny.* New York and London 1943.
Nigg, W. *Das ewige Reich. Geschichte einer Sehnsucht und einer Enttäuschung.* Erlenbach-Zürich 1944.
Norlev, Chr. *Jesus af Nazaret og hans Evangelium set paa Datidens sociale Baggrund.* Copenhagen 1943.
Nygren, A. *Filosofisk och kristen etik.* 2nd edn. Stockholm 1932.
Oepke, A. "Jesus und der Gottesvolkgedanke," in *Luthertum*, 1942, pp. 33-62.
——"E. Hirsch, *Frühgeschichte des Evangeliums*, 1941" (review), in *Theologisches Literaturblatt*, 1942, pp. 137-43.
Olmstead, A. T. *Jesus in the Light of History.* New York 1942.
Orr, J. "Kingdom of God, of Heaven," in *A Dictionary of the Bible*, ed. J. Hastings *et al.*, vol. i, pp. 844-56. Edinburgh 1899; 6th imp. 1905.
Otto, R. *Aufsätze, das Numinöse betreffend.* Munich 1923.
——*Das Heilige. Über das Irrationale in der Idee des Göttlichen und sein Verhältnis zum Rationalen.* Breslau 1917; 7th edn. 1922. Eng. version: *The Idea of the Holy. An Inquiry into the non-rational factor in the idea of the Divine and its relation to the rational*, trans. J. W. Harvey. London and New York 1923, 1950.
——*Geist und Wort nach Luther.* Diss. theol. Göttingen 1898.
——*Kantisch-Fries'sche Religionsphilosophie und ihre Anwendung auf die Theologie.* Tübingen 1909.
——*Leben und Wirken Jesu nach historisch-kritischer Auffassung.* Göttingen 1901; 4th edn. 1905. Eng. version: *Life and Ministry of Jesus according to the Historical and Critical Method*, trans. H. J. Whitby. Chicago 1908.
——*Reich Gottes und Menschensohn. Ein religionsgeschichtliche Versuch.* Munich 1934; 2nd rev. edn. 1940. Eng. version: *The Kingdom of God and the Son of Man. A Study in the History of Religion*, trans. Floyd V. Filson and B. L. Woolf. London 1938.
——*Sünde und Urschuld.* Munich 1929.
Peabody, F. G. *Jesus Christ and the Social Question.* New York 1900.
Pedersen, E. Thestrup. "Kristendommens afmytologisering og Førkyndelsen," in *Dansk Teologisk Tidskrift*, viii (1945), pp. 193-222.
Percy, E. *Die Botschaft Jesu. Eine traditionskritische und exegetische Untersuchung.* Lunds universitets årsskrift, N.F. Ser. i, vol. xlix, No. 5. Lund 1953.
Pfannmüller, G. *Jesus im Urteil der Jahrhunderten, Die bedeutendste. Auffassungen Jesu in Theologie, Philosophie, Literatur und Kunst bis zur Gegenwart.* 2nd edn. Berlin 1939.

PFLEIDERER, O. *Das Urchristentum, seine Schriften und Lehren in geschichtlichem Zusammenhang*; 2 vols. 2nd edn. Berlin 1902. Eng. version: *Primitive Christianity. Its Writings and Teachings in their Historical Connections*, trans. W. Montgomery. 4 vols. London and New York 1906-11.

PIEPENBRING, C. *Jésus historique*. Bibliothèque de critique réligieuse, Nos. 26, 27. Paris 1909. Eng. version: *The Historical Jesus*, trans. L. A. Clare. London and New York 1924.

POHLMANN, H. *Der Gottesgedanke Jesu als Gegensatz gegen den israelitisch-jüdischen Gottesgedanken*. Studien zu deutschen Theologie und Frömmigkeit, VOL. IV. Weimar 1939.

PREISKER, H. *Die urchristliche Botschaft von der Liebe Gottes, im Lichte der vergleichenden Religionsgeschichte*. Aus der Welt der Religion, Bibl. Reihe, No. 5. Giessen 1930.

——*Geist und Leben. Das Telos-Ethos des Urchristentums*. Gütersloh 1933.

PRENTER, R. "Evangeliets afmytologisering," in *S.T.K.*, 1946, pp. 89-108.

PROOST, K. E. *De Bergrede, hare herkomst en strekking*. Amsterdam 1914.

PURDY, A. C. "Das Neue Testament in der amerikanischen Theologie," in *Th.R.*, N.F. III (1931), pp. 367-86.

RAD, G. VON. "βασιλεύς," in *Th.W.B. N.T.*, VOL. I, pp. 563-9.

RAGAZ, L. *Dein Reich komme*. 2nd edn. Basle 1911.

——*Die Gleichnisse Jesu*. Berne 1944.

——*Du Sollst. Grundzüge einer sittlichen Weltanschauung*. 2nd edn. Ossmanstedt bei Weimar 1911.

——*Weltreich, Religion und Gottesherrschaft*. 2 vols. 1922.

RAMSEY, A. M. *From Gore to Temple*. London and New York 1960.

RAUSCHENBUSCH, W. *A Theology for the Social Gospel*. New York 1922.

——*Christianizing the Social Order*. New York 1912.

RAWLINSON, A. E. J. *Christ in the Gospels*. London 1944.

——(ed.). *Essays on the Trinity and the Incarnation, by members of the Anglican communion*. London and New York 1928.

RENAN, E. *La Vie de Jésus*. Paris 1863. Eng. version: *The Life of Jesus*. London 1864.

RICHARDSON, A. *An Introduction to the Theology of the New Testament*. London 1958.

RIDDLE, D. W. *Jesus and the Pharisees*. Chicago 1928.

——"Jesus in modern research," in *J.Rel.*, 1937, pp. 170-82.

——"The bearing of recent Gospel research upon the study of the teaching of Jesus," in *J.Rel.*, 1934, pp. 150-67.

RIESENFELD, H. *The Gospel Tradition and its Beginnings. A study in the Limits of "Formgeschichte."* London 1957.

RITSCHL, A. *Die christliche Lehre von der Rechtfertigung und Versöhnung*. Bonn, VOL. I, 4th edn. 1903; VOL. II, 4th edn. 1900; VOL. III, 3rd edn. 1888. Eng. version of VOL. I: *A Critical History of the Christian Doctrine of Justification and Reconciliation*, trans. J. S. Black, Edinburgh 1872; of VOL. III: *The Christian Doctrine of Justification and Reconciliation. The Positive Development of the Doctrine*, trans. H. R. Mackintosh and A. B. Macaulay, Edinburgh 1900.

——*Unterricht in der christlichen Religion*. 3rd edn. Bonn 1886. Eng. version: *Instruction in the Christian Religion*. Trans. Alice M. Swing. London and New York, 1901.

ROBINSON, J. A. T. *Jesus and His Coming. The Emergence of a Doctrine.* London 1957.

ROBINSON, W. H. *The Parables of Jesus in their relation to His Ministry.* Chicago 1928.

SANDAY, W. "The apocalyptic element in the Gospels," in *Hibbert Journal,* x, No. 1 (1911), pp. 83-109.

——*The Life of Christ in recent Research.* Oxford 1907.

SALVATORELLI, L. "From Locke to Reitzenstein: the historical investigation of the origins of Christianity," in *Harvard Theological Review,* 1929, pp. 263-367.

SCHILDENBERGER, J. "Verheissung und Erfüllung," in *Biblica,* xxiv (1943), pp. 107-24, 205-30.

SCHLATTER, A. *Die Geschichte des Christus.* Stuttgart 1921; 2nd edn. 1923.

——*Die Theologie des Neuen Testaments.* VOL. I, *Das Wort Gottes.* Stuttgart 1909.

SCHMIDT, K. L. "βασιλεύς," in *Th.W.B. N.T.,* VOL. I, pp. 579-92.

——"Das Christuszeugnis der synoptischen Evangelien," in *Jesus Christus im Zeugnis der Heiligen Schrift und der Kirche,* 1936, pp. 7-33.

——"Das überweltliche Reich Gottes in der Verkündigung Jesu," in *Th.Bl.,* 1927, pp. 118-20.

——"Jesus Christus," in *R.G.G.,* 2nd edn. 1929, pp. 110-51.

——*Le Problème du Christianisme primitif. Quatre conférences sur la forme et la pensée du Nouveau Testament.* Paris 1938.

SCHMIEDEL, O. *Die Hauptprobleme der Leben-Jesu-Forschung.* Tübingen 1902; 2nd edn. 1906.

SCHMOLLER, O. *Die Lehre vom Reiche Gottes in den Schriften des Neuen Testaments.* Leiden 1891.

SCHNACKENBURG, R. *Gottes Herrschaft und Reich. Eine biblischtheologische Studie.* Frieburg 1959.

SCHNEDERMANN, G. *Das Judenthum in den Evangelien. Eine Einführung in das geschichtliche Verständnis des Lebens Jesu* (2nd edn. of *Das Judentum und die christliche Verkündigung in den Evangelien,* 1884). Leipzig 1900.

——*Jesu Verkündigung und Lehre vom Reiche Gottes in ihrer geschichtlichen Bedeutung.* 2 vols. Leipzig 1893-95.

——*Über den jüdischen Hintergrund im Neuen Testament.* Leipzig 1890.

——*Wie der Israelit Jesus der Weltheiland wurde.* 2nd edn. Leipzig 1912.

SCHNEIDER, J. *Der Sinn der Bergpredigt. Von der Grundordnung christlichen Lebens.* Berlin n.d.

——"Die biblische Botschaft vom Reiche Gottes," in *Das kommende Reich. Stimmen aus der deutschen christlichen Studentbewegung,* No. 78. Leipzig 1933, pp. 5-26.

——"T. W. Manson, *The Teaching of Jesus*" (review), in *Th.Lz.,* 1932, pp. 556-9.

SCHNIEWIND, J. *Das Evangelium nach Markus.* Das Neue Testament Deutsch, VOL I., PT. I. Göttingen 1937.

——*Das Evangelium nach Matthäus.* Das Neue Testament Deutsch, VOL. I, PT. 2. Göttingen 1937.

——"Zur Synoptiker-Exegese," in *Th.R.,* 1930, pp. 129-89.

SCHRENK, G. "βιάζομαι," in *Th.W.B. N.T.,* VOL. I, pp. 608-13.

SCHUMANN, F. K. *Der Gottesgedanke und der Zerfall der Moderne.* Tübingen 1929.

SCHÜRER, E. *Geschichte des jüdischen Volkes im Zeitalter Jesu Christi,* VOL. II. 2nd edn. Leipzig 1888.

SCHUSTER, H. "Die konsequente Eschatologie in der Interpretation des Neuen Testaments, kritisch betrachtet," in *Z.N.W.*, XLVII (1956), pp. 1-25.

SCHWEITZER, A. *Aus meinem Leben und Denken.* Leipzig 1932. Eng. version: *Out of my Life and Thought: an autobiography,* trans. C. T. Campion. New York 1949.

——*Das Messianitäts- und Leidensgeheimnis. Eine Skizze des Lebens Jesu.* Tübingen and Leipzig 1901; 2nd edn. 1929. Eng. version: *The Mystery of the Kingdom of God. The Secret of Jesus' Messiahship and Passion,* trans. W. Lowrie. London 1956.

——"Die idee des Reiches Gottes im Verlaufe der Umbildung des Eschatologischen Glaubens in den uneschatologischen," in *Schweitzerische Theologische Umschau,* 1953.

——*Geschichte der Leben-Jesu-Forschung.* Tübingen 1913.

——*Von Reimarus zu Wrede. Eine Geschichte der Leben-Jesu-Forschung.* Tübingen 1906. Eng. version: *The Quest of the Historical Jesus: a critical study of its progress from Reimarus to Wrede,* trans. W. Montgomery, 3rd edn. London 1954.

SCOTT, E. F. *The Kingdom and the Messiah.* Edinburgh 1911.

——*The Kingdom of God in the New Testament.* New York 1931.

SEEBERG, E. *Wer ist Christus?* Sammlung gemeinverständ. Vorträge, No. 183. Tübingen 1937.

SEIFERT, P. *Die Religionsphilosophie bei Rudolf Otto. Eine Untersuchung über ihre Entwicklung.* Diss. Bonn 1936.

SEVENSTER, G. *Ethiek en eschatologie in de synoptische Evangelien. Een studie over het typische in Jesus' zedeleer.* Diss. Leiden 1929.

SHARMAN, H. B. *The Teaching of Jesus about the Future according to the Synoptic Gospels.* Chicago 1909.

SIEGFRIED, TH. *Das Wort und die Existenz. Eine Auseinandersetzung mit der dialektischen Theologie:* VOL. II, *Die Theologie der Existenz bei Friedrich Gogarten und Rudolf Bultmann.* Gotha 1933.

SJÖBERG, E. *Der Menschensohn im äthiopischen Henochbuch.* Skrifter utgivna av Kungl. Humanistiska Vetenskapssamfundet i Lund, VOL. XLI. Lund 1946.

——"Ville Jesus vara Messias? Bestridandet av Jesu messiasmedvetande i det sista seklets forskning," in *Svensk Exegetisk Årsbok,* X (1945), pp. 82-151.

SMITH, B. T. D. *The Parables of the Synoptic Gospels. A critical Study.* Cambridge 1937.

SÖDERBLOM, N. *Gå vi mot religionens förnyelse?* Uppsala 1919.

——*Jesu bergspredikan och vår tid.* Stockholm 1899; 2nd edn. Malmö 1930.

——*Kristenhetens möte i Stockholm augusti nittonhundratjugofem.* Stockholm 1926.

——*När stunderna växla och skrida,* VOL. II. Stockholm 1919; 3rd edn. 1935.

STALKER, J.   *The Christology of Jesus: being His teaching concerning Himself according to the Synoptic Gospels.* London 1899.

STAPFER, E.   *Jésus-Christ, sa personne, son autorité, son oeuvre.* 3 vols. Paris 1896-98.

STAUFFER, E.   "Der Stand der neutestamentlichen Forschung," in *Theologie und Liturgie,* ed. L. Henning.   Kassel 1952, pp. 35-105.

——*Die Theologie des Neuen Testaments.*   Theologische Wissenschaft. Stuttgart and Berlin 1941.   Eng. version: *New Testament Theology,* trans. J. Marsh.   London 1955.

——*Jesus, Gestalt und Geschichte.*   Berne 1957.   Eng. version: *Jesus and His Story,* trans. D. M. Barton.   London 1960.

——*Jesus, Paulus und wir.*   Hamburg 1961.

STREETER, B. H.   "Professor Burkitt and the Parables of the Kingdom," in *The Interpreter,* 1910-11, pp. 241-7.

——"Synoptic Criticism and the Eschatological Problem," in *Studies in the Synoptic Problem, by members of the University of London,* ed. W. Sanday.   London 1911, pp. 423-36.

——*The Four Gospels. A study of Origins, Treating of the manuscript tradition, sources, authorship and dates.*   London 1924; 5th imp. 1936.

——"The Historic Christ," in *Foundations: A statement of Christian Belief in terms of modern thought, by seven Oxford Men.*   London 1912, pp. 73-145.

STRÖM, A. V.   *Vetekornet. Studier över individ och kollektiv i Nya Testamentet.* Stockholm 1944.

TASKER, R. W. G.   *The Nature and Purpose of the Gospels.*   London 1944.

TAYLOR, V.   *Jesus and His Sacrifice. A study of the Passion-sayings in the Gospels.*   London 1937.

THEISSING, J.   *Die Lehre Jesu von der ewigen Seligkeit. Ein Beitrag zur neutestamentlichen Theologie.*   Breslauer Studien zur historischen Theologie, N.F., VOL. VI.   Breslau 1940.

THORNTON, L. S.   *The Incarnate Lord. An essay concerning the Doctrine of the Incarnation in its relation to Organic Conceptions.*   London 1928.

THURNEYSON, E.   "Christus und seine Zukunft. Ein Beitrag zur Eschatologie," in *Zwischen den Zeiten,* IX (1931), pp. 187-211.

TITIUS, A.   *Die neutestamentliche Lehre von der Seligkeit und ihre Bedeutung für die Gegenwart;* VOL. I, *Lehre Jesu vom Reiche Gottes.*   Freiburg i. B. and Leipzig 1895.

TRAUB, A.   "Die Gegenwart des Gottesreiches in den Parabeln vom Senfkorn und Sauerteig, von der selbstwachsenden Saat, dem Unkraut und dem Fischnetz," in *Z.Th.K.,* 1905, pp. 58-75.

TYRRELL, G.   *Christianity at the Cross-Roads.*   London 1909; 4th im. 1913.

VIELHAUER, P.   "Gottesreich und Menschensohn in der Verkündigung Jesu," in *Festschrift für Günther Dehn,* ed. W. Schneemelcher.   Neukirchen 1957, pp. 51-79.

VOLKMAR, G.   *Jesus Nazarenus und die erste christliche Zeit, mit den beiden ersten Erzählern.*   Zürich 1882.

WABNITZ, A.   *L'Idéal messianique de Jésus.*   Thèse.   Montauban 1873 or 1878.

WAGENFÜHRER, M.-A. "Der Kirchenbegriff des Neuen Testaments," in *Germanentum, Christentum und Judentum*, VOL. II, ed. W. Grundmann. Leipzig 1942, pp. 273-306.

WARSCHAUER, J. *The Historical Life of Christ*. London 1927.

WEBER, H. E. "Die Kirche im Lichte der Eschatologie," in *Neue Kirchliche Zeitschrift*, 1926, pp. 299-339.

WEIFFENBACH, W. *Die Wiederkunftsgedanken Jesu. Nach den Synoptikern kritisch untersucht und dargestellt*. Leipzig 1873.

WEINEL, H. *Biblische Theologie des Neuen Testaments. Die Religion Jesu und des Urchristentums*. Tübingen 1911; 2nd edn. 1913.

WEISS, B. *Lehrbuch der biblischen Theologie*. 6th edn. Stuttgart and Berlin 1895; 7th edn. 1903.

WEISS, J. "Das Problem der Entstehung des Christentums," in *Archiv für Religionswissenschaft*, 1913, pp. 423-515.

——*Die Idee des Reiches Gottes in der Theologie*, Vorträge der Theol. Konferenz zu Giessen, No. 16. Giessen 1901.

——*Die Predigt Jesu vom Reiche Gottes*. Göttingen 1892; 2nd edn. 1900.

WELLHAGEN, J. *Anden och Riket. Lukas religiösa åskådning med särskild hänsyn till eskatologien*. Uppsala 1941.

WELLHAUSEN, J. *Einleitung in die drei ersten Evangelien*. Berlin 1905.

——*Israelitische und jüdische Geschichte*. Berlin 1894.

WENDLAND, H.-D. *Die Eschatologie des Reiches Gottes bei Jesus. Eine Studie über den Zusammenhang von Eschatologie, Ethik und Kirchenproblem*. Gütersloh 1931.

——*Geschichtsanschauung und Geschichtsbewusstsein im Neuen Testament*. Göttingen 1938.

——"The Kingdom of God and History," in *Church, Community and State*, VOL. III. London 1938, pp. 143-94.

WENDT, H. H. "Das Reich Gottes in der Lehre Jesu," in *Christliche Welt*, 1893, pp. 338-42, 361-5, 386-91, 410-13, 434-9.

——*Die Lehre Jesu*. 2 vols, Göttingen 1886-90; 2nd edn. 1901.

WERNER, M. *Die Entstehung des christlichen Dogmas problemgeschichtlich dargestellt*. Bern and Leipzig 1941. Shortened Eng. version: *The Formation of Christian Dogma. An Historical Study of its Problem*, trans. S. G. F. Brandon. London 1957.

WERNLE, P. *Die Anfänge unserer Religion*. Tübingen and Leipzig 1901; 2nd edn. 1904. Eng. version of 1st edn.: *The Beginnings of Christianity*, trans. G. A. Bienemann. 2 vols. London and New York 1903-4.

——*Die Reichgotteshoffnung in den ältesten christlichen Dokumenten und bei Jesus*. Tübingen and Leipzig 1903.

——*Jesus*. Tübingen 1917.

——"A. Schweitzer, *Von Reimarus zu Wrede*" (review), in *Th.Lz.*, 1906, pp. 501-6.

WINDISCH, H. *Der Sinn der Bergpredigt. Ein Beitrag zum geschichtlichen Verständnis der Evangelien und zum Problem der richtigen Exegese*. Untersuchungen zum Neuen Testament, ed. H. Windisch. Leipzig 1929; 2nd edn. 1937.

——"Die Sprüche vom Eingehen in das Reich Gottes," in *Z.N.W.*, XXVII, (1928), pp. 163-92.

WINDISCH, H. *Jesus und der Geist nach synoptischen Überlieferung.* Studies in Early Christianity, ed. S. Jackson Case. New York 1938.

——"A. Schweitzer, *Von Reimarus zu Wrede*" (review), in *Th.R.*, 1909, p. 146.

WINKEL, M. E. *Der Sohn. Die evangelischen Quellen und die Verkündigung Jesu von Nazareth in ihrer ursprünglichen Gestalt und ihre Vermischung mit jüdischem Geist; nach textlich revidierten kanonischen und ausserkanonisch überlieferten Aussprüchen und Berichten.* Kampen 1935.

WISSING, J. C. *Het begrip van het Koninkrijk Gods, vooral met betrekking tot de religiens-socialen in Zwitzerland,* 1927.

WREDE, W. *Das Messiasgeheimnis in den Evangelien. Zugleich ein Beitrag zum Verständnis des Markusevangeliums.* Göttingen 1901.

——*Vorträge und Studien.* Tübingen 1907.

ZAHN, T. *Grundriss der Neutestamentlichen Theologie.* Leipzig 1928.

Index